MW01286882

Corrections and Social Developmental Needs for Offenders

By

Barry Shelby McCrary, D. Ed.

Abstract

How can the insights of students and corrections workers improve the process of preparing adult offenders for functioning successfully after being released from a corrections system? This research approach was born out of the idea of creating learning environments for students and personnel. The attempt to create a learning organization required the promotion of a new perspective for corrections students and workers moving from providing a service of managing behaviors toward learning about the offender in order to manage and address long-term needs. In order to develop this perspective, a qualitative and quantitative research paradigm was employed. The purposes of this research approach were; (1) to examine the current process by which corrections workers assess and provide supervision and educational program and; (2) to determine if there are valuable insights and undocumented procedures that corrections workers can use to prepare offenders to function successfully after leaving the corrections system. The literature exploring risks/need factors in the predicting of criminal behavior was reviewed along with a sociological, developmental, and criminological perspective. The reason for reviewing the various perspectives was to explore those insights to consider ways to improve treatment to meet social development needs. This approach may provide additional insights for criminal justice practitioners and students to help corrections workers identify those routine program activities which best support long-term success for these offenders. Furthermore, new strategies for preparing offenders and improving the overall system may be discovered.

ACKNOWLEDGMENTS

I give praise and acknowledgement to my dear, late, great father and mother Jack Sr. and Harriette McCrary who taught me the importance of God, family, community, nation, and race, working together and sacrificing to benefit the whole.

I want to thank my loving and encouraging wife, DeHavilland McCrary and two adult children, Barry Jr. and Valeria McCrary.

Introduction and Human Development

"Does it take a village to raise a child or can a parent do it alone?"

Is the village or community a place where chaos comes to order, where crises are resolved, and where everyone begins to work together? Is the village or community a place where young people have mentors, role models and someone looking out for their best interests? Is the community a place where families have support; students have tutors and access to computers? Is the community a place where education is being promoted, love and respect is valued and family and youth relations are nurtured? Is the community safe and secure, where no one goes without a meal and expectations for youth are high? Is the community able to sets high standards, goals and values, and has the power to enforce these standards if there are attempts to lower them? Is human behaviors an individual choice or influenced by environment?

What are Ruins of a village?

Can Ruins of a village or community be unhealthy and dangerous? Can carcasses of a community, produce chaos as a norm, low expectations acceptable, crises not resolved and everyone isn't necessarily working together? From ruins of a community is productive growth nurtured, families supported and everyone looking out for the best interests of the children? From ruins of a community are some children fatherless, lack of role models and guidance from positive people. Are tutors hard to find, computers non-existent, education not being promoted and love and respect replaced by gangs and violence? Are norm to survive replaced with toughness, self-made rules and self-interest? How can living in ruins of a community affect families?

Many parents may ask, "How can the community be rebuilt?" "How can my child and family benefit from a new vision for the future?" "It this too good to be true, and what does the community have to do?"

What is the government's role and responds? The "systems responds" may be, to rebuilding the community we would suggest more police. Yes more police. Yes the criminological perspective may suggest, your child may need more police in the community, more arrest of children committing crimes and charging youth as adults. Based on this approach, police will maintain order, stop and frisk youth, and decrease crime in neighborhoods, and as a result, this policed community will provide juvenile justice court services. In juvenile court, your child will have a juvenile record and access to counselors, tutors, computers, recreational activities, mentors, role models, crisis intervention specialists and drug and alcohol counseling. However, many parents may ask, how can we rebuild the community without criminalizing my child?

And a response from a criminological perspective to that question may be, "if crime is the problem, police may be the solution". But parents and community may ask how can the village, community, and system help to prevent and intervene in behaviors to decrease the likelihood of crime?

With these questions this workbook will attempt to address the various community concerns to address social development needs from different perspectives and students and practitioners will identify what they think will work to improve treatment to meet social developmental needs of youth.

Is human behaviors an individual choice or influenced by environment?

_____

_____

_____

_____

_____

_____

_____

_____

_____

_____

What Happen to Willie

The attempt to improve prevention and intervention work requires understanding

different perspectives of how at-risk youth view their surroundings and for prevention

and intervention workers to become more effective they most continue to understand

youth's perspective to moves away from providing services solely or primarily as a

means of managing behaviors to understanding youth, to facilitate change. To further

understand and gain insight to ways to decrease cycles of failure we suggest looking at a

story created by Dr. Jawanza Kunjufu (1986), about a young man named Willie.

What Happen to Willie

It's 8:30 Monday morning. Willie is lying in the bed watching television and dozing off between commercials. He is twenty years old, six feet tall and 170 pound. His day has been divided between the television and the street corner since age thirteen. Willie was a good student in the primary grades where his natural ability was sufficient, but in the upper grades where discipline and study habits are expected, Willie adhered more to the culture of and rigors of the street and it's highly influential peer group. Willie does not know in retrospect, whether he dropped out or was pushed out of school at the first "legal" age of sixteen. Willie knows that both he and school had been together since day care at the ripe age of three, and that thirteen years of being still and listening to ideas unrelated to his world were enough.

His mother has been working at the phone company all of her life; his older brother works at the post office, and his younger sister presently is in college. Willie has never known his father. From time to time, Willie drops into a community center that offers GED training. He has taken several courses but not the test.

There are large numbers of teenagers and young adults who parallel Willie – male, female, younger and older, from two parent homes as well as single parent welfare dwellings.

Questions:

- **What actually happen to Willie?**

  _____
  _____
  _____
  _____
  _____
  _____

- **When did it happen?**

  _____
  _____
  _____
  _____

- **What prevented Willie from maintaining his development like his brother and sister?**

  _____
  _____
  _____
  _____
  _____

- **What will happen to Willies talents while he watches television?**

  _____
  _____
  _____
  _____
  _____

- **Did someone fail Willie?**

  _____
  _____
  _____
  _____

- **If so, who?**

  _____
  _____
  _____
  _____

- **Was it the family, school, economy, church, or government?**

  _____
  _____
  _____
  _____
  _____

- **What does Willie value?**

  _____
  _____
  _____
  _____

- **How can Willie be motivated?**

  _____
  _____
  _____

- **What are Willie's talents?**

  _____
  _____
  _____
  _____

- **What is the present employment picture for Willie?**

  _____
  _____
  _____
  _____

- **How can Willie become economically self-sufficient?**

  _____
  _____
  _____
  _____
  _____

One of the ways to improve prevention and intervention work toward meeting the social developmental needs of at-risk youth is gathering this type of information that can enable a clear understanding of the value system that underlies the behavior. This knowledge will enhance the ability to develop prevention and intervention training modules for students, service providers, and workers who are attempting to help adults in the corrections system.

Topics

- Community Corrections
  - Community Corrections Technologies Electronic Monitoring TechnologiesAddressing Agencies' Need to Automatically Transfer Offender Tracking Data
    - Data Analysis Has Potential to Improve Community Supervision
    - Evaluating a Location-Based Offender Monitoring System
    - Evaluating the Use of GPS Technology in the Community
    - Market Survey of Offender Tracking Technologies Gives Agencies a Snapshot of Available Products
    - Standards and Testing for Offender Tracking Technologies
  - Executive Session on Community Corrections Papers From the Harvard Executive Session on Community Corrections Programs for Drug-Involved Offenders

- Evaluating Delaware's Decide Your Time Protocol for Drug-Using Offenders Under Community Supervision
  - Sex Offenders About Megan's Law
  - About the Study of Megan's Law in New Jersey
  - Additional Research on the Effectiveness of Sex Offender Registration
  - Other Web Resources on Sex Offenders
  - Sex Offender Management and Risk Assessment
  - Sex Offender Registration and Notification: Research Finds Limited Effects in New Jersey
  - Sex Offender Registration, Notification and Residency Restrictions
  - Sex Offender Residency Restrictions: How Mapping Can Inform Policy
  - Video: Discussing the Future of Justice-Involved Young Adults Corrections Technologies
  - Institutional Corrections
    - Contraband Control and Detection Cell Phones in Prisons
    - Detecting Drugs on Surfaces Quickly and Easily
    - Evaluating Video Visitation Technology for Prisons Exploring the Use of Restrictive Housing in the U.S.: Issues, Challenges, and Future DirectionsImproving Safety in Institutions with Technology Institutional Corrections Technology Working Group Priorities

- Institutional Corrections Technologies Institutional Corrections Technology Priorities Monitoring Inmates Predicting Trouble Spots Within Prisons
  - Suicide Watch Technologies Could Improve Monitoring, Reduce Staff Time
- National Study of Prison Closings Prison Rape About the Prison Rape Elimination Act of 2003
  - Other Agency Responses to the Prison Rape Elimination Act
  - Prison Rape Publications
  - Prison Rape Research Findings
  - Prison Rape: Ongoing Research and Future Directions
  - Prison Rape: Other Web Resources
- Restrictive Housing Offender Reentry
- About the Serious and Violent Offender Reentry Initiative Evaluation of Second Chance Act Demonstration Projects Evaluation of the Serious and Violent Offender Reentry Initiative Reentry: Other Web Resources Research on Reentry and Employment Recidivism

Various Perspectives for human behavior

Socialization

Socialization refers to the preparation of newcomers to become members of an existing group, and to think, feel, and act in ways the group considers appropriate (Persell, 1987). Socialization is also an interactive process through which individuals negotiate their definition of the situation with others. Socialization is a combination of social structure and process that influence individual's free will and human autonomy. There are three distinct aspects of socialization: (1) the context in which it occurs, (2) the actual content and processes people use to socialize others, and (3) the result arising from those contexts and processes (Persell, 1987).

Context of Socialization

Context is the stage in which socialization occurs. Social context includes culture, language, and social structure such as the class, ethnic, and gender hierarchies of a society (Persell, 1987). Expanding cultural understanding of young men will enable the workers to gain a greater awareness of the "why" behind behavioral characteristics and how certain behaviors are interwoven within the culture (Wynn, 1992). Cultural consciousness is important in treatment to meet the social developmental needs of delinquent youth. Most cities are diverse, and communities have people of different genders, age, religions, race, class, sexual orientation, and physical abilities. A treatment approach that neglects cultural consciousness runs the risk of not meeting the needs not only of the youth offender but also of the community in which the offender lives. Valuing cultural diversity begins to address the issue of respecting the rights of others. Culture is the central starting point which influences a person's individual character, personal make up, family structure, society, and the total environment.

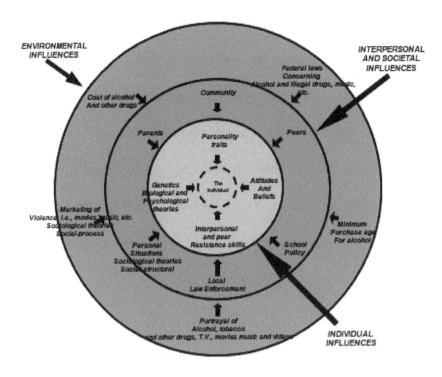

Society's response to anti-social and delinquent behavior

The purpose of this course is to begin the corrections discussion with question about how

society defines human behaviors, and early problem behaviors, and America's societal

response to the various behaviors. This course will attempt to explore the result of societal

responses as the evolution of corrections policy which created corrections system, courts,

programs, corrections practitioners, and research to meet social developmental needs for adult

offenders. This course will attempt to connect the dots from ideology about individual

behaviors, to theories for causes of crime, and societal responses to antisocial and criminal

behaviors by way of the formulation of criminal courts. To address the various pathways to criminal court this corrections methods course will identify various topics to address

corrections. To begin the process of discussing corrections lets first begin the discussion

about behaviors.

Questions to consider:

- **How does American society define human behavior?**

- **What is considered antisocial behavior?**

- **What is meant by juvenile delinquency?**

- **How many juveniles under the age of 18 are arrested by law enforcement officers in the U.S.?**

- <u>**How many juveniles are under juvenile court jurisdiction?**</u>

- **What is the history of America's response to juvenile delinquency?**

- What is <u>human behavior</u>?

    - The potential and expressed capacity for physical, mental, and social activity during the phases of human life.

    - http://www.britannica.com/EBchecked/topic/275332/human-behaviour

- What are <u>antisocial behaviors</u>?

    - We define "antisocial behavior" as a cluster of related behaviors, including disobedience, aggression; temper tantrums, lying, stealing, and violence (see Patterson, 1982). http://aspe.hhs.gov/hsp/prison2home02/eddy.htm

- What is considered delinquent behavior?

- legal definition, individual must be found guilty of offense

- How many juveniles under the age of 18 are arrested by law enforcement officers in the U.S.?

    - 1.8 to 2.2 million juveniles under the age of 18 is arrested by law enforcement officers in the U.S.

- <u>How many juveniles are under juvenile court jurisdiction?</u>

    - In 2000 more than **30 million youth** were under juvenile court jurisdiction but numbers always fluctuate

- What is the history of America's response to juvenile delinquency?

    <u>Juvenile Justice History — Center on Juvenile and Criminal Justice</u>

An approach to managing behaviors

- A developmental approach recognizes the interactions among the individual child or adolescent and the many social systems that surround him or her.

- <u>Antisocial behavior</u> results from the <u>interaction of numerous risk factors</u>, and from the <u>absence of a sufficient number of protective factors</u>.

- The <u>psychological terms</u> associated with antisocial behavior (e.g., **externalizing** versus **internalizing** behaviors; <u>conduct disorders; ADHD</u>, etc.) are introduced briefly.

- Official statistics to set the stage
    - <u>1.8 to 2.2 million juveniles under the age of 18 are arrested</u> by law enforcement officers in the U.S.

- Numbers always fluctuate
    - In 2000 more than **30 million youth** were under juvenile court jurisdiction.

- <u>Nonviolent nature of most offense</u>; young ages

Summary of Key Concepts

Concept	*Definition*
Risk factors	**Experiences & influences** that increase the tendency to become antisocial & delinquent
Protective factors	Experiences & **abilities** that help people adjust & **cope** with negative & adverse events
Competence	Ability to **exert control** over one's life & to adjust to problems effectively

Resilience	Ability to **overcome** risk factors and to function adaptively despite being exposed to serious threats & negative experiences

History

A SHORT HISTORY OF ILLINOIS CORRECTIONS

Public flogging, the pillory for imprisonment, or a short time in county jails comprised the earliest forms of punishment for public offenders after Illinois was chartered in 1818 as the nation's 21st state. The state's few jails consisted of the most part of rude log dwellings.

According to a historian writing of the time, "This prison was ordered to be build of hewn timber, 12 inches square and was considered, in those pioneer times, quite a terror to all who dared trample upon the majesty of the law."

The author was referring to the jail erected in 1818 in Crawford County. Illinois county records reveal that the oldest jail was built five years earlier in Gallatin County. Hans W. Mattick and Ronald P. Sweet, authors of *Illinois Jails*, have described well the procedure for booking prisoners in those rustic structures:

In those days, a typical prisoner would have entered a two-story log structure with three or four narrow, barred windows through the only door, located on the second floor. If he was considered dangerous, he would have been let down to the ground floor on a ladder placed through a hole in the ceiling and later withdrawn. He shared his quarters with the debtors, the insane, the inebriate and other "evil doers." Generally, no heat was

provided and a bucket served his sanitary needs.

It was recognized by thinking men at the time that the prevalent forms of punishment needed changing. But the public's apathy to any increase in taxation prevented adoption of any other policy until 1827. During that year, the General Assembly decided that certain saline lands grated the state by the federal government for the use and support of salt works be sold, if permission could be obtained from Congress. Permission was granted and on agreement within the state, the western portion of Illinois allotted its half of the funds to the building of a penitentiary at Alton. The eastern half of the state took its portion and used the money for other needed public improvements.

The funds allotted for construction were inadequate, however, and in 1831, the General Assembly appropriated an additional $10,000 from the state treasury.

Interestingly, in 1831, the state's criminal code was revised, making public whipping and exposure in the pillory illegal forms of punishment. Instead, public offenders were now to be confined in the Alton penitentiary (whipping, however, apparently did not entirely disappear from use, for in 1845, a report from the Alton prison reveals the lashing of an offender with a rawhide upon his naked back).

Even though the law was changed, public approval of the new system of punishment was slow in coming. The early settlers seemed to resent the denial of one of their cherished forms of popular amusement–public flogging and the pillory.

The Alton institution received its first inmates in 1833. The prison's 24 cells contained beds of straw with coverings of blankets and buffalo robes. Management from 1838 to the penitentiary's close was in the hands of a "lessee," to whom the state leased the

physical property and its men for a fixed sum. The lessee, in turn, furnished supplies,

handled all the products of convict labor, employed guards and exercised the general

powers of the warden.

It soon became apparent that the site for the prison was ill-chosen. The buildings had

been erected on the side of a steep slope extending down to the Mississippi River and

whenever it rained, deep gullies were cut through the yard, undermining the facility's

walls. Constant outlays for repairs were causing a severe drain on the state treasury.

Addressing the General Assembly in February 1847, Dorothea L. Dix was severely

critical of Illinois' treatment of prisoners and of the Alton penitentiary. Having made a

study of the state's care or lack of it, she advised the legislators to stop wasting further

funds on the Alton institution, to abandon it and build another elsewhere. She pointed

out, among other faults, that the prison hospital was located in a damp, unventilated

cellar; that there were not chapel, chaplain, or moral and religious instructors; no

provisions for destitute discharged convicts, whose own clothing was often lost or rotted

by the end of their terms; that there were no bathing facilities; that the dining room had

neither flagging nor flooring, but a dirt floor, which could not be washed; and that this

was the only prison in the United States at the time in which the inmates had to stand

while eating their meals.

The prison population grew rapidly. Writing in 1854, Thomas Ford said, "In the course of

15 years of experience under the new system, I am compelled to say that crime has

increased out of all proportion to the increase in inhabitants." By 1857, the facility contained 256 cells with two men to a cell.

During that year, the General Assembly appropriated funds for erection of a new 1,000-cell prison at Joliet, and in 1860, all prisoners were transferred there from Alton. The federal government then took over the Alton facility for use as a military reservation for Confederate prisoners and dissenters. At one time, nearly 2,000 men were incarcerated there.

The original leasing of prisoners to the lowest bidder, which was still in vogue when the Joliet prison was opened, was abandoned in July 1867 as un-Christian and inhumane. The state took over control and management of the institution and during the last of Governor John R. Palmer's administration (1873), the prison became self-supporting and had a surplus. The institution's favorable cash position was due mainly to the fact that although the leasing plan had been abandoned, another system was devised whereby the state let to private contractors the services of fixed numbers of prisoners to work in specified industries at so much per day per prisoner. As distasteful as the system was, it seems to have been profitable to the state as well as to the contractors. Many men laid the foundations for large fortunes in the shoe, shirt and furniture factories and the foundries of the old Joliet prison.

Opposition to this system began to make itself felt, however, the hue and cry coming principally from organized labor. But it was not until 1904 that the state abandoned contract labor and substituted in its place the prison industries system. Manufacturers and labor soon attacked this system, however, and gradually succeeded in reducing the industries to the vanishing point. In 1931, the present state-use system was adopted

by the General Assembly, after organized manufacturers and labor agreed to the bill.

As the prison population grew, so did the institution itself. New additions were built from

time to time and minor changes in the prisoners' daily routine took place. The inmates

were fed in their cells until May 30, 1903, when a central dining room was opened. The

lock-step was continued until June 1905, when it was abolished.

The Illinois State Reform School at Pontiac was opened on June 23, 1871, being first

used as a facility for male first time offenders aged 16 to 26. The reform school idea

originated from the Illinois Teachers Association, who secured the enactment of the law

creating the facility in 1867. The original site was given to the state by Jesse W. Fell, of

Bloomington, a friend of Abraham Lincoln and to whom Lincoln gave his autobiography.

The Pontiac facility's name was changed in 1892, becoming the Illinois State

Reformatory, and again in 1933, when it became the Pontiac branch of the Illinois State

Penitentiary.

The next penitentiary to be built in Illinois was Menard. The site chosen faces the

Mississippi River, almost opposite the site of old Kaskaskia, the land formerly belonging

to the Menard family. Most of the labor of building the facility was furnished by

prisoners transferred from the Joliet penitentiary. The first cellhouse was completed in

1878, and contained 400 cells. The second cellhouse was built in 1890.

History appears to have been amiss in accounting for the incarceration of female

prisoners. However, in 1889, the General Assembly passed a law requiring that women

be sent to the Joliet prison. For a time, they were housed on the fourth floor of the administration building, and in June 1895, a building for women prisoners was opened. It had accommodations for 100 females, each cell with an outside window. This facility was used until the 1930s, when the State Reformatory for Women was opened at Dwight. The institution at Joliet was remodeled at a cost of $100,000 and converted into a receiving and diagnostic depot.

During the first year of Governor Charles S. Deneen's administration in 1909, a widespread agitation against conditions at the Joliet prison attracted the attention of Illinois' citizens, resulting in a series of investigations. Spirited rebukes of the state for maintaining brutal and inhumane conditions resulted in an act of the legislature, which appropriated initial funding for acquisition of lands for a new prison near Joliet. The idea was that the new facility would absorb the population of the old prison and that plant could be abandoned.

A commission of three had been provided by law to design and erect the penitentiary. By 1917, the walls of the first cellhouse of the new Stateville plant began to creep upward. The architect for the new institution had visited several countries in Europe in quest of ideas and returned home with enthusiastic plans for circular cellhouses. The original plans called for each cell to accommodate one man comfortably and the inclusion of toilet facilities and an outside window. Work progressed until the 65 acres of compound were enclosed by a wall 35-feet high and 6,750-feet long. The wall was completed in the summer of 1920, but other essentials, such as heat and kitchens had not been completed so that the prison could be occupied. The penitentiary was finally completed and prisoners began moving in. Notwithstanding the development of the Stateville branch, an official at the time reported, "The old prison with its tiny cells still has its 1,800 men and in periods of industrial activity, it and its cell blocks are swathed in the smoke and the gases of the steel mills that have been built up to its front gate."

In 1923, when the law was amended so that circuit, county and municipal courts might sentence offenders, the Illinois State Farm at Vandalia came into being. The original 1,200-acre site was designed for misdemeanants found guilty of petty offenses with terms ranging from 60 days to a year.

The State Reformatory for Women at Dwight was established in the early 1930s through combined efforts of the Illinois Federation of Women's Clubs whose members had worked diligently for many years to promote appropriate legislation for creation of such a facility.

A new era in corrections in Illinois was begun on July 22, 1969, when Governor Richard B. Ogilvie created the Task Force on Corrections, and named as its chairman Peter B. Bensinger, chairman of the Illinois Youth Commission. The task force met throughout the summer of 1969 and presented its recommendations to Governor Ogilvie that November.

In presenting his message outlining creation of the new Department of Corrections to the 76th General Assembly, Governor Ogilvie said, "In recommending this department, I emphasize this: we must break the present cycle of arrest, incarceration and release, which in a majority of cases is repeated over and over again. We are faced with the most difficult of all tasks—the understanding and changing of human behavior—and we must approach our job with a full awareness of the failure of past policies.

"In Illinois we keep our adult felons incarcerated for periods longer than 45 other states, yet our rate of recidivism, or return to prison, is one of the highest. We speak of rehabilitation, but we provide only one vocational officer to every 50 custodial officers at Joliet. We have given our state a half-way house program and work release programs, but we have not given a full professional department to administer these programs."

"The proposal which I am submitting to you today for the creation of the Department of Corrections is an adaption of the Model Act for Standard Correctional Services of the National Council on Crime and Delinquency. This Model Act has served as the pattern for penal reform in four states in the last three years. It reflects a joint effort, which we have undertaken with the John Howard Association and the Illinois Committee of the NCCD."

The governor ended his special message to the legislature with the plea, "the threat to our people and our institutions is not of the future–it is a clear and present danger. It must be met with all the skills, the tools, the financial backing and the dedication we can summon to the task. With your help, this administration will take the first vital steps which this present danger demands."

Source: *First Annual Report 1970*

Illinois Department of Corrections

Illinois Department of Corrections-Mission Statement

Mission Statement

"The mission of the Department of Corrections is to protect the public from criminal offenders through a system of incarceration and supervision which securely segregates offenders from society, assures offenders of their constitutional rights and maintains programs to enhance the success of offenders' reentry into society."

Agency Overview

Mission

To serve justice in Illinois and increase public safety by promoting positive change in offender behavior, operating successful reentry programs, and reducing victimization.

Vision

- We will operate safe, secure, and humane correctional facilities.

- We will provide quality services to those who require medical and mental health treatment.

- We will evaluate offenders individually and develop an appropriate course of action based on individual needs.

- We will reduce recidivism by offering seamless, efficient services that are geared toward offender rehabilitation.

- Staff is our greatest asset and we will ensure that all staff is trained to the highest professional level.

- This is a team-based environment where open communication and sharing new ideas are encouraged.

- We value the well-being of IDOC staff and offenders and will serve the people of Illinois with compassion and fairness.

About the Illinois Department of Corrections

The Illinois Department of Corrections (IDOC) was established in 1970. During its creation, the agency combined administration of all state prisons, juvenile centers and adult and juvenile parole services under one direction for the first time. The creation

of the training academy followed in 1974, which helped set the foundation of training the

best staff possible for the agency's correctional facilities. On July 1, 2006, the Illinois

Department of Juvenile Justice was formed, which separated the adult and juvenile

corrections systems.

When IDOC originated, Illinois only operated seven adult facilities. Since that time,

stricter laws have resulted in increased sentencing and longer terms. To address this

steady increase in the inmate population, the agency today operates 25 adult correctional

centers as well as boot camps, work camps and adult transition centers.

Safety is at the forefront of agency operations with an emphasis on frontline staff to

protect and control inmates. A number of initiatives to ensure the safety of employees

and inmates have yielded significant results. Security level designations, controlled line

movement, inmate property boxes and increased monitoring of security threat groups

have contributed to a more secure Illinois prison system.

IDOC's Fiscal Year 2015 budget totals $1,414,403,728. The agency employs

approximately 11,600 employees and is responsible for the management of nearly 44,400

adult inmates and supervision of 28,000 parolees.

Today, inmates and parolees are now given more opportunities for successful reentry into

society than ever before.

All 25 correctional centers participate in reentry summits. The summits help address

reintegration and recidivism by promoting relationships between ex-offenders,

community service providers, policy experts and government agencies. Topics covered

include finance and economics, religion, spirituality, mental health and physical well-being, employment, housing and education as it relates to ex-offenders. Resource

fairs also introduce participants to agencies that can help them with jobs, housing, life

skills and other needs after they are released from prison.

The IDOC Parole Program addresses public safety and enhances parole supervision on

the streets through increased monitoring and graduated sanctions. All parolees receive

direct supervision in the community. The Parole Division has increased its parole agent

numbers and contact with parolees as they return to the community, as well as has case

management programs and specialized parole surveillance units.

IDOC has an aggressive sex offender parole supervision program and specially trained

agents supervise the state's paroled sex offenders. The department has implemented a

Global Positioning System, which uses satellite technology to track high-risk sex

offender parolee movement.

The department has enhanced the community reentry process through its development of

the Community Support Advisory Council (CSAC) in high-impact areas of the state

where a large majority of parolees return. CSACs are community-based partnerships

designed to work collaboratively with parole and other existing community resources to

develop wraparound services for parolees, while assisting other groups with building

community capacity to develop their own resources.

Launched in 2010, another reentry initiative developed by parole are Summit of Hope

events, which provide community expos of services and resources to assist ex-offender

reintegrate safely into the community to reduce recidivism. The Summit of Hope is an

invitation only event for those local parolees in each community. The event is designed to

bring the community together, gather all resources available, and put them under one roof in providing a one-stop environment where parolees can obtain the necessary assistance to move past the barriers which prevent them from success.

As an added focus on community reentry, IDOC assists veterans who are currently incarcerated through the Incarcerated Veterans Transition Program. The program serves to support reentry by accessing the strengths and needs of veteran offenders and identifying programs and services to support their transition into society. The program is in collaboration between IDOC, Illinois Department of Veterans Affairs, the Illinois Department of Employment Security and the Federal Department of Labor. About 18 months prior to release, incarcerated veterans are offered the opportunity to participate in the Incarcerated Veterans Transition Program. The program includes educational modules, employment workshops and counseling and linkage to other benefits and programs, such as health services, housing arrangements and obtaining I.D. cards.

Frequently Asked Questions
FAQ Index
1. What is Sentence Credit?
2. Does Corrections have a program of incarceration payments?
3. What are "C-Number" inmates?
4. How do sentencing laws work?
5. Can I communicate with an inmate over the Internet?
6. What is the situation with older inmates?
7. I am a former inmate of IDOC and would like to have my name removed from the Internet Inmate Search Database. How can I do that?
8. How do I write/correspond with an inmate?
9. How can I send an electronic message to an inmate?
10. What items can I mail to an inmate?
11. How can I send money to an inmate?
12. What is the situation with boot camps in Illinois?
13. What is the procedure for assigning inmates to facilities when they begin to serve their sentence?
14. How long must an inmate be in prison before they can go to a work release center?

15. How can I obtain public archived information about past IDOC inmates?
16. What is the role of the Prisoner Review Board?
17. What are the procedures for receiving collect telephone calls from an inmate?
18. What are the procedures for visiting an inmate?
19. What is IDOC's visitation policy for a proposed visitor who has been convicted of a criminal offense or who has criminal charges pending?
20. Who sets the conditions for parole?
21. How can I obtain public information about a current inmate or parolee?
22. What is reception and classification?
23. What medicines can an offender bring once sentenced to the Illinois Department of Corrections?
24. How does an inmate get transferred to another facility?
25. What is the situation with work release programs in Illinois?
26. As a victim of a crime, is there any information available from the department?
27. How can I be notified of the release, transfer, escape, death, or out-to-court appearance of an inmate who is incarcerated in the Illinois Department of Corrections?
28. How do I obtain medical information about an inmate currently incarcerated?
29. Where can I get information regarding sex offenders?
30. How can an inmate being released to parole be approved to reside at my residence?
31. How can a parolee be transferred to another state?
32. How do I report possible criminal behavior of a parolee or a parole absconder?
33. I am interested in a career with the Illinois Department of Corrections. How can I obtain more information?
34. How can I serve as a volunteer with the Illinois Department of Corrections?
35. What's the difference between a jail and a prison?

Attorney FAQ

•What attorneys need to know about communicating with clients who are incarcerated in the Illinois Department of Corrections

•Legal Mail

•Attorney/Client Visits

•Phone Calls

•How do I serve a subpoena for an inmate's records?

•How do I serve a summons on an IDOC inmate in a civil non-IDOC-related case?

WHAT ATTORNEYS NEED TO KNOW ABOUT COMMUNICATING WITH CLIENTS WHO ARE INCARCERATED IN THE ILLINOIS DEPARTMENT OF CORRECTIONS

All inmates in the Illinois Department of Corrections are allowed to accept confidential mail communications from their attorneys. Additionally, with advance notification, private visiting arrangements can be made for attorneys on the inmate's visiting list. General population inmates may make collect calls to their attorneys on monitored phone lines for non-confidential communications. However, arrangements for unmonitored phone calls between attorneys and clients is an exception provided on a case-by-case basis. Unmonitored calls are generally only approved if other means of communicating are not adequate and the prison is able to accommodate the call.

In determining whether the prison will make arrangements for an unmonitored phone call, the Department will take into account court deadlines, which, if missed, could prejudice the client's legal interest.

The general rules on legal mail, visits, and phone calls are set forth in the Department Rule 525. (See 20 ILAC 525). The following clarifying information is intended to help you communicate with your client.

LEGAL MAIL:

All inmates may receive privileged communications from their attorneys. Attorneys should be aware of the following procedures:

1. On the outside of the envelope, clearly mark privileged mail as "Legal" or "Privileged" and put your name, title and return address.

2. Legal mail may only contain communications from the person whose name is on the outside of the envelope. Including third party correspondence or sending non-legal correspondence as privileged mail is prohibited. Non-legal correspondence may be sent as regular mail subject to inspection.

3. Incoming legal mail shall be opened in the presence of the committed person to whom it is addressed to inspect for contraband, to verify the identity of the sender, and to determine that nothing other than legal matter is enclosed.

4. The Department will not accept faxed communications on behalf of inmates.

Top of Page

ATTORNEY/CLIENT VISITS:

An attorney visiting an inmate as a family member or friend will be subject to the same monitored visiting policy as other visitors. The rules for visits are listed on this website under 'Visitation Rules.'

Requests for confidential attorney-client legal visits may be requested but must be approved in advance. Visiting areas for confidential legal visits are limited. Therefore, in addition to the facility visitation rules, the following additional requirements apply to legal visits:

1.The visit must be scheduled in advance. A request for an attorney/client visit must be in writing from the attorney and faxed to the facility where the client is currently incarcerated at least two business days prior to the requested date of the visit.

2.The written request must contain the following information: a.The client's name and IDOC identification number;

b.The preferred date and time of the requested visit; and

c.The name, telephone number, fax number, e-mail address (optional), and attorney registration number of the attorney requesting the visit.

d.The case name, case number, and court in which the attorney is representing the inmate.

Training Academy

ABOUT THE TRAINING ACADEMY

It is the mission of the Illinois Department of Corrections Training Academy to support and contribute to the mission of the Illinois Department of Corrections (IDOC). This will be accomplished through the development of quality training in all subjects identified as necessary for the discharge of the department's responsibilities. Training given by the academy will be relevant, realistic and current and will be available to appropriate target audiences of this and other agencies. Professionalism, accountability and the highest ethical standards will be emphasized in every curriculum offered.

The IDOC Training Academy is located on the grounds of the agency's headquarters in Springfield, Ill. The academy offers regional training sites located at Pontiac Correctional Center in Pontiac, Ill., for northern region training and on the campus of John A. Logan Community College in Marion, Ill., for southern region training. The academy also provides training where needed at prisons across the state.

The Training Academy's focus is to provide quality and up-to-date training using technology and reality based training, wherever possible, for all new incoming security and non-security staff. In addition, the academy develops and provides training for all existing staff members within the department to maintain and enhance their job performance. Training in the areas of Firearms, Crisis Intervention, Hostage Negotiations, Administration of Discipline, Critical Incident, Command Post, Prison Rape Elimination Act and Instructional Methods, to name a few, are offered throughout the year and taught by both academy instructors and subject-matter experts from throughout the corrections field. The academy also streamlines certain annual mandatory training by featuring it online to better accommodate the department's front line and support staff.

Other core curricula of the Training Academy include a one-week course Pre-service Orientation Training (PSOT) directed toward all non-security staff within the department to provide the skills, tools and knowledge for the management of daily occurrences. The Corrections Training Academy also provides an eight-week pre-service course for all new state correctional parole agents to prepare them in the supervision of parolees in the community. Also included is a weeklong annual in-service course for parole agents that provides instructions on the most up-to-date, efficient and safest tactics and techniques to assist in the performance of their jobs. This is achieved by instructing agents in reality based drills and scenarios, while experienced instructors evaluate the agent's proficiency. Finally, the Training Academy continues to provide support and training for other agencies within the state in the areas of criminal justice and corrections. The core curriculum of the Training Academy is the six-week new Correctional Officer Training or Pre-Service Security Training. Upon hire, the new correctional officer (cadet) will be assigned to attend this training located at the Training Academy in Springfield, Ill. New cadets will be transported from their facility to the Training Academy each week and should be prepared for a strict training schedule to include topics such as Professionalism, Firearms, Control Tactics, Use and Application of Restraints, Report Writing, Inmate Sexual Assault Prevention and Intervention, along with group practical exercises in one of the many facilities throughout the state. The training provided for all new cadets stresses teamwork and professionalism.

Cadets live in one of two dormitory buildings and adhere to strict rules involving property in which they can possess and conditions within their room. A new cadet can expect the following daily schedule:

1. 6:30a.m. - 7:15a.m. Breakfast

2. 7:15a.m. - 7:45a.m. Prepare for Daily Inspection

3. 8:00a.m. - 8:20a.m. Daily Inspection

4. 8:00a.m. - 8:30a.m. Daily Roll Call

5. 8:30a.m. - 11:30a.m. Class

6. 11:30a.m. - 12:30p.m. Lunch

7. 12:30p.m. - 4:00p.m. Class

8. 4:00p.m. - 5:30p.m. Study / Free Time

9. 5:30p.m. - 6:30p.m. Dinner

10. 6:30p.m. - 10:00p.m. Study / Free Time

11. 10:00p.m. Lights Out

Cadets entering the Training Academy will be provided further information by their hiring facility prior to arrival at the Training Academy. The cadet is strongly encouraged to be physically fit at the level required at screening prior to arrival at the Training Academy.

STAFF AND DEVELOPMENT TRAINING

- **Academics**

- **Employee Ethics, Professionalism**

- **Departmental Firearms Training**

- **Security, Custody and Control I and II**

- **Chemical Agents and Oleoresin Capsicum (Pepper Spray)**

- **Control Tactics**

- **Cell, Area, and Vehicle Search**

- **Restraints**

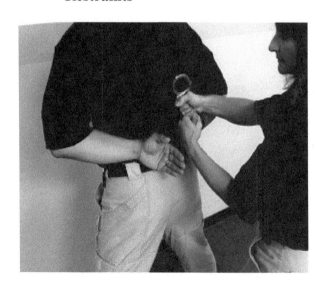

- **Personal Searches**

- **Hostage and Riot**

- **Critical Incident Management and Command Post Training**

- **Fire Emergencies**

- **Final Written Exam**

- **Dormitories**

- **Correctional Officer Trainee Graduation**

IDOC cadets participate in a formal ceremony upon successful completion of 240-hours of Pre-service Security Training at the academy. Marksmanship, Academic, Professional Standards and Instructor Recognition Awards are presented to the outstanding cadets in each category. Cadets are awarded certificates and badges and sworn to the Oath of Office.

"I shall carry out my professional duties in a manner which meets the department's highest ethical standards.

I shall conduct my personal affairs in a manner that reflects positively on my profession and the department.

I shall, in the course of my official duties, treat committed persons equally with fairness and dignity.

I shall act to preserve safety of the staff, committed persons and the public.

I will obey all rules and regulations of the department and all state and federal laws.

I shall uphold the Constitution of the United States and my sovereign State."

3.Information about where an inmate is housed as well as the facility's location and phone number can be obtained on this website under "Inmate Search" and "Facilities".

4.The Attorney will be given confirmation either by fax or e-mail as to whether the proposed visit is granted. Attorneys who arrive at a facility without prior approval for the visit will not be allowed a confidential legal visit.

5.Attorneys must present two forms of identification to enter the prison; one of which must be a photo ID. Identification must include the attorney's date of birth and current address. Attorneys are also required to present their current attorney registration card.

6.Law students (Supreme Court Rule 711 certification) working with an attorney will also be allowed attorney/client visits. A law student must submit proof of 711 certification and a written statement signed by the attorney attesting that the student is working under the attorney's supervision. The written statement must also include the name of the attorney's client with whom the student is seeking a confidential visit.

7.Attorneys arriving for a legal visit are reminded not to bring telephones, pagers, computers, or other similar electronic contraband into the facility. Additionally, tobacco products and metal binding clips are prohibited.

8.Visitation may be temporarily suspended during an institutional lockdown. It is recommended that attorneys contact the facility prior to departure to confirm that the client has not been transferred and that visitations at the facility have not been suspended. Lockdown status for a particular facility can also be found on this website under the link to "Facilities".

Top of Page

PHONE CALLS:

The IDOC is currently updating the attorney/client confidential call procedure. Attorneys wishing to speak with a client concerning confidential and privileged matters should contact the facility where the offender is housed for current procedures.

Top of Page

How do I serve a subpoena for an inmate's records?

A subpoena for records should be served on the prison facility where the records are located and not at the Chicago or Springfield IDOC Offices. The subpoena should be addressed to the facility 'Record Officer Supervisor.' The prison facility of any current inmate or former prison facility of any inmate on parole or mandatory supervised release can be found on the IDOC public website on the 'Inmate Search' link.

Please be advised, there are copying costs for records.

Top of Page

How do I serve a summons on an IDOC inmate in a civil non-IDOC-related case?

For service/summons on an inmate in a civil matter (e.g. home mortgage foreclosure, divorce, etc.), the serving party may serve the inmate through the county sheriff or by mail where allowed by law. For mail service, the inmate alone, and not IDOC, is responsible for returning the service receipt. Or, the serving party may personally serve the inmate through a private process server per the procedure set out in 735 ILCS 5/2-203.2.

IDOC does not transport inmates to court hearings in non-IDOC civil cases except per a court's writ of habeas corpus ad testificandum.

Industries

Illinois Correctional Industries

Illinois Correctional Industries (ICI) mission is to provide inmates with the skills and training necessary to be successful upon release from prison. ICI performs this objective at no cost to the taxpayers of Illinois. The revenue ICI generates from the sale of its products fully funds its entire operation. ICI currently has programs operating in 19 facilities that produce a variety of products and provide various services. These products and services include food, milk and juice, clothing, office and university furniture, eyeglasses, mattresses and pillows, and service dog training, just to name a few. The industry programs situated throughout the state are featured on the map below.

It is with this goal in mind that ICI continues to focus on inmate rehabilitation. Over 950 men and women offenders are voluntarily employed in meaningful work situations that aid in developing useable skills and positive work habits. Each day, they come to their job and learn how to work with others in many situations. They take direction from ICI supervisors and help teach peers new skills, while learning techniques for success at the same time. It is through the development of these work habits that inmates prepare themselves for the challenges of post-release employment.

To qualify as an ICI worker, inmates must demonstrate good disciplinary status; have received a positive review by Internal Affairs; and meet the facility time standard on time left on sentence. Inmates with life sentences are not employed by ICI.

Illinois Correctional Industries sells goods that affect many Illinois communities. For example, in Fiscal Year 2010, Dixon Correctional Industries sold more than 361,000 pairs of eyeglasses and earned gross revenues of almost $10.2 million. The Illinois

Department of Health and Human Services purchased more than 350,000 pairs of

eyeglasses for low income families, adults as well as children.

For more information visit the <u>Illinois Correctional Industries (ICI)</u> website.

Sustainability

In accordance with *20 ILCS 3954 the Green Governments Illinois Act,* the Illinois Department of Corrections is proud to announce the release of its first Sustainability Plan. Building a culture of sustainability in our agency will help to make us better stewards of the resources entrusted to us. We are dedicated to use common sense solutions, encourage innovation, and empower our staff, as well as offenders to help us in shifting the paradigm when it comes to defining our approach to sustainable practices as it relates to our daily operations.

Our paramount mission in the Department of Corrections is maintaining the safety and security of our facilities. Working within those parameters the IDOC launched its Sustainability Initiative on Earth Day 2012. What this means is that the department has committed to conserve energy, reduce our waste, grow more of our food and become a more self-sufficient agency. This multifaceted initiative will save taxpayer dollars, create offender vocational and job training opportunities, while reducing the environmental impacts of our operations.

The sustainable activities occurring in our facilities have been impressively far reaching and will continue flourish. An example of this is the Illinois Correctional Industries (ICI) Menard Recycling Center located at the Menard CC, near Chester, IL in rural Randolph

County. What initially started as a modest effort to pull cardboard from the prison's waste stream as a cost savings measure has grown beyond the prison's wall to a full-fledged Recycling Processing Center serving not only area state facilities but also most of the communities in the area. In light of this success and as a major component in the IDOC's Sustainability Initiative ICI has been tasked to expand this effort and build an internal recycling infrastructure within the agency using the Menard-ICI Program as the template.

For more information about facility specific sustainable efforts, please click on Illinois Correctional Industries or the respective facility name below:

- Big Muddy River Correctional Center

- Centralia Correctional Center

- Concordia Campus

- Danville Correctional Center

- Decatur Correctional Center

- Dixon Correctional Center

- East Moline Correctional Center

- Fox Valley Adult Transition Center

- Graham Correctional Center

- Hill Correctional Center

- Illinois River Correctional Center

- Jacksonville Correctional Center

- James R. Thompson Center

- Lawrence Correctional Center

- Lincoln Correctional Center

- Logan Correctional Center

- Menard Correctional Center

- Peoria Adult Transition Center

- Pinckneyville Correctional Center

- Pontiac Correctional Center

- Robinson Correctional Center

- Shawnee Correctional Center

- Sheridan Correctional Center

- Southwestern Illinois Correctional Center

- Stateville Correctional Center

- Taylorville Correctional Center

- Vandalia Correctional Center

- Vienna Correctional Center

- Western Illinois Correctional Center

IDOC Advisory Board

Illinois Department of Corrections Advisory Board

An advisory board to the agency is established under the Illinois Compiled Statutes. The Adult Advisory Board is established by Chapter 730 Illinois Compiled Statues 5/3-2-6 and is composed of nine persons appointed by the Governor for a term of six years. The Director and Assistant Director serve as ex-officio members of the Board.

The Board advises the Director concerning policy matters and programs of the Department with regard to the custody, care, study, discipline, training and treatment of persons in the State correctional institutions and for the care and supervision of persons released on parole.

Member Names

Baldwin, John

Taylor, Gladyse

Berry, Wilder Kendric

Kunard, Laura

Lape, Keith

Lee, Edna

Olson, David

Quezada-Gomez, Carlos

Watson, H. Richard

Whittington, Philip

Young, Donald

Subcommittee on Women Offenders

The Subcommittee on Women Offenders advises the Advisory Board and the Director on all policy matters and programs of the Department with regard to the custody, care, study, discipline, training and treatment of women in the State correctional institutions and for the care and supervision of women released on parole. The Subcommittee shall be composed of 3 members of the Advisory Board appointed by the Chairman who shall designate one member as the chairman of the Subcommittee. The Subcommittee shall meet no less often than quarterly and at other times at the call of its chairman.

Reference

http://nij.gov/Pages/welcome.aspx

Fulton County

Drug Court

Program Manual

Revised October 5, 2011

Table of Contents

1. Foreword 3

2. Confidentiality 3

3. Key Components of Drug Court 4

4. Referrals to Drug Court 5

5. Eligibility for Drug Court 5
      A. Qualifying Factors 5
      B. Disqualifying Factors 5
      C. Initial Intake Process 6
      D. Drug Court Screening 6
      E. Comprehensive Assessment 7

6. Requirements for Admission to Drug Court 8

7. Judicial Dispositions Allowing Admission to Drug Court 9

8. Successful Graduation of Defendant From Drug Court Program 10

9. Unsuccessful Termination of Defendant From Drug Court 10

10. Drug Court Team Members and Their Responsibilities 10

11. Drug Court Sessions and Procedures 12

12. Drug Court Case Staffings 13

13. Drug Court Program Phases 13

14. Incentives 15

15. Sanctions 15

16. Graduation Requirements 16

17. Termination 17

18. Duties of Drug Court Officer 17

19. Drug Testing Protocol 19

20. Amendments to Drug Court Manual 20

1. Foreword

The Fulton County Drug Court Program is a highly structured judicial intervention process for substance abuse treatment of eligible Defendants. It is a collaborative effort involving the judge, state's attorney, defense counsel, probation officers, substance abuse treatment professionals, law enforcement and community based organizations. It emphasizes early identification and intervention, a non-adversarial approach, a continuum of services, frequent and ongoing judicial interaction, frequent drug testing, a coordinated strategy and response, and measurements for effectiveness.

The Program goals are to effectively address and reduce substance abuse, to assist in creating productive citizens, and to reduce recidivism. Ideally, the reduction of recidivism is best achieved when the Defendant is able to properly function within the community, to be gainfully employed whenever possible, and to live a fulfilling and productive life. The benefits to the community include increasing public safety, providing a more productive workforce, and reducing cost to the criminal justice system and the taxpayers.

Drug Court is a team approach which encourages the Defendant to deal with his/her substance abuse problems. The team uses incentives and sanctions to motivate the Defendant to make positive life changes.

The Fulton County Court Services Department shall appoint one or more of its adult probation officers to serve as a "Drug Court Officer".

The participation of the Fulton County Court Services Department is an inherent part of the Fulton County Drug Court Program. All guidelines and policies applicable to the Ninth Judicial Circuit Court Services Department apply to Court Services Employees Participating in the Drug Court Unit. This Drug Court Program Manual Shall Be an Addendum to the Court Services Departments Manual.

Fulton County Drug Court is authorized by 730 ILCS 166, Drug Court Treatment Act.

2. Confidentiality

All information pertaining to drug court participants is strictly confidential and is not to be shared with any outside party. However, any information may be shared or inspected by the persons on the Drug Court Team upon execution of a proper release signed by the Defendant. All information pertaining to drug court participants may not be shared with anyone not on the Drug Court Team, including other probation officers, except by court order or Defendant's release of information. All such information is not and shall not be a public record.

Drug Court applicants or participants shall be required to sign release of information forms so that relevant information may be shared with appropriate agencies. If an applicant or participant refuses to sign the necessary releases, he or she may be ruled ineligible to participate in the Drug Court Program.

Drug Court probation files, including pre-sentence and post-sentence evaluations or investigations, computer notes, and all other Drug Court materials are considered to be confidential information and are not to be released except by court order or client release of information. Non-Drug Court case information may be released to other probation departments as appropriate.

Any family member, attorney, member of the public, or any other person observing or participating in drug court shall sign a confidentiality agreement promising not to disclose any information obtained from observing or participating in Drug Court.

Drug Court material is protected by federal regulations of confidentiality (42 CFR Part 2) and the Illinois Mental Health Developmental Disabilities Confidentiality Act (740 ILCS 110/1 *et. seq.*). Both federal regulation and state law prohibit the disclosure of treatment records and information without written consent of the recipient of treatment.

3. Key Components of Drug Court

1. Drug Court integrates alcohol and other drug treatment services and, when appropriate, mental health services with justice system case processing.
2. Using a non-adversarial approach, prosecution and defense counsel promote public safety while protecting Defendants' due process rights.
3. Eligible Defendants are identified early and promptly placed in the drug court program.
4. Drug courts provide access to a continuum of alcohol, drug, and related treatment and rehabilitative services.
5. Abstinence is monitored by frequent alcohol and other drug testing.
6. A coordinated strategy governs Drug Court responses to Defendants' compliance.
7. Ongoing judicial interaction with each Drug Court Defendant is essential.
8. Monitoring and evaluation measure the achievement of program goals and gauge effectiveness.
9. Continuing interdisciplinary education promotes effective Drug Court planning, implementation, and operations.
10. Forging partnerships among Drug Courts, public agencies, and community-based organizations generates local support and enhances drug court program effectiveness.

4. Referrals to Drug Court

Referrals to Drug Court may be for Defendants both prior to conviction and after conviction. Referrals may come from any source including the Fulton County State's Attorney, the Fulton County Public Defender, private defense counsel, the Fulton County Court Services Department, a Judge, or the treatment provider.

The Fulton County State's Attorney, upon consultation with the Drug Court Officer of the Court Services Department, shall determine whether or not a referral shall be advanced for further screening and assessment.

5. Eligibility for Drug Court

Initial eligibility for participation in Drug Court shall be determined by the intensity of the substance abuse by the Defendant. While felony cases are given preference, non-felony cases may be considered.

A. Qualifying Factors

In order to qualify for Drug Court, the following factors must apply to the Defendant:

1. Must be a resident of Fulton County.
2. Must be a substance abuser.
3. Must have offenses related to substance abuse.
4. Must be diagnosed as a substance abuser.
5. Must be a non-violent offender as defined by State and Federal statute.
6. Must be an adult offender.
7. May have prior felony convictions.
8. Both male or female offenders may qualify.
9. If the Defendant has probation violations, then the new offenses must be drug related and/or drug related technical violations.

B. Disqualifying Factors

A Defendant shall be excluded from Drug Court participation if any of the following apply:

1. The Defendant is excluded from participation by any statute, including being a violent offender, as defined by any State and Federal statute including 730 ILCS 166/ 20(b)(4):

The Defendant has been convicted of a crime of violence within the past 10 years excluding incarceration time, including but not limited to: first degree murder, second degree murder, predatory criminal sexual assault of a child, aggravated criminal sexual assault, criminal sexual assault, armed robbery, aggravated arson, arson, aggravated kidnaping, aggravated battery resulting in great bodily harm or permanent disability, stalking, aggravated stalking, or any offense involving the discharge of a firearm.

2 Prior completion or discharge from a Drug Court (per statute 730 ILCS 166/20).
3. Denial of addiction, dependency, or abuse.
4. Active participation as a gang member defined by Illinois Criminal Code.
5 Diagnosis of severe mental health issues that would interfere with the ability to work in treatment. A mental health issue does not preclude participation in Drug Court if the Defendant is able to meaningfully participate in Drug Court and treatment.
6. The Defendant has an infectious disease which is a serious health risk to others and appropriable measures to safeguard the health of others are impractical.

C. Initial Intake Process

1. The State's Attorney must approve the Defendant for the initial Drug Court screening upon consultation with the Drug Court Officer in the Court Services Department.
2. If approved by the State's Attorney, the Drug Court Officer shall review the Defendant's criminal history to determine if the Defendant is prohibited from participating in Drug Court.
3. The Drug Court Officer will explain to the Defendant all conditions as well as consequences for non-compliance with the Drug Court Program. It will be the responsibility of the Drug Court Officer to ensure that the Defendant understands his/her obligations to the Court.
4. If the Defendant meets all of the above conditions, the Defendant shall then participate in a Drug Court Screening.
5. The Drug Court Officer will schedule an appointment with the defendant within five working days for a Drug Court Screen Interview.

D. Drug Court Screening

The Defendant will be scheduled for a Drug Court Screen Interview within 5 working days of receipt of the referral.

Drug Court Screening is a process to determine whether an individual is a likely candidate for participation in Drug Court. The Drug Court Officer will interview the Defendant and review Defendant's criminal, social, mental health, and other appropriate records and information to elicit the following factors:

1. Consumption Patterns – The type, frequency, duration, and quantity of substance abuse.
2. Feelings of loss of control related to substance abuse.
3. Extent of physical consequences of substance abuse.
4. Experience with physiological problems related to withdrawal from substance abuse.
5. The Defendant's recognition of problems related to his/her substance abuse.
6. Mental Health – Review the Defendant's ability or capacity to comprehend and participate in Drug Court and treatment.
7. The Drug Court Officer shall conduct a urinalysis and/or other drug/alcohol tests and shall document the results of all information gathered in the screening process.
8. The Drug Court Officer shall provide a written screening report and recommendations to the State's Attorney and the Drug Court Judge. Should the Drug Court Officer deem a candidate inappropriate and the referral source disagrees with this conclusion, the Drug Court Team will review the case for eligibility and further assessment. The decision of the team shall be final, except that the State's Attorney must concur with any decision that the Defendant is eligible for the Comprehensive Assessment.
9. The Drug Court Officer shall have the Defendant sign a release of information to the treatment provider, as well as any other release of information forms deemed appropriate.
10. The Drug Court Officer will send a referral packet to the treatment provider within 3 working days.
11. The Defendant will make an appointment with the Drug Court approved treatment provider within 5 working days of the initial Intake Screen appointment.
12. The treatment provider will perform a Comprehensive Assessment.

E. Comprehensive Assessment

Assessment is a more comprehensive procedure than screening, intended to confirm or refute the screening results. Special attention is given to the specific substance being abused, the extent of the use of such substance, any co-existing health problems (particularly mental health disorders, and the initial formulation of a treatment plan.

The treatment provider will assess each candidate and determine whether the candidate meets the following criteria:

1. There is a relationship between substance abuse and criminality.
2. The Defendant's substance abuse has caused a serious impact on major life areas of his or her life such as family, interpersonal relationships, education, employment, leisure and health.
3. The Defendant is an addict, substance abuser, or is chemically dependent.
4. The Defendant does not have a serious mental illness which would prohibit participation in substance abuse treatment.
5. The Defendant shows a willingness to address his/her substance abuse addiction (and his/her mental health issues, as required).

The treatment provider shall prepare an Assessment Report, which will be provided to the Drug Court Officer who shall distribute the Assessment Report to the State's Attorney, Defense Counsel, Drug Court Judge, and the other Drug Court Team members.

The Drug Court Officer shall submit the Assessment Report from the treatment provider along with a written screening report and recommendations to the State's Attorney and Drug Court Judge. Should the drug court officer deemed a candidate inappropriate and a referral source disagrees with this conclusion, the Drug Court Team shall review the case for eligibility and further assessment. The decision of the team shall be final, except the State's Attorney must concur with any decision that the Defendant is eligible to participate.

6. Requirements for Admission to Drug Court

A Defendant may be admitted to Drug Court if he or she meets all eligibility requirements including, but not limited to, the following:

1. The Defendant has successfully completed his/her initial screening with the Drug Court Officer and has successfully completed the Comprehensive Assessment.

2. The majority of the Drug Court Team members present at an assessment staffing determines, based on the Assessment Report, that the Defendant appears to be eligible for admission to Drug Court (except, however, the State's Attorney shall have an absolute veto to bar the Defendant from participating in Drug Court).

3. The Defendant shall execute a written agreement as to his or her participation in the program and shall agree to all of the terms and conditions of the program including, but not limited to, the possibility of sanctions or incarceration for failing to abide or comply with the terms of the program.

4. If the States Attorney and the Defendant have entered into a written agreement concerning disposition of charges against the Defendant upon successful or unsuccessful completion of the Drug Court Program, such written agreement shall be disclosed to and filed with the Drug Court before admission to the Drug Court Program.

5. The Defendant's attorney shall review with the Defendant the form "Drug Court Conditions and Agreements". If the defendant continues to desire to participate in drug court, then he shall sign that form pursuant to 730 ILCS 166/2 5(c).

6. The Court shall:
   A. Review the assessment and eligibility of the Defendant.
   B. Advise the Defendant of the nature of Drug Court.

C. Advise the Defendant of his responsibilities and determine the Defendant's willingness to participate.

D. Consider any written agreement between the State and the Defendant concerning Defendant's admission into the Drug Court Program and the consequences upon Defendant's successful or unsuccessful completion of the Drug Court Program.

E. Thereafter, the Court shall determine whether the Defendant is accepted into the Drug Court Program.

F. The Judge shall inform the Defendant that if the Defendant fails to meet the conditions of the Drug Court Program, that eligibility to participate in the program may be revoked and the Defendant may be sentenced or the prosecution continued as provided in the Unified Code of Corrections for the crime charged or in any written agreement between the Defendant and the States Attorney.

7. It is recommended that a judge other than the Drug Court Judge shall be the judge who sentences a Defendant to the Drug Court Program.

7. Judicial Dispositions Allowing Admission to Drug Court

Prior to being admitted to the Drug Court Program, the States Attorney and the Defendant may enter into a written agreement concerning disposition of any pending or possible charges against the Defendant. Without limitation, the agreements may be in one of the following forms:

1. Pre-Adjudicatory Dispositions

The Defendant shall tender to the Court a guilty plea to one or more pending criminal charges, and/or to one or more pending Petitions to Revoke; and the Defendant shall waive all time limits for speedy trial, prompt preliminary hearing, or any and all other time limits allowed by law to the Defendant. Thereafter, the Court, by agreement of the parties, shall:

a. Generally continue the criminal prosecution against the Defendant until the Defendant is either successfully or unsuccessfully discharged from the Drug Court Program; and

b. Order the Defendant to comply with all terms and conditions of the Drug Court Program, including being incarcerated in the county jail for a total period not to exceed 180 days as a possible sanctions against the Defendant for non-compliance with the terms and conditions of the Drug Court Program.

2. Post-Adjudicatory Dispositions

The Defendant shall enter a guilty plea to one or more pending criminal charges, and/or one or more pending Petitions to Revoke; thereupon the Defendant shall be sentenced to either:

(a) To a period of probation. One of the terms of probation shall be that the Defendant must successfully complete the Drug Court Program.

(b) To a sentence of confinement in the county jail or the Department of Corrections. Service of such sentence shall be stayed pending successful completion of the Drug Court Program. If the Defendant is unsuccessfully discharged from the Drug Court Program, he shall thereupon commence his sentence of confinement. Any jail time the Defendant has served as a participant of Drug Court for violations of the Drug Court Rules shall not be credited to the original sentence of confinement in the county jail or in the Department of Corrections.

8. Successful Graduation of Defendant From Drug Court Program

Upon successful completion of the terms and conditions of the program, the Court may dismiss the original charges against the Defendant or successfully terminate the Defendant's sentence or otherwise discharge him or her from any further proceedings against him or her in the original prosecution pursuant to 730 ILCS 166/35.

9. Unsuccessful Termination of Defendant From Drug Court Program

If the States Attorney believes that a Defendant should be unsuccessfully discharged from the Drug Court Program, the States Attorney shall file a petition for such relief. Defendant shall be entitled to an evidentiary hearing on such petition and shall be entitled to all due process rights, including an appointed attorney if he or she cannot afford to hire an attorney.

It is recommended that a judge other than the Drug Court Judge be the judge who hears any petition to terminate a Defendant's participation in the Drug Court Program.

10. Drug Court Team Members and Their Responsibilities

The following persons are the core members of the Drug Court Team. Other members may be added as deemed appropriate by the core team members. The following are the major responsibilities for each Drug Court Team member:

Judge:
The judge acts as the lead partner in the Drug Court process. He or she participates in all Drug Court client staffings and presides over the court proceedings. He or she administers effective sanctions and incentives. The judge is a spokesperson to the community advocating Drug Court and support for the program.

State's Attorney:

The State's Attorney is the gatekeeper of the program. He or she participates in client staffings operating in a non-adversarial manner. He or she advocates for effective sanctions and incentives while ensuring community safety. The State's Attorney is a spokesperson to the community advocating Drug Court and support for the program. The State's Attorney may assign an assistant state's attorney to represent the State's Attorney's Office in the Drug Court Program.

Drug Court Officer:

The Court Services Department shall designate an officer or officers to be the Drug Court Officer. He or she has the overall responsibility to assist with the management and coordination of all facets of the Drug Court operations including maintaining the confidential Drug Court files. He or she participates in client staffings by reporting client's progress. He or she advocates for effective sanctions and incentives based upon the day-to-day knowledge of the Drug Court Defendant. The Drug Court Officer is a spokesperson to the community advocating support for the Drug Court Program.

Treatment Provider:

The treatment provider conducts a full assessment to ensure appropriate offenders are entered into Drug Court. He or she develops an individual treatment plan for each Defendant. He or she participates in client staffings by reporting on treatment progress. He or she advocates for effective sanctions and incentives based upon the day-to-day knowledge of the Drug Court Defendant. Treatment providers are spokespersons to the community advocating support for the Drug Court Program.

Law Enforcement:

The Fulton County Sheriff, or one Fulton County Deputy that he or she may appoint, and the City of Canton Chief of Police, or one Canton Police Officer that he or she may appoint, shall be full members of the Drug Court team. They act as a liaison to other law enforcement agencies. Law enforcement will assist with home visits as needed, help collect random drug tests as needed, process and serve warrants on Drug Court clients, and assist with identification of potential Drug Court clients. They shall participate in client staffings by reporting on Defendant's activities in the community. The law enforcement officers are spokespersons to the community advocating support for the Drug Court Program.

Public Defender and Defense Counsel:

The public defender and other defense counsel may, upon a case-by-case basis, be a member of the Drug Court team as they deem appropriate. He or she should monitor the referral and acceptance process. He or she may participate in client staffings, operating in a non-adversarial manner. He or she advocates for effective sanctions and incentives while ensuring the Defendant's legal rights are protected. The public defender and defense counsel is a spokesperson to the community advocating support for the Drug Court Program.

Evaluator:

The evaluators for the Fulton County Drug Court are the Fulton County Court Services Supervisor and the Fulton Circuit Drug Court Program Officer. The evaluators are full members of the Drug Court Team. He or she will work in collaboration with the Drug Court Team. He or she will assist in the collection of data to produce periodic outcome studies on Drug Court Defendants. He or she will lead project evaluation discussions with team members with the results to facilitate project implementation. He or she will help train team members in data collection and assist in preparing reports for statistical purposes. The evaluator is a spokesperson to the community advocating for Drug Court and support of the program.

11. Drug Court Sessions and Procedures

1. Drug Court sessions are held once each week or as otherwise directed by the Drug Court Judge. Defendants are notified in advance of when they are required to appear, and failure to appear when required may result in the issuance of an arrest warrant or a body attachment.

2. Appearances in court by Drug Court Defendants will vary in frequency based upon the Defendant's classification in Phase 1, 2, 3 or 4 of the program. The manner in which the cases are processed in each session remains solely within the discretion of the Drug Court Judge.

3. The Drug Court Officer shall attend all Drug Court staffings prior to Drug Court sessions. The Officer shall attend Drug Court at all times when it is in session. The Drug Court Officer duties include, but are not limited to, the following:

   * Participate in the pre-court staffing between the Drug Court Judge, States Attorney, treatment provider, law enforcement, and other Drug Court Team members.

   * Be prepared to contribute significant information regarding a Defendant's progress or lack thereof at the staffing and provide a written summary.

   * Conduct any drug testing that day as directed by the Court.

   * Meet and discuss any issues with the Defendants participating in the Drug Court Program.

   * Maintain a confidential file for each Defendant regarding proceedings during the Drug Court hearings.

12. Drug Court Case Staffings

Case staffings will be held weekly immediately prior to the Drug Court, with all team members attending. The Drug Court Judge will conduct and lead each staffing, seeking input from all members.

There are two (2) types of staffing:

1. Eligibility staffings are held to determine a Defendant's eligibility for Drug Court.

2. Compliance staffings are held to discuss a Defendant's compliance with the program. Compliance staffings will occur immediately prior to the commencement of court at a time to be determined by the Judge. Such staffings shall be attended by the Drug Court Officer, State's Attorney, Public Defender or Defense Counsel (when applicable), treatment providers, law enforcement, and the Drug Court Judge.

Incentives and sanctions will be agreed upon by the Drug Court Team. The Drug Court Judge will make the final determination for all incentives and sanctions.

13. Drug Court Program Phases

A Defendant must progress through and successfully complete the following four Drug Court Phases before completion and graduation from the Drug Court Program:

Phase 1
*   The Defendant shall meet with the Drug Court Officer or other probation officer as directed at least twice per week at his/her office.
*   The Defendant shall allow the Drug Court Officer to meet the Defendant at Defendant's home at any time the Drug Court Officer appears and requests a home visit.
*   The Defendant shall submit, at any time or place, to any authorized drug testing procedure or breathalyzer procedure requested by the Drug Court Officer or by any law enforcement officer a minimum of three times per week.
*   The Defendant shall attend and participate in any treatment recommended by treatment provider.
*   The Defendant shall attend Drug Court once each week.
*   The Defendant shall attend a Recovery Support or Self-Help Program at least three times per week, verified by sign-in sheets.
*   The Defendant shall attend any other ancillary program or treatment plan as indicated by Drug Court Team.
The Defendant shall not complete Phase 1 in less than 60 days.

Phase 2

*   The Defendant shall meet with the Drug Court Officer at least once per week at his/her office.
*   The Defendant shall allow the Drug Court Officer to meet the Defendant at Defendant's home at any time the Drug Court Officer appears and requests a home visit.
*   The Defendant shall submit, at any time or place, to any authorized drug testing procedure or breathalyzer procedure requested by the Drug Court Officer or by any law enforcement officer a minimum of two times per week.
*   The Defendant shall attend and participate in any treatment recommended by treatment provider.
*   The Defendant shall attend Drug Court once each week.
*   The Defendant shall attend a Recovery Support or Self-Help Program at least three times per week, verified by sign-in sheets.
*   The Defendant shall attend any other ancillary program or treatment plan as indicated by Drug Court Team.
*   The Defendant shall obtain employment or be enrolled in school.

The Defendant shall not complete Phase 2 in less than 60 days.

Phase 3

*   The Defendant shall meet with the Drug Court Officer at least once per week at his/her office.
*   The Defendant shall allow the Drug Court Officer to meet the Defendant at Defendant's home at any time the Drug Court Officer appears and requests a home visit.
*   The Defendant shall submit, at any time or place, to any authorized drug testing procedure or breathalyzer procedure requested by the Drug Court Officer or by any law enforcement officer a minimum of one or two times per week.
*   The Defendant shall attend and participate in any treatment recommended by treatment provider.
*   The Defendant shall attend Drug Court once each month.
*   The Defendant shall attend a Recovery Support or Self-Help Program at least three times per week, verified by sign-in sheets.
*   The Defendant shall attend any other ancillary program or treatment plan as indicated by Drug Court Team.
*   The Defendant shall maintain his/her employment and/or school enrollment.

The Defendant shall not complete Phase 3 in less than 120 days.

Phase 4 – Aftercare

*   The Defendant shall attend Drug Court once each month.
*   The Defendant shall submit to any authorized drug testing procedure or breathalyzer procedure at any time requested by the Drug Court Officer or by any law enforcement officer a minimum of one time per week as determined by the Drug Court Officer.
*   The Defendant shall meet with the Drug Court Officer at least once every other week at his/her office.

* The Defendant shall attend a Recovery Support or Self-Help Program at least one time per week, verified by sign-in sheets.
* The Defendant shall maintain payment plan compliance with regard to payments of all fines, costs, and other financial obligations associated with Drug Court and with Defendant's criminal case(s).
* The Defendant shall maintain employment or school attendance, unless previously waived by the Drug Court Team.

The Defendant shall not complete Phase 4 in less than 120 days.

14. Incentives

The Drug Court Team believes behavior does not change by punishment alone; therefore, incentives are used to reward the offender's positive behavior.

Incentives include, but are not limited to:
* Praise from the Court.
* Called first in court.
* Promotion to next phase.
* Reduction of fines/CSE.
* Calendars.
* Certificates with 12 month progressive seals.
* Recovery coins.
* Recovery books.
* Coupons for food or etc.
* Bikes or toys for their children.
* Raffle (prize given for consistent positive behavior).
* Excuse Cards to allow Defendant to avoid a minor sanction such as a writing assignment.

The team may also develop additional incentives that are unique to the individual.

15. Sanctions

The Drug Court Team believes a sanction is an immediate negative consequence in response to an undesirable behavior.

The intensity of sanctions increases with the number and seriousness of Defendant's non-compliance with the Drug Court Program.

Sanctions may be imposed for violation of the following rules:
* Positive drug test or breathalyzer test.
* Missed drug test or breathalyzer test.
* Adulterated or falsified drug test or breathalyzer test.
* Missed treatment appointment.

* Non-compliance in treatment.
* Unemployed when required to work.
* Missed court appearances.
* Failure to complete community service hours.
* Lack of positive involvement with his/her family, including meeting financial responsibilities and child care responsibilities (if applicable).
* Failure to attend GED or other education program or job training.
* Failure to properly attend a Recovery Support or Self-Help Program.
* Missed Drug Court Officer appointments.
* Failure to cooperate with Drug Court Officer.

Other rule violations, as deemed appropriate by the Court, may receive sanctions.

Sanctions include, but are not limited to:
* Defendant admonished by Court.
* Defendant placed in jury box and remains there until others are done.
* Defendant placed in a holding cell for a period of time.
* Defendant confined in the County Jail for a total not to exceed 180 days.
* Defendant subjected to increased drug testing.
* Defendant subjected to increased supervision.
* Defendant place on curfew.
* Defendant loses established sobriety time.
* Defendant demotion in Phase.
* Defendant subjected to electronic monitoring.
* Defendant ordered to perform community service hours.
* Defendant's recovery support meetings are increased.
* Defendant required to complete a writing assignment.

The team may also develop additional sanctions that are unique to the individual.

16. Graduation Requirements

The following requirements must be met for a Drug Court Defendant to graduate from Drug Court:

1. Completion of substance abuse treatment.
2. Be drug free for 12 months.
3. Be gainfully employed or furthering his or her education.
4. Be actively involved in recovery support activities.
5. Be in a stable living environment.
6. Fines and court costs must be paid in full, or Defendant must be in compliance with a payment plan for the past120 days.

17. Termination

Drug Court Defendants may be terminated from Drug Court for the following reasons:

1. Committing any new offense.
2. Adulteration of saliva or urine samples – multiple times.
3. Absconding from the jurisdiction.
4. Continued non-compliance of Drug Court rules and expectations.

If a petition to revoke probation or any other petition to terminate a Defendant's participation in Drug Court is filed by the State's Attorney's Office, it is recommended that the Drug Court Judge not preside over any such petition.

18. Duties of Drug Court Officer

A. General Duties

The Drug Court Officer is the primary case supervisor for Defendants sentenced to Drug Court. The Drug Court Officer shall be a probation officer of the Fulton County Court Services Department. The Drug Court Officer's responsibility (or his designee) include, but are not limited to, the following activities:

1. Conduct initial intake and screening of potential Drug Court Defendants to determine eligibility and interest, and to explain program requirements.
2. Serve on the Drug Court Team.
3. Inform the Drug Court Team of training opportunities.
4. Maintain cooperative relationships with treatment agencies, community organizations and other involved partners.
5. Attend Drug Court case staffings and court hearings, reporting compliance or noncompliance, and recommending incentives and sanctions. Attend Drug Court at all times when in session.
6. Maintain a confidential Drug Court File in reference to each Defendant recording the proceedings for each Defendant as directed by the Drug Court Judge.
7. Collect data and statistics and work closely with the program evaluator.
8. Promote team integrity.
9. Develop community resources.
10. Monitor client's compliance with Drug Court rules, communicating with the client in accordance with the program standards and phases.
11. Monitor and identify clients for random drug testing.
12. Conduct drug testing either on his own initiative or as directed by the Court, by himself or in cooperation with law enforcement.
13. Meet with and discuss any issues with Defendants who are in the Drug Court Program.

Additional duties and responsibilities may be assigned to the Drug Court Officer as future consideration so indicates.

B. Drug Court Officer's Duties After Defendant is Accepted into Drug Court

Intake:

Once a Defendant has been accepted into Drug Court, the Drug Court Officer will set an appointment for the initial intake. This intake will be held within seven working days of the court hearing accepting the Defendant into Drug Court. If the Defendant is in residential treatment or jail, probation will conduct an initial interview at the respective facility.

An intake will consist of:
* Review of the Drug Court Order.
* Signing of all required Drug Court forms.
* Signing of all required consent forms.
* Obtaining an initial drug screen.
* DNA indexing for felony Defendants, if not previously completed.
* LSI-R interview.
* Developing an initial supervision plan.
* Setting up a reporting schedule.
* Creating a Tracker file.
* Creating an office file.
* Creating a confidential Drug Court File.
* Coordination of treatment staffing.

C. Types of Visits and Contacts with Drug Court Officer
The following is a list of the types of visits and contacts a Drug Court Defendant will have:

Office Visit:

The Defendant will be given a designated day to report to the probation office. Additional office visits may be scheduled by the Drug Court Officer based upon the Defendant's compliance.

On a weekly basis they shall bring address and employment verification, via check stub and a piece of mail. Self-Help sheets (AA/NA attendance sheets) shall be viewed by the Drug Court Officer at each office visit. Random drug screens will be conducted. Supervision and treatment plan will be discussed.

Initial Home Visit:

Initial home visit shall be conducted within ten working days of being sentenced to Drug Court. Initial home visits will be conducted as set by the Ninth Judicial Circuit Court Services Standards and Guidelines.

18

Random Home Visits

Random home visits may be conducted at any time, day or night, without any notice to the Defendant at the Drug Court Officer's discretion.

Employment Visits:

Employment visits may be conducted at the Drug Court Officer's discretion.

Agency Visits:

If the Defendant is in residential treatment, a visit there will be considered a home visit.

Jail Visit:

If the Defendant is sentenced to jail for more than seven days, a jail visit will be conducted and considered a home visit.

Collateral Contacts:

Collateral contacts consist of any contact with agencies, family, employer, self-help sponsor, or others that may have contact or information concerning the Defendant. These contacts by the Drug Court Officer may be in person via the telephone, e-mail, or through progress summaries.

All visits and contacts shall be documented into the Tracker file within 24 working hours of contact, excluding weekends, holidays, and illness.

19. Drug Testing Protocol

"Drug testing" shall include any authorized form of testing including, but not limited to, saliva swabs, breathalyzer testing, urine samples, or blood samples.

The Drug Court Officer and the treatment provider shall coordinate drug testing for the Fulton County Drug Court.

Random and unscheduled drug tests will be conducted on at least a weekly basis. The number of drug screens taken in a week will depend on the phase that the Drug Court Defendant is in. Random drug tests may be taken at any time and at any place.

The drug test shall be administered in accordance with the procedures and guidelines of the department or agency conducting the test. A Consent Form shall be completed by each department or agency.

If there is doubt about any drug test, a second sample may be required.

20. Amendments to Drug Court Manual

This Drug Court Manual may be amended from time to time by the presiding Drug Court Judge, with the advice of the Drug Court Team.

BUILDING AN OFFENDER REENTRY PROGRAM:

A GUIDE FOR LAW ENFORCEMENT

Acknowledgments

This project was supported by grant number 2005-MU-MU-K012 awarded by the U.S. Department of Justice, Office of Justice Programs' Bureau of Justice Assistance. The opinions, findings, and conclusions or recommendations expressed in this document are those of the authors, and do not necessarily represent the official position or policies of the U.S. Department of Justice.

The International Association of Chiefs of Police (IACP) is grateful to a number of individuals who were instrumental in developing this guide. The IACP was fortunate to receive valuable input from approximately 50 law enforcement officials from 21 states and Canada who contributed information on their offender reentry program experiences through their participation in our regional focus groups and site visits. Specifically, we offer our appreciation to:

- Chief David Spenner (retired) and Sergeant Steve Madsen of the Racine (WI) Police Department for lending their experience in a variety of ways to include the production of the video, Offender Reentry: A Police Perspective.
- Those agencies represented at each of the regional focus groups and the sites profiled in this guide.
- Jim Jordan, Chief Alberto Melis, and Lieutenant Blake Miller for their review and contributions to this document.

For more information about law enforcement's role in offender reentry efforts or information contained in this guide, please contact Offender Reentry Project Manager Stevyn Fogg at the IACP: 1-800-THE-IACP ext. 842 or fogg@theiacp.org.

TABLE OF CONTENTS

INTRODUCTION

SECTION I: OFFENDER REENTRY 101

What is Offender Reentry?.. 2
What is Law Enforcement's Role in Offender Reentry?............................... 2
Why would Law Enforcement Participate in Offender Reentry?........................ 3
What are the Benefits to Law Enforcement Participation in Offender Reentry?......... 3
What are the Challenges to Law Enforcement Participation in Offender Reentry? 4
What should Law Enforcement Know Before Participating in Offender Reentry?....... 5

SECTION II: BUILDING AN OFFENDER REENTRY PROGRAM

Needs Assessment.. 8
Components and Activities 9
Funding and Resources...11
Practical Tools and Instruments..12
Building Partnerships...13
Management and Operations..15
Measuring Success 19
Key Recommendations and Advice..21

SECTION III: CURRENT STATE OF PRACTICE EXAMPLES FROM LAW ENFORCEMENT

Campbell County Police Department (KY)..25
Indianapolis Police Department/Marion County Sheriff's Department (IN)............27
Las Vegas Metropolitan Police Department (NV) 29
Louisville Metro Police Department (KY) 31
Lowell Police Department (MA)..33
Minneapolis Police Department (MN)..35
New Haven Department of Police Service (CT) 37
Park City Police Department (UT) 39
Racine Police Department (WI)...41
Redmond Police Department (WA) 43
Savannah Chatham Metropolitan Police Department (GA) 45
Topeka Police Department (KS) 47
High Point Police Department/Winston-Salem Police Department (NC)..............49

GLOSSARY

GLOSSARY 51

RESOURCES AND MATERIALS

RESOURCES AND MATERIALS 51

INTRODUCTION

According to the U.S. Department of Justice (DOJ), Office of Justice Programs (OJP), on an annual basis, more than 650,000 offenders are released from incarceration and return to communities nationwide.[1] Research from OJP's Bureau of Justice Statistics (BJS) indicates that two-thirds of those released are likely to recidivate. Given this, offenders who are released pose a significant challenge to public safety.

In response to the growing number of returning offenders, DOJ launched a reentry initiative that supported the creation of programs at various levels in all 50 states, the District of Columbia, and the U.S. territories. Additionally, federal, state, local, and private agencies and organizations have partnered to study and develop best approaches to offender reentry. The consensus is that offender reintegration requires a concerted effort among criminal justice practitioners to address the impact made by returning offenders. As a result, many programs have been implemented to transition released offenders back into the community and reduce recidivism.

In the 1990s, an increasing number of returning offenders spurred innovation within local law enforcement and among other stakeholders. Intensive supervision partnerships between law enforcement and community corrections, like Boston's Operation Night Light, have been chronicled and championed. While law enforcement and corrections partnerships showed promise, the offender reentry concept was envisioned as a more comprehensive approach. This broadened concept called for support, beyond enforcement, to include provision of needed services such as education, housing, substance abuse treatment, and employment. This reentry concept embodies the figurative "carrot" (services) and "stick" (enforcement) approach. While reentry literature is robust, very little of it addresses the role that law enforcement has or should have. Moreover, reentry programs have flourished while strategic involvement of police has not.

In an effort to determine the state of law enforcement's participation in offender reentry initiatives, the International Association of Chiefs of Police (IACP) partnered with OJP's Bureau of Justice Assistance (BJA) to comprehensively examine law enforcement's role in offender reentry initiatives. IACP's goal, through this project, is to increase law enforcement's participation in offender reentry through the provision of information, sharing of leading practices, and development of products to promote public safety partnerships. The intended outcomes of this effort--through increased law enforcement participation in reentry programs--are reduced recidivism, victimization, and disorder while increasing officer safety.

Due to the limited information available on law enforcement participation in reentry efforts, IACP qualitatively and quantitatively examined the potential for intensified law enforcement involvement in three ways:

1. **Literature Review.** We conducted a review of the literature to determine the mission and critical elements of reentry as it relates to law enforcement. Next, we developed a list of questions arising from a review of research reports and policy statements on reentry and relevant programs. The questions focused on identifying policy and operational gaps within law enforcement as it relates to reentry.

2. **FocusGroups.** In an effort to identify leading practices in law enforcement's participation in offender reentry initiatives, IACP staff conducted a series of focus groups. Approximately 50 law enforcement officials from 21 states and Canada participated in five regional focus groups.

3. **SiteVisits.** IACP staff conducted site visits to more than 15 police and sheriffs' departments. The site visits were designed to document how law enforcement is engaged and to examine the operational aspects of its reentry efforts. Profiles of some of the programs exhibiting potentially replicable and leading practices are located later in this guide.

The information gathered through our efforts provided material for the IACP to develop a guide for law enforcement by law enforcement. The purpose of this guide is to:

- Provide an overview of the information available specifically on law enforcement's current and emerging role in offender reentry.

- Present key strategies, components, and results of law enforcement participation in offender reentry programs.

To illustrate, this resource guide is presented in sections:

- *Section I: Offender Reentry 101* provides an overview of the questions and responses law enforcement has and may have about its role in offender reentry; identifies the benefits and challenges that police experience with reentry programs; and provides examples of how law enforcement agencies have developed, implemented, and managed such programs.

- *Section II: Building an Offender Reentry Program* provides a blueprint for law enforcement interested in implementing an offender reentry program. This section presents real-life examples from the sites visited that exhibit leading practices in law enforcement-involved offender reentry programs.

- *Section III: Current State of Practice: Examples from Law Enforcement* highlights law enforcement agencies that are engaged in offender reentry programs and initiatives.

- The *Glossary* provides definitions of commonly used offender reentry terms.

- The *Resources and Materials* section contains a list of helpful online resources used by offender reentry project staff and profiled agencies.

Reentry programs use a variety of terms to describe offenders who are participating in offender reentry programs. For the purposes of this guide, the term "offender" is used to describe ex-offenders, ex-convicts, former inmates, felons, formerly incarcerated individuals, probationers and parolees, and program participants or candidates in the programs profiled.

SECTION I:
OFFENDER REENTRY 101

WHAT IS OFFENDER REENTRY?

Offender reentry, which is also known as reentry, prisoner reentry, or re-entry, refers to the return of offenders from incarceration back into the community. In general and for the purposes of this guide, reentry refers to persons released from state or federal prisons, individuals discharged from parole, and those under probation. As a concept, reentry involves any program, initiative, or partnership that addresses the issues necessary to ensure that offenders successfully transition and maintain a crime-free existence post-release. These issues commonly include lack of education, job training or vocational experience, housing, and/or substance abuse and mental health treatment. From a law enforcement perspective, offender reentry:

■ Is an issue of officer and community safety.

■ Provides another way for police to use preemptive prevention approaches such as community policing and problem-oriented policing to address the return of high-risk offenders.

Given that law enforcement and the public are aware that offenders are returning to communities across the country, IACP examined the role that law enforcement has and can have in offender reentry efforts.

WHAT IS LAW ENFORCEMENT'S ROLE IN OFFENDER REENTRY?

IACP's review of existing literature revealed that little information is available on what role law enforcement has in offender reentry or on the impact of offender reentry efforts in general. The literature, however, does indicate that law enforcement has long partnered with corrections officials to provide enhanced supervision or fugitive apprehension support. Information collected by the IACP revealed that:

■ The value of police participation is recognized in theory but not in practice. A large percentage of law enforcement officials indicate that they do not participate in reentry initiatives, programs, or activities.

■ Law enforcement agencies are often included in reentry efforts as an afterthought. Law enforcement officials admit that they have either not been invited to join reentry initiatives; have self-invited to participate in reentry efforts; or were invited but did not have decision-making input.

■ Along the enforcement-to-service delivery continuum, law enforcement is most thought of and used as the "stick" while service providers are considered the "carrot".

■ Reentry activities that involve law enforcement span the spectrum from pre-release to post-release participation.

■ Most law enforcement-involved reentry initiatives focus on violent adult or sex offenders.

Law enforcement currently involved in offender reentry efforts has conflicting views about whether it should lead or serve as a collaborative partner in reentry. Some law enforcement officials believe that it is their job as protectors of public safety to lead the effort, while others are of the opinion that it is permissible for police to begin an offender reentry program and later hand it over to social or community service agencies to lead. Law enforcement officials consulted for this project collectively believe that law enforcement's role in offender reentry efforts should be to:

■ Enhance public safety
■ Ensure officer safety
■ Reduce recidivism
■ Decrease crime

Whether as a lead or partner agency, law enforcement's role should also include reducing the impact that unsuccessful offender reintegration has on the community and law enforcement. This can be accomplished through partnership or as a conduit of the process. Law enforcement officials currently involved in reentry efforts advise that:

■ State and local law enforcement serve as strategic collaborative *partners* and resources in offender reentry efforts. Partnerships allow law enforcement to pool its resources with a range of stakeholders to respond to the challenges that returning offenders present. For example, police collaborate with institutional or community corrections officials to enhance community supervision of offenders. This activity increases communication and reduces the chance that offenders will be involved in criminal activities unknown to police or community corrections officers.

■ Law enforcement's role is also to serve as *conduits* for raising offender reentry issues with legislators and educating and informing the public. Law enforcement serves in multiple capacities. For example, law enforcement: 1) Assists in developing and enforcing legislation that affects offenders, 2) Assists in developing reentry plans for returning offenders, and 3) Informs the community about offender reentry in their jurisdiction.

WHY WOULD LAW ENFORCEMENT PARTICIPATE IN OFFENDER REENTRY?

The sheer numbers of offenders released to communities each year poses a significant challenge to law enforcement. For this reason alone, it is important for law enforcement to take a proactive approach to offender reentry. On more than one occasion, law enforcement officials that consulted on this publication remarked, "They're coming home like it or not. Can we afford not to participate?"

WHAT ARE THE BENEFITS OF LAW ENFORCEMENT PARTICIPATION IN OFFENDER REENTRY?

Having an active role in offender reentry efforts can provide tangible benefits to law enforcement and the communities it serves. One of the benefits echoed more than once by participating law enforcement officials is that offenders are not anonymous. Through partnership, law enforcement is made aware of the offenders that will be returning to their community, where the offenders will reside, and what their criminal histories are. Additional benefits realized by the community and police agencies include:

■ A decrease in criminal activity.

■ An increase in perceived improvement in the quality of crime prevention.

■ New or stronger partnerships.

■ A reduction in recidivism.

■ An interruption or break in the cycle of generational crime.

■ An increase in stable families.

■ Increased trust between the community and police.

■ Increased access to information, resources, and shared responsibility for ensuring public safety.

Reentry initiatives also strengthen law enforcement partnerships that already exist and build or increase trust among new partners. Moreover, sharing information with other law enforcement agencies is helpful in that the intelligence can be used to develop leads to solve crimes. Finally, law enforcement's involvement in reentry changes the community's view of law enforcement. Instead of viewing police as an "occupying force," the community sees police as a partner in fighting crime. As a result, law enforcement receives the added benefit of increased credibility as an agency and trust from the community.

WHAT ARE THE CHALLENGES TO LAW ENFORCEMENT PARTICIPATION IN OFFENDER REENTRY?

Law enforcement officials involved in reentry initiatives encountered challenges they categorize into the "Three P's: Politics, Personalities, and Priorities." Politically, offender reentry is a controversial topic that can contribute to a variety of challenges as experienced by existing law enforcement participants. Additionally, a common misunderstanding about law enforcement participation in reentry programs is that law enforcement will be doing social work instead of focusing on crime prevention and public safety. Here are some additional challenges:

- **Changingpolitical priorities.** Responding to "hot-button" issues creates an unstable foundation for law enforcement. Police have not been invited to the table to discuss and make decisions about returning offenders. Therefore, they are reactive rather than proactive to legislation or correctional agency protocols governing returning offenders.

- **Lackof political buy-in.** The local political climate may be resistant to having a program in their community. Critics of such programs verbalize that if a program is created, more offenders will relocate to the community to obtain program services. The local political establishment may not want to absorb additional offenders or make their communities a haven for offenders.

- **Flexibleadministrations.** Shifting administrations and the resulting public policies and laws have the capacity to negatively impact police authority. For instance, a change in the state political structure can unravel statewide

efforts if there are no specific and formalized policies in place. One important example of this impact is the use of warrantless searches by police whether or not a parole or probation officer is present. Where one state may support warrantless searches another may not. Changing existing strategies and activities may require additional resources and procedures to conduct the same activities.

- **Lackof political or government support.** If the governing body of the jurisdiction is not on board with law enforcement's approach, then it may be difficult to participate. Two reasons that such involvement would not receive support are: 1) image and 2) potentially negative press. For the political representatives or decision-making body, it may send the wrong message to become involved in offender reentry or may be in contrast to their politically recognized image.

- **Lackof resources.** Resources for the initiative generally refer to funding and people. Both are necessary to ensure success and may be impacted by:

1) Temporary or inadequate funding. While some reentry programs are implemented by in-kind services, grants, or are absorbed into existing budgets, limited or conditional funding can impact program implementation, resource allocation, and sustainability. It is difficult to begin an initiative only to have the funds removed mid-stream. Lack of consistent funding also creates barriers to committing personnel to offender reentry efforts.

2) Lack of interest and buy-in from law enforcement. Law enforcement-involved offender reentry programs experience a lack of internal buy-in both from the top-down and bottom-up. One reason is resistance to the paradigm shift necessary to participate. Some law enforcement officials may feel that shifting from an intervention and suppression focus to partner with social service agencies makes them look soft on crime or more like social workers. Law enforcement officials involved in such programs

advise that buy-in involve a switch from an "us versus them" to a "help them prevent harm to us" perspective.

3) Lack of community support. Communities across the country have vocalized their opinions against programs that encourage a return of offenders back to "our" community. "Not in my backyard" and other such philosophies can be difficult, but not impossible to overcome.

WHAT SHOULD LAW ENFORCEMENT KNOW BEFORE PARTICIPATING IN OFFENDER REENTRY?

Law enforcement officials involved in offender reentry initiatives were eager to discuss lessons learned, program success stories, and provide advice to agencies that are interested in becoming involved in offender reentry initiatives. Their insights cover law enforcement's perspective; attitudes about offenders; perceptions of other justice disciplines; partnering; community and media engagement; and program results. Here is a sample of the important points to remember before participating in reentry efforts:

- **Law enforcement needs to change the way it does business.** Focusing on what the community *needs* versus what the offender gets in an offender reentry program helps to affect a paradigm shift among law enforcement.

- **Incarceration/punishment alone does not reduce risk or recidivism.** Incarcerating offenders is costly, time-limited, and does little to reduce the risk of re-offending. It is important to focus on holding high-risk offenders accountable and addressing transitional needs.

- **Post-release reentry programs must include transitional services that are responsive to offender needs and require accountability.** Reentry partners consulted for this project reason that the "system" has taught offenders to be victims. As a result, offenders have not properly prepared to transition to their communities.

In their opinion, it is important to replace incarceration-based attitudes with meaningful program-based solutions. Reentry programs teach offenders to be accountable and help to interrupt the cycle of violence.

- **It is important to start small.** Regardless of how many partners are involved or the resources available, it is essential that the effort be manageable. Starting small and building incrementally leads to the best results.

- **It is important to build relationships with potential partner agencies *before* taking on a new initiative.** Having collaborated and leveraged resources on other efforts is helpful when it comes time to introduce a new endeavor.

- **Forming a strong coalition of partners is vital.** A strong coalition includes partner agencies or individuals with the social capital in community programming or power brokers (e.g., mayor, city council) who can determine legislative or local policies. For example, community corrections know which offenders are being released and when and what crimes they have committed. They can help design appropriate community and social controls to assist in maintaining public safety.

- **Adopting the 4-Cs to partnership: collaboration, communication, cooperation, and commitment is key.** Partners must have honest communication. If public safety is a program goal, then cooperation and a commitment to working collaboratively is necessary.

- **Developing a foundation before partnering is essential.** The foundation must include clarification of partner roles, responsibilities, and program protocols. Next, developing a common theme or comprehensive message that every partner agency can buy into further clarifies the program goals. For example, if the goals of the program are to reduce recidivism or enhance public safety, be sure that the agencies invited to partner can contribute to achieving these goals.

- **Itis important to measure and evaluate what the efforts are accomplishing.** Program results and success often lead to additional funding and other positive goals.

- **Programtransparency is significant.** It is important to be open about the program goals and planned accomplishments. This approach includes informing the community of law enforcement's role in addressing the return of offenders, educating them about the challenges inherent in offender reintegration, and obtaining the community's help in ensuring offender accountability. The result of this strategy is solidarity among the community, the justice system, and service providers against potential re-victimization at the hands of returning offenders.

- **Patienceis truly a virtue.** It may take a month or two years to fully realize all program goals.

Benefits of Law Enforcement Participation in Offender Reentry Initiatives

- Increased officer safety.
- Decreased offender anonymity.
- Reduced recidivism.
- Decreased criminal activity.
- Increased quality of crime prevention.
- New or stronger partnerships.
- Increased trust between the community and police.
- Increased access to information, resources, and shared responsibility for ensuring public safety.

SECTION II:

BUILDING AN OFFENDER REENTRY PROGRAM

Section II is designed for law enforcement executives who have determined that their jurisdiction has been impacted by returning offenders. The following material provides a blueprint for developing a reentry program.

NEEDS ASSESSMENT

The first step in establishing an offender reentry program is to assess the needs of the agency. The following is a five-step process many law enforcement agencies have used.

1. Identify/Develop Goals

The majority of law enforcement-involved offender reentry programs featured in this guide were developed for the purposes of:

- Enhancing public and officer safety.

- Reducing crime.

- Reducing recidivism.

The reasons for building or participating in offender reentry programs should be guided by the types of crimes affecting your community and how reentry efforts will achieve program goals. Law enforcement should first evaluate the size, scope, and nature of the problem before implementing reentry activities. This exercise will help develop the goals of the program.

2. Assess Resources

Use program goals to identify program primary and secondary needs.

- Examine whether or not additional or existing personnel or funds will be required to implement a reentry program.

- Consult with the agency's legal staff or human resource department to determine if existing agency protocols will be affected by the implementation of the program.

- Devise a strategy for supporting participation in existing reentry efforts or for implementing a program in-house.

- Ensure that participation does not inundate agency resources and support.

3. Develop Key Program Elements

Criminal justice research has shown that the barriers to successful reintegration of returning offenders are:

- Lack of housing

- Lack of education

- Lack of job training and/or employment

- Lack of substance abuse treatment

- Lack of family support

Program goals should feature key elements designed to meet each of these barriers.

4. Determine Partners

A common misunderstanding about law enforcement participation in reentry programs is that law enforcement will be doing social work. Determining appropriate partners will ensure that law enforcement focuses on crime prevention and public safety. Here are tips for determining potential partner individuals and agencies.

- Identify what agencies to contact based on the program strategy; develop a comprehensive list of partners; and build the partnership around offender needs (i.e., employment, housing, education, treatment) that ensure the goals of the program are met.

- Use existing partnerships to solicit new partners.

- Articulate the goals of the program clearly so that all partners understand what their role will be and what is expected of them.

5. Develop a Strategy

The program strategy or objectives should be guided by program goals and resources. In order to be able to measure program success, the program must have benchmarks against which achievement can be measured. Law enforcement offender reentry strategies could include encouraging offender compliance and accountability, targeting enforcement efforts, exchanging intelligence and information sharing, engaging the community, and brokering social services.

COMPONENTS AND ACTIVITIES

The following section provides an overview of possible program components and activities to implement. We have previously indicated that the following are common reentry goals:

- Enhancing public and officer safety

- Reducing crime

- Reducing recidivism

Program components and activities are developed to meet not only the goals of the program, but other issues unique to the community. For example, officials in New Haven (CT) placed an emphasis on employability. The New Haven Police Chief remarked, "I realized that I don't arrest too many people that have jobs." Similarly, the Reentry Partnership Initiative (RPI) in Lowell (MA) focuses on health, mental health, and substance abuse treatment. Lack of ongoing health and mental health care is one of the reasons for high rates of recidivism among offenders. Many offenders are released without plans for obtaining formerly state-provided medication, with inadequate amounts to sustain them, or with an inability to obtain medication or medical care. For this reason, RPI works with the Massachusetts Department of Medical Assistance or MassHealth to provide returning offenders with health cards at the time of discharge. This provides a continuity of care and treatment to include those with substance abuse and mental health issues. Both of these examples illustrate that while enhanced services are geared toward the offender, they are developed to protect the community at large.

Offender reentry programs that involve law enforcement have components that start while offenders are still incarcerated and/or continue upon the offender's release. In Topeka (KS), offenders meet with a pre-release Accountability Panel to devise graduated sanctions and incentives based on their Individual Release Plan (IRP). Monitoring by the panel continues post-release. Offenders are also moved to correctional institutions closer to Topeka to facilitate release planning and ensure that law enforcement and service providers can participate.

Some programs require mandatory participation, while other programs are voluntary. For instance, North Carolina's sentencing structure has resulted in approximately 10-15 percent of offenders "maxing out" or being released without conditions of supervision. This means that with the exception of sex offenders, offenders are not required to report to any law enforcement, corrections, or court officials post-release. Therefore, participation in program activities for these offenders is voluntary in most cases.

Overall program components encompass a comprehensive traditional approach that incorporates a continuity of care that starts with risk and need assessment and continues with service delivery and closes with offender accountability and compliance. The following describes the program components and activities most often found in law enforcement-involved offender reentry programs:

- **EnhancedSupervision.** This is also referred to as offender monitoring/tracking or increased surveillance. Law enforcement works with community corrections officials to ensure that offenders maintain the conditions of release and supervision. Their involvement includes conducting joint home visits, curfew checks or patrols. Depending on the authority of the community corrections officials, home visits can involve simple notification that law enforcement will be monitoring their activities along with corrections. Home visits can be unscheduled visits and designed to verify that offenders are maintaining the conditions of their release. Visits to the home can include a search of the residence for illegal or unauthorized drugs, guns, and other contraband. Unscheduled visits to their places of employment are conducted to verify that the offender does work there and is reporting as scheduled. Community corrections officials participate in ride-a-longs or joint patrols of known "hot spots" to ensure that their supervisees are not returning to their old patterns. Program officials in Park City (UT) include bar checks as part of their supervision conditions. Park City has a larger than average number of bars for a city of its size and encounters primarily alcohol- and substance abuse-related crimes. Therefore, probation officials visit bars to ensure that offenders who are prohibited from being in bars are following their conditions of supervision.

- **Information Sharing.** Information sharing is critical. Law enforcement meet with partner agencies regularly to obtain data that will help them prepare for the challenges that returning offenders present. From corrections officials, they receive data on who is returning, where they will live, what their levels of risk and needs are, and what partner agencies will be providing services to address the needs. Likewise, police share information with corrections if they have collateral contacts with the offender whether or not it results in arrest or conviction. Police share information on known associates and "hang-out" areas so that corrections officials can monitor offender behavior.

- **Intelligence Exchange.** While similar to information sharing, intelligence exchange is more akin to law enforcement strategies and information. Law enforcement officials work together on committees, task forces or meet regularly to exchange investigative intelligence that may be beneficial to all law enforcement agencies involved. For example, the Minneapolis Anti-Violence Initiative (MAVI) Team includes federal, state, and local law enforcement in Minneapolis that target adult and juvenile offenders with histories of violence, firearms offenses, and gang involvement. Whenever any of the agencies receives information on the targeted offender, investigative approaches are shared to prevent duplication and potential interagency overlap and conflict.

- **Computerized Offender Tracking.** Many of the programs in which law enforcement participates use information management systems to track offender activities and compliance. These methods range from simple spreadsheets and databases to web-based intelligence sharing systems, peer-to-peer networks and mobile alert systems. All are intended to enhance law enforcement's ability to track offender activities and monitor their behaviors. Specific information on these databases can be found in the section on Practical Tools and Instruments.

- **Notifications Sessions.** These sessions are also known as Call-in Meetings, Lever-pulling Meetings, Accountability Panels, and Offender Review Boards. Law enforcement, service providers, and the community gather in a show of solidarity against crime and violence in their neighborhoods. In general, law enforcement informs offenders that they will be working with corrections to monitor offender compliance and will not hesitate to arrest them or impose discipline on offenders who fail to follow through as required. Service providers offer necessary transitional services. The community has an opportunity to identify the individuals responsible for violence in their communities. The sessions impose an element of accountability. In some sessions, law enforcement and service providers interact with offenders in the same room. In other sessions, the offender meets with each faction separately.

- **Community Engagement.** Informing the community of or engaging them in supporting reentry efforts is essential. In High Point (NC), police hold a series of community meetings to gather information, share their reentry strategy, and reveal the offenders they will be focusing on. They communicate the results of these strategies in flyers, newsletters, and through community representatives. Police also engage community members to walk joint patrols. This approach builds trust, shows that the effort is transparent, and develops a relationship whereby residents become the "eyes and ears" of law enforcement.

- **Transitional Social Services.** Transitional services are the "carrots" in reentry programs. Offenders are offered and provided with the services they need to successfully return to the community. Services such as job and housing assistance, educational testing and assessment, life skills training, alcohol and substance abuse counseling and treatment, mentoring, and spiritual guidance are all offered by community and government social service and faith-based organizations.

Depending on program resources, length of time in existence, jurisdiction size, and partners involved, some programs contain other unique and extensive components not commonly found in reentry programs. The following extensive components and activities can be used to expand existing offender reentry programs:

- **Reentry Courts.** Reentry courts are built using the drug court model to serve as another crime prevention tool in that the court has the ability to order sanctions beyond the existing supervision conditions. Law enforcement that partner with Reentry Courts in Indianapolis (IN) and

Las Vegas (NV) report that these courts can be effective accountability tools.

- **Transitional/Reentry Planning.** Law enforcement has input into the post-release supervision conditions of offenders. Police meet with corrections officials to share information on the offender's criminal history in the community and discuss their concerns for the offender's future. Some law enforcement officials make recommendations on which neighborhoods offenders can enter or associates with whom they cannot be seen. Law enforcement officials also serve on post-release accountability panels to monitor whether or not their conditions are being followed.

- **COP Houses.** Community Oriented Policing (COP) houses have been opened in high crime, low socioeconomic areas in Racine (WI). These neighborhoods were chosen as focal points because a high number of offenders return to them. The houses serve as an extension of the collaboration already started between police and community corrections. Police and community corrections are located in the houses to serve as both a resource and crime deterrent in the community.

FUNDING AND RESOURCES

While partnerships are developed to solve localized problems or make specific improvements that enhance the quality of life for the community, lack of funding to support law enforcement participation in offender reentry efforts is a significant barrier. Offender reentry poses an additional challenge to manpower, infrastructure, and technological resources that are necessary to build or participate in offender reentry activities. Therefore, it is important to develop funding and resource guidelines to sustain the program long-term and exhibit program value. Additionally, experienced reentry leaders advise that law enforcement agencies forge the following strategies to address funding and resources:

- **Develop a proposed budget for building or participating in reentry activities.** Include how many personnel hours would be necessary to support and/or participate in such efforts. Also consider infrastructural resources. Will office space or furniture be required to participate? What technological resources for database development and information sharing will be necessary to partnering with other agencies and monitoring offenders?

- **Rely on partner agencies to share program responsibilities.** Once partner agencies are identified, it is important to obtain a firm commitment from them on their specific program contributions. How many people from their agency are they devoting to this effort? What in-kind or financial support are they willing to provide? How will those funds or products be delivered and on what timeline?

- **Recognize that other agencies are experiencing budget cuts and have limited resources.** Similar to changing political priorities, the lack of resources creates an atmosphere of instability because agencies are unable to sustain what they have implemented.

- **Take advantage of community resources.** Tap into the policing, community, and partner volunteer programs. Volunteers can be used to support program activities and spread the word about program efforts.

A lack of appropriate funding and resources impact program effectiveness. Below are examples of funding sources used by law enforcement agencies to participate in offender reentry programs and initiatives:

- **Grants.** The U.S. Department of Justice has provided funding for offender reentry through federal grant programs such as the Serious and Violent Offender Reentry Initiative (SVORI); Project Safe Neighborhoods; and Local Law Enforcement Block Grant (LLEBG) program.

- **Cooperative Agreements.** Another benefit to partnering with other agencies is the ability to combine existing financial resources. Program partners who already receive funding such as housing, workforce development, and schools can pool those funds through a cooperative agreement to maximize the use of these funds for their offender reentry efforts.

- **Special Assessment Taxes.** Local government agencies can levy special taxes for reentry efforts. Many jurisdictions use this as the primary method for supporting emergency and 911 services in their communities.

A fiscally responsible plan that demonstrates long-term investment in a reentry effort is essential to leverage offender reentry components and activities.

Financial Preparation

- Create a budget.
- Consider internal and external funding opportunities in the public sector (i.e., local, regional, state, and federal levels) and private sector (i.e., banks, foundations).
- Obtain financial and in-kind commitments from partner agencies and community resources.

PRACTICAL TOOLS AND INSTRUMENTS

Law enforcement agencies involved in offender reentry efforts employ a variety of strategies and tools to facilitate their participation. Police officials advise that it is important to:

- Use criminogenic tools to assess risk and needs

- Employ technology to gather and share information

- Request and allow access to relevant databases or request funding to build compatible systems to bridge the information gap between partner agencies.

Needs and Risk Assessments. Criminal justice research by Dr. Ed Latessa[2] and others reveal that a large amount of crime is committed by a small percentage of the population in a community. Therefore, many offender reentry programs implement needs and risk assessment components to more precisely target how best to help offenders transition. The most common risk and needs assessment tools currently in use are the Level of Service Inventory-Revised (LSI-R) or diagnostic tests designed to uncover co-occurring and other mental health disorders. These tools are most helpful to corrections officials in determining the offender's level of supervision and to guide staff in making treatment decisions.

Crime Mapping. One of the reasons police agencies instituted reentry programs was to effect change in high crime or "hot spot" areas. Crime mapping is a method used by several agencies to target their resources and efforts, develop partnerships, and create a positive influence. Crime mapping uses specific methods for locating concentrations of crime in a particular area of the community.[3] The method can be as simple as pinpointing areas on a map using thumbtacks to large scale statistical computer models. Crime mapping was instrumental to the Indianapolis Police Department in developing its Violence Impact Program Enhanced Response (**VIPER**) system (see explanation below).

Information Management Systems. Many of the programs in which law enforcement participates use information management systems to track offender activities and compliance, to measure program effectiveness, and communicate internally and externally. These methods range from simple spreadsheets and databases to web-based intelligence-sharing systems, peer-to-peer networks, and mobile alert systems. Information on the impetus for creating them, how they are used, and components of simple to more complex databases are described below:

- The Louisville (KY) Metro Police Department (LMPD) developed and maintains a Microsoft Access-based case management system called **METSYS**. This system includes offender information and their status in the program. LMPD and partner agencies have varying levels of access and input to the information in the database. For example, only LMPD staff can see all screens and fields, but partner agencies have limited visibility. Likewise, inputting data is limited to LMPD staff. The information is used to track offenders' status and to ensure their success.

- The Kansas Department of Corrections (KDOC) provides limited access to their Kansas Adult Supervised Population Electronic Repository (KASPER). **KASPER** is a database that contains information about offenders who are: currently incarcerated; under post-incarceration supervision; and, who have been discharged from a sentence. For the reentry program in Topeka (Shawnee County Reentry Program), this database provides information on the status of an offender currently incarcerated or on post-release supervision within the KDOC system, and is a useful tool for learning where an inmate is housed, demographic data, whether an offender has been released to post-incarceration supervision (parole, conditional release, post-release supervision, compact parole), and where in the state that offender is under supervision. The Topeka Police Department's Reentry Community Police Officer (RCPO) uses KASPER and conducts searches of their own Offender Management Information System **(OMIS)** to check for any warrants or detainers from other jurisdictions in preparation for meeting with the offenders who have been accepted into their reentry program.

- The Indianapolis (IN) Police Department (IPD) developed the Violence Impact Program Enhanced Response **(VIPER)** system to assist them in identifying the most violent offenders in Marion County and to aggressively target those persons for prosecution. IPD staff researched the commonality of the violence within each incident of homicide to create a plan to attack those traits that seem indigenous to each violent event. The elements common to each crime were:

  - History of violence in the lives of both suspects and victims.

  - Proliferation of firearms in many acts of violence committed in the county.

  - Use of drugs and/or alcohol as an aggravating or causative factor in many of the homicides.

VIPER is used to systematically flag a list of up to 200 of the most violent offenders in Marion County who are:

- 18-30 years old

- Charged or arrested on multiple occasions for a defined list of violent crimes

- Involved in groups of known, chronic offenders

- Involved in drug use or sale.

Patrol officers can access VIPER through mobile data terminals in police units. This is helpful in identifying VIPER offenders encountered through collateral contacts.

- The Middle District of North Carolina's **Violent Crimes Task Force Web-Based Database** allows law enforcement

to manage information on violent offenders, criminal involvement, and criminal associations. This database allows multiple law enforcement agencies, prosecutors, probation and parole, researchers, and community resource delivery agencies to view and contribute a variety of information on violent offenders. The database is managed by the Winston-Salem Police Department and is accessible among law enforcement partners from over 50 agencies in 24 counties in North Carolina.

- High Point (NC) Police Department (HPPD) developed a concurrent regional and statewide network for connecting information resources of police departments called **Police-2-Police (P2P) technology**. This network allows access to and the identification of all individuals who have appeared at Call-in/Notification Sessions in any of the states in which the network is used. As of 2005, 64 police departments in North Carolina, Florida, and Texas used this technology.

- HPPD also distributes **e-mail alerts**, which are internal weekly e-mail criminal intelligence messages on crime trends for the purposes of promoting officer safety and sharing gang/group, drug, and anti-terrorist information.

Reentry Tools to Consider

- Needs/Risk Assessments
- Information/Case Management Systems
- Information-sharing Networks

BUILDING PARTNERSHIPS

Partnership is an essential element in addressing offender reentry. Law enforcement and other agencies pool their resources to meet program goals that assist returning offenders in successfully reintegrating back into the community and maintaining a crime-free existence. The agencies critical to partner with in offender reentry efforts include:

- **CommunityCorrections.** This term is used to describe local probation and parole offices. In most cases, law enforcement and community corrections have similar interests—ensuring that offenders abide by the conditions of their release. Community corrections can be an important liaison between law enforcement and the state department of corrections by obtaining information on the number and types of offenders that will be released in the community. In some cases, law enforcement can work with community corrections to develop conditions of supervision, undertake reentry planning, and ensure offender compliance and accountability through enhanced surveillance and supervision efforts (i.e., coordinating joint patrols, home visits, and curfew checks).

- **Government and Community Social Service Agencies.** The term social service agency includes government and community agencies that provide services to assist offenders in successfully returning to the community. These services include:

  - Housing assistance.

  - Obtaining or satisfying basic educational requirements (i.e., GEDs).

  - Job counseling, vocational training or employment referrals.

  - Alcohol or substance abuse treatment and support.

  - Family reunification and re-connection.

In a majority of the sites visited, law enforcement partnered with state- or federally-sponsored Workforce Development Boards to provide job or vocational assistance. Educational assessment and services are provided by local educational institutions, and local shelters or halfway houses to provide emergency or transitional housing for offenders. Family reunification, which is not widely available in reentry programs in which law enforcement is involved, has been offered as part of other mental health treatment or transitional counseling services provided by local churches, community organizations, or social service referrals.

- **Federal, State, and Local Law Enforcement.** Project Safe Neighborhoods (PSN) is very prominently partnered with state and local law enforcement to reduce gun-related violence and promote safe communities. PSN funds have been used to enhance arrests and prosecutions, conduct joint warrant sweeps, exchange investigative

intelligence, and launch marketing plans. It is also important to partner with law enforcement agencies in neighboring jurisdictions. Law enforcement officials in Indianapolis (IN) found that while many of the crimes occurred in identified urban "hot spots," the individuals responsible for committing the crimes lived in the suburbs. By partnering with officials who control areas outside their immediate jurisdiction, they prevented offenders from becoming traveling menaces.

- **Community.** The community is often overlooked as a partner in offender reentry efforts; however, its engagement is essential to program success. Community members can act as the "eyes and ears" for law enforcement by verbalizing their concerns, identifying high crime areas and individuals, and assisting with offender accountability.

- **Research Partner.** If resources do not permit or the law enforcement agency does not have a data collection or crime analysis unit in-house, it is important to have a research partner involved for data analysis. Many programs that take a systematic approach to offender reentry are data-driven; that is, they use quantitative data (i.e., crime rates and recidivism rates), lessons learned, and success stories to implement leading practices. Law enforcement programs in Indianapolis (IN) and Winston-Salem (NC) implemented information management systems to track unbiased, objective data. Other jurisdictions that are partners to PSN programs submit their data to program research partners for analysis and reporting.

Law enforcement officials suggest the following strategies for building partnerships:

- **Identify critical players in the state or community that bring real resources to the table.** Selecting partners based on their willingness and ability to contribute is extremely important. Law enforcement in Louisville (KY) found that it was critical to partner with the U.S. Attorney's Office because offenders receive more time on the federal level if they recidivate. Similarly, officials in Indianapolis (IN) found the faith community to be key to addressing violence. Both are important leveraged resources.

- **Become familiar with the missions, goals, and objectives of potential partner agencies.** This information will provide guidance on how similar the agency's vision is to law enforcement.

- **Identify the benefits of partnering.** Stakeholders will want to know "What is in it for me?" so it is important to be able to detail the benefits of partnering to each stakeholder.

- **Make use of partner agencies.** As soon as partnerships are built, it is important to remember to rely on partners. It is also important not to take on more than one agency can handle. For example, some agencies work with partners to create implementation plans, evaluate their plans, and make program changes accordingly.

- **Establish "gatekeepers" or "champions" at each partner agency.** This will be the contact or "go-to" person that law enforcement can call for information and assistance.

Finally, law enforcement officials who lead or participate in offender reentry programs advise that agencies realize that partnership and collaboration takes a lot of time and effort.

Five Essential Reentry Partners

1. State Departments of Corrections or local community corrections
2. Social service agencies
3. Community- and faith-based organizations
4. Other federal, state, regional, or contiguous law enforcement agency representatives
5. Political bodies responsible for funding and resource support (i.e., mayor or city council)

MANAGEMENT AND OPERATIONS

Two important goals of reentry programs that specifically involve law enforcement are public safety and officer safety. Experienced law enforcement officials indicate that initial participation was deemed "soft on crime." What they have learned from this experience is that it is important to:

Eight Reentry Strategies for Law Enforcement

1. **Build partnerships.** Pool resources with a range of other stakeholders (e.g., corrections, and social services) to achieve program goals.

2. **Enhance offender supervision.** Share offender supervision with community corrections by conducting joint patrols, home visits, or curfew checks to monitor offenders post-release.

3. **Encourage offender compliance and accountability.** Work with institutional and community corrections to develop offender reentry plans that focus on ways to deter future crime and promote pro-social activities.

4. **Target enforcement efforts.** Compile and analyze data on specific places/problem areas or "hot spots" and risks associated with specific individuals or groups to direct patrols and focus resources on community policing and other crime prevention strategies that ensure officer and public safety.

5. **Exchange intelligence and share information.** Work, formally or informally, with other law enforcement and corrections agencies to share information such as offender release dates, supervision conditions, intelligence on known associates of offenders, or ongoing investigations involving high-risk offenders.

6. **Engage the community.** Communicate your position on offender reentry, market program efforts, and seek support from the community and media. For example, police develop brochures, participate in community meetings to educate the public, and use community members as additional "eyes and ears".

7. **Broker social services.** Work with partner agencies to link offenders to programs and services that support successful transition into the community. This includes obtaining their GED or educational assistance, job counseling and training, substance abuse treatment or other health care, and housing.

8. **Ensure public safety.** Collaborate with corrections agencies to notify crime victims of offender release dates and conditions of supervision, share information on and invite crime victim participation in post-release planning, use intelligence to prevent additional crime victims, and engage the family in monitoring offenders' post-release progress.

- Clarify law enforcement's role in determining what its goals are

- Balance "hard line" enforcement with positive reinforcement in reintegrating offenders

- Separate law enforcement's role from the social services role.

In offender reentry programming, policing should remain consistent and stick to law enforcement's main goals, but focus on apprehending offenders before they re-offend. Law enforcement contributors to this guide offered specific management and operational strategies that law enforcement should implement to successfully participate in a reentry initiative.

INSTITUTE A PARADIGM SHIFT IN YOUR AGENCY

Many law enforcement executives believe that they need to embrace reentry as a new way of doing usual business. Getting internal buy-in to participate in offender reentry programs will take time. Contributors to this guide realized that it was more important to work smarter, not harder. In their opinion, to effectively participate in reentry programs, law enforcement needs to affect a paradigm shift in thinking so that officers can better serve the community. Here are a few key ways to do this:

- **Recognize that offenders are coming back to your community.** You cannot stop the process, so it is better to be proactive than reactive. Getting involved early helps to stop certain crimes from occurring or to prevent minor crimes from becoming major crimes.

- **Implement/leverage a community oriented policing philosophy.** According to program leaders, having a community policing philosophy helped partner agencies transition and commit to this initiative.

- **Use information sharing opportunities to get buy-in from the rank-and-file officers.** Start with one officer, share the message, and use those informed officers to spread the message through roll calls, in-service trainings,

meetings, and presentations to the community and their fellow officers. Provide concrete examples (e.g., cost-benefit analysis) of the potential benefits to participating.

- **Recognize that effort equals outcome.** Law enforcement agencies will have to be willing to increase work to decrease crime. For some participating law enforcement agencies, promoting the program is critical. Community meetings, public engagements, and general outreach are some examples.

- **Make a commitment and stick with it.** As soon as a decision to engage in offender reentry initiatives has been made, it is essential that the agency devote adequate resources to support the effort. Police executives must keep the program ever-present among all of the various agency activities s/he manages. One way to do this is to create a tickler system to remind the chief to rotate the topic on the calendar at crime strategy meetings, command staff meetings, or roll call. Using something as simple as Microsoft Outlook® Task List would accomplish this goal.

- **Think long-term.** Law enforcement agencies need to look at this initiative as one piece of a larger process. For the Racine (WI) former police chief, "It is short-sighted to strictly consider the enforcement aspect of law enforcement. It has changed how I assess and measure myself as a chief."

- **Consider the political/policy implications of participation.** Recent police search and seizure laws require that law enforcement officers consider the civil liberty implications for sharing information with non-police. The Supreme Court's decision in the *Knights*[4] case details their perspective on information sharing between law enforcement and corrections. Another issue for consideration concerns joint home visits and whether or not police presence is for enforcement or protection. Identifying gaps and needs for clarification on such laws and new legislation will help obtain buy-in internally and externally.

IMPLEMENT RELEVANT OPERATIONAL CHANGES

Law enforcement needs to understand how to use resources. Probation and parole officers need assistance in reducing their caseloads and law enforcement needs intelligence on criminal activities. These agencies can help each other. Participation in offender reentry initiatives is a decision that needs to come from the top of the law enforcement structure. Accordingly, it is important to choose the right staff members to participate and support the effort, market and coordinate program activities, and serve as the agency's representative. For example, the chief needs to motivate the line staff. It sends a message to officers and offenders about the importance of the initiative when the chief appears at the notification meetings. Command staff must be willing to support reentry as a preventative approach by collaborating with human services and community-based agencies designed to assist offenders. They must also be willing to invest the necessary resources into this effort. Here are a few points to consider:

- **Generate and sustain program support.** Start and maintain regular meetings to keep the lines of communication open and to keep the program going. Ensure "wrap-a-round" or follow-up reporting to all agencies involved. It is essential that partners collect information, reflect, solicit more ideas, and return to share ideas with partner agencies.

- **Select and involve appropriate staff.** The MAVI program in Minneapolis (MN) started by involving personnel with a keen knowledge of street activity, a bigger perspective than their agency, and assertive individuals willing to suggest ideas that represent risk-taking.

- **Involve both command and front-line staff.** Command staff can make operational and policy decisions for front-line staff to implement. Both command and front-line staff must be willing to embrace a new approach to dealing with offenders. Employ first-line supervisors to promote the initiative and obtain buy-in from front-line officers. It is also important to recruit police officers who are interested in serving in the program and genuinely want this effort to succeed.

- **Hire and/or train community-oriented officers.** Today's officers are highly educated and tested on how well they can think, communicate, and prevent harm. Look for quick-thinking officers who are there to serve, protect, and function mostly through communication.

- **Document collateral contacts with supervised offenders.** Use Field Interview Report (FIR) cards whenever an officer has official collateral contact with an offender under community corrections supervision. Sending completed FIR cards to supervising community corrections officers is a good monitoring strategy.

- **Target enforcement efforts.** Police use community policing and other crime prevention strategies such as joint home visits, patrols, and curfew checks to ensure offender accountability. Directed and expanded police-probation patrols in high crime or "hot spot" precincts can also provide much-needed intelligence.

- **Locate probation/police satellite offices in targeted at-risk neighborhoods.** Require officers to talk with residents, establish relationships with probation and parole, supervise specialized caseloads built from the neighborhood geography (i.e., those who reside in and have committed crimes in that neighborhood).

- **Change shift schedules to meet program needs.** If possible, adjust shift schedules to accommodate non-traditional service hours. For example, Campbell County (KY) Police extended day shift hours to enhance offender supervision while maintaining a firm hold on the overtime budget.

- **Rotate program staff.** Campbell County (KY) police officers are rotated to prevent burnout and give interested officers an opportunity to serve in the reentry program.

- **Encourage continued front-line officer involvement.** Once internal buy-in has been obtained from front-line staff, their continued support and active participation should be encouraged. Awarding certificates of appreciation or letters of recognition for a job well done or to acknowledge their elite status in working with this challenging population can set the tone for their continued efforts.

DEVELOP OR ENHANCE YOUR RELATIONSHIP WITH THE COMMUNITY

Managing community relations can be quite challenging for law enforcement involved in offender reentry programs. The residents do not want offenders in the neighborhood and offenders do not trust law enforcement and may question their involvement. It is essential that law enforcement engages the community through initiatives that focus on reducing crime, exchanging information, enhancing crime prevention methods, and addressing livability issues.

The Savannah Chatham (GA) Metropolitan Police Department (SCMPD) officers assigned to their reentry program use two strategies for informing and engaging the public in offender reentry activities. Officers coordinate with SCMPD's Crime Stoppers program to market any program absconders. Through Crime Stoppers, the program can reach the public through print, TV, the Internet, and via a police-monitored tip line. Moreover, every officer is assigned to a community group. They request to be on the community agenda and make presentations to share information on their reentry and other police activities. Here are some other ways to involve the community:

- **Involve citizens from the beginning.** Educate the community on program activities and how it will reduce their risk for victimization; participate in workshops that prepare the offender's family for his or her return; work with victims and their families; and identify and share with the community how their efforts and involvement can be beneficial if they assist the police department.

- **Repackage your agency as a resource rather than an enforcer.** Many programs bring law enforcement in as the enforcer but law enforcement can have far greater input. Police can be a resource, which helps improve public relations by letting offenders know that police are not the enemy, they are there to be supportive. In Racine (WI) community orienting policing (COP) house officers advise that once an officer is assigned to a COP house or a particular neighborhood, that officer is required to go out and make contacts in the community. Officers go door-to-door to introduce themselves to local businesses to make them aware of police presence. Likewise, officers introduce themselves to citizens. Similarly, the High

Point (NC) Police Department wants the community to think of the police as a safe haven to go to; an identified face to approach and talk to; and a resource for referrals. A positive face on the police is something offenders have not often experienced.

- **Focus on victims and other severely impacted residents.** Work with the community to target chronic offenders and give crime victims a voice by ensuring they are notified of the criminal's arrest and sentencing so that the victim can present an impact statement. Additionally, develop relationships with minority communities to provide specialized services.

- **Include rehabilitated offenders in the effort.** They can serve as role models and help educate other offenders and the community on the benefits of the reentry initiative.

IMPLEMENT STRATEGIC MARKETING APPROACHES

It is important to show how valuable the initiative is to enhance public safety and reduce crime and recidivism. Your audience includes not only your officers, funding agencies, political or partner supporters, but also other law enforcement officials. Work with police associations to increase an understanding of the topic and to gain buy-in from a law enforcement perspective. A strategic marketing approach should also focus on:

- Developing a tagline that illustrates what your program hopes to accomplish.

- Developing a positive, proactive relationship with members of the press.

Both approaches are mediums for selling the program communitywide or statewide and reinforcing the idea that offenders are not just returning home to "your" community, but to "their" community as well.

The Indianapolis (IN) Violence Reduction Partnership (IVRP) regularly produces and distributes intelligence newsletters. The newsletters include articles updating partners on each agency's progress. In 2000, IVRP partners jointly planned, produced, and promoted a public service campaign that included television, billboards, truck panels, and IndyGo bus advertisements. The ad campaign slogans were "You Can't Take Back the Violent Act" and "Unlucky Seven/Gun and Crime = Seven Years Hard Time." "Unlucky Seven" refers to the average number of years that an offender received pursuant to a 1999 statute that prohibits a person convicted of one of 26 enumerated violent or drug-related crimes from possessing a firearm.

CONSIDER TRAINING NEEDS

Law enforcement program leaders found that in addition to gaining buy-in, support, and participation, training was necessary for officers and partner agencies. These cross-training activities enhance communication and understanding of agency rights and limitations. For example:

- In Minneapolis (MN), probation officers are not armed, but receive annual defensive tactics training and education from the Minneapolis Police Department (MPD), Hennepin County Sheriff's Office (HCSO), and the Hennepin County Attorney's Office. MPD provides training on search and seizure, use of pepper spray, and handcuffing. HCSO provides training on radio procedures, updates, and related information. The County Attorney's Office provides an overview of search, seizure, and related Fourth Amendment issues. Community corrections representatives make presentations at the MPD academy frequently.

- In 2002, the Savannah (GA) Impact Program (SIP) began providing multi-agency program training so that police would have a better understanding of parole and probation and vice versa. The training covered the limitations, policies, and practices of each agency. For example, the district attorney made a presentation on search and seizure issues and police provided an overview of self-defense, tactical firearms, and interview and interrogation procedures. Other agencies have conducted training on human diversity, cultural attitudes, cultural behaviors, and responses. All of the police officers who staff SIP are certified by the Georgia Peace Officers Standards and Training (POST) Council. Prior to SIP, only probation and parole officers were certified to conduct

drug screening and testing. Now, both police and community corrections staff in SIP are cross-certified.

Offender reentry strategies should also be shared widely for maximum cooperation and exposure at venues such as Regional Community Policing Institutes and police academies and associations. The Redmond (WA) reentry program is so widely known that its program leaders have trained more than 70 other law enforcement agencies to implement similar crime prevention strategies.

MEASURING SUCCESS

Terms like "reducing recidivism" and "maintaining public safety" are important to measure. Gauging success is one of the ways to ensure that the program includes the right partners, is delivering services in a most efficient manner, and that program activities are effectively managed. The overall measure of success for a reentry program can be how few offenders re-offend or commit new crimes. Success has been measured using anecdotal success stories and formal and informal evaluation data. According to the former Chief of the Racine (WI) Police Department, "Absence of crime is the true measure of success [for the Community Re-Entry Program]." Since the program's inception in September 2004, the program has enjoyed a 65 percent employment rate among program participants; 64 percent have remained crime-free; and only 22 percent have recidivated, which is much lower than the national average of 67 percent.

For involvement in offender reentry efforts, measures of success must be determined by the program goals and objectives law enforcement agencies are seeking to achieve. Some of the measures to gauge levels of success by law enforcement agencies are:

- A change in crime rates before and after the return of high-risk offenders.

- An increase in specific re-victimizations attributed to returned offenders.

- Re-arrest rates for returned offenders.

- Lack of new arrests vs. technical violations.

- Arrests vs. convictions.

- Movement/change in supervision status (e.g., movement from intense to regular supervision or removal from supervision).

- Resource delivery, receipt, and impact (i.e., number of offenders who obtained their GED, obtained employment, maintained steady housing, number of offenders who remained clean of illegal substances).

- Frequency and amount of resource delivery.

- Comparison of local recidivism rates to the national average (e.g., crime type, new arrests, and technical violations).

- The number of victims harmed by returned offenders.

- Perceived reduction in fear of crime by the community.

- The number of complaints lodged by residents in response to reentry program activities.

METHODS/TOOLS FOR MEASURING SUCCESS IN OFFENDER REENTRY

Both traditional and non-traditional methods for measuring success can be used. The Racine (WI) Community Re-Entry Program employs quality assurance/program monitoring strategies to ensure program success. This includes a review of case plans, constant communication among partner agencies working with offenders, and a review of arrests and supervision violations. Other examples include:

- Community feedback and/or citizen crime surveys

- Police reports

- Federal Bureau of Investigation (FBI) Uniform Crime Report (UCR) data.

To develop concrete measures of success that illustrate significant reentry program outcomes, it is suggested that agencies:

- Identify the intended results.

- Decide on the measures of success and outcomes from

the beginning and be certain that everyone involved agrees on the same measures of success.

- Create a baseline measure (e.g., reduce community fear of crime) because it is hard to quantify some goals.

- Be certain of what is really being measured (e.g., reduction in crime vs. *perceived* reduction in crime).

- Set achievement benchmarks (e.g., reduction in crime in six months).

- Use criminogenic risk/need assessments tools (e.g., LSI-R) to determine what the offenders' needs (e.g., housing, employment, and education) are pre- or post-release and their level of risk for re-offending.

- Obtain feedback, correct problems, and re-evaluate activities.

- Create systems of documentation to help measure outcomes (e.g., implement a data tracking mechanism to collect, manage, analyze, and report measurement data collected using community surveys and such).

- Make sure service providers are properly trained in using chosen measurement tools.

- Partner with research departments at local colleges and universities to manage data.

Documenting program success is an important component in securing program sustainability through continued funding and resource allocation, partnerships, and community buy-in.

Measuring Success

- Define success for your program.
- Review other reentry program measures of success.
- Choose appropriate methods and tools for measuring your program's success.

KEY RECOMMENDATIONS AND ADVICE

Law enforcement officials involved in strategic roles in offender reentry initiatives shared a variety of recommendations and advice based on their experiences, lessons learned, and success stories for other law enforcement agencies interested in implementing reentry programs or expanding existing programs. Recommendations are categorized by general advice, partnership, potential program impact, outreach, and community engagement.

GENERAL PROGRAM ADVICE

- **Commitment is critical.** Realize that a program like this entails a major commitment on the part of leadership to pursue new directions and take risks regarding the allocation of resources.

- **Start small.** Be willing to start small in terms of partners, activities, and the population to be served. Use a graduated step approach that allows you to add on program components one step at a time before measuring overall success.

- **Consider offender perspective.** Understand that there are offenders reentering the community who do not want to change. One offender-turned-program-supporter remarked, "What made me realize that I had a choice was that I tried it the other way, so I said, let me give this way a try because I could always go back to being a street thug."

- **Programs must be tailored.** Recognize that one size does not fit all. There is no one program that works for every offender.

- **It is important to provide wraparound services.** Reentry programs must address the issues that create barriers to successful reintegration: lack of housing, education, employment, substance treatment, and family support. The Savannah Impact Program (SIP) makes a point to involve families in the offender's progress; they are invited to graduations; and are seen as a support system during aftercare. The family's involvement and support also validates the offender's choice to participate in SIP.

- **Identify the "right" problem and strategies for the jurisdiction.** Law enforcement in Park City (UT) focused on alcohol and substance abuse because they have a high number of bars and encounter high levels of driving under the influence (DUI) crimes. Other jurisdictions need to identify the problem that is most important for them to focus on before moving forward with a reentry effort.

- **It is critical that program leaders do their homework on their neighborhoods.** Gather information on what crimes are occurring and get feedback from the community on what their concerns are.

- **Reentry programs need a full-time person to manage the process.** This person will be the contact for the program, liaison with partner agencies, and be dedicated to nurturing the initiative, monitoring offenders, information sharing, and follow-up.

PARTNERSHIP

- **Invite partners that complement the program.** Program leaders consulted for this guide advise that law enforcement agencies choose partner agencies based on their strengths, social capital, and the services they can deliver. For example, police officers are not job counselors or ministers, so it is important to find partners who can provide the services most needed by returning offenders.

- **Be patient in attempting to gain the trust and confidence of partner agencies.** The Savannah (GA) Impact Program executive director advised providing information or requesting cooperation and/or assistance incrementally. He remarked, "I came with a pistol and not a shotgun" approach to engaging partner agencies.

- **Develop partner selection criteria.** Reentry program leaders suggest that prospective departments develop a list and evaluate agencies based on the following criteria:

  - Is/would this agency/individual be a good, credible stakeholder?

  - Can they provide services or resources we cannot provide?

- Can they provide services in support of an offender's successful reintegration?

- Does it make "sense" to involve this agency in the effort?

- **Coordinate services.** It is important to coordinate services among program partners to ensure that there is no duplication or overlap. While each agency brings a particular type of expertise, communicating about the services to be delivered by each partner agency is extremely important.

- **Maintain partner interest, involvement, and input.** Program leaders admit that almost half of their time and effort is spent encouraging partners to remain a part of the effort. Establish subcommittees to carry out specific tasks to maintain interest and spread the responsibilities around.

- **Establish a strong but manageable core group.** Program leaders advise that having a strong core committee helps keep activities going, but the size of the group must be manageable.

POTENTIAL PROGRAM IMPACT

- **Recognize that technical violations may increase.** Program leaders learned that technical violations will rise when there is increased contact/enhanced surveillance. One of the reasons for this increase is there are more frequent opportunities for community corrections officials to interact and observe offenders.

- **Offenders may relocate.** Another impact of enhanced supervision is that offenders may move to other jurisdictions if the surveillance or conditions are too intense. Program leaders suggest that police and sheriff's departments communicate with/notify their counterparts in neighboring jurisdictions to head off potential problems.

- **Evaluate and define success.** Look to other successful programs for strategies. Implement program activities, evaluate them, tweak them, and remove what does not work. Critique program effectiveness after each meeting. Constantly evaluate what you do and bring partners back to the table.

COMMUNITY ENGAGEMENT AND OUTREACH

- **Devise a marketing strategy that gets the message out.** It is helpful to produce a brochure right away so that program leaders will have something to hand others that explains the program concept, helps to obtain program support, and makes a lasting impression.

- **Conduct program outreach with other law enforcement agencies.** Communicate about your program statewide with law enforcement through state associations.

- **Use the community or partners to address negative criticism about the program.** The best way to counter naysayers is to use other partner agencies—not law enforcement executives—to talk about program successes.

- **Promote an all-inclusive attitude.** Recognize that while the community may see offenders as interlopers returning to "their" community, offenders believe they are coming home to their own communities as well.

- **Develop an easily identifiable motto or tag line.** The motto law enforcement officials who contributed to this guide suggested is, "Structure + Support = Success."

Key Advice

- Identify the problems and strategies specific to your jurisdiction.
- Invite agencies that compliment the program goals and objectives to collaborate.
- Develop a marketing strategy that explains the program concept, helps to obtain support, and makes a lasting impact.

SECTION III:
CURRENT STATE OF PRACTICE EXAMPLES FROM LAW ENFORCEMENT

The IACP conducted site visits to police and sheriff departments to document how law enforcement is engaged and to examine the operational aspects of their reentry efforts. The sites visited were selected because they involve law enforcement in a strategic or decision-making role; engage government and community support; employ a multi-agency collaborative approach across jurisdictions; and utilize leading practice strategies that have yielded results. A review of the demographics of each site visited reveals that law enforcement involvement in reentry efforts is diverse. For example:

- Law enforcement agencies visited are geographically diverse.

- Participating law enforcement agencies represented small, medium, and large departments in rural, suburban, and urban areas.

- The agencies experienced a range of violent, property, and traffic crimes.

- Reentry efforts ranged from simple partnerships and information sharing efforts to large-scale transitional team approaches.

This section offers profiles of 13 offender reentry programs in which 18 law enforcement agencies participate.

AGENCY PROFILE KEY

For contextual purposes, each profile includes a program summary and descriptions of the components, activities, partners, and law enforcement strategies used. A brief snapshot of the criteria for offender participation, unique community challenges or strategies, and key program features is also displayed. The chart below illustrates the general components and activities of the programs highlighted in this guide.

Programs	PROGRAM COMPONENTS/ACTIVITIES								
	Enhanced Supervision	Partnership Building	Information Sharing	Intelligence Exchange	Notification Sessions	Community Outreach/ Engagement	Joint Home Visits	Joint Curfew Checks	Joint Patrols
CRP (WI)	✔	✔	✔	✔	✔	✔	✔		✔
CT-PSN (CT)	✔	✔	✔	✔	✔	✔			
GHP (NV)	✔	✔	✔						
IVRP (IN)	✔	✔	✔	✔	✔	✔	✔		
JIST (KY)	✔	✔	✔	✔			✔		✔
MAVI (MN)	✔	✔	✔	✔		✔	✔		✔
RPI (MA)	✔	✔	✔	✔			✔		
RSVP (KY)	✔	✔	✔	✔	✔	✔	✔	✔	✔
SCORB (UT)	✔	✔	✔	✔	✔	✔	✔		
SCRP (KS)	✔	✔	✔		✔	✔	✔		
SIP (GA)	✔	✔	✔			✔			
SMART (WA)	✔	✔	✔	✔	✔	✔	✔		
VCTF (NC)	✔	✔	✔	✔	✔	✔	✔		

CAMPBELL COUNTY POLICE DEPARTMENT (KENTUCKY)
JUVENILE INTENSIVE SERVICE TEAM (JIST)

Offender Participant Criteria:
- Formerly committed at-risk youth
- Convicted of crimes involving violence, drugs/alcohol or gangs

Unique Community Challenges/Strategies:
This is one of the few offender reentry programs in the country that specifically focuses on juveniles.

Key Program Features:
- Targeted Police Enforcement
- Enhanced Supervision
- Immediate Sanctions
- Transitional Support Services

AGENCY PROFILE

- Population Served: Approx. 88,600
- Sworn Employees: 33
- Onset of Reentry Participation: 2000

PROGRAM SUMMARY

The Juvenile Intensive Service Team (JIST) endeavors to assist juveniles in transitioning from state commitment back to their homes and the community. The impetus for the program was an increase in juvenile crimes accompanied by the relocation of a local high school from the City of Alexandria (KY) into the unincorporated area of Campbell County. The community reported an increase in car vandalisms, petty thefts, and burglaries whose primary perpetrators were juveniles. JIST, a partnership between the Campbell County Police Department (CCPD) and Department of Juvenile Justice, was formed in response to this increase in crime. The program goals are to address juvenile crime, serve youth returning from placement in state-operated facilities, and prevent subsequent out-of-home placement. Juveniles are deemed "high risk" by their age at first court appearance, prior criminal behavior, prior out-of-home placements, identified school problems, substance abuse, and peer relationships. The program has been successful in obtaining high compliance rates among program participants. Success is measured in terms of probation supervision compliance, lack of recidivism, and reduction in juvenile offenses. Monthly statistics are collected and maintained. Based on these criteria, 71 percent of the juveniles in the program have not re-offended.

COMPONENTS AND ACTIVITIES

- Intensive supervision, monitoring, and enforcement
- Interactive juvenile service worker and police teams
- Interagency communication, information sharing, and intelligence exchange
- Coordinated partnerships to provide transitional services

PROGRAM PARTNERS

- Kentucky Department of Juvenile Justice
- Community service agencies: Transitions Substance Abuse Counseling

LAW ENFORCEMENT PARTICIPATION

The CCPD Chief has dedicated command staff to oversee program participation; assigned officers for joint home visits and patrols with probation officials; shared information with program partners; extended or alternated shift schedules to meet program and officer needs; and rotated officers to prevent burnout and give interested officers an opportunity to serve in the program. School Resource Officers (SROs) provide on-site monitoring and intelligence regarding program participants.

PROGRAM STRATEGIES FOR SUCCESSFUL REINTEGRATION

The JIST approach is a unique partnership between law enforcement and juvenile social services. The program features activities found in other such programs, but the focus is on juvenile offenders. The program emphasizes public safety, reduction in crime and recidivism, and provides support services to help juvenile offenders reintegrate back into the community.

CONTACT INFORMATION

Rob Forrest, Kentucky Department of Juvenile Justice: 859-292-6652 or roberte.forrest@ky.gov
http://djj.ky.gov/programs/aftercare.htm

INDIANAPOLIS POLICE DEPARTMENT (INDIANA)

MARION COUNTY SHERIFF'S DEPARTMENT
INDIANAPOLIS VIOLENCE REDUCTION PARTNERSHIP (IVRP)

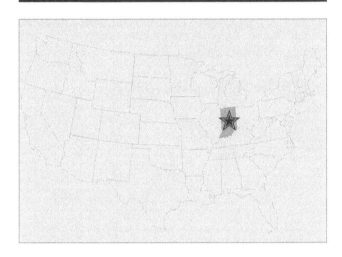

Offender Participant Criteria:
- Adults and juveniles
- History of violence
- Crimes that are gun-related, involve drugs/alcohol

Unique Community Challenges/Strategies:
Indianapolis has been the site of federal parolees who like to "state shop" and relocate to Indianapolis. This puts a great deal of stress on community resources.

Key Program Features:
- Lever-pulling Meetings
- VIPER
- Ongoing Assessment and Evaluation

AGENCY PROFILE

- Population Served: Approx. 781,800
- Sworn Employees: 1,600 (combined)
- Onset of Reentry Participation: 1997

PROGRAM SUMMARY

The Indianapolis Violence Reduction Partnership (IVRP) is a collaborative effort involving all of the criminal justice agencies serving Marion County (IN). The IVRP working group includes members of law enforcement, corrections and probation, prosecutors and court officials, social service providers, university researchers, and faith-based organizations. IVRP has developed a problem-solving methodology wherein violent incidents are analyzed, strategies are implemented, and the efforts assessed and reprogrammed to impact crime. Program goals and objectives include increased arrests and prosecution of the most serious and chronic violent offenders and disruption of illegal firearms markets. IVRP uses a multi-level and multi-agency response that includes Lever-pulling meetings to communicate anti-violence messages to potential offenders and the community, development of community-based prevention components, and offender accountability. Officials within the Indianapolis Police Department (IPD) researched the commonality of violence within each incident of homicide to create a plan to attack those traits that seem indigenous to violent events. Using this information, IPD implemented the Violence Impact Program Enhanced Response (VIPER) program. VIPER is used to identify, flag, and monitor the most violent adult and juvenile offenders. Federal and local prosecutors review and jointly decide how to prosecute VIPER cases. IVRP uses reduction in homicide and violent crime rates, reduction in parole and probation violations, and program effectiveness as measures of success. Researchers from the Hudson Institute and Indiana University have partnered with IVRP to study the effectiveness of the program. Results show a reduction in homicide rates during program operation. Prior to VIPER only 28 percent of those identified were charged. After implementing VIPER, the conviction rates for homicides increased.

COMPONENTS AND ACTIVITIES

- Lever-pulling meetings
- Targeted law enforcement
- Enhanced supervision and prosecution
- Community collaboration
- Coordinated partnerships to provide transitional services
- Ongoing program assessment and evaluation

PROGRAM PARTNERS

- Marion County Justice Agency, Indiana State Police
- Indianapolis Mayor's Office and Courts
- U.S. Attorney's Office, State Attorney's Office
- Indiana Department of Correction, Marion County Probation
- Federal agencies include: Bureau of Alcohol, Tobacco, Firearms and Explosives (ATF); U.S. Marshals Service; Drug Enforcement Administration (DEA); Federal Bureau of Investigation (FBI)
- Government and community social service agencies
- Hudson Institute, Indiana University

LAW ENFORCEMENT PARTICIPATION

IPD joined IVRP to promote a coordinated approach to arresting, prosecuting, and sentencing the most chronic, violent offenders. Officers participate in enhanced supervision activities to include joint home visits and warrant and drug sweeps; deliver anti-violence messages at lever-pulling meetings; attend intelligence exchange meetings with federal and state law enforcement agencies; and report collateral contacts with offenders that are flagged in VIPER.

Specific law enforcement and prosecution strategies have been implemented to work hand-in-hand. IPD added detectives to district neighborhood narcotics units, assigned officers to tactical enforcement units, increased walking beats and mounted police patrols, increased cooperation with the U.S. Marshals Service to apprehend absconders, and re-formed an Aggravated Assault Unit. District detective supervisors began meeting every two weeks to analyze crimes and share information with state and federal prosecutors.

PROGRAM STRATEGIES FOR SUCCESSFUL REINTEGRATION

IVRP employs a problem-solving approach to addressing homicide and serious violence in Indianapolis and Marion County at-large. A working group was implemented to meet regularly to share information and intelligence and prevent overlap. A focused approach was developed that outlined who would be the target of enhanced supervision and prosecution services. VIPER cases are flagged in federal and state prosecutor offices to ensure that these cases receive specialized processing based on the intelligence gathered through the IVRP partnership and VIPER. After a concerted effort to identify offenders, conduct drug sweeps, and serve warrants, homicide rates decreased.

CONTACT INFORMATION

Diana Burleson or Kristina Korobov, Marion County Justice Agency: 317-327-3121
http://www.indygov.org/eGov/County/MCJA/home.htm

LAS VEGAS METROPOLITAN POLICE DEPARTMENT (NEVADA)
GOING HOME PREPARED (GHP) PROGRAM

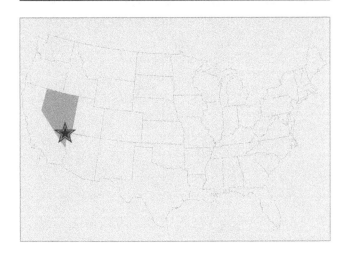

Offender Participant Criteria:
- Adults and juveniles aged 14-35
- Eligible for parole on their last and final sentence
- Serving time/convicted of serious categorical felonies
- Repeat violent offender
- Crimes involving violence, gangs or weapons

Unique Community Challenges/Strategies:
Nevada is one of the fastest growing states characterized by a high degree of transience. Thirty-eight percent of Nevada inmates are incarcerated for crimes of violence; 31% of men and 50% of women are repeat violent offenders.

Key Program Features:
- Enhanced Supervision
- Ongoing Assessment and Evaluation
- Reentry Planning

AGENCY PROFILE

- County Population Served: Approx. 575,973
- Sworn Employees: 2,251
- Onset of Reentry Participation: 2002

PROGRAM SUMMARY

The Nevada Department of Corrections (NDOC) has partnered with law enforcement and community and social service agencies to provide serious and violent offenders with pre-release and transitional services. GHP was created using support from the U.S. Department of Justice's Serious and Violent Offender Reentry Initiative (SVORI) to implement a coordinated offender reentry system. The goals of the Going Home Prepared (GHP) program are to enhance public safety and reduce recidivism. Prior to this effort, there were no coordinated transitional services, state-run halfway houses or day reporting centers. This changed after the implementation of GHP. GHP maintains statistics on measures of success to include recidivism rates and technical violations. Using data obtained through offender tracking, pre- and post-tests, and offender feedback, the program has documented a 39% recidivism rate to include technical violations and absconders. Before the program was implemented, the recidivism rate was around 80 percent.

COMPONENTS AND ACTIVITIES

- Enhanced supervision
- Partnership building, information sharing, and intelligence exchange
- Coordinated transitional services
- Reentry court

PROGRAM PARTNERS

- Nevada Department of Corrections
- Eighth Judicial District Court (reentry court)
- Government and community social services: Southern Nevada Workforce Investment Board, Clark County School District, Salvation Army, the Nevada Welfare Division, the Nevada Treatment Center, HELP of Southern Nevada, Choices Group, and Lutheran Social Services of Nevada.

LAW ENFORCEMENT PARTICIPATION

The Las Vegas Metropolitan Police Department serves on the Advisory Board and has designated contact personnel that the reentry coordinator can contact when a parolee has absconded from supervision.

PROGRAM STRATEGIES FOR SUCCESSFUL REINTEGRATION

GHP was built on the philosophy that reentry gives offenders an option different than what they know and have chosen in the past. GHP is staffed by reentry case workers and clinical social workers to ensure proper pre- and post-release risk and needs assessment. Advisory Board members and program partners work together to provide coordinated service management. Offenders are released with a copy of their reentry plan; copies of their articles of identification; bus tokens and passes; and calendars to plan beneficial activities designed to ensure their post-release success. Lack of health and mental health support has proven to be factors in recidivism among Las Vegas offenders. For this reason, GHP officials have arranged for offenders to receive health cards and treatment services post-release as well as food stamps for a finite period of time. Program officials also work with local halfway houses to arrange for transitional housing for those offenders without homes or family support.

The success of the GHP program has led to the state-supported creation of Casa Grande Transitional Housing Facility, which opened in 2006. Although violent and sex offenders are not eligible to participate in the program, this and other comprehensive "street readiness" programs have arisen since the implementation of GHP.

CONTACT INFORMATION

Dana Serrata, Reentry Coordinator:
702-486-9926 or dserrata@doc.nv.gov

LOUISVILLE METRO POLICE DEPARTMENT (KENTUCKY)
REDUCING SERIOUS VIOLENCE PARTNERSHIP (RSVP) PROGRAM

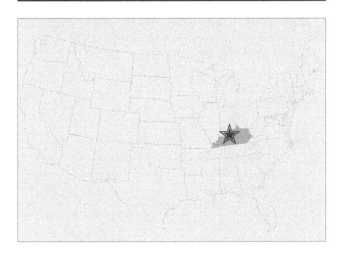

Offender Participant Criteria:
- Adults
- Current conviction involves an index crime, violence or firearms crime
- Individuals who have lost a friend or family member to violence

Unique Community Challenges/Strategies:
In 2003, the Jefferson County and Louisville Police Departments merged to become the Louisville Metro Police Department.

Key Program Features:
- Enhanced Supervision
- Call-in Meetings
- METSYS

AGENCY PROFILE

- Population Served: Approx. 256,231
- Sworn Employees: 574
- Onset of Reentry Participation: 2005

PROGRAM SUMMARY

The Reducing Serious Violence Partnership (RSVP) program is a partnership between criminal justice and social service agencies designed to reduce and deter violent crime in Louisville, enhance public safety, and improve an offender's prospects for successful integration into the community post-release. Key features of the program are its Call-in meetings and data tracking through METSYS. Law enforcement coordinates and participates in call-in meetings every other month. Offenders in the program are told that law enforcement enforces a "no tolerance" for violence perspective. Meetings are mandatory, but held in seclusion without community input. Offender tracking is conducted using METSYS, a Microsoft Access-based case management system maintained by the police department. This system includes offender information and their status in the program. Program success is defined by the rate of murders, gun violence, and whether or not program participants have committed new crimes. The first cycle of program participation began in March 2005. For a one-year period, approximately 87 offenders participated in program activities. Of the 87, 17 percent successfully completed the program; 60 percent continue to be actively involved in program activities; and 19 percent were returned to prison.

COMPONENTS AND ACTIVITIES

- Intensive supervision and monitoring
- Interagency communication, information sharing, and intelligence exchange
- Coordinated partnerships to provide transitional services
- Offender tracking through METSYS

PROGRAM PARTNERS

- Kentucky Department of Corrections; Probation and Parole Department
- U.S. Attorney's Office, Commonwealth's Attorney's Office; County Attorney's Office
- Community service agencies: Kentuckiana Works, Louisville Urban League/Workforce Development, Metro Health Department; faith community

LAW ENFORCEMENT PARTICIPATION

The police chief has dedicated staff to managing program activities, coordinating Call-in meetings, tracking offender status, and conducting joint home visits, curfew checks, and ride-a-longs.

PROGRAM STRATEGIES FOR SUCCESSFUL REINTEGRATION

Program components integrate enhanced probation/parole supervision, partnership building and maintenance, information sharing, and intelligence exchange. Future program activities will include outreach to judges to encourage their cooperation with recommendations made by probation and parole for non-compliant offenders; program expansion to include juveniles; and outreach to community colleges to award scholarships for successful participants.

CONTACT INFORMATION

Diana Darby, Louisville Metro Police Department: 502-574-2430 or Diana.darby@lmpd.loukymetro.org
http://www.louisvilleky.gov/MetroPolice

LOWELL POLICE DEPARTMENT (MASSACHUSETTS)
REENTRY PARTNERSHIP INITIATIVE (RPI)

Offender Participant Criteria:
- Adults
- Histories of violence
- Returning to or relocating to Lowell

Key Program Features:
- Targeted Police Enforcement
- Enhanced Supervision
- Intelligence Exchange

Unique Community Challenges/Strategies:
Seventy-five percent of offenders in Massachusetts "max out" their sentences. Lowell is the recipient of a large number of returning offenders and increased ethnic gang activities.

AGENCY PROFILE

- Population Served: Approx. 105,167
- Sworn Employees: 249
- Onset of Reentry Participation: 1999

PROGRAM SUMMARY

The Reentry Partnership Initiative (RPI) is a corrections, law enforcement, and community-based program that seeks to positively increase officer safety, enhance public safety, and reduce recidivism. These goals are accomplished by improving risk management of released offenders, enhancing surveillance and monitoring, strengthening individual and community support systems, and repairing the harm done to victims.

COMPONENTS AND ACTIVITIES

- Intensive supervision and monitoring of offenders through joint home visits
- Offender tracking for re-arrest or new convictions
- Interagency communication, information sharing, and intelligence exchange
- Coordinated partnerships to provide transitional services

PROGRAM PARTNERS

- Massachusetts Department of Corrections, Middlesex County House of Corrections, Massachusetts Probation Service, Regional Reentry Centers
- Department of Youth Services
- Community service agencies: Safety First, South Middlesex Opportunity Council (SMOC), Vision New England

LAW ENFORCEMENT PARTICIPATION

The Lowell police chief has increased involvement of neighborhood officers to participate in home visits, pre-release orientation panels, and other activities designed to assist offenders in successfully transitioning. Lowell Police Department (LPD) staff have received access to the Massachusetts Department of Corrections database for pre-release data. This allows LPD staff to collect, track, and analyze offender data to ensure program effectiveness and to ensure offender accountability. Dedicated staff attends collaborative meetings with community and partner agencies. The Chief also conducts meetings with district command staff that focus on crimes and high crime areas. This information is shared with other relevant program partners and used to enhance program services.

PROGRAM STRATEGIES FOR SUCCESSFUL REINTEGRATION

Overall, RPI includes a combination of pre- and post-release program components that include information sharing, home visits, offender monitoring, and information dissemination. LPD staff: 1) Participate in inmate discharge planning; 2) Conducts presentations at pre-release orientation meetings to describe the program and its services; and, 3) Informs offenders that they are not anonymous. LPD staff compiles released offender information to include the offender's demographic information, a brief summary of the criminal history (including past or present gang involvement and risk level), and a list of any open criminal matters. This information is included in the reentry blotters and daily crime intelligence bulletins. This information is also entered into a computer tracking database that is used to monitor offender arrest patterns. Law enforcement coordinates service delivery for offenders through the state corrections system and parole board-managed Regional Reentry Centers (RRCs). RRCs are staffed by reentry officers and probation supervisors who review offender release plans and coordinate community-based, shared case management and ongoing support as needed. Access to mental health and substance abuse treatment are accomplished through issuance of MassHealth cards.

CONTACT INFORMATION

Jennifer Ball, Lowell Police Department: 978-937-3228 or jball@ci.lowell.ma.us
http://www.lowellpolice.com/about_lpd/policing_ini/reentry.htm

MINNEAPOLIS POLICE DEPARTMENT (MINNESOTA)
MINNEAPOLIS ANTI-VIOLENCE INITIATIVE (MAVI) AND COMMUNITY JUSTICE PROGRAM

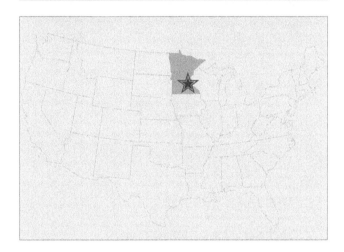

Offender Participant Criteria:
- Adult and juveniles
- Histories of violence
- Previous firearms use, arrest, convictions
- Suspected or proven gang involvement

Unique Community Challenges/Strategies:
Minneapolis is host to various diverse, but concentrated populations such as American Indian, Somali, and Hmong people.

Key Program Features:
- Targeted Police Enforcement
- Enhanced Supervision
- Intelligence Exchange

AGENCY PROFILE

- Population Served: Approx. 382,618
- Sworn Employees: 861
- Onset of Reentry Participation: 1997

PROGRAM SUMMARY

The Minneapolis Anti-Violence Initiative (MAVI) is a collaborative approach to reduce serious violent crime in Minneapolis. The program targets adult and juvenile offenders with histories of violence, firearms offenses, and gang involvement who are on community supervision. The Community Justice Program is a partnership that focuses on reducing the prison population in Minnesota and helping restore offender relationships with the community through faith-based mentoring and support. Both MAVI and the Community Justice Program focus on crime reduction as their measure of success. Probation officers and police track information on how long offenders stay out after their release, what resources they receive, any new crimes they are charged with, and the outcomes of services received. MAVI crime rates have steadily declined since the program's inception in 1997.

COMPONENTS AND ACTIVITIES

- Intensive supervision, monitoring and enforcement
- Interactive community corrections and police teams
- Interagency communication, information sharing, and intelligence exchange
- Coordinated partnerships to provide transitional services

PROGRAM PARTNERS

- Hennepin County Sheriff's Office
- Minnesota Department of Corrections, Department of Community Corrections
- Minnesota Department of Public Safety, Metro Gang Strike Force, Minneapolis Park Police
- U.S. Attorney's Office, Bureau of Alcohol, Tobacco, Firearms and Explosives (ATF), U.S. Marshals Service; Drug Enforcement Administration (DEA), Federal Bureau of Investigation (FBI, Immigration and Customs Enforcement (ICE)
- Community service agencies: Citizens and Law Enforcement Action Network (CLEAN), CourtWatch, Greater Minneapolis Council of Churches

LAW ENFORCEMENT PARTICIPATION

The Minneapolis Police Department (MPD) has developed open lines of communication and built partnerships with the Hennepin County Sheriff's Office (HCSO) and other federal and state law enforcement agencies. Law enforcement officers participate in expanded and intensive home visits, warrant sweeps, focused patrols, and community outreach called "walk and talks." Crime prevention specialists are assigned to conduct enhanced supervision and patrols in high-risk communities as part of the Crime Prevention/Safety for Everyone (CCP/SAFE) program. MAVI Team members participate in cross-training opportunities to include annual defensive tactics training (use of pepper spray and handcuffing), radio procedures, and overview of search, seizure, and related Fourth Amendment issues. The MAVI intelligence team meetings are an excellent opportunity for local, state, and federal law enforcement agencies to discuss and share information about high-risk offenders. Information is compiled using offense reports, and cross-referenced with probation supervision lists and conditions to develop a profile of offenders who may have violated their conditions. Discussions regarding gang affiliations or other associations take place.

PROGRAM STRATEGIES FOR SUCCESSFUL REINTEGRATION

Law enforcement participates in transitional planning, information sharing, and intelligence gathering and exchange. Another reentry-focused effort in which MPD is involved is the Citizens and Law Enforcement Action Network (CLEAN) and Court Watch. CLEAN:

- Compiles a list of people who chronically violate the law
- When one of these individuals is arrested, MPD contacts the Community Safety Center (CSC)
- The CSC staff contacts all victims or residents affected by the crime
- Those victims write a community impact statement with the assistance of CSC staff
- The impact statement is presented to the court for consideration before sentencing of individuals on the CLEAN roster.

This, and many other strategies, has contributed to lowering the crime rate in Minneapolis.

CONTACT INFORMATION

For MAVI: David Hile, Hennepin County Department of Community Corrections: 612-348-9215 or david.hile@co.hennepin.mn.us

For Community Justice Program: Hillary Freeman, Crime Prevention Specialist: 612-673-2892 or hillary.freeman@ci.minneapolis.mn.us
http://www.ci.minneapolis.mn.us/police/outreach

NEW HAVEN DEPARTMENT OF POLICE SERVICE (CONNECTICUT)
CONNECTICUT PROJECT SAFE NEIGHBORHOODS (CT-PSN) PROGRAM

Offender Participant Criteria:
- Violent crime
- Gun-related

Unique Community Challenges/Strategies:
According to the police chief, New Haven is one of the poorest cities in the country and is plagued by high levels of unemployment.

Key Program Features:
- "Timezup" Notification Meetings
- Transitional Services
- Community Outreach

AGENCY PROFILE

- Population Served: Approx. 123,600
- Sworn Employees: 407
- Onset of Reentry Participation: 1999

PROGRAM SUMMARY

Since 1999, the New Haven Department of Police Service (NHPD) has implemented or participated in a variety of crime prevention programs and strategies. Project One and the New Haven Guns Project were two such efforts that focused on gun violence and involved partnerships with law enforcement at the federal and state level. Both efforts merged and later folded into the Project Safe Neighborhoods (PSN) program managed by the U.S. Attorney's Office in Connecticut. PSN is a national comprehensive, strategic approach to reducing gun violence and promoting safe neighborhoods. PSN combats gun violence by bringing together law enforcement officials, prosecutors, and community leaders to implement a multi-faceted strategy to deter and punish gun violence. The goals of their offender reentry efforts are to make New Haven a safer place to live, work, and raise children; break the barriers to offender success by providing transitional services; and reduce crime by addressing causation before citizens become victims, perpetrators or witnesses. Success is measured in terms of crime and recidivism rates, level of partner resources, and increased partner communication.

COMPONENTS AND ACTIVITIES

- "Timezup" notification meetings
- Coordinated partnerships to include a Core Group and Community Advisory Board
- Wraparound transitional services that include: participant and family assessment, job and educational assistance, life skills training, alcohol and substance abuse counseling, social services, and faith-based spiritual guidance

PROGRAM PARTNERS

- U.S. Attorney's Office, State Attorney's Office
- U.S. Probation Office, State Department of Corrections, Court Support Services (State Probation), State Board of Parole
- Bureau of Alcohol, Tobacco, Firearms and Explosives (ATF), Connecticut Statewide Firearms Trafficking Task Force
- Community: Crossroads, Strive New Haven, Connecticut Works/Workforce Alliance

LAW ENFORCEMENT PARTICIPATION

The police department has gone from traditional, reactive and incident-based, 911-driven approach to a community policing approach that employs proactive methods for crime prevention. New Haven police are committed to reducing crime and the fear of crime to improve the quality of life for all people by institutionalizing this policing philosophy and implementing innovative strategies. Community Substation Management Teams have been formed to help identify and examine neighborhood problems and to develop strategies utilizing local resources. The composition of Management Teams varies by neighborhood, but is generally comprised of the police supervisor, beat officers, block watch members, representatives of neighborhood-based agencies, and any citizen who takes an active interest in neighborhood improvement.

PROGRAM STRATEGIES FOR SUCCESSFUL REINTEGRATION

Partnership, intelligence sharing, offender accountability, community outreach, social services, and "Timezup" notification meetings are the strategies used in this program. The relevant agencies come together to track and monitor offender behavior, hold offenders accountable through supervision and attendance at the community-attended "Timezup" meetings, and employ police to encourage offender compliance through collateral contacts.

CONTACT INFORMATION

John Marrella, U.S. Attorney's Office: 203-821-3700
http://www.usdoj.gov/usao/ct/psn_cities.html#NewHaven

PARK CITY POLICE DEPARTMENT (UTAH)
SUMMIT COUNTY OFFENDER REVIEW BOARD (SCORB)

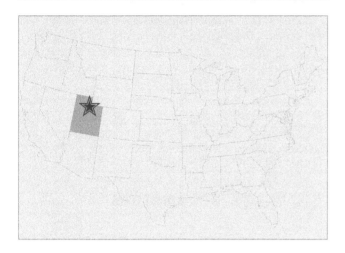

Offender Participant Criteria:
- Adults at-risk for recidivism
- Convicted of driving under the influence (DUIs) or substance-related crimes

Unique Community Challenges/Strategies:
Park City has the largest number of bars per capita in the state. The community is plagued by high incidents of DUIs.

Key Program Features:
- Offender Review Board
- Community Engagement
- Bar Checks

AGENCY PROFILE

- Population Served: Approx. 7,371
- Sworn Employees: 31
- Onset of Reentry Participation: 2005

PROGRAM SUMMARY

The Summit County Offender Review Board (SCORB) is a partnership designed to reduce crime, recidivism, and technical violations among individuals under probation and parole supervision. It serves to increase awareness among the community that offenders reside in the community; achieves a high level of cooperation among local, state, and federal agencies for supervising, monitoring, and successfully reintegrating returning offenders; increases both the quality and quantity of supervision contacts; and assists offenders in accessing available treatment, programming, and community resources. Unlike most municipalities with offender reentry programs, Park City primarily experiences traffic- and substance-related crimes rather than violent crimes. Due to the large number of bars in the area, most offenders are arrested on alcohol-related crimes such as driving under the influence (DUI) or substance abuse. Reduced recidivism rates and gun rates are measures of success. Recidivism rates are lower than those of comparable jurisdictions based on anecdotal evidence. Offense data reveals a decrease in gun crimes.

COMPONENTS AND ACTIVITIES

- Partnership and collaboration
- Information sharing
- Enhanced supervision, joint home visits, bar checks
- Offender case management
- Offender Review Board meetings
- Community engagement
- Partner cross-training

PROGRAM PARTNERS

- Summit County Sheriff's Office
- Utah Department of Corrections, Office of Probation and Parole, Salt Lake Adult Probation and Parole Day Reporting Center
- U.S. Attorney's Office
- Community service agencies: Transitional, and alcohol and substance abuse treatment

LAW ENFORCEMENT PARTICIPATION

Both the Park City Police and Summit County Sheriff's Office have assigned four officers and four deputies each to conduct joint home visits and patrols. Program activities have been absorbed into police and sheriff agency budgets or are conducted by officers and deputies on a voluntary basis when they are not on-call. Law enforcement is involved in the management and coordination of program activities. A reserve officer is assigned to take photos of offenders and obtain signed contracts at Offender Review Board (ORB) meetings.

PROGRAM STRATEGIES FOR SUCCESSFUL REINTEGRATION

The program employs a high level of cooperation among local, state, and federal agencies to monitor, supervise, and reintegrate offenders back into the community. Offenders are assessed and offered relevant treatment and service options to ensure their successful return. Program leaders also employ unique techniques to ensure maximum use of resources and offender accountability. For example, a community volunteer compiles offender profiles for each ORB meeting and maintains meeting minutes. Similarly, a reserve officer is employed to take updated photographs of each offender every time they come before the Board. This officer also arranges for offenders to sign a letter immediately after their ORB appearance attesting to the ORB meeting agreements. This letter serves as an unofficial contract with the offender and is a measure of offender accountability.

CONTACT INFORMATION

Lt. Phil Kirk, Park City Police Department:
435-615-5512 or pkirk@parkcity.org
http://www.parkcity.org/citydepartments/police/index.html

RACINE POLICE DEPARTMENT (WISCONSIN)
COMMUNITY RE-ENTRY PROGRAM (CRP)

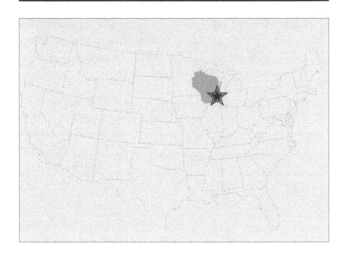

Offender Participant Criteria:
- Adults
- Convicted of violent, gun-related crime
- Involved in gangs or drugs
- Live in or spend significant time in COP neighborhoods

Unique Community Challenges/Strategies:
Racine is a small town located between the Milwaukee and Chicago metropolitan areas with a high rate of unemployment.

Key Program Features:
- Enhanced Supervision
- Community Meetings
- COP Houses

AGENCY PROFILE

- County Population Served: Approx. 81,855
- Sworn Employees: 195
- Onset of Reentry Participation: 2004

PROGRAM SUMMARY

The Community Re-Entry Program (CRP) emerged as an extension of the community policing philosophy governing the Racine Police Department (RPD). The program applies a holistic community-based approach to reduce violent offender recidivism and enhance public safety. RPD and the Division of Community Corrections co-lead this multi-agency partnership geared toward helping offenders with violent pasts reintegrate back into one of Racine's four community oriented policing (COP) neighborhoods. Key components of the program are its Community Re-Entry meetings and police-probation teams assigned to satellite offices in COP houses. Measures of success for this program include rates of recidivism and technical violations. Program leaders employ quality assurance/program monitoring strategies to ensure program success. Since 2004, the program has enjoyed a 65 percent employment rate among program participants and 64 percent of participants have remained crime-free.

COMPONENTS AND ACTIVITIES

- Enhanced supervision through joint patrols, curfew checks, and home visits
- Community reentry meetings
- Partnership building, information sharing, intelligence exchange
- Coordinated transitional services

PROGRAM PARTNERS

- Wisconsin Department of Corrections, Division of Corrections, Racine Correctional and Youthful Offender Correctional Facilities
- U.S. Attorney's Office
- Racine Vocational Ministries
- Gateway Technical College
- Government and community social services: Racine County Workforce Development, Racine Safe Neighborhood Alliance, Neighborhood Watch; City Council

LAW ENFORCEMENT PARTICIPATION

CRP was created, implemented, and is jointly managed by a sergeant in the Racine Police Department (RPD) along with community corrections and community service agencies. This individual and other patrol officers are dedicated to program activities to include sharing satellite COP houses with probation and parole agents. RPD also uses community-based activities to facilitate community relations. They developed a Children's Garden outside of one of the COP houses for the neighborhood children to maintain along with designated COP officers. Another COP house hosts a gang diversion program that targets juveniles. Yet another police-sponsored program is the Cops n' Kids Reading Center through which books are collected and distributed from a COP house. Because this project requires children to interact with police in order to obtain reading materials, it has the joint benefits of forging relationships with the community and enhancing literacy skills of neighborhood children.

PROGRAM STRATEGIES FOR SUCCESSFUL REINTEGRATION

Program leaders developed a program that involves the community, addresses a known problem, and includes relevant partners. CRP includes a combination of wraparound support services, enhanced surveillance, and strict enforcement of rules to achieve program goals. Constant communication among partner agencies ensures that participants are unable to manipulate "the system," and partnering with the U.S. Attorney's Office ensures the stricter penalties that the federal system can apply.

CONTACT INFORMATION

Dwayne Windham, Community Re-Entry Coordinator: 262-633-9591 or crpdwayne@sbcglobal.net

REDMOND POLICE DEPARTMENT (WASHINGTON)
SUPERVISION MANAGEMENT AND RECIDIVIST TRACKING (SMART) PARTNERSHIPS

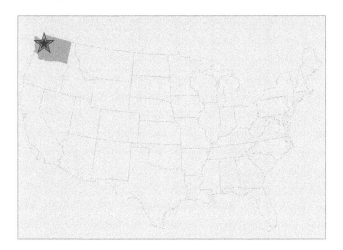

Offender Participant Criteria:
- Adults at-risk for recidivism

Unique Community Challenges/Strategies:
To date, the Redmond Police Department has trained almost 70 police departments on offender reentry strategies.

Key Program Features:
- Enhanced Supervision
- Formalized Information Exchange
- Training

AGENCY PROFILE

- Population Served: Approx. 45,256
- Sworn Employees: 74
- Onset of Reentry Participation: 1992

PROGRAM SUMMARY

The Supervision Management and Recidivist Tracking (SMART) Partnerships were created in 1992 as a method for increasing community safety. This partnership, which initially included the Redmond Police Department (RPD) and the Bellevue Office of the Department of Corrections, has expanded to include federal-, regional-, and state-level law enforcement and other officials. The program includes four components: direct monitoring of high-risk individuals under community supervision who live or work in Redmond; a formal system of information exchange between police and community corrections agencies about released offenders; documentation of collateral contacts between offenders and external entities; and training other law enforcement agencies.

COMPONENTS AND ACTIVITIES

- Partnership and collaboration
- Formal information sharing
- Enhanced supervision
- Documenting collateral contacts using Field Interview Report (FIR) cards
- Training other law enforcement agencies

PROGRAM PARTNERS

- Washington Department of Corrections
- Redmond Office of Community Corrections

LAW ENFORCEMENT PARTICIPATION

In addition to creating the SMART program, RPD is also involved with the FireArm Crime Enforcement (FACE) Coalition of King County. FACE is a Project Safe Neighborhoods (PSN) partner whose goal is to decrease the use of firearms in the commission of crimes. RPD command staff serves on the "Behind the FACE" panel to provide valuable information to offenders on the ramifications of firearms possession and the penalties of repeat offenses post-release. RPD also coordinates and aggressively investigates crimes involving firearms.

PROGRAM STRATEGIES FOR SUCCESSFUL REINTEGRATION

Overall program components integrate enhanced community corrections supervision, partnership building and maintenance, information sharing, intelligence exchange, FACE panel participation, and law enforcement training.

CONTACT INFORMATION

Commander Terry Morgan, Redmond Police Department: 425-556-2523 or tmorgan@redmond.gov
http://www.ci.redmond.wa.us/insidecityhall/police/police.asp

SAVANNAH CHATHAM METROPOLITAN POLICE DEPARTMENT (GEORGIA)
SAVANNAH IMPACT PROGRAM (SIP)

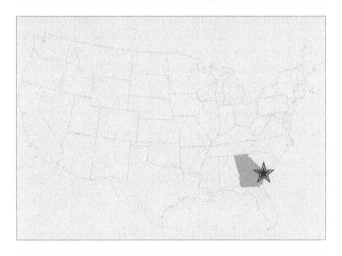

Offender Participant Criteria:
- High risk, high-profile, high-need adults, and juveniles under supervision
- Lived or committed their crime in Savannah

Unique Community Challenges/Strategies:
The SIP program purchased the building in which the program is housed to cut down on overhead costs.

Key Program Features:
- Enhanced Supervision
- Education/Literacy Assistance
- *Work Ventures* Vocational Training

AGENCY PROFILE

- Population Served: Approx. 131,510
- Sworn Employees: 575
- Onset of Reentry Participation: 2001

PROGRAM SUMMARY

The Savannah Impact Program (SIP) is an intensive probation/parole supervision, juvenile outreach and offender employment program. The mission of the program is to protect the public from high-risk offenders who are on parole or probation. The program uses a collaborative community corrections approach to enhance an offender's reentry into the community. Program goals include reducing recidivism by high-risk offenders; maintaining a continuum of supervision pre- to post-release; providing resources to re-direct an offender's life into law-abiding paths; and providing transitional services for offenders post-release. SIP uses the revocation rate, number and types of collateral interactions (i.e., field and office visits, drug screenings, and referrals), offender employment, and program completion as measures of success. The program reports a 15 percent revocation rate based on 749 offenders supervised during 2004.

COMPONENTS AND ACTIVITIES

- Intensive supervision and monitoring of offenders
- GED instruction
- Substance abuse and cognitive thinking counseling
- Employment and vocational training
- Juvenile Intervention Program
- Family support and reunification
- Cross-agency training

PROGRAM PARTNERS

- Georgia Department of Corrections, Probation and Parole Department, Georgia Board of Pardons and Parole
- City of Savannah, County of Chatham
- Richard Arnold Adult Education Center

LAW ENFORCEMENT PARTICIPATION

The SIP program was created, implemented, and managed by the Savannah Chatham Metropolitan Police Department. A dedicated police and probation team approach was implemented. Teams co-manage and provide intense supervision and support to offenders who deserve a second chance at building a sustainable crime-free, economically independent life through education, training, skills programs, and employment opportunities. The program executive director fashioned the program work area as a police squad room because this approach is beneficial to information sharing given their co-management work style.

PROGRAM STRATEGIES FOR SUCCESSFUL REINTEGRATION

In addition to dedicating staff to this program, SIP has implemented many significant strategies. Police officers were partnered with parole and probation officers to co-manage and supervise returning offenders. The program implemented multi-agency cross-training on the limitations, policies, and practices of each partnering agency; and, instruction on search and seizures, self-defense, tactical firearms, and interview and interrogation techniques. SIP staff receives training on human diversity, cultural attitudes, cultural behaviors, and responses. All police officers who staff SIP are certified by the Georgia Peace Officers Standards and Training (POST) Council. SIP established contracts with the City Departments of Sanitation and Parks and Trees to provide vocational training. Their vocational training program teaches safety, work ethic, structure, accountability, responsibility, and life skills. This program also involves the family to provide offender support in making a successful transition.

CONTACT INFORMATION

Keith Vermillion, SIP Executive Director,
Savannah Chatham Metropolitan Police Department:
912-651-4360 or kvermillion@ci.savannah.ga.us
http://www.ci.savannah.ga.us/cityweb/SPD.nsf/

TOPEKA POLICE DEPARTMENT (KANSAS)
SHAWNEE COUNTY REENTRY PROGRAM (SCRP)

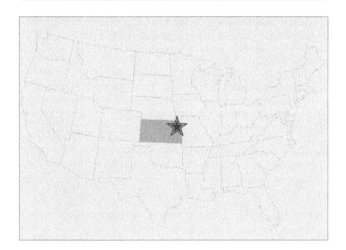

Offender Participant Criteria:
- Adults at-risk for violence or recidivism

Unique Community Challenges/Strategies:
Shawnee County is one of the sites in which approximately 71% of offenders coming out of Kansas state prisons will return.

Key Program Features:
- Computerized Offender Tracking
- Accountability Panel
- Extensive Transitional Service Delivery
- Warrant/Detainer Checks
- Assistance Obtaining Identification

AGENCY PROFILE

- Population Served: Approx. 122,377
- Sworn Employees: 296
- Onset of Reentry Participation: 2002

PROGRAM SUMMARY

The Shawnee County Reentry Program (SCRP) is a comprehensive program that prepares and assists offenders with their transition back into the community. Program strategies emphasize preventing failure as a proactive means to ensuring community safety. Participants receive tools to reduce risk and foster success. The pre- and post-release program components include a continuity of care that starts with assessment and continues with the delivery of education and training, housing, financial planning, job preparedness, and substance abuse and mental health service delivery. Recent reports from the Kansas Department of Corrections reveal that the recidivism rate among program participants was 13.7 percent. This is based on the data collected while tracking high-risk program participants in 2003.

COMPONENTS AND ACTIVITIES

- Partnership and collaboration
- Information sharing
- Pre-release assessment of risks and needs
- Offender data tracking and case management
- Program evaluation
- Cross-agency training
- Collaboration with a boundary spanner to resolve inter-agency conflicts
- Parole officers certified by DMV to administer pre-release written driver license exams

PROGRAM PARTNERS

- Kansas Department of Corrections, Kansas Parole Board
- Kansas Board of Education; Topeka Public Schools, University of Kansas
- Workforce Network of Kansas, Mayor of Topeka
- Community service agencies: Faith organizations and local agencies specializing in mental health, law, victim services, and substance abuse

LAW ENFORCEMENT PARTICIPATION

The police department has dedicated a Reentry Community Police Officer (RCPO) to serve as the program point of contact, serve arrest and detainer letters/warrants, conduct prison transition visits, conduct presentations and outreach, and to share information with program partners.

PROGRAM STRATEGIES FOR SUCCESSFUL REINTEGRATION

Engaging all necessary partners, establishing a structure for statewide support, and involving the community in meaningfully supporting offenders in their return are the strategies employed in this program. Many offenders have difficulty implementing reentry plans due to lack of appropriate state- or federal-issued identification. One of the unique strategies of the program is its focus on assisting offenders in getting their drivers' licenses or other official forms of identification prior to release. This program collaborates with other agencies to assist offenders in obtaining proper identification. The program unites the community and provides social service support to assist offenders in effectively transitioning from prison into society as productive, law-abiding citizens. Offenders leave correctional institutions with supervision and reentry plans that require them to be accountable; to focus on their risk and needs; to obtain job training; and to safely reconnect with their families and other helpful support networks.

CONTACT INFORMATION

Janene Falley, Reentry Community Police Officer, Topeka Police Department:
785-368-9247 or jfalley@topeka.org
http://www.topeka.org/policedepartment/index.shtml

VIOLENT CRIMES TASK FORCE (MIDDLE DISTRICT OF NORTH CAROLINA)
HIGH POINT POLICE DEPARTMENT
WINSTON-SALEM POLICE DEPARTMENT

Offender Participant Criteria:
- Adults at-risk for recidivism
- Histories of violence
- Gun- and drug-related crime

Unique Community Challenges/Strategies:
The sentencing structure in North Carolina has resulted in approximately 10-15% of offenders "maxing out" or being released without conditions of community supervision.

Key Program Features:
- Enhanced Supervision
- Call-in/Notification Sessions
- VCTF web-based Intelligence Sharing
- Police-2-PoliceTechnology

AGENCY PROFILE (HIGH POINT)

- Population Served: Approx. 85,839
- Sworn Employees: 224
- Onset of Reentry Participation: 1998

AGENCY PROFILE (WINSTON-SALEM)

- Population Served: Approx. 187,776
- Sworn Employees: 465
- Onset of Reentry Participation: 1998

PROGRAM SUMMARY

Both the High Point Police Department (HPPD) and the Winston-Salem Police Department (WSPD) have implemented comprehensive offender reentry efforts in their jurisdictions. The Violent Crimes Task Force (VCTF) is a comprehensive, collaborative, data-driven strategic approach created to improve the quality of life for residents and reduce violent crime in High Point and Winston-Salem. Both departments work with other agencies to identify violent repeat and/or group offenders and employ techniques to stop the violence. This innovative approach has received national recognition and serves as a model for other cities across the nation. HPPD officials report that there has been a 20 percent reduction in crime citywide and a 40 percent reduction in crime in "hot spot" neighborhoods. Furthermore, the recidivism rate in High Point is half the state average.

COMPONENTS AND ACTIVITIES

- Partnership and collaboration
- Formal information sharing
- Enhanced supervision
- Call-in/Notification sessions
- VCTF web-based intelligence sharing
- Electronic and other technological offender tracking and officer notification techniques

PROGRAM PARTNERS

- North Carolina Department of Corrections, local community corrections agencies
- U.S. Attorney's Office for the Middle District of North Carolina, local District Attorney's Office
- Project Safe Neighborhoods coordinator with the Durham (NC) Police Department
- Government, community, faith, and social service organizations

LAW ENFORCEMENT PARTICIPATION

While the WSPD commissioned the creation of and manages the VCTF web database, High Point contributes to the database. Likewise, both agencies attend local call-in meetings and notification sessions.

PROGRAM STRATEGIES FOR SUCCESSFUL REINTEGRATION

Overall program components integrate enhanced community corrections supervision, partnership building and maintenance, information sharing, intelligence exchange, call-in meetings and notification session participation, law enforcement training, and community outreach.

CONTACT INFORMATION

Detective Kyle Pratt, High Point Police Department: 336-887-7855 or kyle.pratt@highpointnc.gov
http://www.high-point.net/police/index.cfm

Detective John Leone, Winston-Salem Police Department: 336-773-7700 or jleone@wspd.org
http://www.cityofws.org/Home/Departments/Police

GLOSSARY

Criminogenic—Relates to the causes, characteristics, or factors identified by research as predictors of crime and/or related to recidivism.

Discretionary Parole—Is awarded by a Board of Parole or Pardons that has authority to conditionally release prisoners based on a statutory or administrative determination of eligibility.

Mandatory Parole—Is generally given in jurisdictions using determinate sentencing statutes. Offenders are conditionally released from incarceration after serving a specified portion of their original sentence minus any good time earned.

Offender—Refers to individuals who have received and served a sentence in a correctional institution.

Parole—Involves a period of conditional supervised release following incarceration in a correctional institution. Offenders "may be released either by a parole board decision or by mandatory conditional release. If the conditions of supervision are violated, the parolee can be returned to prison to serve any of the remaining portion of the sentence."[5]

Parole Violators—Refers to offenders returned to prison for violating the conditions of their release or for a new offense committed while under parole supervision.

Probation—Includes offenders who have been sentenced to a period of correctional supervision in the community in lieu of incarceration or following a period of incarceration in a local or state facility.

Recidivism—Occurs when a previously convicted offender is re-arrested, re-convicted, or returned to incarceration with or without a new sentence during a three-year period following his or her release.

Reentry—Is a broad term used to refer to issues related to the transition of offenders from prison to community supervision. In this guide, reentry refers to persons released from state or federal prisons or discharged from state parole, federal parole, or who are under federal or state probation.

RESOURCES AND MATERIALS

International Association of Chiefs of Police (IACP)
www.theiacp.org

U.S. DEPARTMENT OF JUSTICE:

- Bureau of Justice Assistance (BJA)
  http://www.ojp.usdoj.gov/bja
- Bureau of Justice Statistics (BJS)
  http://www.ojp.usdoj.gov/bjs/
- Community Capacity Development Office
  http://www.ojp.usdoj.gov/ccdo/
- National Institute of Justice (NIJ)
  http://www.ojp.usdoj.gov/nij/
- Office of Community Oriented Policing Services (COPS)
  http://www.cops.usdoj.gov

- Office of Justice Programs (OJP)
  http://www.ojp.usdoj.gov
- Project Safe Neighborhoods (PSN)
  http://www.psn.gov

OTHER ORGANIZATIONS:

- Council of State Governments,
  Re-Entry Policy Council
  http://www.reentrypolicy.org/reentry/default.aspx
- National Governors Association (NGA),
  NGA Center for Best Practices
  http://www.nga.org/portal/site/nga/
- Urban Institute
  http://www.urban.org

REFERENCE MATERIALS

Basile, V.D. (2002). Model for Developing a Reentry Program. *Federal Probation*, 66 (3), 55-58, http://www. uscourts.gov/fedprob/2002decfp.pdf (accessed August 22, 2005).

Byrne, J.M. & Hummer, D. (2004). Examining the Role of the Police in Reentry Partnership Initiatives. *Federal Probation*, 68 (2), 62-69, http://www.uscourts.gov/fedprob/ September_2004/endnotes.html#initiatives (accessed August 25, 2005).

Council of State Governments, Re-Entry Policy Council, *Report of the Re-Entry Policy Council*, http://www. reentrypolicy.org (accessed August 22, 2005).

LaVigne, Nancy G., Amy Solomon, Karen A. Beckman and Kelly Dedel, *Prisoner Reentry and Community Policing: Strategies for Enhancing Public Safety*, Washington, DC. Urban Institute, March 2006. http://www.urban.org/url. cfm?ID=411061 (accessed April 7, 2006).

National Institute of Corrections, *Transition from Prison to Community Initiative* (2002), http://nicic.org/WebPage_ 222.htm (accessed July 25, 2005).

National Governors Association, NGA Center for Best Practices, Issue Brief: *NGA Prisoner Reentry Police Academy*, Washington, DC: National Governors Association, January 5, 2005, http://www.nga.org/portal/site/nga/menuitem/ af6 24995eb41697a4ddcbeeb501010a0/vgne (accessed August 22, 2005).

Parent, D. & Snyder, B., *Police-Corrections Partnerships Programs*, Washington, DC: U.S. Department of Justice, Office of Justice Programs, National Institute of Justice, 1999,http://www.ncjrs.gov/pdffiles1/175047.pdf#search=% 22Police%20Corrections%20Partnerships%22.

Taxman, F.S., Byrne, J.M. & Young, D. (2002). Targeting for Reentry: Matching Needs and Services to Maximize Public Safety, College Park, MD: University of Maryland-College Park, Bureau of Governmental Research, http://www.ncjrs.gov/pdffiles1/nij/grants/196491.pdf (accessed August 22, 2005).

Taxman, F.S., Young, D., Byrne, J.M., Holsinger, A., & Anspach, D. (2002). From Prison Safety to Public Safety: Innovations in Offender Reentry, College Park, MD: University of Maryland-College Park, Bureau of Governmental Research, http://www.bgr.umd.edu/pdf/ May_2003_From_Prison.pdf (accessed August 22, 2005).

U.S. Department of Justice, Office of Justice Programs. *Reentry State Activities & Resources.* http://www.ojp.usdoj. gov/reentry/sar/welcome.html (accessed August 22, 2005).

U.S. Department of Justice, Office of Justice Programs, *Learn About Reentry*, http://www.ojp.usdoj.gov/reentry/ learn.html (accessed August 22, 2005).

U.S. Department of Justice, Bureau of Justice Statistics, *Reentry Trends in the U.S.: Recidivism*, 2002 by Timothy Hughes and Doris James Wilson (Washington, DC) http:// www.ojp.usdoj.gov/bjs/reentry/recidivism.htm (accessed March 10, 2006).

U.S. Department of Justice, Office of Justice Programs, Bureau of Justice Statistics, *Recidivism of Prisoners Released in 1994*, June 2002 by Patrick A. Langan and David J. Levin (Washington, DC) http://www.ojp.usdoj.gov/bjs/abstract/ rpr94.htm (accessed August 22, 2005).

END NOTES

[1] U.S. Department of Justice, Office of Justice Programs, *Learn About Reentry*, (Washington, DC), http://www.ojp.usdoj.gov/reentry/learn.html, August 22, 2005.

[2] University of Cincinnati. Dr. Latessa has published over 75 works in the area of criminal justice, corrections, and juvenile justice. He has directed over 60 funded research projects, including studies of day reporting centers, juvenile justice programs, drug courts, intensive supervision programs, halfway houses, and drug programs. He and his staff at the University of Cincinnati have also assessed over 350 correctional programs throughout the United States, (Cincinnati, OH), http://www.uc.edu/criminaljustice/faculty.html, November 30, 2005.

[3] U.S. Department of Justice, National Institute of Justice, "Mapping Crime: Understanding Hot Spots," March 2006, http://www.ncjrs.gov/pdffiles1/nij/209393.pdf.

[4] Cornell Law School, *United States v. Knights* 534 U.S.112 , 219 f.3d 1138 (2001), (Ithaca, NY), http://www.law.cornell.edu/supct/html/00-1260.ZO.html, July 13, 2006.

[5] U.S. Department of Justice, Bureau of Justice Statistics, "Probation and Parole in the United States, 2004," November 2005, http://www.ojp.usdoj.gov/bjs/abstract/ppus04.htm.

International Association of Chiefs of Police
515 North Washington St, Alexandria, VA USA 22314   p: 703.836.6767/1.800.THE IACP   www.theiacp.org

U.S. Department of Justice
Office of Justice Programs
Bureau of Justice Statistics

June 2016, NCJ 249849

Background Checks for Firearm Transfers, 2013–14 - Statistical Tables

Jennifer C. Karberg
Ronald J. Frandsen
Joseph M. Durso
Trent D. Buskirk, Ph.D.
Regional Justice Information Service
Allina D. Lee
Bureau of Justice Statistics

More than 180 million applications for firearm transfers or permits were subject to background checks since the effective date of the Brady Handgun Violence Prevention Act on February 28, 1994, through December 31, 2014. During this period, about 2.8 million applications (1.6%) were denied. In 2014, nearly 15 million applications were subject to background checks, and 193,000 (1.3%) were denied, including about 91,000 denied by the FBI and about 102,000 denied by state and local agencies.

Data in this report were obtained from the Bureau of Justice Statistics' (BJS) Firearm Inquiry Statistics (FIST) program. The FIST program collects information on firearm applications and denials and combines this information with the FBI's National Instant Criminal Background Check System (NICS) transaction data to produce an estimated number of background checks for firearm transfers or permits since the effective date of the Brady Act.

These statistical tables describe trends in background check activities that occurred in 2014 and include partial data for 2013. Data include the number of firearm transaction applications processed by the FBI and by state and local agencies, the number of applications denied, reasons for denial, and estimates of applications by jurisdiction and by each type of approval system.

Summary findings

- Since the effective date of the Brady Act on February 28, 1994, through December 31, 2014, more than 180 million applications for firearm transfers or permits were subject to background checks. More than 2.8 million applications (1.6%) were denied (**table 1**).

- Nearly 15 million applications for firearm transfers were received in 2014, down from an estimated 17.6 million in 2013.

- About 1.3% of the nearly 15 million applications for firearm transfers or permits in 2014 were denied—about 91,000 by the FBI and about 102,000 by state and local agencies. An estimated 193,000 applications for firearm transfers or permits in 2013 were denied—about 88,000 by the FBI and about 104,000 by state and local agencies (**table 2**).

- Among state agencies, denial rates in 2014 were 3.1% for purchase permits, 1.5% for instant checks, 0.9% for other approval checks, and 1.0% for exempt carry permits. Denial rates in 2013 were estimated to be 1.9% for purchase permits, 1.2% for instant checks, 0.8% for other approval checks, and 0.9% for exempt carry permits (**table 3**).

- Among local agencies, the denial rates in 2014 were 4% for purchase permit checks and 1.2% for exempt carry permit checks (**table 4**).

- A felony conviction (42%) was the most common reason for the FBI to deny an application in 2014, followed by a fugitive from justice status (19%) (**table 5**).

- Among the 18 state agencies that reported reasons for denial, a state law prohibition (26%) was the most common reason to deny an application in 2014, followed by a felony conviction (22%).

- Excluding other prohibitions, of the approximately 330 local agencies that reported reasons for denial, a state law prohibition (20%) was the most common reason to deny an application in 2014.

- Among all agencies that reported reasons for denial in 2014, denial of an application due to a felony conviction, indictment, charge, or arrest accounted for approximately 42% of denials **(table 6)**.

- Bureau of Alcohol, Tobacco, Firearms and Explosives (ATF) field offices investigated 7,978 NICS denials that were referred by the FBI in 2014—up from 6,257 in 2013. Among denials, a felony conviction was the most common reason for referral to a field office in 2014 (37%) and in 2013 (33%) **(table 7)**.

Tables

TABLE 1
Estimated number of firearm applications received and denied since the effective date of the Brady Act, 1994–2014

TABLE 2
Firearm applications received and denied, by type of agency and type of check, 2013 and 2014

TABLE 3
Firearm applications received and denied by state agencies, by type of check, 2013 and 2014

TABLE 4
Firearm applications received and denied by local agencies, by community size and type of permit, 2014

TABLE 5
Reasons for denial of firearm transfer and permit applications, by checking agencies, 2013 and 2014

TABLE 6
Percent change in the number of applications, denials, and reasons for denial, 1999–2014

TABLE 7
Bureau of Alcohol, Tobacco, Firearms and Explosives investigation of National Instant Criminal Background Check System denials by the FBI, 2013 and 2014

TABLE 8
Number of checking agencies in the 2014 Firearm Inquiry Statistics survey

Appendix tables

APPENDIX TABLE 1
Estimated standard errors for firearm applications received and denied by local agencies, 2014

APPENDIX TABLE 2
Standard errors for table 4: Firearm applications received and denied by local agencies, by community size and type of permit, 2014

APPENDIX TABLE 3
Firearm applications received and denied by jurisdiction, 2014

APPENDIX TABLE 4
Firearm applications received and denied by jurisdiction, 2013

APPENDIX TABLE 5
Reasons for denial of firearm transfer and permit applications, by checking agencies, 2013 and 2014

APPENDIX TABLE 6
Prohibited person records in the National Instant Criminal Background Check System Index, 2014

APPENDIX TABLE 7
Prohibited person records in the National Instant Criminal Background Check System Index, 2013

APPENDIX TABLE 8
Reasons for denial of firearm transfer and permit applications, December 31, 2014

APPENDIX TABLE 9
Agencies conducting firearm background checks, December 31, 2014

APPENDIX TABLE 10
National Instant Criminal Background Check System checking agencies, FBI, or state Point of Contact for firearm transfers, 2014

APPENDIX TABLE 11
Forums for appeals of firearm transfer and permit denials, 2014

Background

The Brady Handgun Violence Prevention Act of 1993 (Pub. L. No. 103-159, 107 Stat. 1536 (1993), codified as amended at 18 U.S.C. § 921 et seq.) mandates that a criminal history background check be performed on any person who attempts to purchase a firearm from a Federal Firearms Licensee (FFL). The permanent provisions of the Brady Act established the NICS, which the FBI or a state Point of Contact (POC) accesses prior to approval or denial of a firearm transfer. The NICS is a system comprised of data on persons who are prohibited from purchasing or possessing a firearm under federal or state law.

The Gun Control Act (18 U.S.C. § 922) prohibits transfer of a firearm to a person who—

- is under indictment for, or has been convicted of, a crime punishable by imprisonment for more than 1 year

- is a fugitive from justice

- is an unlawful user of, or addicted to, a controlled substance

- has been adjudicated as a mental defective or committed to a mental institution

- is an illegal alien or has been admitted to the United States under a nonimmigrant visa

- was dishonorably discharged from the U.S. Armed Forces

- has renounced U.S. citizenship

- is subject to a court order restraining him or her from harassing, stalking, or threatening an intimate partner or child

- has been convicted of a misdemeanor crime of domestic violence

- is under age 18 for long guns or under age 21 for handguns.

An FFL contacts either the FBI or a state POC to determine whether a prospective purchaser is prohibited from receiving a firearm. During 2014, the FBI conducted all NICS checks for 30 states, the District of Columbia, and U.S. territories. POC agencies, which may be statewide or local, conducted all NICS checks for 13 other states. In the remaining 7 states, POC agencies conducted NICS checks on handgun transfer applicants, and the FBI conducted checks on long gun transfer applicants. Several states require an additional background check that does not access the NICS. State laws may require a check on a permit applicant or a person who seeks to receive a firearm from an unlicensed seller. For more information on the NICS, visit the FBI's Criminal Justice Information Service (CJIS) website at http://www.fbi.gov/about-us/cjis/nics.

BJS began the FIST program in 1995 to provide national estimates of the total number of firearm applications received and denied pursuant to the Brady Act and similar state laws. The FIST program collects counts of firearm transfers and permit checks conducted by state and local agencies and combines this information with the FBI's NICS transaction data. In addition, FIST collects information on reasons for denials and law enforcement actions taken by the FBI and ATF against denied persons.

Overview of the national firearm check system

About 1,300 federal, state, and local agencies conduct background checks on persons who apply to purchase a firearm or for a permit that may be used to make a purchase.

Prospective firearm applicants must either undergo a NICS background check that has been requested by a dealer or present a state permit that ATF has qualified as an alternative to the point-of-transfer check.

ATF-qualified permits are those that—

- allow an applicant to possess, acquire, or carry a firearm

- were issued not more than 5 years earlier by the state where the transfer is to take place, after an authorized government official verified that possession of a firearm by the applicant would not be a violation of law.

All permits issued since November 29, 1998, must have included a NICS check. Many NICS-alternative permits may be used for multiple purchases while valid. State laws often provide that a permit will be revoked if the holder is convicted of an offense or otherwise becomes ineligible after receiving the permit.

NICS-alternative permit changes occurred in two states during 2013 and 2014. Alaska reinstated processing of NICS-alternative permits (called NICS exempt carry permits within the state) in 2013. West Virginia carry permits were qualified by ATF as a NICS alternative in 2014, after amendments to state laws.

Prior to transferring a firearm under the permanent Brady provisions, an FFL is required to obtain a completed Firearm Transaction Record (ATF form 4473) from the applicant. An FFL initiates a NICS check by contacting either the FBI or the state POC. Most inquiries are initiated by telephone. In 2002, the FBI added E-Check to allow FFLs to request a check electronically. The FBI or state POC queries available federal, state, local, and tribal systems and notifies the FFL that the transfer may proceed, may not proceed, or must be delayed pending further review of the applicant's record.

When an FFL initiates a NICS background check, a name and descriptor search is conducted to identify any matching records in three nationally held databases managed by the

FBI's CJIS. The following databases are searched during the background check process:

- The Interstate Identification Index (III) maintains individual criminal history records. As of January 8, 2015, the NICS accessed and searched 85,909,018 III records during a background check.[1]

- The National Crime Information Center (NCIC) contains data on persons who are the subjects of protection orders or active criminal warrants, immigration violators, and others. As of December 31, 2014, the NICS searched 5,598,974 NCIC records during a background check.

- The NICS Index, a database created specifically for the NICS, collects and maintains information contributed by federal, state, local, and tribal agencies pertaining to persons prohibited from receiving or possessing a firearm pursuant to federal and state law. Typically, the records maintained in the NICS Index are not available via the III or the NCIC. As of December 31, 2014, the NICS Index contained 12,881,223 records.

- The U.S. Immigration and Customs Enforcement (ICE) databases contain information on non-U.S. citizens who attempt to receive firearms in the United States. In 2014, the NICS Section and POC states sent 104,828 such queries to ICE. From February 2002 to December 31, 2014, ICE conducted more than 622,771 queries for the NICS.[2]

An applicant who is denied a firearm transfer or permit may appeal to the FBI or a POC. Some jurisdictions allow a further appeal to a court. A denied person who submitted a false application or has an outstanding warrant may be subject to arrest and prosecution under federal or state laws.

State and local NICS participation

Each state government determines the extent of its involvement in the NICS process. Three levels of state involvement currently exist:

- A full POC requests a NICS check on all firearm transfers originating in the state.

- A partial POC requests a NICS check on all handgun transfers. FFLs in the state are required to contact the FBI for NICS checks for long gun transfers.

[1]Data are reported through January 8, 2015, because the FBI did not run data through December 31, 2014, in the 2014 report, *National Instant Criminal Background Check System Operations*, available at https://www.fbi.gov/about-us/cjis/nics/reports/2014-operations-report. See also *Survey of State Criminal History Information Systems, 2014*, available at https://www.ncjrs.gov/pdffiles1/bjs/grants/249799.pdf.

[2]For more information about the NICS background check process, see the 2014 report, *National Instant Criminal Background Check System Operations*, available at https://www.fbi.gov/about-us/cjis/nics/reports/2014-operations-report.

TABLE 1
Estimated number of firearm applications received and denied since the effective date of the Brady Act, 1994–2014

	Number of applications		
	Applications	Denials	Percent denied
Total	180,244,000	2,817,000	1.6%
Brady interim period[a]			
1994–1998	12,740,000	312,000	2.4%
Permanent Brady[b]	167,504,000	2,505,000	1.5%
1998[c]	893,000	20,000	2.2
1999	8,621,000	204,000	2.4
2000	7,753,000	153,000	2.0
2001	8,068,000	150,000	1.9
2002	7,926,000	136,000	1.7
2003	7,883,000	126,000	1.6
2004	8,133,000	126,000	1.6
2005	8,324,000	132,000	1.6
2006	8,772,000	135,000	1.6
2007	8,836,000	136,000	1.6
2008	10,131,000	147,000	1.5
2009	11,071,000	150,000	1.4
2010	10,643,000	153,000	1.5
2011[d]	12,135,000	160,000	1.3
2012	15,718,000	192,000	1.2
2013[d]	17,602,000	193,000	1.1
2014	14,993,000	193,000	1.3

Note: Counts are rounded to the nearest 1,000. Detail may not sum to total due to rounding. For more information on reporting agencies and sample design, see *Methodology*.
[a]From March 1, 1994, to November 29, 1998, background checks on applicants were conducted by state and local agencies, mainly on handgun transfers. See *Presale Handgun Checks, the Brady Interim Period, 1994–98* (NCJ 175034, BJS web, June 1999).
[b]NICS began operations in 1998. Checks on handgun and long gun transfers are conducted by the FBI and state and local agencies.
[c]November 30 to December 31, 1998, counts are from the NICS operations report for the period and may include multiple transactions for the same application.
[d]Totals for 2011 and 2013 were estimated. For more information on estimation methods, see *Methodology*.
Sources: Bureau of Justice Statistics, Firearm Inquiry Statistics program, 1996–2014; and FBI, National Instant Criminal Background Check System Transaction Statistics, 1998–2014.

- The state does not maintain a POC. FFLs are required to contact the FBI for NICS checks on all firearm transfers originating in the state.

Other uses of the NICS

In addition to NICS background checks required by the Brady Act, use of the NICS is limited to providing information to criminal justice agencies in connection with the issuance of a firearm- or explosives-related permit or license, or responding to an inquiry from ATF in connection with a civil or criminal law enforcement activity relating to federal firearm laws (28 CFR § 25.6). Firearm-related permits include ATF-qualified alternative permits and other permits issued by state or local agencies. In addition to checks on new and renewed applications, rechecks may be conducted on current permit holders.

TABLE 2
Firearm applications received and denied, by type of agency and type of check, 2013 and 2014

Type of checks conducted	2013			2014			1999–2014[a,b]		
	Applications	Denials	Percent denied	Applications	Denials	Percent denied	Applications	Denials	Percent denied
National total (FIST and FBI)	17,601,671	192,564	1.1%	14,993,408	193,363	1.3%	167,504,390	2,504,970	1.5%
FBI total	9,315,963	88,203	0.9	8,256,688	90,895	1.1	93,453,528	1,166,676	1.2
State and local total (FIST)	8,285,708	104,361	1.3	6,736,720	102,468	1.5	74,050,862	1,338,294	1.8
State agencies	7,216,496	83,477	1.2%	5,951,358	85,998	1.4%	62,723,892	1,124,194	1.8%
Instant checks[c]	4,433,318	52,866	1.2	3,757,906	56,343	1.5	41,791,852	804,830	1.9
Purchase permits[d]	699,845	13,549	1.9	412,175	12,741	3.1	6,236,277	151,300	2.4
Exempt carry permits[e]	972,147	8,299	0.9	805,185	7,878	1.0	5,838,101	79,908	1.4
Other approvals[f]	1,111,186	8,763	0.8	976,092	9,036	0.9	8,857,663	88,157	1.0
Local agencies[g]	1,069,212	20,884	2.0%	785,362	16,470	2.1%	11,326,970	214,099	1.9%
Purchase permits[d]	424,579	14,693	3.5	289,080	11,548	4.0	6,165,722	149,056	2.4
Exempt carry permits[e]	437,208	4,919	1.1	359,207	4,247	1.2	3,792,733	54,182	1.4
Other approvals[f]	207,425	1,273	0.6	137,075	675	0.5	1,368,516	10,862	0.8

[a]Includes December 1998.

[b]Includes estimates for local agencies and some state agencies in 2011 and 2013, when FIST was not collected. For details on the estimation procedure used, see *Methodology*.

[c]Require a seller to transmit a buyer's application to a checking agency by telephone or computer. The agency is required to respond immediately or as soon as possible.

[d]Require a buyer to obtain, after a background check, a government-issued document (such as a permit, license, or identification card) that must be presented to a seller before the buyer can receive a firearm.

[e]State concealed weapons permits, issued after a background check, that exempt the holder from a new check at the time of purchase under a Bureau of Alcohol, Tobacco, Firearms and Explosives ruling or state law.

[f]Require a seller to transmit an application to a checking agency, with transfers delayed until a waiting period expires or the agency completes a check.

[g]Totals were estimated. For more information, see *Methodology*.

Sources: Bureau of Justice Statistics, Firearm Inquiry Statistics program, 2013 and 2014; and FBI, National Instant Criminal Background Check System Transaction Statistics, 2013 and 2014.

TABLE 3
Firearm applications received and denied by state agencies, by type of check, 2013 and 2014

Type of check and jurisdiction	2013			2014		
	Applications	Denials	Percent denied	Applications	Denials	Percent denied
Instant check	4,433,318	52,866	1.2%	3,757,906	56,343	1.5%
Colorado	396,955	7,351	1.9	314,976	6,068	1.9
Connecticut	145,552	210	0.1	115,460	91	0.1
Florida	869,560	11,493	1.3	774,363	11,372	1.5
Illinois[a]	505,009	1,448	0.3	401,899	1,616	0.4
Nevada	120,891	1,908	1.6	95,427	1,716	1.8
New Hampshire	50,700	350	0.7	43,000	340	0.8
New Jersey	123,553	620	0.5	95,267	464	0.5
Oregon	263,283	2,151	0.8	233,878	1,590	0.7
Pennsylvania[b]	759,316	8,952	1.2	655,457	9,620	1.5
Tennessee	473,610	13,267	2.8	428,017	17,832	4.2
Utah	110,623	1,587	1.4	91,437	1,985	2.2
Virginia	479,253	2,412	0.5	405,838	2,661	0.7
Wisconsin	135,013	1,117	0.8	102,887	988	1.0
Other approval	1,111,186	8,763	0.8%	976,092	9,036	0.9%
California	960,179	7,493	0.8	931,037	8,569	0.9
Maryland	129,359	1,125	0.9	28,633	346	1.2
Rhode Island[c]	21,648	145	0.7	16,422	121	0.7
Purchase permit	699,845	13,549	1.9%	412,175	12,741	3.1%
Connecticut	55,742	60	0.1	17,904	21	0.1
District of Columbia	1,154	10	0.9	1,366	10	0.7
Hawaii[c]	22,765	232	1.0	19,365	148	0.8
Illinois[a]	324,921	6,893	2.1	170,178	7,941	4.7
Maryland	4,775	46	1.0	16,306	251	1.5
Massachusetts[c]	125,491	3,144	2.5	68,906	2,600	3.8
Michigan[c]	58,831	1,228	2.1	43,702	952	2.2
New Jersey[c]	106,166	1,936	1.8	74,448	818	1.1
Exempt carry	972,147	8,299	0.9%	805,185	7,878	1.0%
Alaska	1,774	12	0.7	2,018	12	0.6
Arizona	71,104	364	0.5	52,049	358	0.7
Arkansas	58,699	431	0.7	41,725	920	2.2
Kansas	31,004	72	0.2	21,976	146	0.7
Kentucky	58,706	1,098	1.9	31,889	560	1.8
Michigan[c]	129,900	1,662	1.3	115,601	2,081	1.8
Minnesota[c,d]	62,950	540	0.9	43,315	422	1.0
Mississippi[b]	22,030	3	--	19,496	3	--
Nebraska	14,513	84	0.6	10,557	98	0.9
North Dakota	13,900	950	6.8	6,900	750	10.9
South Carolina	84,284	1,272	1.5	65,360	948	1.5
Texas	243,329	688	0.3	247,102	776	0.3
Utah	176,137	1,030	0.6	144,645	728	0.5
Wyoming	3,817	93	2.4	2,552	76	3.0

Note: Applications include transfers and permits. Types of firearms included in a jurisdiction's checks or permits are described in *Jurisdiction notes*. For more information on reporting agencies and sample design, see *Methodology*.

--Less than 0.05%.

[a]Number of applications and denials was estimated for 2013. See *Methodology*.

[b]Number of denials was estimated. See *Methodology*.

[c]Totals for local agencies were compiled by a state agency.

[d]Permits are only exempt under state law. Other carry permits listed have a federal exemption.

Source: Bureau of Justice Statistics, Firearm Inquiry Statistics program, 2013 and 2014.

TABLE 4
Firearm applications received and denied by local agencies, by community size and type of permit, 2014

Population served	Applications	Denials	Percent denied
Purchase permits	289,080	11,548	4.0%
Population served			
9,999 or fewer	23,399	316	1.4%
10,000–99,999	119,177	4,724	4.0
100,000–199,999	67,658	2,360	3.5
200,000 or more	78,846	4,148	5.3
Exempt carry permits	359,207	4,247	1.2%
Population served			
9,999 or fewer	12,361	117	0.9%
10,000–99,999	153,905	1,747	1.1
100,000–199,999	87,128	1,468	1.7
200,000 or more	105,813	915	0.9

Note: Detail may not sum to total due to rounding. Counts are from agencies that provided data. For more information on reporting agencies and sample design, see *Methodology*. See appendix table 2 for standard errors.

Source: Bureau of Justice Statistics, Firearm Inquiry Statistics program, 2014.

TABLE 5
Reasons for denial of firearm transfer and permit applications, by checking agencies, 2013 and 2014

Reason for denial	2013 FBI[a]	2013 State	2014 FBI[a]	2014 State	2014 Local
Total	100%	100%	100%	100%	100%
Felony indictment/charge	5.6%	3.5%	5.5%	8.7%	2.7%
Felony conviction	42.9	27.1	42.2	22.3	16.1
Felony arrest with no disposition	~	7.7	~	4.4	2.5
Fugitive from justice	18.2	12.9	19.1	10.8	3.2
Domestic violence misdemeanor	6.1	6.3	6.8	6.1	15.0
Domestic violence restraining order	3.1	5.5	2.9	4.9	4.7
Drug user/addict	10.4	3.7	10.4	5.3	4.6
Mental health commitment/adjudication	3.3	3.5	3.9	5.3	6.9
Illegal/unlawful alien	1.3	2.4	1.6	2.7	1.2
State law prohibition	8.8	23.9	7.3	25.7	19.9
Local law prohibition	/	/	/	/	2.3
Other prohibitions[b]	0.3	3.5	0.2	4.0	21.0

Note: Applications include transfers and permits. Reasons for denial were based on 18 U.S.C. § 922 and state laws. Totals were based on agencies that reported counts on reasons for denial. Local data are not available for 2013. For more information on reporting agencies and sample design, see *Methodology*. See appendix table 4 for counts.

~Not applicable. This is a not a federal disqualifier, but a disqualifer that is used in certain states.

/Not reported. This does not apply to the FBI or state agency reporters.

[a]During 2008, the FBI began a new classification system and reclassified all denials from 1999 to 2008. Therefore, totals are not comparable with those in editions of this report prior to 2008.

[b]Includes juveniles, persons dishonorably discharged from the U.S. Armed Forces, persons who have renounced U.S. citizenship, and other unspecified persons.

Sources: Bureau of Justice Statistics, Firearm Inquiry Statistics program, 2013 and 2014; and FBI, National Instant Criminal Background Check System Section Federal Denials, 2013 and 2014.

TABLE 6
Percent change in the number of applications, denials, and reasons for denial, 1999–2014

	1999	2014	Percent change, 1999–2014
Applications	8,621,000	14,993,000	73.9%
Denials[a]	204,000	193,000	-5.4%
Felony denials	148,000	82,000	-44.6
All other reasons	56,000	111,000	98.2
Percent felony[b]	72.5%	42.2%	~
Felony denials per 1,000 applications	17.2	5.5	~

Note: Applications include transfers and permits. Counts are rounded to the nearest 1,000. Annual counts may not sum to totals in other tables. Estimates were based on data reported by the FBI and state agencies that reported reasons for denial via the FIST program. Counts of some local agencies are included in the calculation for the distribution of felony denials. For more information on reporting agencies and sample design, see *Methodology*.

~Not applicable.

[a]During 2008, the FBI began a new classification system and reclassified all denials from 1999 to 2008. Therefore, totals are not comparable with those in editions of this report prior to 2008.

[b]The felony percentage is calculated from reported reasons for denial and is multiplied by the total number of denials to estimate the total number of felony denials.

Sources: Bureau of Justice Statistics, Firearm Inquiry Statistics program, 1999 and 2014; and FBI, National Instant Criminal Background Check System Background Checks—FBI Denials, 1999 and 2014.

TABLE 7
Bureau of Alcohol, Tobacco, Firearms and Explosives investigation of National Instant Criminal Background Check System denials by the FBI, 2013 and 2014

	2013		2014	
	Total	Percent	Total	Percent
FBI denials referred to ATF DENI Branch	93,993	100%	95,934	100%
DENI Branch referrals to ATF field divisions[a]				
Total referred to field	6,257	6.7%	7,978	8.3%
Delayed denials[b]	2,740	2.9	2,514	2.6
Standard denials[c]	3,517	3.7	5,464	5.7
Not referred to field	82,828	88.1%	83,440	87.0%
Not referred and overturned	4,858	5.2%	4,453	4.6%
Canceled[d]	50	0.1%	36	--
Awaiting response[e]	0	0.0%	27	--
Reasons for referrals to ATF field divisions				
Convicted felon	2,083	33.3%	2,917	36.6%
Subject to protective order	1,400	22.4	1,592	20.0
Domestic violence misdemeanor	1,042	16.7	1,434	18.0
Unlawful user of controlled substance	553	8.8	646	8.1
Fugitive from justice	430	6.9	536	6.7
Under indictment/information[f]	408	6.5	433	5.4
Adjudicated mentally defective	277	4.4	336	4.2
Illegal/unlawful alien	53	0.8	74	0.9
Career armed criminal	4	0.1	6	0.1
Dishonorable discharge	5	0.1	4	0.1
State prohibition	1	--	0	0.0
U.S. State Department subject	1	--	0	0.0

Note: Detail may not sum to total due to rounding.

--Less than 0.05%.

[a]A denial is referred if it is likely to merit prosecution under Bureau of Alcohol, Tobacco, Firearms and Explosives and U.S. Attorney criteria.

[b]A firearm may be obtained during an open transaction, where the FBI has not completed a check in 3 business days and the dealer is allowed to transfer the firearm. If the FBI completes the check and finds that the buyer is prohibited, a delayed denial referral is made to ATF.

[c]Involves a person who is not allowed to receive a firearm because the FBI found a prohibitory record within 3 business days.

[d]Represents NICS checks that should not have been conducted and were canceled by the FBI.

[e]DENI Branch specialist has contacted a court or law enforcement agency for additional information and is waiting for the results.

[f]An information is a formal accusation of a crime. It differs from an indictment because it is made by a prosecuting attorney rather than a grand jury.

Source: Bureau of Justice Statistics, based on data from Bureau of Alcohol, Tobacco, Firearms and Explosives, Denial Enforcement and NICS Intelligence Branch, Firearm Denial Statistics, 2013 and 2014.

Methodology

Data used for this report were prepared by the Regional Justice Information Service (REJIS) through a cooperative agreement with the Bureau of Justice Statistics (BJS) under the Firearm Inquiry Statistics (FIST) program. The FIST program collects information on background checks for firearm transfers or permits from federal, state, and local agencies.

FIST frame generation

State statutes determine which agencies conduct background checks for a firearm permit or transfer. To generate the FIST sampling frame for the 2014 collection, REJIS, under the direction of BJS, used multiple data sources combined with a large known pool of past FIST responders. First, REJIS included local agencies from the 2012 FIST frame that were known to have responded to the FIST survey at least once in the previous 3 years and had a verified status of conducting background checks or processing applications for firearm transfers or permits. REJIS used other data sources and resources to verify the frame, including the 2008 Census of State and Local Law Enforcement and a 2011 Originating Agency Identifier file of law enforcement agencies obtained from the FBI.

The 2014 FIST universe was composed of the following:

- **FBI**—30 states and the District of Columbia rely on the FBI's National Instant Criminal Background Check System (NICS) to conduct firearm background check activities for handguns and long gun transfers. In seven other states, the FBI's NICS conducts checks for long gun transfers only.

- **State reporting agencies**—31 state agencies and the District of Columbia police provide complete statewide counts of applications for firearm transfers or permits, denials of applications, and (when reported) reasons for denial for at least one type of check.

- **Local reporting agencies**—1,287 local checking agencies in 11 states issue permits, track applications and denials, or conduct background checks for various types of firearm permit or transfer systems.[3]

---

[3]The FIST program obtains data from local law enforcement agencies that conduct background checks and issue permits as well as from other types of local agencies that conduct these activities, such as probate courts (in Georgia) and county clerks or other types of administrative offices (in New York). In such cases, the agency surveyed may not actually conduct a background check but rather issue a permit, track a permit that was issued, or track a transfer check. For the FIST program, collecting application and denial data from agencies that conduct background checks or track permit or transfer applications is considered to be the most accurate and sometimes the only means available to assess background check activity. Additionally, populations covered by local agencies (for basic NICS checks and permits, not including other types of checks and permits, such as separate state-level checks and ATF-exempt carry permits) account for only 7% of the total U.S. population.

For the FIST program, it is important to distinguish between local agencies that are authorized by statute to conduct background checks and those that actually conduct the checks. Although local agencies in certain states are legally authorized to conduct background checks for firearm transfers or permits, these agencies are not required to do so. When developing the 2014 FIST frame, REJIS identified a few instances where a local agency (usually a municipal police department) that was legally authorized by state statute to conduct a background check had never actually conducted background check activities and was unlikely to ever do so. Instead, transfer or permit applicants who might use such a local agency are directed to another local authority (usually the county sheriff) with jurisdiction to conduct a transfer check or issue a permit. Agencies that did not conduct background check activities were considered to be out of scope for the 2014 data collection.

For the FIST data collection, BJS determined that eligible agencies in the frame should be those that are authorized to conduct and are known to conduct or maintain information on background checks. Such agencies collect or maintain data on the critical FIST data elements: applications, denials, and (when reported) the reasons for denial. Agencies that only have delegated background check functions are considered out of scope because they do not actually conduct firearm background check activities nor track information on such activities, which are the critical data collection items on the survey. Smaller law enforcement agencies that had closed since the construction of the FIST frame were determined to be out of scope for the 2014 data collection.

FIST sample

The 2014 FIST survey was designed to provide state-level estimates of background check activity. BJS produced a national estimate of the number of applications for firearms received and denied pursuant to the Brady Act by combining data obtained from state agencies and local checking agencies with FBI's NICS transaction data obtained from the FBI's NICS Section.[4]

REJIS collected state-level data from the state reporting agencies via survey or extracted publicly available online reports from the state website. Except for one state (Pennsylvania) in which denials were estimated, all data collected by state agencies are considered to be complete counts. To obtain FIST data in 2014, REJIS surveyed local agencies in 11 states with local checking agencies that were authorized to conduct firearm background check activities or process applications. Totals were estimated for states where the reporters were local agencies.

Local agencies in 8 (Idaho, Iowa, Montana, Nebraska, North Carolina, Nevada, New York, and West Virginia) of the 11 states were enumerated, and local agencies in 3 (Georgia, Minnesota, and Washington) of the states were sampled in 2 of the 4 sample strata due to the large number of potential reporters. REJIS created a stratified random sample proportionate to state and stratum size in each of the 3 states sampled based on population size that roughly equates to—

- Stratum 1: rural—places of less than 10,000 population

- Stratum 2: small cities—places of between 10,000 and 99,999 population

- Stratum 3: small metropolitan areas—places of between 100,000 and 199,999 population

- Stratum 4: large metropolitan areas—places of 200,000 or more population.

BJS created a reserve sample to account for potential low response rates for the 2014 collection. In total, a 30% reserve sample was drawn for each of the three sampled states; it was split into two reserve samples yielding a 15% sample per reserve sample. Because all agencies in strata 3 and 4 were surveyed, the reserve sample only affected strata 1 and 2

[4]The FBI reports on NICS transaction data in its annual *NICS Operations Report*. The FBI tracks the number of applications and denials processed by the NICS system. However, the FBI only reports reasons for denials made by the NICS Section and does not include reasons for denials issued at the state and local levels (information that FIST collects). In 2014, the FBI reported more than 12.7 million state Point of Contact transactions, compared to the approximately 6 million reported by FIST. This variation can be attributed to several factors, notably within the category of state firearm permits. The FIST counts include applications for two types of state firearm permits: (1) permits required for a transfer (purchase permits) and (2) concealed carry permits that may be used to exempt the holder from a background check at the time of transfer (exempt carry permits). At yearend 2014, 21 states had an exempt carry permit, and 29 other states had concealed carry permits that were not exempt and were not included in FIST. At least some of those 29 states used NICS for checks on applicants, and those checks have been included in the FBI statistics. The largest difference within the state firearm permit category was caused by periodic rechecks that at least two state agencies ran on all current carry permit holders. The rechecks were included in FBI transaction counts but not in FIST counts because they were not connected to a firearm transfer, and the FIST reporting agency was able to separately report new and renewed permit applications.

of the sampled agencies. The first reserve sample was to be used if one of the sampled states had a response rate of less than 85% for the initial data collection period. The second reserve sample was to be used if one of the sampled states had a response rate of less than 75% after the first reserve sample was collected. REJIS used the first and second reserve samples for Georgia in 2014. No reserve samples were used for the sampled agencies in Minnesota and Washington.

The final designated sample included 561 enumerated (self-representing or SR) local agencies and 274 sampled (non-self-representing or NSR) local agencies. After adjusting for agencies that were ineligible to participate in the survey, the final sample consisted of 845 state and local agencies. The overall response rate was 80%. All (100%) state agencies and 80% of local agencies responded to the survey **(table 8)**.

BJS and REJIS updated the 2013–14 FIST survey form. To minimize respondent burden, the form was changed to provide clearer instructions tailored to terminology used by individual state agencies to describe the permit or permits of interest. BJS removed questions from the 2014 FIST survey on arrests, appeals, and reversals of denied applications because only a small number of agencies historically reported these data, which significantly limited the ability to draw reliable conclusions about the data. To increase survey response, REJIS used multiple survey modes (e.g., online form, paper survey, and fax) and a rigorous nonresponse follow-up contact strategy.

Estimation

Data obtained from state and local agencies were combined with the FBI's federal NICS transaction data to create an estimate of the total number of firearm transfer and permit applications received and denied nationally. REJIS applied design weights and nonresponse adjustment factors for enumerated and sampled local agencies to generate estimates of the number of applications and denials at the state level.

TABLE 8
Number of checking agencies in the 2014 Firearm Inquiry Statistics survey

Checking agencies	Total	Sample	Responses	Response rate
Total	1,319	845	679	80%
Statewide*	32	32	32	100%
Local	1,287	813	647	80%
Population served				
9,999 or fewer	574	289	223	77%
10,000–99,999	600	411	338	81
100,000–199,999	64	64	48	75
200,000 or more	49	49	38	78

Note: Agencies that were ineligible to participate in the FIST survey were deemed out of scope and removed from all counts of checking agencies.
*The same agencies were also surveyed for 2013 data. The response rate among state agency reporters for 2013 was 97% (31 responses).
Source: Bureau of Justice Statistics, Firearm Inquiry Statistics program, 2014.

The 2014 FIST data collection provides for two basic weighting structures for local respondent agencies: a weight applied to SR agencies and a weight applied to NSR agencies.

SR agencies (enumerated)

Each local checking agency within the eight states in which all known eligible agencies were contacted received a design weight of 1 (w1 = 1). In addition to the design weight, a nonresponse adjustment (w2) was applied to responding agencies to compensate for the agencies that did not respond.

NSR agencies (sampled)

The process for calculating weights for NSR agencies was similar to that for SR agencies, except these agencies (the small agencies in strata 1 and 2 of the sampled states) received a design weight of greater than 1 (w1 > 1) according to the population-based stratum and the state in which they reside. This weight reflects the inverse of the probability of selection for the state and stratum size (cell) in which the agency resides. The reserve samples for Minnesota and Washington were not released. In these cases, the design weights were further adjusted to compensate for the reserve subsampling. Agencies in strata 3 and 4 (large agencies) were selected with certainty and were therefore given a weight of 1. Weights were adjusted for any agencies that were out of scope in the sampled states.

Nonresponse adjustment

The nonresponse adjustment accounts for agencies that were ineligible (out of scope) and for nonrespondents. It consists of a ratio adjustment of the sum of the weighted eligible agencies (per state and population size stratum) to the sum of weighted respondent agencies (also per state and population size stratum). A nonresponse adjustment was applied to each cell (stratum within state) if there was any nonresponse. This created a specific adjustment for each cell that applies to all states, whether enumerated or sampled.

Partial-year reporting adjustment

A weight (w3), consisting of a small ratio adjustment to account for missing months of data, was applied to adjust for any agency that reported only partial-year data. This adjustment to account for missing months was necessary for six local agencies and to calculate reasons for denial from Pennsylvania.

Final weights

The final weights (Fw) applied to each FIST case are the product of a design weight applied to each agency, a nonresponse adjustment weight, and the partial-year reporting weight (Fw = w1 × w2 × w3).

Item nonresponse imputation for local agencies

For the 2014 FIST collection, REJIS determined that there were very few cases in which information on applications for firearm transfers or permits was missing. There were more cases of missing data for denials, but this was a small number compared to other missing data (e.g., reasons for denial). To count partial responses, agencies were required to report either the number of applications received or the number of denials issued. If neither was present, the agency was considered a nonrespondent. Fifteen agencies provided denials but not applications. Twenty-eight agencies provided the number of applications but not denials. In the instances of missing data on applications or denials, REJIS used a conditional mean imputation to estimate the number of applications and denials.

To yield the most reliable estimates, REJIS replaced missing values with the mean number of applications of other agencies in the same state that were in the same population category. In population stratum 1, this approach was deemed sufficient because all agencies served a population of less than 10,000. In population stratum 2, the population size covered a broad range (10,000 to 99,999). As such, a traditional group-mean replacement would have produced unacceptably imprecise approximations. To address this, for agencies with complete data, REJIS employed a basic multiple imputation strategy that took into account the number of denials, the actual population size served, and the number of applications to calculate the estimated number of applications in instances of missing data. The result was a within-state and stratum group-based sum of imputed values, but it was proportionate to the population allocation of imputed applications or denials per agency.

Estimates for 2013 data

BJS collected 2013 and 2014 data from federal agencies and from the 31 state agency reporters and the District of Columbia. Due to various factors, including time spent revising the survey to incorporate more accurate terminology familiar to respondents, complexities associated with trying to collect multiple years of data from local jurisdictions, and BJS's objective to report more timely FIST data, BJS collected only 2014 data from local checking agencies.[5] To account for the missing 2013 local agency data in the national estimate, REJIS used available FIST

---

[5]To mitigate reporting burden, BJS collected only 2014 data from local checking agencies. While state agencies are more likely to maintain the requested data in an automated format (e.g., a database), local agencies, especially those in smaller jurisdictions, may not have access to these same resources. These agencies may need to gather FIST data from files or other sources that require manual counts, and requesting multiple years of data could result in an unnecessary increase in respondent burden when reliable estimates can be produced in a different way.

2012, 2013, and 2014 state data to estimate the number of applications and denials from local agencies.[6] Specifically, REJIS used a random intercept linear regression spline model with one knot at 2013 to incorporate the hierarchical structure of the data (multiple time points and total application and denials estimates per state) to separately model total applications and total denials. The spline models were selected over conditional growth models (linear or quadratic) to allow for nonlinearity in the trends in total applications (and denials) over time across all states. To improve the overall imputations, these models also incorporated either a fixed or time varying covariate shown to be highly correlated with the FIST applications and denials totals over time.

Adjustments to data

REJIS obtained concealed carry permit data from Michigan by fiscal year, which were used to provide estimates for calendar years 2013 and 2014.

Mississippi reported applications for 2013 and 2014 but did not report denials for either year. Because sufficient data from prior years were unavailable to calculate an estimate using a linear trend, the ratio of denials to applications reported by Mississippi in 2012 was used to calculate a simple ratio that was applied to the number of applications to estimate the number of denials.

Pennsylvania reported the number of instant checks for 2013 and 2014, which are included in the FIST national estimate. The proportion of all Pennsylvania transactions that were instant checks was used to estimate the number of denials of instant checks and reasons for denials.

Standard errors

Standard error calculations were computed for the estimates of total applications, total denials, and the ratio of denials to total applications for three types: purchase, transfer and concealed carry permits across states, and size of region for local agencies. The standard error computations take into account several aspects of the FIST design, including stratification of data collection by a combination of state and population served categories and finite population sampling (without replacement) across the states and population categories of interest. REJIS approximated the FIST design by generating 68 final strata defined as combinations of state and population categories. Data from SR agencies were treated as certainty samples with an initial selection probability of one. For these states and population category combinations, complete responses would have a negligible contribution to the overall standard errors for a given estimate. To account for this and the fact that finite population correction (FPC) factors for the samples

generated by the FIST design were very small, FPCs were directly incorporated into the standard error computations. Finally, estimates for local agencies included one additional subdomain of agency type: local or state (centralized reporting). All computations were generated using the FIST final sampling weight, which incorporated adjustments for missing values, nonresponse, and an overall population eligibility or coverage adjustment. In some cases, standard error computations were not possible, as only one agency reported information from a given type of application in areas where more than one agency was queried (via sample or census). In these cases, no standard error computations were provided.

Reasons for denial

BJS has collected information about reasons for denial since the FIST program's inception in 1996. The FIST survey includes 12 categories that reflect the most common reasons for denial and closely match the categories of federal prohibitors. NICS POC agencies enforce federal prohibitors and state law prohibitors that may vary from the federal categories (see appendix table 6 for a list of federal and state prohibitors). Agencies that responded to the FIST survey were asked to record their denials in the most appropriate categories. When REJIS obtained data from an agency's website or internal report that did not match with an existing FIST denial category, REJIS determined which denial category best matched the reported reason and verified the classification with the responding agency.

In 2014, the FBI, 18 state agencies, and approximately 330 local agencies reported reasons for denials. There are two major difficulties in reporting reasons for denial.

First, among reporting agencies there was a high degree of nonresponse on items that asked about reasons for denial. Among local agencies, nonresponse was high in most states and population strata. Local agencies in one state (New York) did not report any reasons for denial. In 2014, the FBI and some state agencies provided a reason for each denial. Other state agencies provided reasons only for some denials, and some state agencies did not provide any reasons for denials.

Second, the method by which agencies record or track reasons for a denial varies among state and local agencies. Of those that report any reasons for a denial, approximately three-quarters of local agencies report all of the reasons found on a background check that disqualify a permit or transfer seeker from obtaining a firearm, while a quarter of agencies report only one reason for a denial. This proportion is reversed among state agencies, for which a third report all of the reasons a permit or transfer was denied and two-thirds report only one reason. Another difficulty among some state and local agencies that report one reason for a denial is that some report only the most serious charge listed

---

[6]Data were also estimated for the state agency reporter from Illinois, as data were not provided for 2013.

on a background check, others list the first reason found, and others do not indicate how they determined which reason to report.

Due to the high nonresponse and variation in the way reasons for denial are reported, a simple estimation for the number of reasons for denial by local agencies was calculated. Estimates used only the agency base weight rather than the final weight that was applied to all other local agency estimates. (See *Final weights* section.) This was done to bring the representation of responses from sampled agencies in line with those from states in which a census of agencies was conducted. The FBI and state agency reasons for denial counts are reported, and no estimation on these counts was conducted.

Definitions

Application for firearm transfer is information submitted by a person to a state or local checking agency to purchase a firearm or obtain a permit that can be used for a purchase. Information may be submitted directly to a checking agency or forwarded by a prospective seller.

Denial occurs when an applicant is prohibited from receiving a firearm or a permit that can be used to receive a firearm because a disqualifying factor was found during a background check.

Exempt carry permit is a state carry permit (issued after a background check) that exempts the holder from a check at the time of purchase under an ATF regulation or state law.

Federal Firearms Licensee (FFL) is also known as a federally licensed firearms dealer. A dealer must be licensed by the Bureau of Alcohol, Tobacco, Firearms and Explosives (ATF) to be classified as an FFL and must be enrolled with the FBI's NICS to request a NICS check.

Firearm is any weapon that is designed to or may readily be converted to expel a projectile by the action of an explosive.

Handgun is a firearm that has a short stock and is designed to be held and fired using a single hand, such as a pistol or revolver.

Instant check (instant approval) systems require a seller to transmit a purchaser's application to a checking agency by telephone or computer, after which the agency is required to respond as quickly as possible.

Long gun is a firearm with a barrel extended to about 30 inches to improve accuracy and range, commonly with a shoulder butt, and designed to be fired with two hands, such as a rifle or shotgun.

National Instant Criminal Background Check System (NICS) is a national system that checks available records to determine if prospective transferees are disqualified from receiving firearms.

Other approval systems require a seller to transmit a purchaser's application to a checking agency by telephone or other means. The agency is not required to respond immediately but must respond before the end of the statutory time limit.

Purchase permit systems require a prospective firearm purchaser to obtain, after a background check, a government-issued document (called a permit, license, or identification card) that must be presented to a seller to receive a firearm.

Transactions are inquiries to the federal NICS system and may include more than one inquiry per application.

Jurisdiction notes

The following notes provide additional information about changes in jurisdictions that occurred and about the types of firearms included in a jurisdiction's instant checks, purchase permits, exempt carry permits, or other approval checks in 2013 and 2014. Jurisdiction statutes should be consulted for complete details on a jurisdiction's firearm laws.

Alaska—A state agency conducted background checks on applicants for exempt carry permits that may have been used for handgun or long gun transfers.

Arizona—A state agency conducted background checks on applicants for exempt carry permits that may have been used for handgun or long gun transfers.

Arkansas—A state agency conducted background checks on applicants for exempt carry permits that may have been used for handgun or long gun transfers.

California—A state agency conducted other approval checks on applicants for handgun and long gun transfers.

Colorado—A state agency conducted instant checks on applicants for handgun and long gun transfers.

Connecticut—The state authorized two types of purchase permits, and every handgun transferee was required to obtain one of the permits. Beginning April 1, 2014, a purchase permit was also required for a long gun. In addition, a state agency conducted instant checks at the point of transfer on applicants for handgun and long gun transfers.

District of Columbia—The chief of police conducted checks on applicants for a registration certificate (categorized by the FIST as a purchase permit), which was required to obtain a handgun or a long gun. In addition, the FBI conducted NICS checks requested by dealers who transferred a firearm after receiving a buyer's registration certificate.

Florida—A state agency conducted instant checks on applicants for handgun and long gun transfers.

Georgia—Local agencies issued exempt carry permits that may have been used for handgun or long gun transfers.

Hawaii—A purchase permit was required to obtain a handgun or a long gun. Local agencies conducted checks on purchase permit applicants.

Idaho—Local agencies issued exempt carry permits that may have been used for handgun or long gun transfers.

Illinois—A purchase permit was required to obtain a handgun or a long gun. In addition, a state agency conducted instant checks at the point of transfer on applicants for handgun and long gun transfers.

Iowa—A purchase permit was required to obtain a handgun. An exempt carry permit may have been substituted for the purchase permit. Both types of permits may have been used to acquire a long gun. Local agencies conducted checks on applicants for purchase and exempt carry permits.

Kansas—A state agency conducted background checks on applicants for exempt carry permits that may have been used for handgun or long gun transfers.

Kentucky—A state agency conducted background checks on applicants for exempt carry permits that may have been used for handgun or long gun transfers.

Maryland—A purchase permit issued by a state agency was required to obtain a handgun after October 1, 2013. In addition, a state agency conducted other approval checks on applicants for transfers of handguns and assault weapons, which were designated by state law as regulated firearms.

Massachusetts—A purchase permit was required to obtain a handgun or a long gun. Three types of purchase permits were included in the FIST survey data. Local agencies conducted checks on permit applicants.

Michigan—A purchase permit was required for a handgun transfer between two individuals who were not licensed dealers. An exempt carry permit may have been substituted for the purchase permit and may have also been used to acquire a long gun. Local agencies conducted checks on purchase permit and exempt carry permit applicants.

Minnesota—A purchase permit was required to obtain a handgun or an assault weapon. An exempt carry permit may have been substituted for the purchase permit. Local agencies conducted checks on purchase and exempt carry permit applicants.

Mississippi—A state agency conducted background checks on applicants for exempt carry permits that may have been used for handgun or long gun transfers.

Montana—Local agencies issued exempt carry permits that may have been used for handgun or long gun transfers.

Nebraska—Local agencies conducted checks on applicants for a purchase permit, which was required to obtain a handgun. An exempt carry permit issued by a state agency may have been substituted for the purchase permit. Both types of permits may have been used to acquire a long gun.

Nevada—A state agency conducted instant checks on applicants for handgun and long gun transfers. Local agencies issued exempt carry permits that may have been used for handgun or long gun transfers.

New Hampshire—A state agency conducted instant checks on applicants for handgun transfers.

New Jersey—A purchase permit was required to obtain a handgun or a long gun. Local agencies and the state police conducted checks on purchase permit applicants. In addition, the state police conducted instant checks at the point of transfer on applicants for handgun and long gun transfers.

New York—The state's purchase permit was required to obtain a handgun and certain types of long guns. Local agencies conducted checks on purchase permit applicants.

North Carolina—A purchase permit was required to obtain a handgun. An exempt carry permit may have been substituted for the purchase permit. Both types of permits may have been used to acquire a long gun. Local agencies conducted checks on applicants for purchase and exempt carry permits.

North Dakota—A state agency conducted background checks on applicants for exempt carry permits that may have been used for handgun or long gun transfers.

Oregon—A state agency conducted instant checks on applicants for handgun and long gun transfers.

Pennsylvania—A state agency conducted instant checks on applicants for handgun and long gun transfers.

Rhode Island—Local agencies conducted other approval checks on applicants for handgun and long gun transfers.

South Carolina—A state agency conducted background checks on applicants for exempt carry permits that may have been used for handgun or long gun transfers.

Tennessee—A state agency conducted instant checks on applicants for handgun and long gun transfers.

Texas—A state agency conducted background checks on applicants for exempt carry permits that may have been used for handgun or long gun transfers.

Utah—A state agency conducted instant checks on applicants for handgun and long gun transfers, and conducted background checks on applicants for exempt carry permits.

Virginia—A state agency conducted instant checks on applicants for handgun and long gun transfers.

Washington—Local agencies conducted other approval checks on applicants for handgun transfers.

West Virginia—Local agencies issued exempt carry permits that may have been used for handgun or long gun transfers on or after June 4, 2014, when the permit was qualified by ATF as an alternative to the NICS transfer check.

Wisconsin—A state agency conducted instant checks on applicants for handgun transfers.

Wyoming—A state agency conducted background checks on applicants for exempt carry permits that may have been used for handgun or long gun transfers.

Related Publications

Background Checks for Firearm Transfers - Statistical Tables, 2012 (NCJ 247815, December 2014)

Background Checks for Firearm Transfers - Statistical Tables, 2010 (NCJ 238226, February 2013)

Background Checks for Firearm Transfers - Statistical Tables, 2009 (NCJ 231679, October 2010)

Background Checks for Firearm Transfers - Statistical Tables, 2008 (NCJ 227471, August 2009)

Background Checks for Firearm Transfers - Statistical Tables, 2007 (NCJ 223197, July 2008)

Background Checks for Firearm Transfers - Statistical Tables, 2006 (NCJ 221786, March 2008)

Background Checks for Firearm Transfers, 2005 (NCJ 214256, November 2006)

Background Checks for Firearm Transfers, 2004 (NCJ 210117, October 2005)

Background Checks for Firearm Transfers, 2003: Trends for the Permanent Brady Period, 1999–2003 (NCJ 204428, September 2004)

Background Checks for Firearm Transfers, 2002 (NCJ 200116, September 2003)

Background Checks for Firearm Transfers, 2001 (NCJ 195235, September 2002)

Background Checks for Firearm Transfers, 2000 (NCJ 187985, July 2001)

Background Checks for Firearm Transfers, 1999 (NCJ 180882, June 2000)

Data on this subject for the Brady Interim period prior to the permanent provisions are available in *Presale Handgun Checks, the Brady Interim Period, 1994–98* (NCJ 175034, June 1999)

Enforcement of the Brady Act, 2010: Federal and State Investigations and Prosecutions of Firearm Applicants Denied by a NICS Check in 2011
https://www.ncjrs.gov/pdffiles1/bjs/grants/239272.pdf

Enforcement of the Brady Act, 2009: Federal and State Investigations and Prosecutions of Firearm Applicants Denied by a NICS Check in 2009
https://www.ncjrs.gov/pdffiles1/bjs/grants/234173.pdf

Enforcement of the Brady Act, 2008: Federal and State Investigations and Prosecutions of Firearm Applicants Denied by a NICS Check in 2008
http://www.ncjrs.gov/pdffiles1/bjs/231052.pdf

Enforcement of the Brady Act, 2007: Federal and State Investigations and Prosecutions of Firearm Applicants Denied by a NICS Check in 2007
http://www.ncjrs.gov/pdffiles1/bjs/grants/227604.pdf

Enforcement of the Brady Act, 2006
http://www.ncjrs.gov/pdffiles1/bjs/grants/222474.pdf

Federal Firearms Cases, FY 2008
http://www.ncjrs.gov/pdffiles1/bjs/grants/229420.pdf

Federal Firearms Cases, FY 2007
http://www.ncjrs.gov/pdffiles1/bjs/grants/224890.pdf

Summary of State Firearm Transfer Laws, December 31, 2013
https://www.ncjrs.gov/pdffiles1/bjs/grants/248657.pdf

The following BJS surveys provide an overview of the firearm check procedures in each of the states and the states' interaction with NICS:

Survey of State Procedures Related to Firearm Sales, 2005 (NCJ 214645, November 2006)

Survey of State Procedures Related to Firearm Sales, Midyear 2004 (NCJ 209288, August 2005)

Survey of State Procedures Related to Firearm Sales, Midyear 2003 (NCJ 203701, August 2004)

Survey of State Procedures Related to Firearm Sales, Midyear 2002 (NCJ 198830, April 2003)

Survey of State Procedures Related to Firearm Sales, Midyear 2001 (NCJ 192065, April 2002)

Survey of State Procedures Related to Firearm Sales, Midyear 2000 (NCJ 186766, April 2001)

Survey of State Procedures Related to Firearm Sales, Midyear 1999 (NCJ 179022, March 2000)

Survey of State Procedures Related to Firearm Sales, 1997 (NCJ 173942, December 1998)

Survey of State Procedures Related to Firearm Sales, 1996 (NCJ 160705, September 1997)

Survey of State Procedures Related to Firearm Sales (NCJ 160763, May 1996)

The following BJS survey examines the quality and accessibility of certain criminal and noncriminal records when states conduct a firearm presale background check:

Survey of State Records Included in Presale Background Checks: Mental Health Records, Domestic Violence Misdemeanor Records, and Restraining Orders, 2003 (NCJ 206042, August 2004)

Trends for Background Checks for Firearm Transfers, 1999–2008 http://www.ncjrs.gov/pdffiles1/bjs/grants/231187.pdf

APPENDIX TABLE 1
Estimated standard errors for firearm applications received and denied by local agencies, 2014

	Applications	Denials	Percent denied
Total	19,265	731	0.07%
Purchase permits	13,860	678	0.20%
Exempt carry permits	7,957	171	0.04
Other approvals	7,658	56	0.04

Source: Bureau of Justice Statistics, Firearm Inquiry Statistics program, 2014.

APPENDIX TABLE 2
Standard errors for table 4: Firearm applications received and denied by local agencies, by community size and type of permit, 2014

	Applications	Denials	Percent denied
Purchase permits	13,860	678	0.20%
Population served			
9,999 or fewer	1,972	36	0.10%
10,000–99,999	5,904	245	0.30
100,000–199,999	5,902	184	0.30
200,000 or more	10,886	604	0.50
Exempt carry permits	7,957	171	0.04%
Population served			
9,999 or fewer	436	12	0.10%
10,000–99,999	4,274	115	0.10
100,000–199,999	3,528	106	0.10
200,000 or more	5,693	68	0.10

Source: Bureau of Justice Statistics, Firearm Inquiry Statistics program, 2014.

APPENDIX TABLE 3
Firearm applications received and denied by jurisdiction, 2014

Jurisdiction	Applications	Standard error	Denials	Standard error	Percent denied	Standard error
Alaska						
Exempt carry	2,018	~	12	~	0.6%	~
Arizona						
Exempt carry	52,049	~	358	~	0.7%	~
Arkansas						
Exempt carry	41,725	~	920	~	2.2%	~
California						
Other approval	931,037	~	8,569	~	0.9%	~
Colorado						
Instant check	314,976	~	6,068	~	1.9%	~
Connecticut	133,364		112		0.1%	
Instant check	115,460	~	91	~	0.1	~
Purchase permit	17,904	~	21	~	0.1	~
District of Columbia						
Purchase permit	1,366	~	10	~	0.7%	~
Florida						
Instant check	774,363	~	11,372	~	1.5%	~
Georgia						
Exempt carry[a]	154,189	5,920	2,053	130	1.3%	0.1%
Hawaii						
Purchase permit	19,365	~	148	~	0.8%	~
Idaho						
Exempt carry[a]	28,248	1,716	134	13	0.5%	0.03%
Illinois	572,077		9,557		1.7%	
Instant check	401,899	~	1,616	~	0.4	~
Purchase permit	170,178	~	7,941	~	4.7	~
Iowa	43,836	834	1,161	144	2.6%	0.3%
Purchase permit[a]	16,170	296	835	140	5.2	0.9
Exempt carry[a]	27,666	556	326	9	1.2	0.0
Kansas						
Exempt carry	21,976	~	146	~	0.7%	~
Kentucky						
Exempt carry	31,889	~	560	~	1.8%	~
Maryland	44,939		597		1.3%	
Other approval	28,633	~	346	~	1.2	~
Purchase permit	16,306	~	251	~	1.5	~
Massachusetts						
Purchase permit	68,906	~	2,600	~	3.8%	~
Michigan	159,303		3,033		1.9%	
Purchase permit	43,702	~	952	~	2.2	~
Exempt carry	115,601	~	2,081	~	1.8	~
Minnesota[b]	100,081		1,439		1.4%	
Purchase permit[a]	56,766	5,359	1,017	80	1.8	0.2%
Exempt carry[c]	43,315	~	422	~	1.0	~
Mississippi						
Exempt carry	19,496	~	3	~	0.0%	~
Montana						
Exempt carry[a]	13,215	1,632	141	11	1.1%	0.1%
Nebraska[b]	41,030	~	887	~	2.2%	~
Purchase permit[a]	30,473	457	789	22	2.6	0.1%
Exempt carry	10,557	~	98	~	0.9	~
Nevada[b]	108,748	~	1,763	~	1.6%	~
Instant check	95,427	~	1,716	~	1.8	~
Exempt carry[a]	13,321	800	47	4	0.4	0.0%

Continued on next page

Firearm applications received and denied by jurisdiction, 2014

Jurisdiction	Applications	Standard error	Denials	Standard error	Percent denied	Standard error
New Hampshire						
Instant check	43,000	~	340	~	0.8%	~
New Jersey	169,715	~	1,282	~	0.8%	~
Instant check	95,267	~	464	~	0.5	~
Purchase permit	74,448	~	818	~	1.1	~
New York						
Purchase permit[a]	58,747	10,070	1,668	186	2.8%	0.4%
North Carolina	233,856	11,823	8,681	672	3.7%	0.2%
Purchase permit[a]	126,925	7,853	7,238	632	5.7	0.3
Exempt carry[a]	106,931	4,617	1,443	109	1.3	0.1
North Dakota						
Exempt carry	6,900	~	750	~	10.9%	~
Oregon						
Instant check	233,878	~	1,590	~	0.7%	~
Pennsylvania						
Instant check[a]	655,457	~	9,620	~	1.5%	~
Rhode Island						
Other approval	16,422	~	121	~	0.7%	~
South Carolina						
Exempt carry	65,360	~	948	~	-1.5%	~
Tennessee						
Instant check	428,017	~	17,832	~	-4.2%	~
Texas						
Exempt carry	247,102	~	776	~	0.3%	~
Utah	236,082	~	2,713	~	1.1%	~
Instant check	91,437	~	1,985	~	2.2	~
Exempt carry	144,645	~	728	~	0.5	~
Virginia						
Instant check	405,838	~	2,661	~	0.7%	~
Washington						
Other approval[a]	137,075	7,658	675	56	0.5%	0.0%
West Virginia						
Exempt carry[a,d]	15,636	636	104	8	0.7%	0.1%
Wisconsin						
Instant check	102,887	~	988	~	1.0%	~
Wyoming						
Exempt carry	2,552	~	76	~	3.0%	~

Note: For more information on reporting agencies and sample design, see *Methodology*. Types of firearms included in a jurisdiction's checks or permits are described in *Jurisdiction notes*.

~Not applicable. Complete counts were obtained and no sampling error is present.

[a]Totals were estimated (denials only for Pennsylvania).

[b]Standard errors not applicable to total because a portion of the estimate came from a state reporter.

[c]Permits are only exempt under state law. Other carry permits listed have a federal exemption.

[d]Totals are for June 4 to December 31, 2014.

Source: Bureau of Justice Statistics, Firearm Inquiry Statistics program, 2013.

APPENDIX TABLE 4
Firearm applications received and denied by jurisdiction, 2013

Jurisdiction	Applications	Denials	Percent denied	Jurisdiction	Applications	Denials	Percent denied
Alaska				**Mississippi**			
Exempt carry	1,774	12	0.7%	Exempt carry	22,030	3	0.0%
Arizona				**Nebraska**			
Exempt carry	71,104	364	0.5%	Exempt carry	14,513	84	0.6%
Arkansas				**Nevada**			
Exempt carry	58,699	431	0.7%	Instant check	120,891	1,908	1.6%
California				**New Hampshire**			
Other approval	960,179	7,493	0.8%	Instant check	50,700	350	0.7%
Colorado				**New Jersey**	229,719	2,556	1.1%
Instant check	396,955	7,351	1.9%	Instant check	123,553	620	0.5
Connecticut	201,294	270	0.1%	Purchase permit	106,166	1,936	1.8
Instant check	145,552	210	0.1	**North Dakota**			
Purchase permit	55,742	60	0.1	Exempt carry	13,900	950	6.8%
District of Columbia				**Oregon**			
Purchase permit	1,154	10	0.9%	Instant check	263,283	2,151	0.8%
Florida				**Pennsylvania**[a]			
Instant check	869,560	11,493	1.3%	Instant check	655,457	9,620	1.5%
Hawaii				**Rhode Island**			
Purchase permit	22,765	232	1.0%	Other approval	21,648	145	0.7%
Illinois[a]	829,930	8,341	1.0%	**South Carolina**			
Instant check	505,009	1,448	0.3	Exempt carry	84,284	1,272	1.5%
Purchase permit	324,921	6,893	2.1	**Tennessee**			
Kansas				Instant check	473,610	13,267	2.8%
Exempt carry	31,004	72	0.2%	**Texas**			
Kentucky				Exempt carry	243,329	688	0.3%
Exempt carry	58,706	1,098	1.9%	**Utah**	286,760	2,617	0.9%
Maryland	134,134	1,171	0.9%	Instant check	110,623	1,587	1.4
Other approval	129,359	1,125	0.9	Exempt carry	176,137	1,030	0.6
Purchase permit	4,775	46	1.0	**Virginia**			
Massachusetts				Instant check	479,253	2,412	0.5%
Purchase permit	125,491	3,144	2.5%	**Wisconsin**			
Michigan	188,731	2,890	1.5%	Instant check	135,013	1,117	0.8%
Purchase permit	58,831	1,228	2.1	**Wyoming**			
Exempt carry	129,900	1,662	1.3	Exempt carry	3,817	93	2.4%
Minnesota[b]							
Exempt carry	62,950	540	0.9%				

Note: For more information on reporting agencies and sample design, see *Methodology*. Types of firearms included in a jurisdiction's checks or permits are described in *Jurisdiction notes*.

[a]Totals were estimated (denials only for Pennsylvania).

[b]Permits are only exempt under state law. Other carry permits listed have a federal exemption.

Source: Bureau of Justice Statistics, Firearm Inquiry Statistics program, 2013.

APPENDIX TABLE 5
Reasons for denial of firearm transfer and permit applications, by checking agencies, 2013 and 2014

	2013		2014		
Reason for denial	FBI[a]	State	FBI[a]	State	Local
Total	88,203	37,738	90,895	49,979	7,022
Felony indictment/charge	4,907	1,316	4,956	4,334	187
Felony conviction	37,843	10,228	38,379	11,126	1,133
Felony arrest with no disposition	~	2,922	~	2,179	179
Fugitive from justice	16,071	4,879	17,400	5,413	225
Domestic violence misdemeanor	5,342	2,375	6,190	3,034	1,052
Domestic violence restraining order	2,761	2,066	2,650	2,447	327
Drug user/addict	9,178	1,391	9,449	2,632	322
Mental health commitment/adjudication	2,932	1,336	3,557	2,650	484
Illegal/unlawful alien	1,121	898	1,431	1,325	81
State law prohibition	7,795	9,018	6,661	12,851	1,396
Local law prohibition	/	/	/	/	159
Other prohibitions[b]	253	1,309	222	1,988	1,477

Note: Applications include transfers and permits. Reasons for denial were based on 18 U.S.C. § 922 and state laws. Totals were based on agencies that reported counts on reasons for denial. Local data are not available for 2013. For more information on reporting agencies and sample design, see *Methodology*.

~Not applicable. This is a not a federal disqualifier, but a disqualifer that is used in certain states.

/Not reported. This does not apply to the FBI or state agency reporters.

[a]During 2008, the FBI instituted a new classification system and reclassified all denials from 1999 to 2008. Therefore, totals are not comparable with those in editions of this report prior to 2008.

[b]Includes juveniles, persons dishonorably discharged from the U.S. Armed Forces, persons who have renounced U.S. citizenship, and other unspecified persons.

Sources: Bureau of Justice Statistics, Firearm Inquiry Statistics program, 2013 and 2014; and FBI, National Instant Criminal Background Check System Section Federal Denials, 2013 and 2014.

APPENDIX TABLE 6
Prohibited person records in the National Instant Criminal Background Check System Index, 2014

Type of record	January 1, 2014 Total	Submissions Federal	Submissions State*	December 31, 2014 Total	Submissions Federal	Submissions State*	Percent change
Total	11,166,690	6,893,076	4,273,614	12,881,223	7,721,667	5,159,556	15.4%
Felony conviction	1,647,906	966,413	681,493	1,889,892	1,021,660	868,232	14.7%
Under indictment/information	34,222	33,791	431	32,975	32,439	536	-3.6
Fugitive from justice	392,138	6,012	386,126	469,578	6,676	462,902	19.7
Drug user/addict	33,909	16,160	17,749	24,281	12,527	11,754	-28.4
Mental health commitment/ adjudication	3,260,730	191,458	3,069,272	3,774,301	235,998	3,538,303	15.8
Illegal/unlawful alien	5,621,440	5,621,373	67	6,346,095	6,346,012	83	12.9
Dishonorable discharge	10,328	10,295	33	10,524	10,486	38	1.9
Renounced U.S. citizenship	23,807	23,794	13	27,240	27,220	20	14.4
Protection/restraining order	5,321	223	5,098	47,296	273	47,023	788.9
Misdemeanor domestic violence	93,812	21,582	72,230	112,799	23,030	89,769	20.2
Federally denied persons	33,005	0	33,005	30,285	0	30,285	-8.2
State law prohibition	10,072	1,975	8,097	115,957	5,346	110,611	1,051.3

Note: The NICS Index is used exclusively for NICS checks and contains records of persons who are prohibited by federal or state law from receiving or possessing a firearm. For more information on reporting agencies and sample design, see *Methodology*.

*State totals include U. S. territories.

Source: FBI, National Instant Criminal Background Check System Index, 2014.

APPENDIX TABLE 7
Prohibited person records in the National Instant Criminal Background Check System Index, 2013

Type of record	January 1, 2013 Total	Submissions Federal	Submissions State*	December 31, 2013 Total	Submissions Federal	Submissions State*	Percent change
Total	8,323,931	5,526,483	2,797,448	11,166,690	6,893,076	4,273,614	34.2%
Felony conviction	727,255	79,940	647,315	1,647,906	966,413	681,493	126.6%
Under indictment/information	865	505	360	34,222	33,791	431	3,856.3
Fugitive from justice	378,463	3,834	374,629	392,138	6,012	386,126	3.6
Drug user/addict	18,174	11,186	6,988	33,909	16,160	17,749	86.6
Mental health commitment/ adjudication	1,821,217	161,813	1,659,404	3,260,730	191,458	3,069,272	79.0
Illegal/unlawful alien	5,216,732	5,216,675	57	5,621,440	5,621,373	67	7.8
Dishonorable discharge	10,163	10,135	28	10,328	10,295	33	1.6
Renounced U.S. citizenship	20,654	20,649	5	23,807	23,794	13	15.3
Protection/restraining order	4,101	198	3,903	5,321	223	5,098	29.7
Misdemeanor domestic violence	90,199	20,306	69,893	93,812	21,582	72,230	4.0
Federally denied persons	34,746	1	34,745	33,005	0	33,005	-5.0
State law prohibition	1,362	1,241	121	10,072	1,975	8,097	639.5

Note: The NICS Index is used exclusively for NICS checks and contains records of persons who are prohibited by federal or state law from receiving or possessing a firearm. For more information on reporting agencies and sample design, see *Methodology*.

*State totals include U. S. territories.

Source: FBI, National Instant Criminal Background Check System Index, 2013.

APPENDIX TABLE 8
Reasons for denial of firearm transfer and permit applications, December 31, 2014

Jurisdiction	Felony[a]	Misdemeanor[b]	Fugitive from justice	Mental health commitment/ adjudication[c]	Court order[d]	Drug user/ addict[e]	Alcohol abuse[e]	Minor age	Juvenile offense	Unlawful/ illegal alien[f]
Federal	X	X	X	X	X	X	~	X	~	X
District of Columbia	X	X	~	X	X	X	X	X	~	~
State	49	28	15	34	31	31	19	49	27	17
Alabama	X	~	~	X	~	X	X	X	~	~
Alaska	X	~	~	~	X	X	X	X	X	~
Arizona	X	X	~	X	~	~	~	X	X	X
Arkansas	X	~	~	X	X	~	~	X	~	~
California	X	X	~	X	X	X	~	X	X	~
Colorado	X	~	~	~	~	~	~	X	X	~
Connecticut	X	X	~	X	X	~	~	X	X	X
Delaware	X	X	X	X	X	X	X	X	X	~
Florida	X	X	~	X	X	X	X	X	X	~
Georgia	X	X	~	~	~	~	~	X	X	~
Hawaii	X	X	X	X	X	X	X	X	X	X
Idaho	X	~	~	~	~	~	~	X	~	~
Illinois	X	X	~	X	X	X	~	X	X	X
Indiana	X	X	~	X	X	X	X	X	X	~
Iowa	X	X	~	~	X	~	~	X	X	~
Kansas	X	~	~	X	~	X	X	X	X	~
Kentucky	X	~	~	~	~	~	~	X	X	~
Louisiana	X	X	~	~	X	~	~	X	~	~
Maine	X	~	X	X	X	~	~	X	~	~
Maryland	X	X	X	X	X	X	X	X	X	~
Massachusetts	X	X	X	X	X	X	X	X	X	~
Michigan	X	X	~	X	X	~	~	X	~	X
Minnesota	X	X	X	X	X	X	~	X	X	X
Mississippi	X	~	~	~	~	X	X	X	~	~
Missouri	X	~	X	X	~	X	X	X	~	~
Montana	X	X	~	~	X	~	~	X	~	~
Nebraska	X	X	X	~	X	~	~	X	~	~
Nevada	X	~	X	X	X	X	~	X	~	X
New Hampshire	X	~	~	~	X	X	-	X	~	~
New Jersey	X	X	~	X	X	X	X	X	X	~
New Mexico	X	~	~	~	~	~	~	X	~	~
New York	X	X	X	X	X	X	~	X	~	X
North Carolina	X	~	X	X	X	X	~	X	~	X
North Dakota	X	X	~	X	~	~	~	X	~	~
Ohio	X	~	X	X	~	X	X	X	X	~
Oklahoma	X	~	~	X	~	X	X	X	X	~
Oregon	X	X	X	X	~	~	~	X	~	~
Pennsylvania	X	X	X	X	X	X	X	X	X	X
Rhode Island	X	~	X	X	X	X	~	X	~	X
South Carolina	X	~	X	X	~	X	X	X	~	X
South Dakota	X	X	~	~	~	X	~	X	~	~
Tennessee	X	X	~	X	X	X	X	X	~	~
Texas	X	X	~	~	X	X	X	X	~	~
Utah	X	~	~	X	~	X	~	X	X	X
Vermont	~	~	~	~	~	~	~	X	~	~
Virginia	X	X	~	X	X	X	~	X	X	X
Washington	X	X	~	X	X	X	~	X	X	X

Continued on next page

Reasons for denial of firearm transfer and permit applications, December 31, 2014

Jurisdiction	Felony[a]	Misdemeanor[b]	Fugitive from justice	Mental health commitment/ adjudication[c]	Court order[d]	Drug user/ addict[e]	Alcohol abuse[e]	Minor age	Juvenile offense	Unlawful/ illegal alien[f]
West Virginia	X	X	~	X	X	X	X	X	~	X
Wisconsin	X	~	~	X	X	~	~	X	X	~
Wyoming	X	~	~	~	~	~	~	~	~	~

Note: Federal prohibitors in 18 U.S.C. § 922 are the minimum standard nationwide. Table does not show state laws that incorporate federal prohibitions. A jurisdiction may have other prohibitions not listed in the table. Types of firearms, offenses, and dispositions covered by statutes vary by jurisdiction. See *Jurisdiction notes*.

X Indicates a basis under the jurisdiction's laws for prohibition of firearm transfers or possession or for denial of a permit required for a firearm transfer. Concealed carry permit restrictions are not included.

~Not applicable.

[a]An offense with a penalty of imprisonment for 1 year or more or designated a felony by law.

[b]An offense with a penalty of incarceration for less than 1 year or designated a misdemeanor by law. Includes domestic violence offenses and other offenses.

[c]Includes adjudications of mental illness or incapacity and involuntary or voluntary commitments for inpatient or outpatient mental health treatment.

[d]An order to prevent domestic violence, witness intimidation, stalking, or other criminal acts.

[e]A substance-related conviction, addiction to a substance, or intoxication during a firearm transfer.

[f]An illegal alien or a non-U.S. citizen not entitled to an exception that allows firearm possession.

Source: Bureau of Justice Statistics, Firearm Inquiry Statistics program, 2014.

APPENDIX TABLE 9
Agencies conducting firearm background checks, December 31, 2014

| Jurisdiction | Name or description of checking agencies | |
	Purchase check or permit	Exempt carry permit[a]
United States	Federal Bureau of Investigation	---
Alabama	---	---
Alaska	---	Department of Public Safety
Arizona	---	Department of Public Safety
Arkansas	---	State police
California	Department of Justice Firearms Division	---
Colorado	Bureau of Investigation Insta-Check Unit	---
Connecticut	State Police Special Licensing & Firearms	---
Delaware	---	---
District of Columbia	Metropolitan Police Department	---
Florida	Department of Law Enforcement	---
Georgia	---	County probate courts
Hawaii	Police departments	---
Idaho	---	County sheriffs
Illinois	State Police Firearm Owners Identification and Firearm Inquiry Transfer Program units	---
Indiana	---	---
Iowa	County sheriffs	Department of Public Safety / county sheriffs
Kansas	---	Attorney general
Kentucky	---	State police
Louisiana	---	---
Maine	---	---
Maryland	State Police Licensing Division	---
Massachusetts	Police departments	---
Michigan	Sheriffs and police departments	County licensing boards
Minnesota	Sheriffs and police departments	County sheriffs
Mississippi	---	Department of Public Safety
Missouri	---	---
Montana	---	County sheriffs
Nebraska	Sheriffs and police departments	State patrol
Nevada	Department of Public Safety	County sheriffs
New Hampshire	Department of Safety	---
New Jersey	State police /local police departments	---
New Mexico	---	---
New York[b]	Sheriffs and police departments	---
North Carolina	County sheriffs	County sheriffs
North Dakota	---	Bureau of Criminal Investigation
Ohio	---	---
Oklahoma	---	---
Oregon	State Police Firearms Unit	---
Pennsylvania	State Police Firearms Division	---
Rhode Island	Police departments	---
South Carolina	---	Law Enforcement Division
South Dakota	---	---
Tennessee	Bureau of Investigation Tennessee Instant Check System Unit	---
Texas	---	Department of Public Safety
Utah	Bureau of Criminal Identification	Bureau of Criminal Identification
Vermont	---	---
Virginia	State Police Firearms Transaction Program	---
Washington	Sheriffs and police departments	---
West Virginia	---	County sheriffs
Wisconsin	Department of Justice Firearms Unit	---
Wyoming	---	Attorney general

--- FBI conducts purchase checks or jurisdiction has no exempt permits.

[a]Agencies listed issue carry permits that may be used to waive a purchase check.

[b]License required for purchase may also allow carrying.

Source: Bureau of Justice Statistics, Firearm Inquiry Statistics program, 2014.

APPENDIX TABLE 10
National Instant Criminal Background Check System checking agencies, FBI, or state Point of Contact for firearm transfers, 2014

State	FBI conducts checks for all firearms[a]	POC conducts checks for all firearms	POC checks handguns FBI checks long guns	State	FBI conducts checks for all firearms[a]	POC conducts checks for all firearms	POC checks handguns FBI checks long guns
Total	30	13	7	Montana	X	~	~
Alabama	X	~	~	Nebraska[b]	~	~	X
Alaska	X	~	~	Nevada	~	X	~
Arizona	X	~	~	New Hampshire	~	~	X
Arkansas	X	~	~	New Jersey	~	X	~
California	~	X	~	New Mexico	X	~	~
Colorado	~	X	~	New York	X	~	~
Connecticut	~	X	~	North Carolina[b]	~	~	X
Delaware	X	~	~	North Dakota	X	~	~
Florida	~	X	~	Ohio	X	~	~
Georgia	X	~	~	Oklahoma	X	~	~
Hawaii[b]	~	X	~	Oregon	~	X	~
Idaho	X	~	~	Pennsylvania	~	X	~
Illinois	~	X	~	Rhode Island	X	~	~
Indiana	X	~	~	South Carolina	X	~	~
Iowa[b]	~	~	X	South Dakota	X	~	~
Kansas	X	~	~	Tennessee	~	X	~
Kentucky	X	~	~	Texas	X	~	~
Louisiana	X	~	~	Utah	~	X	~
Maine	X	~	~	Vermont	X	~	~
Maryland	~	~	X	Virginia	~	X	~
Massachusetts	X	~	~	Washington[b]	~	~	X
Michigan	X	~	~	West Virginia	X	~	~
Minnesota	X	~	~	Wisconsin	~	~	X
Mississippi	X	~	~	Wyoming	X	~	~
Missouri	X	~	~				

Note: Includes checks on purchases or on permits required for purchase.

X Indicates agency conducting background checks.

~Not applicable.

[a]The FBI also conducts all National Instant Criminal Background Check System checks for American Samoa, the District of Columbia, Guam, Northern Mariana Islands, Puerto Rico, and the U.S. Virgin Islands.

[b]States with multiple Points of Contact.

Source: Bureau of Justice Statistics, Firearm Inquiry Statistics program, 2014.

APPENDIX TABLE 11
Forums for appeals of firearm transfer and permit denials, 2014

Jurisdiction	Denying agency	Other agency	Court system	Jurisdiction	Denying agency	Other agency	Court system
Federal				**Mississippi**			
Instant check	X	~	X	Exempt carry	X	~	X
Alaska				**Montana**			
Exempt carry	X	~	~	Exempt carry	~	~	X
Arizona				**Nebraska**			
Exempt carry	X	~	X	Purchase permit	~	~	X
Arkansas				Exempt carry	X	~	X
Exempt carry	X	~	X	**Nevada**			
California				Instant check	X	~	~
Other approval	X	~	~	Exempt carry	~	~	X
Colorado				**New Hampshire**			
Instant check	X	~	~	Instant check	X	~	X
Connecticut				**New Jersey**			
Instant check	X	~	~	Instant check	X	~	~
Purchase permit	~	X	~	Purchase permit	~	~	X
District of Columbia				**North Carolina**			
Purchase permit	X	~	X	Purchase permit	~	~	X
Florida				Exempt carry	~	~	X
Instant check	X	~	~	**North Dakota**			
Georgia				Exempt carry	X	~	X
Exempt carry	~	~	X	**Oregon**			
Idaho				Instant check	X	~	~
Exempt carry	~	~	X	**Pennsylvania**			
Illinois				Instant check	X	X	X
Instant check	X	~	X	**South Carolina**			
Purchase permit	X	~	X	Exempt carry	X	~	~
Iowa				**Tennessee**			
Purchase permit	~	~	X	Instant check	X	~	~
Exempt carry	~	~	X	**Texas**			
Kansas				Exempt carry	~	~	X
Exempt carry	X	X	X	**Utah**			
Kentucky				Instant check	X	~	~
Exempt carry	X	~	X	Exempt carry	~	X	~
Maryland				**Virginia**			
Other approval	X	~	X	Instant check	X	~	X
Purchase permit	X	~	X	**Washington**			
Massachusetts				Other approval	~	~	X
Purchase permit	~	~	X	**Wisconsin**			
Michigan				Instant check	X	~	X
Purchase permit	~	~	X	**Wyoming**			
Exempt carry	~	~	X	Exempt carry	X	~	X
Minnesota							
Purchase permit	~	~	X				
Exempt carry	X	~	X				

X Indicates statute or regulation provides a specific procedure to appeal a denial of a firearm transfer or permit. In addition, some denying agencies may reconsider a decision even if not required to do so by law.

~Not applicable.

Source: Bureau of Justice Statistics, Firearm Inquiry Statistics program, 2014.

The Bureau of Justice Statistics (BJS) of the U.S. Department of Justice is the principal federal agency responsible for measuring crime, criminal victimization, criminal offenders, victims of crime, correlates of crime, and the operation of criminal and civil justice systems at the federal, state, tribal, and local levels. BJS collects, analyzes, and disseminates reliable and valid statistics on crime and justice systems in the United States, supports improvements to state and local criminal justice information systems, and participates with national and international organizations to develop and recommend national standards for justice statistics. Jeri M. Mulrow is acting director.

The Regional Justice Information Service (REJIS) prepared these tables under the supervision of Allina D. Lee of BJS. Allen Beck, Ph.D., of BJS provided statistical consultation. Trent D. Buskirk, Ph.D., of REJIS provided statistical and sample design consultation. The tables were prepared under BJS cooperative agreement #2011-BJ-CX-K017. The BJS-sponsored Firearm Inquiry Statistics program collects information on firearm background checks conducted by state and local agencies and combines this information with Federal Bureau of Investigation National Instant Criminal Background Check System transaction data to create a national estimate of the number of applications received and denied annually pursuant to the Brady Handgun Violence Prevention Act of 1993 and similar state laws.

Morgan Young edited the report. Barbara Quinn produced the report.

June 2016, NCJ 249849

NCJ249849

Office of Justice Programs
Innovation • Partnerships • Safer Neighborhoods
www.ojp.usdoj.gov

Bureau of Justice Statistics
Special Report

January 2003, NCJ 195670

Education and Correctional Populations

By Caroline Wolf Harlow, Ph.D.
BJS Statistician

About 41% of inmates in the Nation's State and Federal prisons and local jails in 1997 and 31% of probationers had not completed high school or its equivalent. In comparison, 18% of the general population age 18 or older had not finished the 12th grade.

Between 1991 and 1997, the percent of inmates in State prison without a high school diploma or GED remained the same — 40% in 1997 and 41% in 1991. Of inmates in State prisons, 293,000 in 1991 and 420,600 in 1997 had entered prison without a high school diploma, a 44% increase.

Over 9 in 10 State prisons provided educational programs for their inmates. Half of State prison inmates reported they had participated in an educational program since their most recent admission to prison. About a quarter of State inmates had taken basic education or high school level courses, and almost a third, vocational training.

Data for this report were taken from the Survey of Inmates in State and Federal Correctional Facilities, 1997 and 1991, the Survey of Inmates in Local Jails, 1996 and 1989, and the Survey of Adults on Probation, 1995, sponsored by the Bureau of Justice Statistics (BJS), the Current Population Survey, 1997, sponsored by the Bureau of

Highlights

Educational attainment for correctional populations and the general population

Educational attainment	Total incarcerated	Prison inmates State	Prison inmates Federal	Local jail inmates	Probationers	General population
Some high school or less	41.3%	39.7%	26.5%	46.5%	30.6%	18.4%
GED	23.4	28.5	22.7	14.1	11.0	...
High school diploma	22.6	20.5	27.0	25.9	34.8	33.2
Postsecondary	12.7	11.4	23.9	13.5	23.6	48.4

... Not available.

• 68% of State prison inmates did not receive a high school diploma.

• About 26% of State prison inmates said they had completed the GED while serving time in a correctional facility.

• The groups of State prison inmates who had not completed high school or the GED included —
    40% of males and
42% of females
    27% of whites, 44% of blacks, and 53% of Hispanics
    52% of inmates 24 or younger and 35% of inmates 45 or older
    61% of noncitizens and 38% of U.S. citizens
    59% with a speech disability, 66% with a learning disability, and 37% without a reported disability
    47% of drug offenders
    12% of those with military service and 44% with no military service.

• Although the percentage of State prison inmates who reported taking education courses while confined fell from 57% in 1991 to 52% in 1997, the number who had participated in an educational program since admission increased from 402,500 inmates in 1991 to 550,000 in 1997.

• The following groups of State prison inmates had participated in an educational program since their most recent admission to prison:
    54% without a high school diploma, 60% with a GED,
42% with a high school diploma, and 43% with postsecondary education
    52% of males and 50% of females
    49% of whites, 54% of blacks, and 53% of Hispanics
    58% who were 24 or younger and 47% of those 45 or older
    54% of noncitizens and 52% of U.S. citizens.

Labor Statistics, and the National Adult Literacy Survey, 1992, sponsored by the National Center for Educational Statistics.

In personal interviews with nationally representative samples of inmates in State and Federal prisons and local jails and of persons on probation, respondents were asked about past educational achievements and recent educational experiences, as well as about their offenses, criminal history, and other characteristics.

The National Adult Literacy Survey, another personal interview survey, assessed the literacy levels of persons in the general population and included a short questionnaire about personal characteristics, including educational attainment.

The Current Population Survey (CPS) primarily collects monthly data on labor force participation from a nationally representative sample of the civilian noninstitutional population. In March of each year the CPS also collects additional information, including educational attainment.

In addition, some information on educational programs conducted in correctional settings from the BJS Census of Local Jails, 1999, and the BJS Census of State and Federal Adult Correctional Facilities, 2000 and 1995, has been used. (See *Methodology* for further information on these data.)

Correctional populations less educated than the general population

Correctional populations — including State and Federal prison inmates, local jail inmates, and probationers — differ substantially in educational attainment from persons 18 and older in the general civilian noninstitutional population.

Correctional populations report lower educational attainment than do those in the general population. An estimated 40% of State prison inmates, 27% of Federal inmates, 47% of inmates in local jails, and 31% of those serving probation sentences had not completed high school or its equivalent while about 18% of the general population failed to attain high school graduation (table 1).

Persons in correctional populations were more likely than those in the general population to have passed a test which indicates the same level of knowledge as those with a high school diploma. The Center for Adult Learning and Educational Credentials of the American Council on Education develops the General Educational Development (GED) test for persons who are not enrolled in a school. The test assesses academic skills and knowledge expected of high school graduates. Employers and educational institutions usually accept the GED as the equivalent of a high school diploma.

For a quarter of State prison inmates, a fifth of Federal inmates, a seventh of jail inmates, and a tenth of probationers, as for about 4% of the general population,* passing the GED testing process was the highest level of education they attained.

Participation in college-level courses or post-secondary vocational classes was less common for those in correctional populations than for persons in the general population. An estimated 11% of State prison inmates, 24% of Federal inmates, 14% of jail inmates, and 24% of probationers attended some college or other postsecondary institution compared to 48% in the general population.

———
*National Center for Education Statistics, National Adult Literacy Survey, 1992, "Adult Literacy in America," table 1.1, page 18.

Table 1. Educational attainment for State and Federal prison inmates, 1997 and 1991, local jail inmates, 1996 and 1989, probationers, 1995, and the general population, 1997

| | Prison inmates | | | | Local jail inmates | | Proba- | General |
| | State | | Federal | | | | tioners | population |
Educational attainment	1997	1991	1997	1991	1996	1989		
8th grade or less	14.2%	14.3%	12.0%	11.0%	13.1%	15.6%	8.4%	7.2%
Some high school	25.5	26.9	14.5	12.3	33.4	38.2	22.2	11.2
GED*	28.5	24.6	22.7	22.6	14.1	9.2	11.0	...
High school diploma	20.5	21.8	27.0	25.9	25.9	24.0	34.8	33.2
Postsecondary/some college	9.0	10.1	15.8	18.8	10.3	10.3	18.8	26.4
College graduate or more	2.4	2.3	8.1	9.3	3.2	2.8	4.8	22.0
Number	1,055,495	706,173	88,705	53,677	503,599	393,111	2,029,866	192,352,084

Note: Probationers have been excluded from the general population. General population includes the noninstitutional population 18 or older. Detail may not add to 100% due to rounding.
*General Educational Development certificate.
...Not available in the Current Population Survey.

Sources: BJS, Survey of Inmates in State and Federal Correctional Facilities, 1997 and 1991; BJS, Survey of Inmates in Local Jails, 1996 and 1989; BJS, Survey of Adults on Probation, 1995; Bureau of Labor Statistics, Current Population Survey, March supplement, 1997.

Numbers of prison inmates without a high school education increased from 1991 to 1997

The percentage of State inmates without a high school diploma remained about the same between the 1991 and 1997 prisoner surveys. About 40% in 1997 and 41% in 1991 did not have a high school diploma or GED. In Federal prisons, 23% in 1991 and 27% in 1997, a small but significant increase, had not finished.

An estimated 420,600 State prison inmates in 1997 and 293,000 in 1991 did not have a high school education or a GED — over a third more in 1997 compared to 1991. In Federal prisons, almost twice as many, 23,500 in 1997 and 12,600 in 1991, fit that category.

Three-quarters of State prison inmates did not earn a high school diploma

Inmate survey respondents who did not complete high school were asked if they had received a GED. Respondents who had completed the 12th grade or who had attended college-level courses or post-secondary vocational classes were asked if they

had a high school diploma or a GED. All inmates who completed less than 12 years of schooling and those who received a GED were classified as not completing high school. About 75% of State prison inmates, almost 59% of Federal inmates, and 69% of jail inmates did not complete high school (table 2).

About 35% of State inmates, 33% of Federal inmates, 22% of jail inmates, and 11% of probationers had successfully passed the GED. Of those with a GED, at least 7 in 10 State and Federal inmates obtained their GED while incarcerated.

Jail inmates and the general population reported why they dropped out of school

Approximately 1 in 6 jail inmates dropped out of school because they were convicted of a crime, sent to a correctional facility, or otherwise involved in illegal activities.

Over a third of jail inmates and a sixth of the general population said the main reason they quit school was because of academic problems, behavior problems, or lost interest. About a fifth

of jail inmates and two-fifths of the general population gave economic reasons for leaving school, primarily going to work, joining the military, or needing money.

Most important reason for dropping out of school	Local jail inmates	General population
Behavior or academic problems or lost interest	34.9%	17.2%
Family or personal problems	16.4	18.6
Convicted of crime, sent to correctional facility	11.1	...
Involved in illegal activities	4.8	...
Went to work or the military	13.0	23.9
Financial problems	8.8	15.3
Pregnancy	3.7	6.4
Other	1.1	17.7
No reason	6.3	0.9

Note: General population includes persons 18 or older.
...Not available.

Sources: BJS, Survey of Inmates in Local Jail, 1996; National Center for Educational Statistics, National Adult Literacy Survey, 1992.

Table 2. High school completion, for State and Federal prison inmates, 1997, local jail inmates, 1996, and probationers, 1995

High school completion	Prison Inmates		Local jail inmates	Probationers
	State	Federal		
Completed high school	25.5%	40.6%	31.1%	58.4%
Did not complete high school[a]	74.5	59.4	68.9	41.6
Earned GED[b]	34.8	32.8	22.3	11.0
Since admission	8.3	9.4	...	...
Other incarceration	17.4	14.0	...	...
Outside prison/jail	9.1	9.4	...	...
Did not earn GED	39.7	26.5	46.6	30.6

Note: For the Survey of Inmates in State and Federal Correctional Facilities and the Survey of Inmates in Local Jails, all respondents, regardless of educational attainment, were asked if they received a GED. For the Survey of Adults on Probation, only those respondents who had not completed 12th grade were asked if they had a GED.
Detail may not add to total due to rounding.
...Not available.
[a]Included in those who did not complete high school were inmates who completed less than 12 years of schooling and those who received a GED.
[b]General Educational Development certificate.

Sources: BJS, Survey of Inmates in State and Federal Correctional Facilities, 1997; BJS, Survey of Inmates in Local Jails, 1996; BJS, Survey of Adults on Probation, 1995.

Educational attainment defined as the last completed year of school

The definitions and numbers in this report are as consistent as possible with those of the National Center for Educational Statistics and the Bureau of Labor Statistics. Persons who did not complete a full year of college were classified as persons with a high school diploma, and seniors who did not complete their last year were coded as having some college but no college degree. Any person with 12 or fewer grades of school and a GED were included in the group with a GED.

Some numbers in this report may differ from those in previously published BJS reports for which other definitions were used.

9 in 10 State prisons offer educational programs

About 9 in 10 State prisons, all Federal prisons, and almost 9 in 10 private prisons provide educational programs for their inmates (table 3). These facilities generally hold persons sentenced to at least a year in prison, giving inmates a long period to concentrate on achieving educational goals. By contrast, local jails house persons from arraignment through conviction and for short sentences. Approximately 6 in 10 local jails provide educational programs for their inmates, even though jail inmates generally stay for short time periods.

The percent of State and private prisons offering educational programs to their inmates increased from 1995 to 2000. In 1995, 88% of State prisons and 72% of private prisons provided

educational programs; in 2000, 91% of State prisons and 88% of private prisons offered educational opportunities. During this period all Federal prisons offered courses.

Secondary education programs, which focus on preparing for the GED, were the most prevalent type of courses in 2000. Over 8 in 10 State prisons, almost all Federal prisons, about 7 in 10 private prisons, and over half of jails offered high school level classes. Next most common were classes in basic arithmetic and reading, with 8 in 10 State prisons, almost all Federal prisons, 6 in 10 private prisons, and 1 in 4 local jails offering basic education programs.

In State prisons between 1995 and 2000, the percentages of prisons offering classes increased for basic education (76% to 80%), high school courses

(80% to 84%), and special education programs (33% to 40%), while the percentage with college classes went down (31% to 27%).

Vocational training, special programs designed to train participants for a job, were reported by 56% of State prisons, 94% of Federal prisons, 44% of private prisons, and 7% of local jails.

Over half of inmates reported taking an educational program since their most recent prison admission

Many inmates have taken advantage of educational opportunities while they were incarcerated. About 52% of State prison inmates, 57% of Federal inmates, 14% of jail inmates, and 23% of probationers said they had taken education classes since admission to a correctional facility or their most recent sentence to probation (table 4).

Table 3. Educational programs offered in State, Federal, and private prisons, 2000 and 1995, and local jails, 1999.

Educational programs	State prisons		Federal prisons		Private prisons		Local jails
	2000	1995	2000	1995	2000	1995	1999
With an education program	91.2%	88.0%	100.0%	100.0%	87.6%	71.8%	60.3%
Basic adult education	80.4	76.0	97.4	92.0	61.6	40.0	24.7
Secondary education	83.6	80.3	98.7	100.0	70.7	51.8	54.8
College courses	26.7	31.4	80.5	68.8	27.3	18.2	3.4
Special education	39.6	33.4	59.7	34.8	21.9	27.3	10.8
Vocational training	55.7	54.5	93.5	73.2	44.2	25.5	6.5
Study release programs	7.7	9.3	6.5	5.4	28.9	32.7	9.3
Without an education program	8.8	12.0	0.0	0.0	12.4	28.2	39.7
Number of facilities	1,307	1,278	*	*	242	110	2,819

Note: Detail may not add to total because facilities may have more than one educational program.
*Changed definitions prevent meaningful comparisons of the numbers of Federal facilities, 1995 and 2000.

Sources: BJS, Census of State and Federal Adult Correctional Facilities, 2000 and 1995; BJS, Census of Jails, 1999.

Table 4. Participation in educational programs since most recent incarceration or sentence, for State and Federal prison inmates, 1997 and 1991, for local jail inmates, 1996, and for probationers, 1995

Educational programs	Prison inmates				Local jail inmates	Probationers
	State		Federal			
	1997	1991	1997	1991		
Total	51.9%	56.6%	56.4%	67.0%	14.1%	22.9%
Basic	3.1	5.3	1.9	10.4	0.8	0.4
GED/high school	23.4	27.3	23.0	27.3	8.6	7.8
College courses	9.9	13.9	12.9	18.9	1.0	6.1
English as a second language	1.2	...	5.7	...	...	...
Vocational	32.2	31.2	31.0	29.4	4.8	7.0
Other	2.6	2.6	5.6	8.4	2.1	3.4
Number of inmates	1,046,136	709,042	87,624	53,753	501,159	2,055,942

Note: Detail may not add to total due to rounding or inmates' participation in more than one educational program.
...Not available.

Sources: BJS, Survey of Inmates in State and Federal Correctional Facilities, 1997 and 1991; BJS, Survey of Inmates in Local Jails, 1996; BJS, Survey of Adults on Probation, 1995.

State and Federal inmates had higher participation rates in 1991 than in 1997. In 1991, 57% of State prison inmates and 67% of Federal inmates said they had taken educational courses since entering prison.

Though the rate of participation decreased, the number of State prison inmates educated in prison increased 37% — from 402,500 in 1991 to 550,000 in 1997 — and the number of Federal inmates increased 39% — from 36,200 to 50,300. At the same time, the total number of inmates in State prisons increased 49% and in Federal prisons 65%. Participation in prison education programs did not expand as rapidly as the population, and as a result the percentage of inmates in educational programs fell.

Vocational programs and high school or GED preparation classes were most popular. About a third of State and Federal prison inmates had participated in vocational training to learn particular job skills. About a quarter of prison inmates took high school level classes. Among jail inmates, 5% had vocational training and 9%, high school classes.

State prisoners without a high school diploma more likely to have taken classes since admission

Prison educational resources were concentrated on those with the greatest need — those without a high school diploma. Approximately 54% of State inmates who had not completed the 12th grade and 61% with a GED reported that they had participated in educational programs since being admitted to prison (table 5). In contrast, about 4 in 10 with a high school diploma or postsecondary courses participated in an educational program.

More than a third of those who did not have a high school diploma or GED took high school classes, and a quarter participated in a vocational training opportunity. About 28% of those with a GED were enrolled in a high school program and 44% were in vocational education.

Women in State prison better educated than men

Women in State prisons were more likely than men to have received a high school diploma or attended an institution of higher learning. About 36% of women and 32% of men had graduated from high school or attended a postsecondary institution (table 6).

Women in State prison were more likely to have completed high school than men and less likely to have passed the GED. Approximately 30% of women and 25% of men received high school diplomas; 28% of women and 35% of men had a GED. About 4 in 10 men and women failed to graduate from high school or pass the GED test.

About half of female and male inmates had participated in an educational program since admission. About 21% of women and 24% of men took high school or GED classes; 30% of women and 32% of men were enrolled in a vocational program.

Table 5. Participation in educational programs since most recent admission, by educational attainment, for State prison inmates, 1997

	State prison inmates with –			
Educational programs	Less than high school diploma	GED	High school diploma	Postsecondary/ college
Total	53.5%	60.4%	42.0%	42.8%
Basic	6.4	1.4	0.8	0.4
GED/high school	36.1	28.0	4.6	2.0
College courses	0.7	16.5	13.5	18.9
English as a second language	2.0	0.6	0.9	0.6
Vocational	24.3	43.7	31.8	31.6
Other	1.5	3.1	3.3	4.2
Number of prison inmates	413,759	298,912	214,439	119,027

Note: Detail may not add to total due to rounding or inmates' participation in more than one educational program.

Source: BJS, Survey of Inmates in State and Federal Correctional Facilities, 1997.

Table 6. Education, by gender for State prison inmates, 1997

	Percent of State prison inmates	
	Male	Female
Educational attainment		
8th grade or less	14.3%	13.6%
Some high school	25.3	28.2
GED	28.9	22.3
High school diploma	20.4	21.6
Postsecondary/ some college	8.8	11.2
College graduate	2.3	3.1
High school completion		
Completed high school	25.2%	30.3%
Earned GED	35.2	27.9
In prison/jail	26.3	15.9
Ouside prison/jail	8.9	11.9
Educational programs		
Total	52.0%	50.1%
Basic	3.1	3.3
GED/high school	23.6	21.3
College	10.0	9.1
English as a second language	1.2	0.5
Vocational	32.4	29.5
Other	2.5	3.8
Number of prison inmates	989,419	66,076

Note: Detail may not add to total due to rounding or inmates' participation in more than one educational program.

Source: BJS, Survey of Inmates in State and Federal Correctional Facilities, 1997.

Minority State prison inmates less likely than whites to have a high school diploma or GED

Minority State inmates were generally less educated than their white peers. About 44% of black State prison inmates and 53% of Hispanic inmates had not graduated from high school or received a GED compared to 27% of whites in State prisons (table 7).

Minorities were less likely than whites to have attended college or some other institution of higher learning. About 1 in 10 blacks and 1 in 13 Hispanics had studied beyond high school compared to 1 in 7 whites. Minorities were also less likely than whites to have earned a high school diploma or a GED: 26% of blacks and 17% of Hispanics, compared to 30% of whites, had a high school diploma; 30% of blacks and Hispanics passed the GED compared to 43% of whites.

Prison staff had concentrated educational services to those most in need of further learning. Higher percentages of blacks and Hispanics, compared to whites, had taken educational classes in prison — about 54% of blacks, 53% of Hispanics, and 49% of whites. About a quarter of minorities were enrolled in high school or GED classes while 34% of blacks and 29% of Hispanics took vocational training.

Table 7. Education, by race/Hispanic origin, for State prison inmates, 1997

	Percent of State prison inmates		
	White	Black	Hispanic
Educational attainment			
8th grade or less	10.9%	11.7%	27.9%
Some high school	16.3	32.4	25.1
GED	35.2	24.8	24.7
High school diploma	22.8	21.0	14.9
Postsecondary/some college	11.4	8.4	5.5
College graduate or more	3.5	1.6	1.9
High school completion			
Completed high school	29.9%	25.5%	17.2
Earned GED	42.9	30.4	29.7
In prison/jail	30.0	23.2	23.4
Outside prison/jail	12.9	7.2	6.3
Educational programs after admission			
Total	48.8%	53.8%	52.6
Basic	2.1	3.3	4.8
GED/high school	18.7	26.1	25.4
College	12.4	9.0	7.1
English as a second language	0.1	0.1	6.4
Vocational	32.0	33.7	29.1
Other	3.0	2.5	1.8
Number of prison inmates	351,742	490,384	179,301

Note: Detail may not add to total due to rounding or inmates' participation in more than one educational program.

Source: BJS, Survey of Inmates in State and Federal Correctional Facilities, 1997.

White, black, and Hispanic male inmates ages 20 through 39 markedly less educated than their counterparts in the general population

Males between the ages of 20 and 39 dominate the State prison population; they constituted about two-thirds of all State prison inmates in 1997. Approximately 21% of the State prison population were white males between the ages of 20 and 39, 33% were black males in that age range, and 12% were Hispanics. In the general population these groups constituted a significantly smaller percentage of the total population — 22%. White males ages 20 through 39 were 17% of the general population, and blacks and Hispanics of any race about 3% each.

Within the 20 through 39 age group, male inmates consistently had lower academic achievement than their counterparts in the general population. Young white and black male inmates were about twice as likely as their counterparts in the general population to have not completed high school or its equivalent — (14% versus 28% for whites and 16% versus 44% for blacks). Young Hispanic males' educational achievement did not differ by such magnitude; 52% in prison and 41% in the general population did not have a high school diploma or its equivalent.

Four times as many young males in the general population as in the prison population had attended some college classes or postsecondary courses — 54% of whites in the general population and 11% in prison, 44% of blacks in the general population and 8% in prison, and 32% of Hispanics in the general population and 7% in prison.

Educational attainment of males, ages 20 through 39, by race/Hispanic origin, for State prison inmates and the general population

	Percent of males ages 20 through 39 by race/Hispanic origin					
	White		Black		Hispanic	
Educational attainment	General population	State prison inmates	General population	State prison inmates	General population	State prison inmates
8th grade or less	4.3%	9.9%	2.3%	9.9%	20.9%	24.1%
Some high school	9.6	17.8	13.3	34.0	20.4	27.7
High school diploma	32.1	61.0	40.5	47.9	27.0	41.6
Postsecondary/ some college	30.7	9.3	32.4	7.1	22.8	5.3
College graduate or more	23.4	1.9	11.5	1.1	8.9	1.4

Note: Probationers excluded from general population. Detail may not add to 100% due to rounding.

Sources: BJS, Survey of Inmates in State and Federal Correctional Facilities, 1997; Bureau of Labor Statistics, Current Population Survey, March supplement, 1997.

Young inmates less well educated than older inmates

Young State inmates were more likely than older inmates to have failed to complete high school or its equivalent. Over half of inmates 24 or younger had not completed the 12th grade or the GED (52%), while just over a third of those 35 or older did not have a high school diploma or GED (34% for those 35-44 and 35% for those 45 or older) (table 8).

Relatively few young inmates had pursued a post secondary education, particularly compared to older inmates. An estimated 4% of those 24 or younger, 10% of those 25 to 34, 14% of those 35 to 44, and 21% of those 45 or older had attended college or another postsecondary institution.

About a third in each age group had earned a GED. Over 7 in 10 of those earning their GED had done so in a correctional facility.

Young inmates were more likely than older ones to have participated in an educational program since their admission to prison (58% for those 24 or younger, 52% of those 25 to 34, 50% of those 34 to 44, and 47% of those 45 and older). While about 3 in 10 in all age groups had been enrolled in a vocational program, higher percentages of young inmates compared to older groups were enrolled in GED or high school courses (36% of those 24 or younger and 15% of those 45 or older).

Inmates with military service better educated than those who had not served

About 88% of State inmates who had served in the Army, Navy, Air Force, Coast Guard, Marines, or other military service and 56% who had not been in the military had completed high school or its equivalent and may have enrolled in postsecondary courses (table 9). Some of this difference can be explained because persons who have served in the Armed Forces meet high entrance requirements at enlistment and may subsequently be trained while serving in the Armed Forces.

Half of inmates with military service obtained a high school diploma and over a third passed the GED; less than a quarter who did not serve in the armed forces obtained a high school diploma and about a third a GED.

Since fewer inmates (12%) with military experience had not completed high school or a GED compared to those without military service

---

Table 8. Education, by age, for State prison inmates, 1997

| | Percent of State prison inmates | | | |
| | Age | | | |
	24 or younger	25-34	35-44	45 or older
Educational attainment				
8th grade or less	16.3%	12.1%	12.7%	20.7%
Some high school	35.3	27.2	21.7	13.9
GED	31.2	29.4	27.8	23.1
High school diploma	13.6	21.5	23.5	21.3
Postsecondary/ some college	3.6	8.3	11.3	14.2
College graduate or more	0.1	1.5	3.0	6.9
High school completion				
Completed high school	14.1%	25.4%	30.0%	33.4%
Earned GED	34.4	35.3	35.5	32.0
In prison/jail	27.4	26.3	25.0	22.3
Outside prison/jail	6.9	9.0	10.5	9.6
Educational programs since admission				
Total	57.8%	52.4%	49.6%	46.5%
Basic	2.5	3.0	3.2	4.3
GED/high school	35.5	23.3	19.0	15.4
College	6.4	10.1	11.4	11.6
English as a second language	0.8	1.1	1.4	1.6
Vocational	30.5	34.0	32.5	28.7
Other	2.3	2.5	2.9	2.8
Number of prison inmates	208,955	402,693	310,405	133,442

Note: Detail may not add to total due to rounding or inmates' participation in more than one educational program.

Source: BJS, Survey of Inmates in State and Federal Correctional Facilities, 1997.

Table 9. Education, by military service, for State prison inmates, 1997

| | Percent of State prison inmates | |
| | Military service | |
	Yes	No
Educational attainment		
8th grade or less	4.4%	15.6%
Some high school	7.4	28.1
GED	27.2	28.7
High school diploma	32.5	18.8
Postsecondary/some college	22.2	7.1
College graduate or more	6.2	1.8
High school completion		
Completed high school	49.9%	22.0%
Earned GED	38.3	34.3
In prison/jail	18.7	26.7
Outside prison/jail	19.6	7.6
Educational programs since admission		
Total	47.7%	52.5%
Basic	1.3	3.4
GED/high school	9.9	25.4
College	16.9	8.9
English as a second language	0.4	1.3
Vocational	35.6	31.7
Other	2.8	2.6
Number of prison inmates	132,178	922,715

Note: Detail may not add to total due to rounding or inmates' participation in more than one educational program.

Source: BJS, Survey of Inmates in State and Federal Correctional Facilities, 1997.

(44%), fewer had enrolled in high school/GED classes since their admission to prison. A tenth of those with military service and a quarter without had taken high school or GED classes since admission. About 17% with a military career and 9% without had postsecondary courses.

61% of noncitizens had not completed high school or a GED

Noncitizens, who may or may not speak English fluently, are less likely than citizens to have completed high school or its equivalent. An estimated 61% of noncitizens and 38% of in-

mates with U.S. citizenship had not graduated from high school or obtained a GED (table 10). Aliens were less likely than citizens to have received a high school diploma (19% versus 26%) or a GED (20% versus 36%).

Just over half of both aliens (54%) and citizens (52%) had been in an educational program since admission. About 15% of aliens were taking a course in English as a second language. A quarter of both citizens and aliens were studying at the high school level.

Inmates raised without two parents less likely to have a high school diploma or a GED

State prison inmates who grew up in homes without two parents, with an incarcerated parent, or on welfare or in subsidized housing were less likely than other inmates to have obtained a high school diploma/GED or attended a postsecondary institution.

A larger percentage of State prison inmates who were raised by a single parent or other adult, including relatives, friends, or other adults, compared to those who lived in a two parent household, failed to obtain a high school diploma or pass the GED; 43% of inmates raised by one parent, 47% by others, and 34% by both parents did not complete a high school diploma/GED (table 11).

Table 10. Education, by citizenship, for State prison inmates, 1997

	Percent of State prison inmates having citizenship in —	
	USA	Other countries
Educational attainment		
8th grade or less	12.8%	40.3%
Some high school	25.7	20.5
GED	29.2	15.6
High school diploma	20.8	14.2
Some college	9.2	5.8
College graduate or more	2.3	3.7
High school completion		
Completed high school	25.9%	18.8%
Earned GED	35.6	20.2
In prison/jail	26.2	15.0
Outside prison/jail	9.3	5.3
Educational programs since admission		
Total	51.8%	54.3%
Basic	3.0	6.1
GED/high school	23.4	24.5
College	10.2	4.4
English as a second language	0.4	15.1
Vocational	32.5	27.0
Other	2.7	1.4
Number of prison inmates	1,001,304	52,613

Note: Detail may not add to total due to rounding or inmates' participation in more than one educational program.

Source: BJS, Survey of Inmates in State and Federal Correctional Facilities, 1997.

Table 11. Educational attainment of State prison inmates, by characteristics of their family and background, 1997

		Educational attainment			
Background characteristics	Number	Less than high school	GED	High school diploma	Postsecondary/ some college
Lived with growing up					
Both parents	463,900	34.4%	26.9%	24.2%	14.5%
Single parent	446,873	42.7	30.6	18.0	8.8
Other	139,525	47.4	27.4	16.3	9.0
Parent ever incarcerated	190,560	43.2%	34.4%	16.1%	6.3%
Parent never incarcerated	849,170	38.8	27.3	21.5	12.5
Parent received welfare or inmate lived in public housing	427,097	46.9%	30.4%	16.1%	6.6%
Parent did not receive welfare and inmate did not live in public housing	619,605	34.5	27.4	23.5	14.7
Parent abused alcohol or drugs	332,971	38.7%	33.8%	18.5%	9.0%
Parent did not abuse alcohol or drugs	711,567	40.0	26.1	21.4	12.5
Peers engaged in illegal activity while growing up	792,560	38.7%	31.9%	19.3%	10.0%
Peers did not engage in any illegal activity	255,476	42.1	18.3	24.1	15.5

Note: Detail may not add to 100% due to rounding.

Source: BJS, Survey of Inmates in State and Federal Correctional Facilities, 1997.

Table 12. Educational attainment, by presence of selected disabilities, for State prison inmates, 1997

| Educational attainment | None | Disabilities | | | | |
		Total*	Learning	Speech	Physical	Mental condition
8th grade or less	11.9%	17.5%	30.3%	24.8%	16.4%	17.3%
Some high school	24.9	26.4	35.8	33.9	23.9	24.1
GED	30.4	25.6	16.5	19.0	25.6	27.5
High school diploma	21.3	19.3	14.1	15.2	20.6	19.0
Some college	9.1	8.9	3.0	6.1	10.6	9.4
College graduate or more	2.3	2.3	0.2	1.0	2.9	2.7
Number of prison inmates	636,443	417,776	103,789	39,166	125,257	169,904

Note: Detail may not add to 100% due to rounding.
*Total disability includes a limiting condition, difficulty seeing, difficulty hearing, learning disability, speech disability, physical disability, and mental or emotional condition.

Source: BJS, Survey of Inmates in State and Federal Correctional Facilities, 1997.

Inmates who reported that a parent had been incarcerated were less likely to have completed 11th grade at most, compared to inmates who did not have a parent serve time in a correctional institution (43% versus 39%). Among inmates with an incarcerated parent, twice as many received a GED as their final educational achievement as received a high school diploma (34% versus 16%).

An estimated 47% of inmates who reported that they had either received welfare or lived in publicly-supported housing and 35% who received no government aid did not finish high school. Those who received public assistance were likely to obtain a GED as their highest level of attainment; 30% received a GED compared to 16% who completed high school.

66% of State prison inmates with learning disabilities did not complete high school or a GED

Among inmates who reported a disability — such as a limiting condition, difficulty seeing or hearing, a learning, speech or physical disability, or a mental or emotional condition — about 44% did not finish high school or its equivalent (table 12). Thirty-seven percent of those without a disability did not complete high school.

Two-thirds with a learning disability and 6 in 10 with a speech disability did not complete 12th grade or a GED.

47% of drug offenders did not have a high school diploma or a GED

Almost half of State prison inmates serving their sentence for selling or using illegal drugs had not graduated from high school or passed the GED (table 13). About 4 in 10 inmates serving a sentence for a violent or property offense had not finished high school. Violent offenses include homicide, sexual assault, robbery, and assault, and property crimes include burglary, larceny/theft, motor vehicle theft, and fraud. An estimated 42% of those in prison for a public-order offense — primarily weapons, obstruction of justice, and violations of supervised release — did not complete high school or its equivalent.

Table 13. Educational attainment, by offense, for State prison inmates, 1997

| Educational attainment | Offense | | | |
	Violent	Property	Drug	Public-order
8th grade or less	14.9%	12.0%	15.0%	14.7%
Some high school	22.3	25.9	31.6	27.0
GED	32.0	30.1	21.1	25.1
High school diploma	20.1	19.8	21.1	21.2
Postsecondary/some college	8.6	9.6	8.9	9.4
College graduate or more	2.2	2.5	2.3	2.5
Number of prison inmates	492,398	229,262	215,644	102,707

Note: Detail may not add to 100% due to rounding.

Source: BJS, Survey of Inmates in State and Federal Correctional Facilities, 1997.

Inmate unemployment before admission varied with education

Approximately 38% of inmates who completed 11 years or less of school were not working before entry to prison (table 14). Unemployment was lower for those with a GED (32%), a high school diploma (25%), or education beyond high school (21%). About 20% without a high school diploma, 19% with a GED, 14% with a high school diploma, and 13% with training beyond high school were not looking for work.

Official labor statistics exclude persons not looking for work. Using that definition, the unemployment rate for State prison inmates at admission was 22% for those with less than a high school diploma, 15% for those with a high school diploma/GED, and 9% with education beyond high school. Of all inmates, 17% were unemployed at admission. From 1990 to 1997 when 9 in 10 inmates entered prison, national unemployment ranged from 7.5% in 1992 to 4.9% in 1997. In 1997 unemployment in the general population was 8.1% for those 25 or older without a high school diploma/GED, 4.3% for high school graduates, and 2.6% for those educated beyond high school. (See: <http://www.bls.gov/cps/#empstat> tables 1 and 7.)

Better educated inmates were more likely to receive wage income. While 57% of those with less than a high school education received wages, 76% with a postsecondary education had wage income. Those without a high school diploma/GED were more likely than those with training after high school to have income from family or friends (20% versus 12%), or from welfare (11% versus 8%). A seventh of those with some postsecondary training and almost a third without a high school diploma had lived with persons who received government assistance.

Less educated inmates more likely than more educated to be recidivists

State prison inmates without a high school diploma and those with a GED were more likely to have a prior sen-

tence than those with a diploma or some college or other postsecondary courses. About 77% who did not complete high school or a GED, 81% with a GED, 71% who finished high school, and 66% with some college were recidivists (table 15).

Less educated inmates were more likely than those with more education to have been sentenced as a juvenile. Approximately 40% without a high school diploma, 45% with a GED, 26% with a high school diploma, and 21%

Table 14. Economic and life style characteristics prior to admission, by educational attainment, for State prison inmates, 1997

| | Percent of State prison inmates | | | |
	Less than high school diploma	GED	High school diploma	Post-secondary/ some college
Employment in month before arrest[a]				
Full time	47.7%	56.4%	63.8%	69.9%
Part time	14.8	11.9	11.3	9.0
Looking for work	17.3	13.1	11.0	7.8
Not looking for work	20.2	18.6	13.9	13.2
Income sources in month before arrest				
Wages	57.1%	64.4%	70.7%	75.9%
Illegal sources	23.3	32.3	24.4	25.9
Family/friends	19.8	20.8	15.9	12.1
Transfer payments	18.4	12.7	14.1	14.8
Welfare	11.0	7.8	7.7	7.5
Supplemental Security Income or Social Security	7.4	3.8	5.3	5.4
Compensation payments	1.5	2.1	2.5	3.6
Investments	0.5	1.4	1.6	7.7
Other[b]	1.4	2.1	2.6	6.9
Personal income in month before arrest				
Less than $1,000	63.3%	51.7%	47.4%	32.7%
$1,000 to $1,999	21.6	25.9	29.5	28.7
$2,000 to $4,999	8.9	13.2	14.6	24.8
$5,000 or more	6.3	9.2	8.5	13.8
Homeless in year before admission	11.6%	10.6%	10.0%	8.2%
Number of persons in household				
Lived alone	16.5%	16.9%	20.7%	25.1%
Lived with one other person	17.7	21.5	23.0	24.2
Household totaled 3 to 5 persons	49.8	50.8	47.6	43.5
Household totaled 6 or more	16.0	10.8	8.7	7.2
Lived with persons who received welfare	31.5%	24.5%	19.3%	14.2%

Note: Detail may not add to total due to rounding or inmates had more than one income source.
[a]Excludes inmates not free at least 1 month before arrest.
[b]Includes pension, alimony, educational assistance, and other income sources.
Source: BJS, Survey of Inmates in State and Federal Correctional Facilities, 1997.

Table 15. Current and prior sentences, by educational attainment, for State prison inmates, 1997

| | Percent of State prison inmates | | | |
Current and prior sentences	Less than high school diploma	GED	High school diploma	Post-secondary/ some college
First time offender	22.6%	18.8%	28.7%	33.8%
For violent offense	12.7	13.8	18.6	20.8
For other offense	10.0	5.0	10.1	13.0
Prior sentences as a juvenile	40.1	45.2	26.3	20.7
To incarceration	18.8	21.8	11.6	9.7
To probation only	21.3	23.4	14.7	11.1
Prior sentences as an adult only	37.3	36.0	45.0	45.4
To incarceration	26.0	26.0	30.5	31.7
To probation only	11.3	10.0	14.5	13.7
Number of prison inmates	417,338	299,959	215,281	119,002

Note: Detail may not add to total due to rounding.
Source: BJS, Survey of Inmates in State and Federal Correctional Facilities, 1997.

with some college had prior sentences as a juvenile either to a facility or probation. About 1 in 5 without a high school diploma or with a GED and 1 in 10 with a diploma or some college had been incarcerated as a juvenile.

Methodology

The following data sets were used in this report.

Bureau of Justice Statistics Surveys

For a description of methods for these surveys see the following BJS publications:

Survey of Inmates in State and Federal Correctional Facilities, 1997 and 1991	*Survey of State Prison Inmates*, 1991, NCJ 136949 3/93; *Substance Abuse and Treatment, State and Federal Prisoners*, 1997 NCJ 172871 1/99.
Survey of Inmates in Local Jails, 1996 and 1989	*Profile of Jail Inmates, 1989*, NCJ 129097 4/91; *Profile of Jail Inmates, 1996*, NCJ 164620 11/98.
1995 Survey of Adults on Probation	*Characteristics of Adults on Probation*, 1995, NCJ 164267 12/9.
Census of State and Federal Adult Correctional Facilities, 1995 and 2000	*Census of State and Federal Adult Correctional Facilities, 1995*, NCJ 164266 8/9.
Census of Jails, 1999	*Census of Jails, 1999*, NCJ 186633 9/01.

National Adult Literacy Survey

The National Adult Literacy Survey, sponsored by the National Center for Education Statistics, was conducted in 1992 to assess literacy skills in the general population and background characteristics related to those skills. A four-stage stratified area sample was used to select respondents 16 years of age and older from the noninstitutional population in the United States. Black and Hispanic respondents were sampled at a higher rate than the remainder of the population in order to increase their representation in the sample. Data collection instruments included the screener, designed to enumerate household members and select survey respondents, a background questionnaire, and a literacy exercise booklet. The background questionnaire collected data on language and educational background, political, social, and labor force participation, literacy activities and demographic information. Respondents also took a test designed to

measure their prose, document, and quantitative literacy skills. Approximately 25,000 persons, paid $20 to participate, were interviewed for the study. The response rates were as follows: 89.1% answered the screener, 81% of those answered the background questions, and 95.8% of those took the literacy test.

Current Population Survey March supplement

The Current Population Survey (CPS), sponsored by the Bureau of Labor Statistics, collects labor force data about the civilian noninstitutional population every month. In March of each year, in addition to the regular questions, educational attainment is also asked. A multistage stratified clustered sample design is used to select approximately 50,000 housing units each month for interview. Generally about 6.5% of the housing units are not interviewed in a given month due to refusals or failure to make contact with persons in the dwelling unit. Data are collected on all persons 15 and older in each household. Information is obtained each month for about 94,000 persons 15 years of age or older.

The accuracy of sample surveys

Sampling error is the variation that may occur by chance because a sample rather than a complete enumeration of the population was conducted. The sampling error, as measured by an estimated standard error, varies by the size of the estimate and the size of the base population.

Estimates of the standard error of some numbers used in this report are found in the appendix tables.

Some standard errors have been calculated to provide estimates of the sampling variability around percents in this report. For example, the 95-percent confidence interval around the percentage of State inmates whose high school graduation was their ultimate educational attainment is approximately 20.5% plus or minus 1.96 times the standard error of .4 (or 19.7% to 21.3%) (appendix table 1).

Standard errors may also be used to test the significance of the difference between two sample statistics or estimates from two surveys. This is done by pooling the standard errors of the two sample estimates.

Appendix table 1. Standard error for estimates of educational attainment

Educational attainment	Prison inmates				Local jail inmates		Probationers	General population
	State		Federal					
	1997	1991	1997	1991	1996	1989		
8th grade or less	0.4%	0.5%	0.7%	0.5%	0.5%	0.6%	0.7%	0.1%
Some high school	0.5	0.6	0.7	0.5	0.7	0.8	1.0	0.1
GED	0.5	0.6	0.9	0.6	0.6	0.5	0.8	...
High school diploma	0.4	0.6	0.9	0.7	0.7	0.7	1.2	0.2
Some college	0.3	0.4	0.8	0.6	0.5	0.5	1.0	0.2
College graduate or more	0.2	0.2	0.6	0.4	0.3	0.3	0.5	0.2

...Not available.

Sources: BJS, Survey of Inmates in State and Federal Correctional Facilities, 1997 and 1991; BJS, Survey of Inmates in Local Jails, 1996 and 1989; BJS, Survey of Adults on Probation, 1995; Bureau of Labor Statistics, Current Population Survey, 1997.

Appendix table 2. Standard error for estimates of educational participation

Educational programs	State		Federal		Local jail inmates	Probationers
	1997	1991	1997	1991		
Total	0.5%	0.7%	1.0%	0.7%	0.6%	1.0%
Basic	0.2	0.3	0.3	0.5	0.1	0.2
GED/high school	0.5	0.6	0.9	0.7	0.5	0.7
College	0.3	0.5	0.7	0.6	0.1	0.6
English as a second language	0.1	...	0.5	...	...	...
Vocational	0.5	0.6	1.0	0.7	0.4	0.4
Other	0.2	0.2	0.5	0.4	0.2	0.6

...Not available.

Sources: BJS, Survey of Inmates in State and Federal Correctional Facilities, 1997 and 1991; BJS, Survey of Inmates in Local Jails, 1996; BJS, Survey of Adults on Probation, 1995.

U.S. Department of Justice
Office of Justice Programs
Bureau of Justice Statistics

Washington, DC 20531

Appendix table 3. Standard error for estimates of participation in educational programs by educational attainment for State prison inmates

Participation in educational programs	Less than a high school diploma	GED	High school diploma	Some college or more
Total	0.9%	1.0%	1.2%	1.6%
Basic	0.4	0.2	0.2	0.2
GED/High school	0.8	0.9	0.5	0.5
College	0.1	0.8	0.8	1.3
English as a second language	0.2	0.2	0.2	0.2
Vocational	0.7	1.0	1.1	1.5
Other	0.2	0.4	0.4	0.6

Sources: BJS, Survey of Inmates in State and Federal Correctional Facilities, 1997.

The Bureau of Justice Statistics is the statistical agency of the U.S. Department of Justice. Lawrence A. Greenfeld is director.

Caroline Wolf Harlow of BJS wrote this report. Doris James Wilson provided verification. Carolyn C. Williams produced and edited the report. Jayne Robinson administered final production.

January 2003, NCJ 195670

The standard error of the difference between State and Federal inmates who earned a high school diploma as their top educational achievement would be 0.8% (or the square root of the sum of the squared standard errors for each group). The 95-percent confidence interval around the difference would be 1.96 times 0.8% (or 1.5%). Since the difference of 6.5% (27.0% minus 20.5%) is greater than 1.5%, the difference would be considered statistically significant.

For additional documentation, questionnaires, and the data for BJS surveys, see <http://www.icpsr.umich.edu/NACJD/bjs.html#siscf> for the prison inmate surveys, <http://www.icpsr.umich.edu/NACJD/bjs.html#silj> for the jail inmate surveys, <http://www.icpsr.umich.edu/NACJD/bjs.html#sap> for the survey of probationers, <http://www.icpsr.umich.edu/NACJD/bjs.html#csfacf> for the prison censuses, and <http://www.icpsr.umich.edu/NACJD/bjs.html#njc> for the jail census. See <http://nces.ed.gov/naal/analysis/

This report in portable document format and in ASCII, its tables, and related statistical data are available at the BJS World Wide Web Internet site: <http://www.ojp.usdoj.gov/bjs/>

resources.asp> for data and documentation for the National Adult Literacy Survey, and <http://www.census.gov/population/www/socdemo/educ-attn.html> for tables from the Current Population Survey on educational attainment.

U.S. Department of Justice
Office of Justice Programs

Bureau of Justice Statistics
Special Report

September 2001, NCJ 186765

Hate Crimes Reported in NIBRS, 1997-99

By Kevin J. Strom
BJS Statistician

Over the past decade, Federal and State legislation has mandated the identification and reporting of offenses known as hate crimes. Today nearly every State and the Federal Government have laws which require sentencing enhancements for offenders who commit hate crimes. These incidents, also referred to as bias crimes, are criminal offenses motivated by an offender's bias against a race, religion, disability, sexual orientation, or ethnicity (FBI, 1999). Bias crimes are not separate types of offenses but are crimes against persons, property, or society identified by a specific motivation of the offender.

The Hate Crime Statistics Act of 1990 (P.L. 101-275) required the establishment of a system to provide information on the nature and prevalence of hate crimes. This responsibility was given to the Federal Bureau of Investigation's (FBI) Uniform Crime Reporting (UCR) program, which began compiling hate crime statistics reported to law enforcement departments in 1990. The UCR data reflected aggregate counts of incidents, victims, suspected offenders, and categories of bias motivation.

In recent years a growing number of law enforcement agencies has reported incident-level crime data to the FBI's National Incident-Based Reporting System (NIBRS).

Highlights

NIBRS hate crime data from 1997-99 showed that —

• In 60% of hate crime incidents, the most serious offense was a violent crime, most commonly intimidation or simple assault.*

• In nearly 4 out of 10 incidents the most serious crime was a property offense, 73% of which were damage, destruction, or vandalism of property.

• Sixty-one percent of hate crime incidents were motivated by race, 14% by religion, 13% by sexual orientation, 11% by ethnicity, and 1% by victim disability.

• The majority of incidents motivated by race, ethnicity, sexual orientation, or disability involved a violent offense, while two-thirds of incidents motivated by religion involved a property offense, most commonly vandalism.

• Of incidents motivated by hatred of a religion, 41% targeted Jewish victims and 31%, unspecified religious groups.

___
*Intimidation, defined as verbal or related threats of bodily harm, is one of the additional offenses collected in NIBRS.

Ages of victims of violent hate crimes

Percent of victims of violence

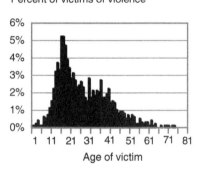

Age of victim

• Racially motivated hate crimes most frequently targeted blacks. Six in ten racially biased incidents targeted blacks, and 3 in 10 targeted whites.

• Younger offenders were responsible for most hate crimes. Thirty-one percent of violent offenders and 46% of property offenders were under age 18.

• Thirty-two percent of hate crimes occurred in a residence, 28% in an open space, 19% in a retail/commercial establishment or public building, 12% at a school or college, and 3% at a church, synagogue, or temple.

NIBRS represents a more comprehensive and detailed crime reporting system, with the ability to capture a wide range of information on specific incidents. In 1997, 1,878 agencies from 10 States submitted NIBRS data to the FBI, representing 6% of the U.S. population. In 1999, 3,396 agencies submitted NIBRS data, from 17 States (Colorado, Connecticut, Idaho, Iowa, Kentucky, Massachusetts, Michigan, Nebraska, North Dakota, Ohio, South Carolina, Tennessee, Texas, Utah, Vermont, Virginia, and West Virginia) representing 13% of the total population.

This report analyzes those NIBRS cases identified by law enforcement agencies as hate crimes from 1997 to 1999. Overall, bias crimes accounted for a relatively small percentage of all criminal incidents reported in NIBRS during this period. Of the nearly 5.4 million NIBRS incidents reported by law enforcement agencies between 1997 and 1999, about 3,000 were identified as hate crimes.

Bias motivation

NIBRS reporting requirements dictate that hate crimes be categorized according to the perceived bias motivation of the offender. Due to the difficulty in determining an offender's motivations, law enforcement agencies record hate crimes only when investigation reveals facts sufficient to conclude that the offender's actions were bias motivated. Evidence used to support the existence of bias could include oral comments, written statements, or gestures made by the offender at the time of the incident or drawings or graffiti left at the crime scene. Other factors, including victim reporting and law enforcement procedure, can also impact the quality and accuracy of hate crime reporting. (See *Methodology*.)

Among those bias incidents reported by NIBRS-participating States from 1997 to 1999, 61% were motivated by racial bias, 14% by religious bias, 13% by sexual orientation bias, 11% by

Table 1. Hate-bias incidents, by type of bias motivation, 1997-99

Type of bias motivation	Hate crime incidents	
	Number	Percent
Total	2,976	100%
Race	1,820	61.2%
Anti-black	1,059	35.6
Anti-white	561	18.9
Anti-multiracial	92	3.1
Anti-Asian	60	2.0
Anti-American Indian	48	1.6
Religion	431	14.4%
Anti-Jewish	177	5.9
Anti-other religious group	132	4.4
Anti-Catholic	29	1.0
Anti-Protestant	30	1.0
Anti-Islamic	30	1.0
Anti-multireligious group	28	0.9
Anti-atheist	5	0.2
Ethnicity	329	11.1%
Anti-Hispanic	199	6.7
Anti-other ethnicity or national origin	130	4.4
Sexual orientation	379	12.7%
Anti-male homosexual	167	5.6
Anti-homosexual	103	3.5
Anti-female homosexual	65	2.2
Anti-bisexual	32	1.1
Anti-heterosexual	12	0.4
Disability	17	0.6%
Anti-physical disability	12	0.4
Anti-mental disability	5	0.2

Note: Unit of count is incidents (n = 2,976).

ethnicity or national origin bias, and 1% by disability bias (table 1).
• Among racially motivated hate crimes, 6 in 10 targeted blacks and 3 in 10 targeted whites.
• Among crimes motivated by bias against a religion, the majority were anti-Jewish crimes or crimes against unnamed religious groups.
• Almost all incidents resulting from bias against a sexual orientation were committed against male or female homosexuals.
• Crimes motivated by hatred of an ethnicity or national origin most frequently targeted Hispanics.

Offense committed during hate crime incidents

The majority of offenses committed during NIBRS hate crimes were violent. This compared to all NIBRS offenses

Table 2. Most serious offense committed during hate-bias incidents, 1997-99

Most serious offense	Hate crime incidents	
	Number	Percent
Total	2,976	100%
Violent offenses	1,785	60.0%
Homicide	3	0.1
Forcible rape	6	0.2
Robbery	38	1.3
Assault, aggravated	385	12.9
Assault, simple	651	21.9
Assault, intimidation	687	23.1
Kidnaping/abduction	4	0.1
Other sexual assault	11	0.4
Property offenses	1,139	38.3%
Arson	21	0.7
Burglary	88	3.0
Larceny/theft	153	5.1
Motor vehicle theft	13	0.4
Forgery/fraud	18	0.6
Vandalism	832	28.0
Other	14	0.5
Other offenses	52	1.7%
Drugs	22	0.7
Weapons	26	0.9
Other	4	0.1

Note: Data reflect the most serious offense that occurred in the incident. Overall, 95% of incident reports include a single offense. See *Methodology* for details. Homicide includes murder and negligent and nonnegligent manslaughter. Other sexual assault includes all forcible sex offenses except for forcible rape. Other property includes embezzlement, extortion, and stolen property.
Unit of count is incidents (n = 2,976).

reported between 1997-99, of which about 1 in 5 involved a violent offense. In 60% of hate crime incidents, the most serious offense was a violent crime while property crimes were the most serious offenses reported in 38% of incidents (table 2). In about 2% of hate crime incidents the most serious crime reported was a drug, weapon, or other type of offense.

Intimidation, simple assault, and aggravated assault were the most commonly reported violent hate crime offenses, representing the most serious offense in nearly 6 in 10 of all bias incidents combined. Intimidation, which refers to verbal or related threats of bodily harm, was the most serious offense reported in 23% of incidents. Simple assault, which defines physical attacks without a weapon or serious victim injury, was the most serious offense recorded in 22% of incidents.

Aggravated assault, which refers to attacks in which the offender uses or displays a weapon and/or the victim suffers serious injury, was the most serious offense reported in 13% of incidents. In an additional 1% of hate crime incidents, the most serious offense was robbery, and in less than 1%, murder and nonnegligent or negligent manslaughter.

Property crimes were the most serious offense recorded in nearly 4 in 10 hate crime incidents, most commonly involving the damage, destruction, or vandalism of personal or public property. Overall, damage, destruction, or vandalism of property was the most serious offense recorded in 28% of all bias incidents. Arson was the most serious crime reported in nearly 1% of bias incidents.

Offense type by bias motivation

While hate crimes predominantly involved assault-related or vandalism offenses, the type of offense differed by bias motivation (table 3). Racially and ethnically motivated incidents were the most likely to be violent. Overall, 66% of race-related incidents and 69% of ethnic-related incidents involved a violent crime. In a quarter of racial or ethnically motivated incidents, intimidation was the most serious offense.

Table 3. Most serious offense, by type of bias motivation, 1997-99

| Most serious offense | Type of bias motivation | | | | |
	Race	Religion	Ethnicity	Sexual orientation	Disability
Total	100%	100%	100%	100%	100%
Violent offenses	66.1%	29.9%	69.3%	56.2%	70.6%
Homicide	0.2	0.0	0.0	0.0	0.0
Forcible rape	0.2	0.2	0.0	0.3	0.0
Robbery	1.0	0.7	3.0	1.3	5.9
Assault, aggravated	14.3	3.9	18.5	11.9	11.8
Assault, simple	24.1	8.4	22.8	24.8	41.2
Assault, intimidation	25.9	16.5	24.6	16.4	11.8
Kidnaping/abduction	0.2	0.0	0.3	0.0	0.0
Other sexual assault	0.2	0.2	0.0	1.6	0.0
Property offenses	31.8%	68.9%	30.1%	42.2%	23.5%
Arson	0.5	1.2	0.6	1.1	0.0
Burglary	2.4	4.4	3.6	3.4	5.9
Larceny/theft	4.5	8.4	4.3	5.8	0.0
Motor vehicle theft	0.4	0.7	0.3	0.5	0.0
Forgery/fraud	0.4	1.2	0.6	0.5	5.9
Vandalism	23.1	52.7	20.7	30.3	11.8
Other	0.5	0.5	0.0	0.5	0.0
Other offenses	2.1%	1.2%	0.6%	1.6%	5.9%
Drugs	0.9	0.7	0.3	0.5	0.0
Weapons	1.1	0.2	0.3	0.8	5.9
Other	0.1	0.2	0.0	0.3	0.0
Number of incidents	1,820	431	329	379	17

Note: Unit of count is incidents (n = 2,976).

Among crimes motivated by sexual orientation bias, 56% were violent and 42% were property offenses. Simple or aggravated assault was the most serious offense recorded in 37% of these incidents, intimidation in 16%, and rape or sexual assault in 2%. Violent crimes were reported in 12 of the 17 incidents motivated by disability bias recorded in NIBRS between 1997 and 1999.

In contrast to other bias crimes, the majority of crimes motivated by religious bias involved property offenses. In 53% of these incidents the most serious offense reported was damage, destruction, or vandalism of property.

Measuring hate crime victimizations not reported to the police

In general, the majority of crimes experienced by the public are not reported to the police. To examine both reported and unreported crime, BJS has collected data through its National Crime Victimization Survey (NCVS) since 1972. In the NCVS, representative national samples of the population are interviewed, with each victim of a crime queried about whether the victimization they experienced was reported to a law enforcement agency. In 2000 just under half of violent crimes and just over a third of property crimes were brought to the attention of the police.

NIBRS hate crime data reflect only those incidents in which a law enforcement agency was notified and properly recorded the event (see *Methodology* for further discussion). On July 1, 2000, BJS initiated the addition of new items to the NCVS designed to uncover hate crime victimizations which go unreported to law enforcement agencies. The NCVS hate crime questions ask victims about the basis for their belief that the crime they experienced was motivated by prejudice or bigotry, as well as the specific behavior of the offender or evidence which may have led to the victim's perception of bias.

Preliminary data from the first 6 months of fielding these questions indicate that the majority of hate crime victims, like victims of many other crimes, do not report the incident to law enforcement.

For the list of questions used in the NCVS to measure hate crime victimization see p. 21 of <http://www.ojp.us doj.gov/bjs/pub/pdf/ncvs2.pdf>.

Table 4. Type of hate crime victims, 1997-99

Victim type	Hate crime victims	
	Number	Percent
Total	3,534	100%
Individual	2,962	84%
Business/financial institution	215	6
Government	155	4
Religious organization	74	2
Society/public	62	2
Other/unknown	66	2

Note: NIBRS allows for the reporting of multiple victims per incident. Unit of count is victims (n = 3,534).

Victim characteristics

Type of victim

The targets of hate crimes were most commonly individuals (84%) as opposed to targets such as businesses or religious organizations (table 4). Businesses or financial institutions represented 6% of bias victims, governments 4%, religious organizations 2%, and society or the general public represented 2%.

Victim demographics

Overall, victims of bias crimes were relatively evenly distributed by age, with slightly smaller percentages reported among victims age 45 or older (table 5). The age of hate crime victims varied according to the nature of the offense, as a larger percentage of victims of violent hate crime were young (figure 1). More than half of victims of violence were age 24 or under, and nearly a third were under

Table 5. Victim characteristics, by most serious offense type, 1997-99

Victim characteristic	All offenses	Most serious offense	
		Violent	Property
Total	100%	100%	100%
Age			
0-12	6%	8%	1%
13-17	17	21	7
18-24	21	23	17
25-34	21	21	19
35-44	19	17	24
45 or older	16	10	32
Gender/race			
White male	40%	40%	41%
Black male	20	23	12
Other male	2	2	2
White female	25	22	33
Black female	12	13	10
Other female	1	1	1

Note: Male (3%) and female (1%) victims of unknown race not included. Victim age was missing in 4% and gender in 1% of cases. Unit of count is person victims (n=2,962).

18. In comparison, of all violent crime victims reported in NIBRS between 1997-99, about 2 in 10 were under age 18 and more than 4 in 10 were under age 25.

Among hate crime victims of aggravated assault, 30% were under 18, as were 34% of victims of simple assault (not shown in table). Victims of intimidation tended to be older, as nearly 40% were age 35 or over. About 3 out of 4 property crime victims were 25 or older, and nearly a third were 45 or older.

Forty percent of all hate crime victims were white males, 25% white females, 20% black males, and 12% black females. An additional 2% of victims

Ages of victims of violent hate crimes

Percent of victims of violence

Figure 1

were Asian, and nearly 1% were American Indian. Overall, blacks represented 36% of violent hate crime victims and 22% of property crime victims. Whites represented 62% and 74%, respectively.

Victim-offender relationships

NIBRS allows specification of the relationship between the victim and offender for violent offenses and nonviolent sex offenses. Among victims of violent hate crimes, 38% listed their attackers as acquaintances, 26% as strangers, and 7% as intimates, relatives, or friends (table 6). The victim-offender relationship remained unknown or unreported for 30% of bias victims. Among cases in which the victim and offender were acquaintances, 82% provided no additional information other than the offender was known to the victim, 16% reported that the offender was a neighbor, and 2% that the offender was an employer or employee (not shown in table).

Younger victims were more likely to be victimized by persons known to them (not shown in table). Of violent victims age 12 or younger, 67% were victimized by an acquaintance, 19% by a stranger, and 3% by a relative or friend. For the remainder, the victim-offender relationship was unknown. Among victims age 13 to 17, 46% were victimized by an acquaintance, 18% by a stranger, and 4% by a relative or friend. In comparison, 21% of victims age 21 or older were victimized by an acquaintance, 20% by a stranger, and 6% by an intimate, relative, or friend.

Table 6. Relationship of victim to offender, by most serious offense committed during incident, 1997-99

Most serious offense	Number of victims	Primary victim-offender relationship				
		Total	Intimate, relative, or friend	Acquaintance	Stranger	Unknown
All violent incidents	2,204	100%	7%	38%	26%	30%
Homicide	3	100%	0%	33%	33%	33%
Forcible rape	6	100	0	50	50	0
Robbery	42	100	0	12	48	40
Assault, aggravated	504	100	7	32	34	27
Assault, simple	815	100	10	45	25	19
Assault, intimidation	819	100	2	36	21	41
Kidnaping/abduction	4	100	25	0	25	50
Other sexual assault	11	100	36	45	9	9

Note: See *Methodology* for coding of victim-offender relationship involving multiple offenders. Unit of count is victims of violence (n = 2,204).

Table 7. Group victimization patterns among violent incidents, by most serious offense, 1997-99

Most serious offense	Number of incidents	Percent of incidents with — Single victim	Multiple victims
Total	1,785	83%	17%
Homicide	3	67%	33%
Forcible rape	6	100	0
Robbery	38	87	13
Assault, aggravated	385	77	23
Assault, simple	651	83	17
Assault, intimidation	687	86	14
Kidnaping/ abduction	4	75	25
Other sexual assault	11	82	18

Note: Unit of count is violent incidents (n = 1,785).

Table 8. Offender characteristics, by most serious offense type, 1997-99

Offender characteristic	Most serious offense		
	All offenses	Violent	Property
Total	100%	100%	100%
Age			
0-12	4%	4%	6%
13-17	29	27	40
18-24	29	29	25
25-34	17	18	12
35-44	13	13	11
45 or older	9	9	6
Gender/race			
White male	62%	60%	69%
Black male	20	21	12
Other male	2	2	1
White female	11	10	15
Black female	5	6	2
Other female	1	1	1

Note: Unit of count is known offenders (n = 3,072). Offender age was missing in 19% and gender/race in 14% of data. In an additional 812 incidents the offender was listed as unknown.

Table 9. Group offending patterns among violent offenses, by most serious offense, 1997-99

Offense type	Number of incidents	Percent of incidents with — Single offender	Multiple offenders
Total	1,582	75%	25%
Homicide	2	100%	0%
Forcible rape	6	100	0
Robbery	32	34	66
Assault, aggravated	352	67	33
Assault, simple	602	70	30
Assault, intimidation	575	85	15
Kidnaping/ abduction	2	50	50
Other sexual assault	11	91	9

Note: Unit of count is violent incidents with a known offender (n = 1,582).

Group victimization patterns

More than 4 out of 5 violent hate crime incidents reported in NIBRS involved the victimization of a single individual within a single incident (table 7). Two or more victims were involved in nearly a quarter of incidents in which the most serious offense was aggravated assault (23%). Violent incidents in which the most serious offense was rape (0 cases out of 6), robbery (13%), or intimidation (14%) were the least likely to involve multiple victims.

Offender characteristics

Offender demographics

Similar to characteristics of the victims, the characteristics of hate crime offenders varied according to offense. Among all NIBRS hate crime incidents, 33% of known offenders, which implies only that some characteristic of the suspect was identified, were age 17 or younger; 29%, age 18 to 24; 17%, age 25 to 34; and 21%, age 35 or older (table 8). Violent offenders were generally older than property offenders (figures 2 and 3). Of violent offenders, 31% were age 17 or younger and 60% were age 24 or younger. Of property offenders, 46% were age 17 or younger and 71% were age 24 or younger.

The majority of persons suspected of committing hate crimes were white males (table 8). Among those suspected of violent hate crimes, 60% were white males, 21% black males, 10% white females, and 6% black females. Whites also represented a larger share of persons suspected of committing property-related hate crimes, as 69% of property offenders were white males and 15% were white females.

By bias motivation, whites represented the majority of offenders suspected of committing hate crimes: religious, (88%), disability (85%), sexual orientation (84%), ethnic (82%), and racial (66%) (not shown in table). Among racially motivated incidents, 56% of suspected offenders were white males, 25% black males,11% white females, and 6% black females.

Group offending patterns

About 3 in 4 violent hate crimes involved a single offender in a single incident (table 9). Two or more offenders were involved in 66% of robbery incidents, in 33% of aggravated assaults, in 30% of simple assaults, and 15% of intimidation incidents.

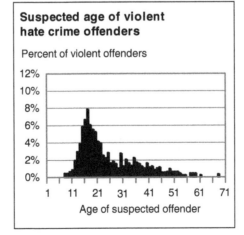

Suspected age of violent hate crime offenders

Percent of violent offenders

Age of suspected offender

Figure 2

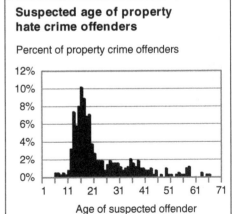

Suspected age of property hate crime offenders

Percent of property crime offenders

Age of suspected offender

Figure 3

Incident characteristics

Location of hate crime incidents

Of all bias incidents reported in NIBRS, 32% were committed in a residence, 28% in an open space, 19% in a commercial/retail business or public building, 12% in a school or college, 7% in another or unknown location, and 3% in a church, synagogue or temple (table 10). (See *Methodology* for definitions.) Open spaces primarily refer to roadways and parking garages or parking lots. Thirty percent or more of racial, ethnic, and disability-biased incidents were committed in an open space. Among incidents motivated by sexual orientation bias, 41% occurred at a residence, 23% in an open space, 16% at a school or college, and 15% at a commercial/retail business or public building. A third of religious-biased crimes occurred at an educational or religious institution.

Weapons in hate crimes

Weapons were reported to have been used in about 18% of all violent hate crimes. Firearms were used or brandished in 4% of violent incidents, knives or sharp objects in 4%, and a blunt object in 4% (table 11). By specific offense, homicides (3 out of 3 incidents) and aggravated assaults were the most likely to involve the use or presence of a weapon. Firearms were used or brandished in 17% of aggravated assault incidents, knives in 17%, and blunt objects in 19%.

The differences in weapon use and offense type correspond to victim injury, with aggravated assault victims the most likely to sustain a serious injury (not shown in table). Among all hate-related violent cases that provided information on injury outcome, 47% reported no injury to the victim, 45% a minor injury, 3% a severe laceration,

Table 10. Location of hate crime incidents, by type of bias motivation, 1997-99

| Location | All incidents | Bias motivation | | | | |
		Racial	Religious	Ethnic	Sexual	Disability
Total	100%	100%	100%	100%	100%	100%
Commercial/retail	19%	20%	16%	20%	15%	12%
Open space	28	31	17	34	23	41
Church/synagogue	3	0	16	1	1	0
School/college	12	10	16	9	16	6
Residence	32	30	29	31	41	41
Other/unknown	7	8	6	5	4	0

Note: Unit of count is incidents (n = 2,976). Commercial/retail category includes public buildings.

Table 11. Violent hate crime incidents, by type of weapon, 1997-99

| Weapon type | All violent incidents | Most serious offense reported in incident | | | | | |
		Homicide	Forcible rape	Robbery	Aggravated assault	Simple assault	Intimidation
Total	100%	100%	100%	100%	100%	100%	100%
Weapon used in incident	18%	100%	17%	24%	70%	8%	0%
Firearm	4	67	17	3	17	0	0
Knife/sharp object	4	0	0	8	17	0	0
Blunt object	4	33	0	13	19	0	0
Motor vehicle	1	0	0	0	5	0	0
Other weapon	5	0	0	0	11	8	0
Personal weapon	35%	0%	83%	63%	27%	74%	0%
No weapon/not reported	47%	0%	0%	13%	4%	18%	100%

Note: Personal weapons refers to cases in which offenders used hands, feet, or fists.
Unit of count is violent incidents (n = 1,789). For small number of incidents in which multiple weapons were reported, the most lethal weapon was selected, such as firearm or knife.

2% broken bones, and 3% some other type of major injury. In comparison, more than half of aggravated assault victims sustained some type of injury and 1 in 5 reported a more serious injury such as broken bones, an internal injury, or a severe laceration.

Time of day of hate crime incidents

The time of day at which violent hate crimes were reported to have occurred was related to the age of the victim. Victims age 17 or younger were most likely to be victimized during the day, as nearly two-thirds of these incidents occurred between 7 a.m. and 6 p.m., with a peak between 2 p.m. and 4 p.m.

Other research has also reported this afternoon period as a peak time for juvenile victimization.*

In comparison, violent hate crimes involving victims age 18 to 24 were more likely to occur in the late evening, with a peak around midnight. More than a quarter of violent incidents involving victims age 18 to 24 occurred between 10 p.m. and 1 a.m.

*For additional information see Howard N. Snyder, *Sexual Assault of Young Children as Reported to Law Enforcement: Victim, Incident, and Offender Characteristics*, BJS, 2000, NCJ 182990; and Howard N. Snyder and Melissa Sickmund, *Juvenile Offenders and Victims: 1999 National Report*, Office of Juvenile Justice and Delinquency Prevention, 1999, NCJ 178257.

Table 12. Hate crimes cleared by arrest or exceptional means, by most serious offense, 1997-99

Offense type	Percent of incidents — Cleared*	Not cleared
Total	25%	75%
Violent offenses	32%	68%
Homicide	67	33
Forcible rape	67	33
Robbery	32	68
Assault, aggravated	40	60
Assault, simple	39	61
Assault, intimidation	21	79
Kidnaping/abduction	50	50
Other sexual assault	36	64
Property offenses	12%	88%
Arson	10	90
Burglary	15	85
Larceny/theft	14	86
Motor vehicle theft	23	77
Forgery/fraud	39	61
Vandalism	10	90
Other	29	71
Other offenses	56%	44%
Drugs	59	41
Weapons	58	42
Other	25	75

*Includes cases cleared by arrest or exceptional means when some element outside law enforcement control precludes arrest. Unit of count is incidents (n = 2,976).

Law enforcement response

Clearance rates

NIBRS data indicate that 1 in 4 hate crime incidents were cleared either by arrest or exceptional means (table 12). Overall, an arrest was made in about 20% of hate crime incidents. An additional 5% of cases were cleared by exceptional means, which most commonly refers to cases in which either the victim refused to cooperate or prosecution was declined because of a lack of evidence.

Table 13. Arrestee characteristics, by arrest offense type, 1997-99

Arrestee characteristic	All offenses	Arrest offense Violent	Property
Total	100%	100%	100%
Age			
17 or under	34%	28%	56%
18-24	27	29	20
25-34	18	21	13
35-44	14	15	8
45 or older	6	7	2
Gender/race			
White male	66%	63%	78%
Black male	18	20	8
Other male	1	1	1
White female	9	8	11
Black female	5	7	1
Other female	1	1	2

Note: Thirty-two arrestees were arrested for multiple incidents. Unit of count is arrestees (n = 808).

Crimes in which the most serious offense was homicide (67% of cases cleared), forcible rape (67% cleared), kidnaping (50% cleared), aggravated assault (40% cleared), simple assault (39% cleared), or forgery/fraud (39% cleared) were the most likely to be cleared through arrest or exceptional means. In comparison, cases in which the most serious offense was intimidation (21%), vandalism (10%), arson (10%), or burglary (15%) were the least likely to be cleared.

Arrestee characteristics

In NIBRS, more than a third of persons arrested for hate crimes were under 18, and over a half were under 25 at the time of arrest (table 13). Younger persons were more likely to be arrested for property-related offenses. Fifty-six percent of persons arrested for property offenses were age 17 or younger compared to 28% of persons arrested for violent hate crimes.

Offenders under age 18 comprised sizable proportions of persons arrested for simple assault (29%), intimidation (33%), and damage, destruction, or vandalism of property (66%) offenses. Three-fourths of hate crime arrestees were white. Eighty-five percent were male, including 66% white males and 18% black males.

The vast majority (93%) of persons arrested for hate crimes were not armed at the time of arrest. About 2% of arrestees were armed with a firearm, 2% with a knife, and 3% with another type of weapon such as a blunt object (not shown in table).

About 38% of hate crime arrests reported in NIBRS were listed as on-view arrests, suggesting that the officer caught the offender during or shortly following the incident (not shown in table). An additional 25% of arrests involved the issuance of a citation or summons in which the offender was not taken into custody, and 37% involved apprehensions in which suspects were taken into custody in connection with warrants or earlier crime incidents.

Of cases providing data, two-thirds indicated that arrestees were residents of the locality in which the crime occurred. Among persons under 18 at the time of arrest, nearly 3 out of 4 were residents of the locality where the incident took place.

National hate crime statistics reported through summary UCR, 1991-99

In 1990 the FBI began collecting information on hate crimes reported by law enforcement agencies as part of their Uniform Crime Reporting (UCR) Program. Since 1991 participation in the program has increased substantially. In 1999, 12,122 agencies in 48 States and the District of Columbia reported summary hate crime data to the FBI.

While the number of participating agencies has grown, most agencies continue to submit zero hate crimes for the year (figure). In 1991, 27% of the 2,771 participating agencies submitted 1 or more hate crime incidents, compared to 15% of the 12,122 participating agencies in 1999.

Nationally, the number of hate crimes reported has fluctuated between about 6,000 and 9,000 incidents annually since 1991. In 1996, 8,759 bias incidents were reported to the FBI; in 1999, 7,876 incidents. In the 1997-99 period covered in this report, NIBRS accounted for nearly 13% of the 23,680 hate crime incidents reported nationally through the UCR program.

Overall, the characteristics of hate crimes reported nationally through the UCR Hate Crime Data Collection Program were similar to those bias incidents reported in NIBRS-participating States. The Summary UCR figures do reflect a higher percentage of intimidation offenses (37% versus 22%), and the NIBRS figures include a slightly higher percentage of simple assault offenses (21% versus 19%).

National UCR Hate Crime Reporting Program

Number of agencies

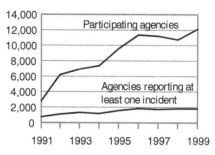

Bias motivation types were similar across both Summary UCR and NIBRS reporting agencies. For additional information on hate crime statistics, as well as a copy of the UCR hate crime incident form and hate crime collection guidelines go to <http://www.fbi.gov/ucr.htm>.

Methodology

To analyze the characteristics of hate crime incidents four files were constructed from the 1997, 1998, and 1999 NIBRS master files. Cases with incident dates prior to 1997 were excluded, as were incidents from States that had not yet been officially certified by the FBI to report NIBRS data. The first file constructed was an incident-level file that included characteristics of the 2,976 hate crime incidents reported in NIBRS, including offense type, time of day, incident location, use or presence of weapons, and the proportion of crimes cleared by arrest or exceptional means. The second file was a victim-level file containing information on the 3,534 hate crime victims reported in NIBRS over the 3-year period. The third file was an offender-level file that contained information on 3,072 known hate crime offenders, which implies that some characteristic of the suspect was identified distinguishing him/her from an unknown offender. The fourth file was an arrestee-level file that contained records on the 808 persons arrested for hate crime offenses.

Variable recoding

Victim-offender relationship was based on calculations from the victim-level file. For cases involving multiple offenders, the victim-offender relationship reflects a hierarchy from best known to least known to the victim. For example, if two of the offenders were coded as strangers and one as an acquaintance to the victim, the victim-offender relationship was coded as acquaintance.

Certain incident locations were recoded into more general categories. Open spaces includes offenses committed at construction sites, field or woods, highway/road/alleys, lakes or waterways, and parking lots or garages. The category retail/commercial establishments and public buildings includes incidents that occurred in air/bus/train terminals, banks, bars or nightclubs, office buildings, convenience stores, department or specialty stores, grocery stores or supermarkets, drug stores or hospitals, liquor stores, rental storage, government or other types of public buildings, gas stations, hotels or motels, and restaurants. Incidents occurring in jails or prisons

were recoded into the other/unknown category.

Multiple offenses reported for single incident

The NIBRS reporting structure allows for two or more offenses to be recorded for a single incident. Overall, multiple offenses were reported in about 5% of all NIBRS hate crime incidents. For those incidents in which multiple offenses were reported the "hierarchy rule" was used to determine the most serious Part I offense in the incident (See *Effects of NIBRS on Crime Statistics*, BJS Special Report, NCJ 178890, July 2000, for details). The only exception to this rule was for arson. If arson was committed in an incident along with other property crimes, arson was considered the most serious property offense. For Part II offenses the following hierarchy was used: violent, property, drugs, and weapons offenses.

Of those secondary hate crime offenses that occurred during an incident in the 1997-99 period, nearly 2 out 3 were damage, destruction, or vandalism offenses. In cases in which vandalism was reported as a secondary offense, the most serious offense in the incident was most frequently burglary (31%), intimidation (30%), simple assault (19%), or aggravated assault (11%).

Limitations of NIBRS hate crime statistics

At present the NIBRS data reported by law enforcement agencies are not a nationally representative sample of hate crimes incidents throughout the country. In particular, large urban areas are underrepresented in NIBRS. One city with a population of 500,000 or more and 12 cities with a population of 200,000 or more participated in the reporting system as of yearend 1999 (see appendix table). Despite these limitations, the total number of hate crime incidents in the NIBRS universe and the detailed characteristics provided in this reporting system represent a unique opportunity for a better understanding of hate crime incidents.

A number of factors can impact the quality and accuracy of national hate crime statistics. Many of these factors are summarized in the BJS-funded report, *Improving the Quality and Accuracy of Bias Crime Statistics Nationally: An Assessment of the First Ten Years of Bias Crime Data Collection* (September 2000), available at <http://www.dac.neu.edu/cj/crimereport.pdf>.

This report suggests that the barriers to hate crime reporting can be separated into two general categories: (1) victim-related reporting factors and (2) factors that effect police recording bias incidents or reporting them to the FBI. The report identifies 7 decision-making points necessary for accurate national reporting:

1. The victim acknowledges a crime was committed;
2. The victim recognizes that hate bias was a motivating factor for the crime;
3. The victim or another party contacts police about the incident;

4. The victim or another party communicates to police that bias was a motivating factor;
5. Law enforcement recognizes the element of hate;
6. Law enforcement documents the type of bias, which could lead to the suspect being charged with a civil rights or bias offense;
7. Law enforcement records the incident and submits the information to the FBI's UCR Hate Crime Reporting Unit.

Selected NIBRS offense definitions

Arson: To unlawfully and intentionally damage, or attempt to damage, any real or personal property by fire or incendiary device.

Assault, aggravated: An unlawful attack by one person upon another wherein the offender uses a weapon or displays it in a threatening manner, or the victim suffers obvious severe or aggravated bodily injury involving apparent broken bones, loss of teeth, possible internal injury, severe laceration, or loss of consciousness. This also includes assault with disease (as in cases when the offender is aware that he/she is infected with a deadly disease and deliberately attempts to inflict the disease by biting, spitting, etc.).

Assault, simple: An unlawful attack by one person upon another where neither the offender displays a weapon nor the victim suffers obvious severe or aggravated bodily injury.

Assault, intimidation: To unlawfully place another person in reasonable fear of bodily harm through the use of threatening words and/or other conduct, but without displaying a weapon or subjecting the victim to actual physical attack.

Destruction/damage/vandalism of property: To willfully or maliciously destroy, damage, deface, or otherwise injure real or personal property without the consent of the owner or the person having custody or control of it.

Appendix table. Population covered by agencies reporting NIBRS hate crime incidents, 1997-99

Population group	Number of incidents	Percent distribution
Total	2,976	100%
Cities		
500,000-999,999	36	1.2%
250,000-499,999	109	3.7
100,000-249,999	198	6.7
50,000-99,999	310	10.4
25,000-49,999	431	14.5
10,000-24,999	609	20.5
2,500-9,999	436	14.7
Less than 2,500	236	8.3
Non-MSA counties		
25,000-99,999*	90	3.0%
10,000-24,999	93	3.1
Less than 10,000	43	1.4
MSA counties		
100,000 or more	200	6.7%
25,000-99,999	145	4.9
10,000-24,999	11	0.4
Less than 10,000	19	0.6

*Includes one incident in 1999 from a county with a population greater than 100,000.

(Note: This offense is reported only if the reporting agency deems that substantial injury to the property has occurred. The offense includes a broad range of injury to property, from deliberate, extensive destruction to less extensive damage. It does not include destruction or damage to property caused by the crime of arson.)

Forcible sex offenses: Any sexual act directed against another person, forcibly and/or against the person's will; or not forcibly or against the person's will where the victim is incapable of giving consent. Forcible rape, forcible sodomy, sexual assault with an object, and forcible fondling are included in this category.

Forcible rape: The carnal knowledge or a person, forcibly, and/or against that person's will; or not forcibly or against the person's will where the victim is incapable of giving consent because of his/her temporary or permanent mental or physical incapacity (or because of his/her youth).

Homicide: The killing of one human being by another.

Murder and nonnegligent manslaughter: The willful (nonnegligent) killing of one human being by another.

Negligent manslaughter: The killing of another person through negligence.

Kidnaping/abduction: The unlawful seizure, transportation, and/or detention of a person against his/her will, or of a minor without the consent of his/her custodial parent(s) or legal guardian.

Robbery: The taking, or attempting to take, anything of value under confrontational circumstances from the control, custody, or care of another person by force or threat of force or violence and/or by putting the victim in fear of immediate harm.

The Bureau of Justice Statistics is the statistical agency of the U.S. Department of Justice. Lawrence A. Greenfeld is acting director.

Kevin J. Strom wrote this report under the supervision of Steven K. Smith, Chief, Law Enforcement, Adjudication, and Federal Statistics. Ramona Rantala gave statistical assistance and provided statistical review. Greg Steadman also provided statistical review. Victoria Major, Sharon Propheter, Christopher Enourato, Cynthia Barnett and Thomas Edwards of the Criminal Justice Information Services Division of the FBI reviewed and commented on the report. Ellen Goldberg and Tom Hester edited the report. Jayne Robinson prepared the report for publication.

September 2001, NCJ 186765

This report and others from the Bureau of Justice Statistics are available through the Internet — **http://www.ojp.usdoj.gov/bjs/**

U.S. Department of Justice
Office of Justice Programs
Bureau of Justice Statistics

SPECIAL REPORT

JUNE 2016

NCJ 249743

Recidivism of Offenders Placed on Federal Community Supervision in 2005: Patterns from 2005 to 2010

Joshua A. Markman, Matthew R. Durose, and Ramona R. Rantala, *BJS Statisticians*
Andrew D. Tiedt, Ph.D., *Former BJS Statistician*

During fiscal year 2005, approximately 43,000 offenders were placed on federal community supervision, including nearly a quarter (23%) who were directly sentenced to probation and more than three-quarters (77%) who began a term of supervised release following a prison sentence. Overall, 35% of these offenders were arrested within 3 years and 43% were arrested within 5 years of placement on community supervision.

This report examines the extent to which offenders placed on federal community supervision were arrested by federal and nonfederal (i.e., state and local) law enforcement agencies prior to and following their placement on community supervision. It also compares the recidivism rates of former federal prisoners to those of former state prisoners released in 2005.

Criminal history and prison records were used to document recidivism patterns

To measure recidivism, this study used a combination of arrest charge, court disposition, incarceration sentence, and custody information found in national criminal history records and other data sources to measure recidivism. Depending on the measure used, the percentage of offenders classified as recidivists will decline as the recidivism measurement progresses from arrest to imprisonment. In other words, of those persons arrested, a smaller percentage are charged, and an even smaller percentage are imprisoned. In the criminal history records, the proportion of arrests that included information on the offender's adjudicated guilt or innocence and, if convicted, on the sentence imposed (e.g., prison, jail, or probation) varied across jurisdictions. This could be due to natural state-variations in criminal justice practice or in criminal history reporting practices. The variations also may have been caused by a lack of reporting court dispositions to criminal history repositories or because the repository could not connect a reported court disposition to a specific arrest.

The analytical approach used in this research sought to minimize the effect on recidivism statistics posed by variations in criminal history reporting policies, coding practices, and coverage. The analysis excluded traffic offenses because those events were not commonly recorded on the criminal history records across states. However, some variations in the content of rap sheets remained and could not be remediated, such as the nature of the charging decision. For example, when a person

HIGHLIGHTS

- Nonfederal (i.e., state and local) law enforcement agencies were responsible for approximately three-quarters (76%) of prior arrests of offenders placed on federal community supervision in 2005.

- Nonfederal charges accounted for more than two-thirds (68%) of all arrests that occurred during the 5 years following placement on federal community supervision.

- Within 1 year following placement in 2005 on community supervision, 18% of the federal offenders had been arrested at least once.

- Among those conditionally released from federal prison, nearly half (47%) were arrested within 5 years, compared to more than three-quarters (77%) of state prisoners released on community supervision.

- About 3 in 10 federal prisoners released to a term of community supervision returned to prison within 5 years, while nearly 6 in 10 state prisoners conditionally released returned in 5 years.

- On average, offenders released from federal prison had fewer prior arrests (5.6) than those released from state prison (10.8).

- Across demographic characteristics or extent of prior criminal offending, state prisoners consistently had higher rates of recidivism than federal prisoners within 5 years after release.

on parole is arrested for committing a burglary, some local law enforcement agencies code the arrest offense as a parole violation, some code it as a burglary, and others code both the burglary and the parole violation. It is difficult to discern from the rap sheets, given that this is often a local coding decision, which charging approach was employed at each arrest.

Offenders placed on federal community supervision averaged five prior arrests

In 2005, the total correctional population was 7,055,600 of which 304,500 were federal offenders. The total community supervision population was 4,946,600 of which 117,900 were offenders under federal community supervision.[1]

Eighty percent of the approximately 43,000 offenders who were placed on federal community supervision in 2005 were male (table 1). More than a third (41%) were white and nearly a third (31%) were black. Approximately 30% were age 29 or younger and about 40% were age 40 or older. The average criminal history of these offenders included approximately five prior arrests. More than a third (38%) of the federal

[1]See *Correctional Populations in the United States, 2014,* NCJ 249513, BJS web, December 2015.

offenders were sentenced to community supervision for a drug offense (table 2).

During their criminal careers prior to being placed on federal community supervision in 2005, these offenders were arrested approximately 210,000 times (table 3). This total included arrests made by federal, state, and local law enforcement agencies in all 50 states, the District of Columbia, and U.S. territories. Federal law enforcement agencies accounted for approximately 24% of all prior arrests. State and local law enforcement agencies were responsible for the other 76% of prior arrests. Almost 45% of federal offenders placed on community supervision in 2005 had 4 or more prior arrests. The large majority (78%) of federal offenders had only one prior federal arrest, which was the arrest that led to the 2005 community supervision sentence. Approximately 70% of

TABLE 1
Percent of offenders placed on federal community supervision in 2005, by demographic characteristics

Characteristic	Total
Total	100%
Sex	
Male	79.7%
Female	20.3
Race/Hispanic origin	
White[a]	41.3%
Black/African American[a]	31.2
Hispanic/Latino	21.8
Other[a,b]	5.7
Age	
24 or younger	11.5%
25–29	16.1
30–34	16.7
35–39	13.9
40–44	14.4
45–49	10.9
50 or older	16.3
Number of prior arrests per offender[c]	
Mean	4.9
Median	3.0
Number of offenders placed on federal community supervision in 2005	42,977

[a]Excludes persons of Hispanic or Latino origin.

[b]Includes American Indian, Alaska Native, Asian, Native Hawaiian, Other Pacific Islander, and persons of two or more races.

[c]Number of times an offender was arrested before being placed on federal community supervision in 2005, including the arrest that led to the 2005 sentence.

Source: Bureau of Justice Statistics, Recidivism of Offenders Placed on Federal Community Supervision in 2005 data collection.

TABLE 2
Percent of offenders placed on federal community supervision in 2005, by most serious conviction offense

Most serious conviction offense	Percent
Total	100%
Violent[a]	6.2
Property	24.1
Drug	38.3
Other public order[b]	23.9
Sex offense[c]	1.9
Immigration	5.7
Number of offenders placed on federal community supervision in 2005	42,977

[a]Excludes rape and sexual assault.

[b]Excludes immigration and other sex offenses.

[c]Includes rape and sexual assault; possession, distribution, and production of child pornography; and transportation for illegal sexual purposes.

Source: Bureau of Justice Statistics, Recidivism of Offenders Placed on Federal Community Supervision in 2005 data collection.

TABLE 3
Number of prior arrests before placement on federal community supervision in 2005, by federal or nonfederal law enforcement agencies

Prior arrests[a]	All	Federal	Nonfederal[b]
Total	100%	100%	100%
No prior arrests	0.0%	0.0%	30.1%
One or more prior arrests	100%	100%	69.9%
1	29.6	78.0	15.6
2–3	25.6	19.1	19.5
4–7	24.5	2.6	19.0
8 or more	20.4	0.3	15.8
Number of prior arrests[c]	210,000	50,000	160,000

Note: Detail may not sum to total due to rounding. Offenders could have a federal arrest, a nonfederal arrest, or both.

[a]Number of times an offender was arrested before being placed on federal community supervision in 2005, including the arrest that led to the 2005 sentence.

[b]Includes state and local law enforcement agencies only.

[c]Number of prior arrests rounded to nearest 1,000.

Source: Bureau of Justice Statistics, Recidivism of Offenders Placed on Federal Community Supervision in 2005 data collection.

federal offenders had at least one prior nonfederal arrest, with more than a third (35%) having four or more prior nonfederal arrests.

2 in 5 offenders placed on federal community supervision were arrested within 5 years

At the end of the 5-year follow-up period, 43% had been arrested (table 4). Nearly half of those who were arrested within the 5-year follow-up period were arrested within the first year after being placed on community supervision in 2005. Within 1 year following placement on community supervision in 2005, 18% of federal offenders had been arrested at least once. By the end of the third year, 35% had been arrested.

Aggregate trends of the first arrest following placement on federal community supervision appeared to diverge when decomposing these arrests as federal and nonfederal charges. Within 2 years after placement on community supervision, 18% of the federal offenders had been arrested for at least one federal charge, and 19% had been arrested for at least one nonfederal charge (figure 1). After 2 years, a higher proportion of new first-time arrests were by nonfederal law

enforcement agencies. As a result, within 5 years of being placed on community supervision in 2005, a quarter (25%) of federal offenders had at least one federal arrest, while more than a third (34%) of federal offenders had at least one nonfederal arrest. During the 5-year follow-up period, 8% had two or more federal arrests, while 18% had two or more nonfederal arrests (table 5). When examining the first arrest

FIGURE 1
Cumulative percent of offenders placed on federal community supervision in 2005 who were arrested for a new crime, by type of arrest, 2005–10

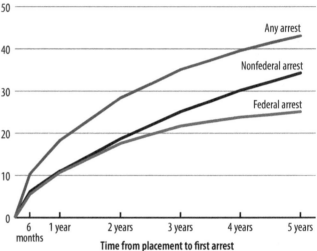

Note: Nonfederal arrests consist of those made by state and local law enforcement agencies. Offenders could have a federal arrest, a nonfederal arrest, or both. See appendix table 1 for percentages.

Source: Bureau of Justice Statistics, Recidivism of Offenders Placed on Federal Community Supervision in 2005 data collection.

TABLE 4
Cumulative percent of offenders placed on federal community supervision in 2005 who were arrested for a new crime, by time from release, 2005–10

Cumulative percent arrested within—	First arrest
6 months	10.3%
1 year	18.2
2 years	28.3
3 years	35.0
4 years	39.5
5 years	43.0

Source: Bureau of Justice Statistics, Recidivism of Offenders Placed on Federal Community Supervision in 2005 data collection.

TABLE 5
Number of arrests following placement on federal community supervision in 2005, by type of arrest, 2005–10

Number of arrests	Any arrest	Federal	Nonfederal
Total	100%	100%	100%
No arrests	57.0%	75.0%	65.8%
One or more arrests	43.0%	25.0%	34.2%
1	16.8	16.9	16.8
2	10.2	5.9	7.7
3	6.3	1.6	4.0
4	3.7	0.5	2.3
5 or more	6.2	0.1	3.5

Note: Detail may not sum to total due to rounding. Nonfederal arrests consist of those made by state and local law enforcement agencies. Offenders could have a federal arrest, a nonfederal arrest, or both.

Source: Bureau of Justice Statistics, Recidivism of Offenders Placed on Federal Community Supervision in 2005 data collection.

after placement on federal supervision, nearly two-thirds of arrests were for nonfederal charges (65%). Among all arrests that occurred within the 5-year follow-up period, 68% were arrests for nonfederal charges (figure 2).

After being placed on federal community supervision in 2005, the offense involved in the first arrest was related to the type of arresting agency. Charges for public order offenses were more likely to occur among the federal arrests. Public order offenses accounted for 33% of nonfederal arrests and 90% of federal arrests, including 68% for a probation or parole violation (table 6). After public order offenses, small proportions of federal offenders on community supervision were first arrested by federal law enforcement agencies for drug (6%), property (2%), and violent offenses (1%). For nonfederal arrests, the distribution was more uniform. Public order offenses were the most common nonfederal offense type at first arrest after placement on federal community supervision (33%), followed by property (23%), violent (21%), and drug (21%) offenses.

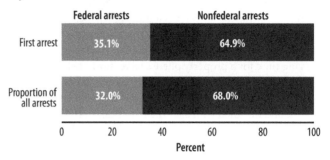

FIGURE 2
Percent of arrests by federal or nonfederal law enforcement agencies following placement on federal community supervision in 2005, 2005–10

Note: Nonfederal arrests are those made by state and local law enforcement agencies.
Source: Bureau of Justice Statistics, Recidivism of Offenders Placed on Federal Community Supervision in 2005 data collection.

TABLE 6
First arrest for offenders following placement on federal community supervision in 2005, by most serious charge and type of arrest, 2005–10

Most serious arrest charge	Any arrest	Federal arrest	Nonfederal arrest
Total	100%	100%	100%
Violent	14.5%	1.3%	21.4%
Homicide	0.3	0.0	0.5
Rape/sexual assault	0.7	0.1	1.0
Robbery	1.6	0.9	2.2
Assault	11.0	0.3	16.5
Other	0.9	0.1	1.2
Property	15.5%	2.3%	22.6%
Burglary	1.5	0.0	2.5
Larceny/motor vehicle theft	5.8	0.3	8.9
Fraud/forgery	5.2	1.8	6.6
Other	3.0	0.1	4.6
Drug	15.6%	5.8%	21.2%
Possession	7.0	1.3	10.4
Trafficking	5.7	3.0	7.0
Other	2.8	1.5	3.7
Public order	53.1%	89.7%	33.1%
Weapons	1.5	1.0	2.0
Driving under the influence	8.7	0.5	12.4
Probation/parole violation	25.0	67.6	2.4
Other	17.8	20.6	16.3
Unspecified	1.4	0.9	1.7%

Note: Detail may not sum to total due to rounding. Nonfederal arrests are those made by state and local law enforcement agencies. Offenders could have a federal arrest, a nonfederal arrest, or both. See *Methodology* for recidivism definitions.
Source: Bureau of Justice Statistics, Recidivism of Offenders Placed on Federal Community Supervision in 2005 data collection.

State prisoners have higher recidivism rates than federal prisoners

BJS examined the recidivism patterns of the approximately 405,000 offenders released from state prison from 30 states in 2005 and tracked for 5 years following release.[2] That study found that recidivism rates varied with the attributes of the inmate. For example, state prisoners released after serving time for a property offense were most likely to be arrested for a new crime compared to other offense types. In addition, recidivism was highest among males and young adults, and declined with age. The recidivism rates of state prisoners after release increased as the extent of their criminal history increased.

[2]See *Recidivism of Prisoners Released in 30 States in 2005: Patterns from 2005 to 2010*, NCJ 244205, BJS web, April 2014.

Comparing federal and state prisoner post-release recidivism patterns

This report compares state prisoners released conditionally in 2005 and persons placed on federal community supervision in 2005 after a period of incarceration. State prisoners released conditionally include those released on discretionary parole, mandatory parole, post-custody probation, and other unspecified conditional releases and excludes those released unconditionally (e.g., expirations of sentences, commutations, and other unspecified unconditional releases).

In addition to measuring recidivism as an arrest for a new crime, this study examined recidivism as an admission to prison for a technical parole or other community supervision violation (e.g., failing a drug test or missing an appointment with a probation officer) or a sentence for a new crime. The availability of this information varied in the criminal history records by state and federal jurisdictions. Given the inconsistent reporting of such custody information in the criminal history records, the return-to-prison measure relied on a combination of data sources.

For released federal prisoners, BJS used the federal prison admission records from the Bureau of Prisons (BOP) (part of BJS's Federal Justice Statistics Program) to supplement the criminal history records by capturing returns to prison both with or without a new sentence. For released state prisoners, state prison admission records from the BJS National Corrections Reporting Program (NCRP) were used to supplement the criminal history data by capturing returns to prison with or without a new sentence. The measure for the state prisoners was based on those released from the 23 states in the study that had the necessary data.

To observe differences in recidivism outcomes, the following section compares recidivism rates for prisoners placed on federal community supervision to those conditionally released from state prisons. (See *Comparing federal and state prisoner post-release recidivism patterns* text box.)

Demographic characteristics and criminal histories differed among federal and state prison populations released in 2005. Four in 10 federal prisoners were age 40 or older, compared to 3 in 10 released state prisoners (table 7). Females were more prevalent among federal prisoners (17%) than state prisoners (10%). The racial distribution within both groups of prisoners was similar.

TABLE 7
Characteristics of federal and state prisoners released on community supervision in 2005

Characteristic	Federal prisoners	State prisoners in 30 states
Total	100%	100%
Sex		
Male	83.5%	89.7%
Female	16.5	10.3
Race/Hispanic origin		
White[a]	38.7%	38.8%
Black/African American[a]	32.8	38.3
Hispanic/Latino	23.3	20.4
Other[a,b]	5.2	2.5
Age at release		
24 or younger	10.1%	17.3%
25–29	16.9	19.2
30–34	18.0	15.9
35–39	14.7	15.9
40–44	14.5	14.4
45–49	10.5	9.7
50 or older	15.2	7.6
Most serious commitment offense		
Violent[c]	7.2%	21.6%
Property	20.0	29.5
Drug	45.5	33.0
Other public order[d]	25.2	11.0
Sex offense[e]	2.2	4.9
Number of prior arrests per released prisoner[f]		
Mean	5.6	10.8
Median	4.0	8.0

Note: Federal and state prisoners are those conditionally released from prison. See appendix table 2 for standard errors.
[a]Excludes persons of Hispanic or Latino origin.
[b]Includes American Indian, Alaska Native, Asian, Native Hawaiian, Other Pacific Islander, and persons of two or more races.
[c]Excludes rape and sexual assault.
[d]Excludes other sex offenses.
[e]Includes rape and sexual assault; possession, distribution, and production of child pornography; and transportation for illegal sexual purposes.
[f]Number of times a prisoner was arrested before being released in 2005, including the arrest that led to the 2005 release.
Source: Bureau of Justice Statistics, Recidivism of Offenders Placed on Federal Community Supervision in 2005 and Recidivism of State Prisoners Released in 2005 data collections.

The two groups diverged regarding their prior offending histories. Seven percent of released federal prisoners were in prison for a violent crime, compared to 22% of released state prisoners. Among most serious commitment offenses, nearly half (46%) of federal prisoners were committed for a drug offense, compared to 33% for state prisoners. Two in 10 (20%) federal prisoners were in prison for a property crime, compared to about 3 in 10 (29%) state prisoners. On average, the released federal prisoners (6 arrests) had fewer prior arrests than released state prisoners (11 arrests).

Overall, the recidivism rates of released federal prisoners were lower than those of state prisoners. Among federal prisoners released on community supervision during 2005, 47% were arrested within 5 years, while 77% of the state prisoners conditionally released in 30 states in 2005 were arrested within 5 years (table 8). Compared to state prisoners, released federal prisoners also had lower recidivism rates within demographic subgroups. Differences among federal and state prisoners also were observed when examining the number of prior arrests; however, the difference in post-arrest rates decreased as the number of prior arrests increased. For example, the gap between post-arrest rates among state prisoners with two or fewer prior arrests (52%) and federal prisoners with two or fewer prior arrests (27%) declined when comparing post-arrest rates among state prisoners with 10 or more prior arrests (86%) to federal prisoners with 10 or more prior arrests (72%).

TABLE 8

Percent of state and federal prisoners released on community supervision in 2005 who were arrested for a new crime or returned to prison, by demographic characteristics, 2005–10

Characteristic	Federal prisoners		State prisoners	
	Arrest	Return to prison[a]	Arrest[b]	Return to prison[a,c]
All released prisoners	47.2%	31.6%	76.5%	59.4%
Sex				
Male	49.6%	33.4%	77.5%	56.4%
Female	35.4	22.1	68.1	44.9
Race/Hispanic origin				
White[d]	39.7%	26.2%	73.1%	53.2%
Black/African American[d]	55.1	35.7	80.6	55.6
Hispanic/Latino	48.3	33.1	75.7	57.8
Other[d,e]	48.5	38.5	74.2	58.8
Age at release				
24 or younger	64.7%	45.8%	84.2%	62.2%
25–29	59.3	40.7	80.6	57.3
30–34	52.9	34.7	77.0	54.8
35–39	48.6	31.9	78.1	56.0
40–44	44.5	29.4	74.2	55.0
45–49	37.7	24.7	69.0	48.8
50 or older	23.5	14.7	58.8	41.9
Most serious commitment offense				
Violent[f]	58.1%	44.3%	73.8%	51.0%
Property	39.5	26.1	82.2	62.5
Drug	44.0	27.1	76.7	53.2
Other public order[g]	57.0	40.2	73.0	54.2
Sex offense[h]	36.7	33.9	61.0	45.4
Number of prior arrests[i]				
1–2	27.0%	16.3%	52.4%	31.1%
3–4	46.4	29.6	67.3	44.3
5–9	59.9	40.8	75.6	53.8
10 or more	72.2	52.4	86.3	65.8

Note: Offenders were tracked for 5 years. See *Methodology* for recidivism definitions. See appendix table 3 for standard errors.
[a]Includes returns to a federal or state prison.
[b]Based on prisoners released conditionally in 30 states.
[c]Based on prisoners released conditionally in 23 states that provided the necessary prison admission data.
[d]Excludes persons of Hispanic or Latino origin.
[e]Includes American Indian, Alaska Native, Asian, Native Hawaiian, Other Pacific Islander, and persons of two or more races.
[f]Excludes rape and sexual assault.
[g]Excludes other sex offenses.
[h]Includes rape, sexual assault, and sexual abuse; possession, distribution, and production of child pornography; and transportation for illegal sexual purposes.
[i]Number of times a prisoner was arrested before being released in 2005, including the arrest that led to the 2005 release.
Source: Bureau of Justice Statistics, Recidivism of Offenders Placed on Federal Community Supervision in 2005 and Recidivism of State Prisoners Released in 2005 data collections.

While federal prisoners placed on community supervision had lower overall recidivism rates than state prisoners conditionally released, the pattern changed when examining the types of arrests prisoners had following release. Thirty-seven percent of federal prisoners had a nonfederal arrest (by a state or local law enforcement agency) within 5 years following release, compared to 75% of state prisoners (figure 3). However, 29% of federal prisoners had a federal arrest within 5 years after release, while 4% of state prisoners had a federal arrest. Within 2 years following release, federal prisoners were nearly as likely to have had a nonfederal arrest as a federal arrest. Starting at 3 years after release and extending through the end of the 5-year follow-up period, the likelihood for nonfederal arrests increased at a rate faster than federal arrests.

Compared to the state prisoners conditionally released, federal prisoners on community supervision were less likely to return to prison following release (figure 4). This finding was observable within a year after release and continued to the end of the follow-up period. Among released federal prisoners, 32% returned to prison within 5 years for either a revocation or an arrest that led to a new sentence. Among state prisoners released in 2005 in 23 states with available recidivism imprisonment data, 59% had either a parole or probation violation or an arrest for a new offense within 5 years that led to a return to prison.

In addition to having a lower recidivism rate following release, federal prisoners had fewer arrests for a new crime overall than state prisoners (table 9). For released federal prisoners, 18% had two to three arrests and 12% had four or more arrests for a new crime. In comparison, 27% of released state prisoners had two to three arrests and 31% had four or more arrests for a new crime.

FIGURE 4
Percent of state and federal prisoners released on community supervision in 2005 who were returned to prison, by time from release to first arrest, 2005–10

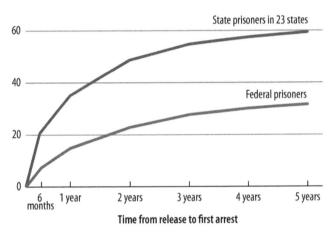

Note: Offenders were tracked for 5 years. See *Methodology* for recidivism definitions. See appendix table 5 for percentages and standard errors. Based on persons released in 23 states that provided the necessary prison admission data.
Source: Bureau of Justice Statistics, Recidivism of Offenders Placed on Federal Community Supervision in 2005 and Recidivism of State Prisoners Released in 2005 data collections.

FIGURE 3
Percent of state and federal prisoners released on community supervision in 2005 who were arrested, by type of arrest and time from release, 2005–10

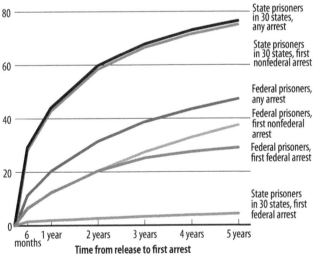

Note: Offenders were tracked for 5 years. Nonfederal arrests consist of those made by state and local law enforcement agencies. Offenders could have a federal arrest, a nonfederal arrest, or both. See appendix table 4 for percentages and standard errors.
Source: Bureau of Justice Statistics, Recidivism of Offenders Placed on Federal Community Supervision in 2005 and Recidivism of State Prisoners Released in 2005 data collections.

TABLE 9
Percent of state and federal prisoners released on community supervision in 2005 who were arrested for a new crime, by number of arrests, 2005–10

Number of new arrests	Federal prisoners	State prisoners in 30 states
Total	100%	100%
No arrests	52.8%	23.5%
1 or more arrests	47.2%	76.5%
1	17.3	19.2
2–3	18.4	26.8
4–7	9.8	22.3
8 or more	1.7	8.2

Note: Offenders were tracked for 5 years. See appendix table 6 for standard errors.
Source: Bureau of Justice Statistics, Recidivism of Offenders Placed on Federal Community Supervision in 2005 and Recidivism of State Prisoners Released in 2005 data collections.

Both federal and state prisoners were most likely to have a first-arrest charge for a public order offense, followed by drug, property, and violent offenses (table 10).

TABLE 10
First new arrest for state and federal prisoners released on community supervision in 2005 who were arrested for a new crime, by type of crime, 2005–10

First arrest following release	Federal prisoners	State prisoners in 30 states
Total	100%	100%
Violent	14.5%	15.3%
Homicide	0.4	0.3
Rape/sexual assault	0.6	0.8
Robbery	1.8	2.1
Assault	10.9	11.2
Other	0.9	0.8
Property	14.8%	22.3%
Burglary	1.6	3.8
Larceny/motor vehicle theft	5.5	8.8
Fraud/forgery	4.8	4.7
Other	2.9	4.9
Drug	16.1%	24.9%
Drug possession	6.1	6.5
Drug trafficking	7.1	12.0
Other	2.9	6.4
Public order	54.5%	37.5%
Weapons	1.5	2.1
Driving under the influence	7.8	4.9
Probation/parole violation	26.3	15.4
Other	18.9	15.0

Note: Detail may not sum to total due to rounding. Offenders were tracked for 5 years. See appendix table 7 for standard errors.

Source: Bureau of Justice Statistics, Recidivism of Offenders Placed on Federal Community Supervision in 2005 and Recidivism of State Prisoners Released in 2005 data collections.

For both federal and state prisoners released on community supervision, an arrest for a new crime following release was more likely an arrest for a nonfederal charge than a federal charge. Sixty-seven percent of all arrests for a new crime among released federal prisoners were for nonfederal charges, compared to 98% of arrests among state prisoners (table 11).

TABLE 11
Percent of state and federal prisoners on community supervision in 2005 who were arrested, by type of arrest, 2005–10

	Federal prisoners	State prisoners in 30 states
First arrest	100%	100%
Federal	36.5	2.8
Nonfederal*	63.5	97.2
All arrests	100%	100%
Federal	33.1	2.1
Nonfederal*	66.9	97.9

Note: Offenders were tracked for 5 years. See appendix table 8 for standard errors.

*Includes state and local law enforcement agencies.

Source: Bureau of Justice Statistics, Recidivism of Offenders Placed on Federal Community Supervision in 2005 and Recidivism of State Prisoners Released in 2005 data collections.

Methodology

Background

In 2008, the Bureau of Justice Statistics (BJS) entered into a data sharing agreement with the FBI's Criminal Justice Information Services (CJIS) Division and the International Justice and Public Safety Network (Nlets) to provide BJS access to criminal history records (i.e., rap sheets) through the FBI's Interstate Identification Index (III). A data security agreement was executed between BJS, the FBI, and Nlets to define the operational and technical practices used to protect the confidentiality and integrity of the criminal history data during data exchange, processing, and storage.

The FBI's III is an automated pointer system that allows authorized agencies to determine whether any state repository has criminal history records on an individual. Nlets is a computer-based network that is responsible for the interstate transmissions of federal and state criminal history records. It allows users to query III and send requests to states holding criminal history records on an individual. The FBI also maintains criminal history records that it has sole responsibility for disseminating. The identification bureaus that operate the central repositories in each state respond automatically to requests over the Nlets network. Responses received via Nlets represent an individual's national criminal history record.

Under the Criminal History Records Information Sharing (CHRIS) Project (award 2008-BJ-CX-K040), Nlets developed an automated collection system for BJS to use to retrieve national criminal history records from the FBI and state repositories on samples of offenders. Nlets produced software to parse the fields from individual criminal history records into a relational database. The database consists of state- and federal-specific numeric codes and text descriptions (e.g., criminal statutes and case outcome information) in a uniform record layout.

The Conversion of Criminal History Records into Research Databases (CCHRRD) Project (grant 2009-BJ-CX-K058) funded NORC at the University of Chicago to develop software that standardizes the content of the relational database produced by Nlets into a uniform coding structure that supports national-level recidivism research. The electronic records accessed by BJS through III for this study are the same records used by police officers to determine the current criminal justice status (e.g., on probation, parole, or bail) of a suspect; by judges to make pretrial and sentencing decisions; and by corrections officials to determine inmate classifications, parole releases, and work furloughs.

Data collection

This study is based on the 42,977 offenders placed on federal community supervision during fiscal year 2005 (October 1, 2004, to September 30, 2005). Federal supervision includes offenders directly sentenced in the federal courts to probation supervision in the community and offenders entering supervision following release from prison to serve a term of supervised release in the community. BJS obtained information on these offenders from the Office of Probation and Pretrial Services (OPPS) of the Administrative Office of the U.S. Courts' Probation/Pretrial Services Automated Case Tracking System (PACTS). This information included each offender's date of birth, sex, race and Hispanic origin, most serious conviction offense, length of community supervision sentence, and the start date of the sentence. OPPS also provided BJS with the FBI identification numbers needed to obtain criminal history records on the federal offenders. The first start date for a federal community supervision sentence during 2005 was selected for those with multiple start dates during the year. As part of the Recidivism of Offenders on Federal Community Supervision Project (award 2010-BJ-CX-K069), Abt Associates assisted BJS with assembling and analyzing the data.

BJS received approval from the FBI's Institutional Review Board (IRB) to access criminal history records through III for this study. This study employed a 5-year follow-up period. In February 2012, BJS sent the FBI identification numbers supplied by OPPS to III via Nlets to collect the criminal history records on the offenders. These records included arrests and court dispositions from all 50 states and the District of Columbia prior to and following the start of the offender's sentence in 2005. Juvenile offenses were rarely included in the criminal history records unless the offender was charged or tried in court as an adult. Over a 3-week period, Nlets electronically collated the responses received from the FBI and state criminal history repositories into a relational database.

To ensure that the records received using the federal offenders' FBI identification numbers were correct, BJS compared other individual identifiers in the PACTS data to those reported in the criminal history records. A federal offender's date of birth in the PACTS data exactly matched his or her birthdate in the criminal history records 98% of the time. Nearly 100% of the PACTS data and criminal history records matched on sex and race at the person level.

BJS reviewed the composition of the criminal history records for distributional differences and inconsistencies in reporting practices and observed some variations across states. During the data processing and analysis phases, steps were taken to standardize the information used to measure recidivism and to minimize the impact these variations had on the overall recidivism estimates. Administrative (e.g., a criminal registration or the issuance of a warrant) and procedural (e.g., transferring a suspect to another jurisdiction) records embedded in the arrest data that did not refer to an actual arrest were identified and removed from the study. Traffic offenses (except for vehicular manslaughter, driving while intoxicated, and hit-and-run) were also excluded from the study because the coverage of these events in the criminal history records varied widely by state. Among offenders placed on federal community supervision in 2005, approximately 2% of their arrests prior to and for 5 years after being placed on community supervision were for traffic offenses.

The criminal history records from some states recorded sentence modifications that occurred after the original court disposition and sentence while records from other states did not. To ensure that consistent counting rules were employed when recidivism was measured across states, the initial court disposition was captured for any arrest charge that had subsequent sentence modifications reported within the same arrest cycle. For instance, if a court adjudication was originally deferred and then later modified to a conviction, the deferred adjudication was coded as the disposition for that arrest charge.

Deaths during the follow-up period

BJS determined that 934 of the 43,911 offenders placed on federal community supervision in 2005 died during the 5-year follow-up period. These offenders were removed from the recidivism analysis. Initial identification of those who died within the 5-year period was done using death information contained in the criminal history record and OPPS's PACTS data. Additional deaths were identified by probabilistically linking the federal offenders to individuals identified as dead in the Social Security Administration's (SSA) public Death Master File (DMF).

Link Plus, a probabilistic record linkage program developed by the Centers for Disease Control and Prevention (CDC), was used to create and score potential matches between the federal offenders' records and the public DMF, using common identifiers found on each file.[3] For persons with multiple Social Security numbers and names and dates of birth, all possible combinations were tested for matches. The software computed a probabilistic record linkage score for each matched record, with the score representing the sum of the agreement and disagreement weights for each matching variable (the higher the score, the greater the likelihood that the match made is a true match). To differentiate true matches from false matches, the scores of the linked records were manually evaluated to ascertain the appropriate upper and

lower bound cutoff scores. During this review, records with a score of 20.0 or higher were determined to be exact matches of name, Social Security number, and date of birth, and scores of less than 10.9 indicated that none of the personally identifiable information matched.

Accordingly, these cutoffs were used as the upper and lower cutoff scores to automatically designate true matches and nonmatches. All remaining pairs that fell between the upper and lower cutoff scores were manually reviewed by two independent reviewers and independently categorized. All discrepancies where the reviewers did not agree (less than 1%) were jointly classified.

The number of released prisoners who were identified as dead in the DMF likely represents an undercount of the actual number of deaths within the sample. This is partly due to the limitations of the public DMF. Specifically, due to state disclosure laws, the public DMF does not include information on certain protected state death records (defined as records received via SSA's contracts with the states). This change, which occurred in November 2011, resulted in SSA removing more than 4 million state-reported death records from the public DMF and adding more than 1 million fewer records annually to the public DMF thereafter. As a result, the public DMF contains an undercount of annual deaths.

How extensively the public DMF undercounts the annual number of deaths is not known. Preliminary analyses of deaths in the public DMF compared to those reported via the CDC's mortality counts suggest that, in 2005, the public DMF undercounted the overall number of deaths in the United States by around 10%. The undercount has increased each year since 2005. As of 2010, the public DMF contained around half (45%) of the deaths reported by the CDC.

Furthermore, the coverage of the public DMF differs by decedent age, with younger decedents being less likely to appear in the public file. Because of this, the death count of offenders placed on federal community supervision in 2005 is likely an undercount of the actual number of deaths.

Missing criminal history records

Among the 42,977 eligible offenders known to have not died during the follow-up period, BJS did not obtain criminal history records on 2,961 offenders because either OPPS was unable to provide their FBI or state identification number or the offender had an FBI identification number that did not link to a criminal history record either in the FBI or state record repositories. To account for the missing data and to ensure the recidivism rates were representative of all 42,977 offenders in the analysis, the data regarding the 40,016 offenders with criminal history information required statistical adjustments to account for those offenders without criminal history information. A joint distribution of the offenders was produced based on sex, race and Hispanic origin, age, and most serious conviction offense. This

---

[3]Centers for Disease Control and Prevention. (2006). Link Plus Version 2.10 probabilistic record linkage software. Atlanta, GA: Centers for Disease Control and Prevention.

distribution documented the number of offenders who fell into each of 236 specific subpopulations defined by crossing 5 categories of age, 2 categories of sex, 4 categories of race and Hispanic origin, and 4 categories of conviction offenses. Within each of the subgroups, statistical weights were applied to the offenders with criminal history information to account for those without criminal history information. When this weight was applied to data on the federal offenders, the standard errors around the estimates were relatively small. For instance, an estimated 43% of persons placed on federal community supervision in 2005 were arrested for a new crime within 5 years. The standard error around this estimate was 0.004%.

Comparison group of released state prisoners

To examine the differences in the recidivism rates of the federal offenders in this study compared to those of state offenders, this report used the findings from a previous BJS study that collected national criminal history records on a sample of offenders released from state prisons in 30 states in 2005. Using data reported by state departments of corrections to BJS's National Corrections Reporting Program (NCRP), 68,597 released prisoners were randomly selected to represent the 404,638 inmates released at that time. In 2005, these 30 states were responsible for about three-quarters of all state prisoners released nationwide. States were selected for the study based on their ability to provide prisoner records and the FBI or state identification numbers of offenders released from correctional facilities in 2005. For more information on this study, see *Recidivism of Prisoners Released in 30 States in 2005: Patterns from 2005 to 2010* (NCJ 244205, BJS web, April 2014).

Conducting tests of statistical significance

This report examines how the recidivism rates of offenders released from federal prisons in 2005 compared with the recidivism rates of offenders released conditionally from state prisons in 30 states during the same year. Because the recidivism study of state prisoners was based on a sample and not a complete enumeration, the estimates are subject to sampling error (i.e., a discrepancy between an estimate and a population parameter based on chance). One measure of the sampling error associated with an estimate is the standard error. The standard error can vary from one estimate to the next. In general, for a given metric, an estimate with a smaller standard error provides a more reliable approximation of the true value than an estimate with a larger standard error. Estimates with relatively large standard errors are associated with less precision and reliability and should be interpreted with caution. BJS conducted tests to determine whether differences in the estimates based on the state prisoners were statistically significant once sampling error was taken into account.

All differences discussed in this report are statistically significant at or above the 95% confidence interval. Standard errors were generated using SUDAAN and SPSS statistical software packages that estimate sampling error from complex sample surveys.

Recidivism measures

This study used three types of events to measure recidivism: arrest, incarceration, and return to prison.

Arrest: An arrest within 5 years of being placed on federal community supervision in 2005. Information presented on the number of arrests is based on unique arrest dates, not individual charges. An arrest can involve more than one type of charge. For instance, one arrest could include a charge for a violent crime and a charge for a drug crime. BJS uses the most serious offense charge when characterizing the arrest offense type.

Return to prison—offenders from federal prison: An arrest within 5 years of being released from a federal prison in 2005 that resulted in a return to prison. When the type of facility (e.g., prison or jail) where an incarceration sentence was to be served was not reported in the criminal history records, a sentence of a year or more was defined as imprisonment. Information on the number of prison sentences is based on each unique arrest date that led to a prison sentence, not the date that the sentence was imposed.

A return to prison also may result from an arrest for a new crime or a technical violation of a condition of release within 5 years of being released from a federal prison in 2005. This recidivism measure incorporates the criminal history records from the FBI and state repositories, and the federal prison admission records obtained from the Bureau of Prisons (BOP). The criminal history records provided information on arrests that resulted in a prison sentence during the 5-year follow-up period. Using a common set of identifiers, BJS supplemented the criminal history records with information on the federal prisoners who returned to prison for a technical violation that did not involve a sentence for a new crime according to the BOP admission records.

Return to prison—offenders released from state prison: An arrest within 5 years of being released from a state prison in 2005 that resulted in a return to prison. When the type of facility (e.g., prison or jail) where an incarceration sentence was to be served was not reported in the criminal history records, a sentence of a year or more was defined as imprisonment. Information on the number of prison sentences is based on each unique arrest date that led to a prison sentence, not the date that the sentence was imposed.

A return to prison also may result from an arrest for a new crime or a technical violation of a condition of release within 5 years of being released from a state prison in 2005. This recidivism measure incorporates the criminal history records from the FBI and state repositories and state prison admission records obtained from state departments of corrections through the BJS National Corrections Reporting Program (NCRP). Criminal history records provided information on arrests that resulted in a prison sentence during the 5-year follow-up period. BJS used NCRP files from 2005 through 2010 to supplement the criminal history records with information on state prisoners who returned to prison for a technical violation or a sentence for a new crime.

Prisoners released from Maryland, Nebraska, Nevada, Ohio, Pennsylvania, and Virginia were excluded from the return-to-prison analysis because the individual identifiers or complete prison admission data needed to locate returns to prison during the entire 2005 through 2010 observation window were not available. Louisiana prisoners were also excluded from the return-to-prison analysis because the sentencing information in the criminal history records from this state was generally not linked to the associated arrest.

Measuring recidivism as an arrest for a new crime compared to a revocation

This report focuses on the arrests and incarcerations found in official criminal history records. Recidivism may also be defined as a revocation of the community supervision when the person violates terms or conditions which may or may not result in a return to prison and which may or may not be recorded in criminal history records. As part of this study, BJS obtained revocation information from OPPS's PACTS data on the 43,000 offenders placed on federal community supervision in 2005. To understand the extent to which revocations affect the recidivism patterns based solely on criminal history records, BJS separately tracked recidivism rates of federal offenders based on a combination of arrests in the criminal history records and revocations in the PACTS data. BJS employed the same methods to standardize arrest

measures, including removal of administrative, procedural, and traffic violation-related records. The differences in the level of observed recidivism using the two measures were consistent during the follow-up period. Within 1 year of being placed on community supervision in 2005, approximately 18% of offenders were arrested while 20% had either an arrest, revocation, or both (figure 5). At the end of the 5 years, 43% had an arrest and 45% had an arrest, a revocation, or both. In summary, while independent revocation information may add some insight, criminal history records on their own provide a nearly complete assessment of arrest-based recidivism rates and trends.

FIGURE 5

Percent of offenders placed on federal community supervision in 2005 who had an arrest or an arrest or revocation, 2005–10

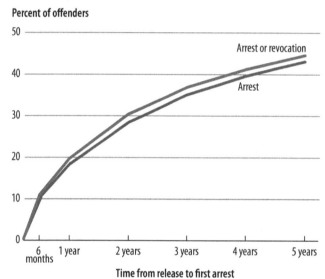

Note: Offenders were tracked for 5 years. See *Methodology* for recidivism definitions.
Source: Bureau of Justice Statistics, Recidivism of Offenders Placed on Federal Community Supervision in 2005 collection.

Offense definitions

Violent offenses include homicide, rape or sexual assault, robbery, assault, and other miscellaneous or unspecified violent offenses.

Homicide includes murder, nonnegligent manslaughter, negligent manslaughter, and unspecified homicide offenses.

Rape or sexual assault includes (1) forcible intercourse (vaginal, anal, or oral) with a female or male, (2) forcible sodomy or penetration with a foreign object (sometimes called deviate sexual assault), (3) forcible or violent sexual acts not involving intercourse with an adult or minor, (4) nonforcible sexual acts with a minor (such as statutory rape or incest with a minor), and (5) nonforcible sexual acts with someone unable to give legal or factual consent because of mental or physical defect or intoxication.

Robbery is the unlawful taking of property that is in the immediate possession of another, by force or the threat of force. It includes forcible purse snatching, but excludes nonforcible purse snatching.

Assault includes aggravated and simple and unspecified assault. Aggravated assault includes (1) intentionally and without legal justification causing serious bodily injury, with or without a deadly weapon, or (2) using a deadly or dangerous weapon to threaten, attempt, or cause bodily injury, regardless of the degree of injury, if any. The category also includes attempted murder, aggravated battery, felonious assault, and assault with a deadly weapon. Simple assault includes intentionally and without legal justification causing less than serious bodily injury without a deadly or dangerous weapon, or attempting or threatening bodily injury without a dangerous or deadly weapon.

Other violent offenses is a category that encompasses a range of crimes, including intimidation, illegal abortion, extortion, cruelty towards a child or wife, kidnapping, hit-and-run with bodily injury, and miscellaneous or unspecified crimes against the person.

Property offenses include burglary, fraud/forgery, larceny, motor vehicle theft, and other miscellaneous or unspecified property offenses.

Burglary is the unlawful entry of a fixed structure used for regular residence, industry, or business, with or without the use of force, to commit a felony or theft.

Larceny is the unlawful taking of property other than a motor vehicle from the possession of another, by stealth, without force or deceit. Includes pocket picking, nonforcible purse snatching, shoplifting, and thefts from motor vehicles. Excludes receiving or reselling stolen property or both, and thefts through fraud or deceit.

Motor vehicle theft is the unlawful taking of a self-propelled road vehicle owned by another. Includes the theft of automobiles, trucks, and motorcycles, but not the theft of boats, aircraft, or farm equipment (classified as larceny). Also includes receiving, possessing, stripping, transporting, and reselling stolen vehicles, and unauthorized use of a vehicle (joyriding).

Fraud/forgery includes using deceit or intentional misrepresentation to unlawfully deprive persons of their property or legal rights. It also includes offenses such as embezzlement, check fraud, confidence game, counterfeiting, and credit card fraud.

Other property offenses include arson, stolen property offenses, possession of burglary tools, damage to property, trespassing, and miscellaneous or unspecified property crimes.

Drug offenses include possession, trafficking, and other miscellaneous or unspecified drug offenses.

Drug possession includes possession of an illegal drug, but excludes possession with intent to sell. It also includes offenses involving drug paraphernalia and forged or unauthorized prescriptions.

Drug trafficking includes manufacturing, distributing, selling, smuggling, and possession with intent to sell.

Other drug offenses include offenses involving drug paraphernalia, forged or unauthorized prescriptions, and other miscellaneous or unspecified drug offenses.

Public-order offenses include weapons offenses, driving under the influence, and other miscellaneous or unspecified offenses.

Weapons include the unlawful sale, distribution, manufacture, alteration, transportation, possession, or use of a deadly or dangerous weapon or accessory.

Driving under the influence (DUI) is driving under the influence of drugs or alcohol and driving while intoxicated.

Other public-order offenses are those that violate the peace or order of the community or threaten the public health or safety through unacceptable conduct, interference with governmental authority, or the violation of civil rights or liberties. The category also includes probation or parole violations, escape, obstruction of justice, court offenses, nonviolent sex offenses, commercialized vice, family offenses, liquor law violations, bribery, invasion of privacy, disorderly conduct, contributing to the delinquency of a minor, and other miscellaneous or unspecified offenses.

APPENDIX TABLE 1
Percentages for figure 1: Cumulative percent of offenders placed on federal community supervision in 2005 who were arrested for a new crime, by type of arrest, 2005–10

Cumulative percent arrested within—	Any arrest	Federal arrest	Nonfederal arrest
6 months	10.3%	5.5%	6.1%
1 year	18.2	10.7	11.0
2 years	28.3	17.6	18.6
3 years	35.0	21.7	25.1
4 years	39.5	23.7	30.1
5 years	43.0	25.0	34.2

Source: Bureau of Justice Statistics, Recidivism of Offenders Placed on Federal Community Supervision in 2005 collection.

APPENDIX TABLE 2
Standard errors for table 7: Characteristics of state prisoners released on community supervision in 2005

Characteristic	State prisoners in 30 states
Total	0.16%
Sex	
Male	--
Female	--
Race/Hispanic origin	
White	0.36%
Black/African American	0.35
Hispanic/Latino	0.35
Other	0.12
Age at release	
24 or younger	0.28%
25–29	0.30
30–34	0.28
35–39	0.28
40–44	0.27
45–49	0.23
50 or older	0.21
Most serious commitment offense	
Violent	0.31%
Property	0.35
Drug	0.36
Other public order	0.23
Sex offense	0.17
Number of prior arrests per released prisoner	
Mean	0.075

-- Less than 0.005%.
Source: Bureau of Justice Statistics, Recidivism of State Prisoners Released in 2005 data collection.

APPENDIX TABLE 3
Standard errors for table 8: Percent of state and federal prisoners released on community supervision in 2005 who were arrested for a new crime or returned to prison, by demographic characteristics, 2005–10

Characteristic	State prisoners	
	Arrest	Return to prison
All released prisoners	0.33%	0.41%
Sex		
Male	0.36%	0.45%
Female	0.65	0.74
Race/Hispanic origin		
White	0.51%	0.61%
Black/African American	0.47	0.64
Hispanic/Latino	0.88	1.06
Other	2.08	2.44
Age at release		
24 or younger	0.65%	0.92%
25–29	0.70	0.94
30–34	0.87	1.07
35–39	0.82	1.03
40–44	0.92	1.08
45–49	1.18	1.38
50 or older	1.56	1.67
Most serious commitment offense		
Violent	0.75%	0.92%
Property	0.57	0.73
Drug	0.58	0.73
Other public order	1.00	1.17
Sex offense	2.03	2.13
Number of prior arrests		
1–2	1.00%	0.92%
3–4	0.92	1.03
5–9	0.62	0.74
10 or more	0.45	0.62

Source: Bureau of Justice Statistics, Recidivism of State Prisoners Released in 2005 data collection.

Percentages and standard errors for figure 3: Percent of state and federal prisoners released on community supervision in 2005 who were arrested, by type of arrest and time from release, 2005–10

Cumulative percent arrested within—	Federal prisoners			State prisoners in 30 states					
				Any arrest		First federal arrest		First nonfederal arrest	
	Any arrest	First federal arrest	First nonfederal arrest	Percent	Standard error	Percent	Standard error	Percent	Standard error
6 months	11.3%	6.3%	6.6%	29.2%	0.36%	1.5%	0.12%	28.0%	0.36%
1 year	20.3	12.3	12.0	44.0	0.37	1.9	0.12	42.7	0.37
2 years	31.4	20.3	20.4	59.7	0.34	2.6	0.14	58.3	0.35
3 years	38.6	25.1	27.3	67.8	0.32	3.3	0.16	66.5	0.33
4 years	43.4	27.5	32.9	73.0	0.30	3.8	0.16	71.6	0.32
5 years	47.2	28.9	37.4	76.5	0.29	4.3	0.17	75.1	0.30

Source: Bureau of Justice Statistics, Recidivism of Offenders Placed on Federal Community Supervision in 2005 and Recidivism of State Prisoners Released in 2005 data collection.

Percentages and standard errors for figure 4: Percent of state and federal prisoners released on community supervision in 2005 who were returned to prison, by time from release to first arrest, 2005–10

Cumulative percent returned to prison within—	Federal prisoners	State prisoners in 23 states	
		Percent	Standard error
6 months	7.3%	20.7%	0.34%
1 year	14.8	35.1	0.37
2 years	22.9	48.8	0.37
3 years	27.6	54.8	0.36
4 years	30.1	57.5	0.36
5 years	31.6	59.4	0.36

Source: Bureau of Justice Statistics, Recidivism of Offenders Placed on Federal Community Supervision in 2005 and Recidivism of State Prisoners Released in 2005 data collections.

Standard errors for table 9: Percent of state prisoners released on community supervision in 2005 who were arrested for a new crime, by number of arrests, 2005–10

Number of new arrests	State prisoners in 30 states
No arrests	0.29%
1 or more arrests	0.29%
1	0.29
2–3	0.34
4–7	0.34
8 or more	0.24

Source: Bureau of Justice Statistics, Recidivism of State Prisoners Released in 2005 data collection.

APPENDIX TABLE 7
Standard errors for table 10: First new arrest for state prisoners released on community supervision in 2005 who were arrested for a new crime, by type of crime, 2005–10

First arrest following release	State prisoners in 30 states
Total	0.33%
Violent	0.24%
Homicide	0.04
Rape/sexual assault	0.05
Robbery	0.10
Assault	0.20
Other	0.06
Property	0.28%
Burglary	0.13
Larceny/motor vehicle theft	0.19
Fraud/forgery	0.15
Other	0.14
Drug	0.31%
Drug possession	0.16
Drug trafficking	0.23
Other	0.17
Public order	0.36%
Weapons	0.11
Driving under the influence	0.14
Probation/parole violation	0.34%
Other	0.37

Source: Bureau of Justice Statistics, Recidivism of State Prisoners Released in 2005 data collection.

APPENDIX TABLE 8
Standard errors for table 11: Percent of state prisoners on community supervision in 2005 who were arrested, by type of arrest, 2005–10

	State prisoners in 30 states
First arrest	
Federal	0.17%
Nonfederal	0.17
All arrests	
Federal	0.11%
Nonfederal	0.11

Source: Bureau of Justice Statistics, Recidivism of State Prisoners Released in 2005 data collection.

The Bureau of Justice Statistics of the U.S. Department of Justice is the principal federal agency responsible for measuring crime, criminal victimization, criminal offenders, victims of crime, correlates of crime, and the operation of criminal and civil justice systems at the federal, state, tribal, and local levels. BJS collects, analyzes, and disseminates reliable and valid statistics on crime and justice systems in the United States, supports improvements to state and local criminal justice information systems, and participates with national and international organizations to develop and recommend national standards for justice statistics. Jeri M. Mulrow is acting director.

This report was written by Joshua A. Markman, Matthew R. Durose, and Ramona R. Rantala, BJS Statisticians, and Andrew D. Tiedt, Ph.D., former BJS Statistitican. Alexia D. Cooper, Ph.D., verified the report.

Lynne McConnell and Jill Thomas edited the report, and Tina Dorsey and Barbara Quinn produced the report.

June 2016, NCJ 249743

Office of Justice Programs
Innovation • Partnerships • Safer Neighborhoods
www.ojp.usdoj.gov

U.S. Department of Justice
Office of Justice Programs
Bureau of Justice Statistics

National Former Prisoner Survey, 2008

Sexual Victimization Reported by Former State Prisoners, 2008

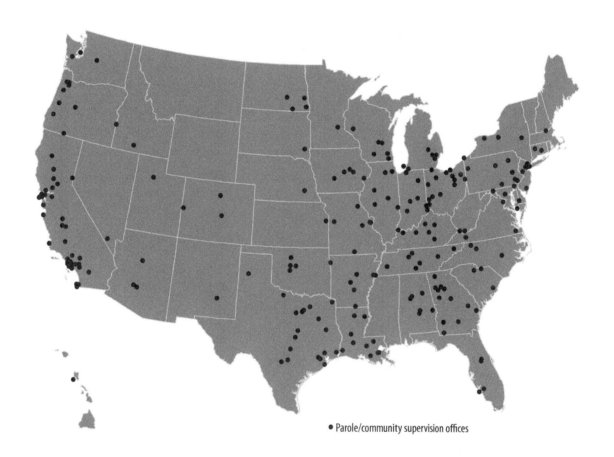

● Parole/community supervision offices

Allen J. Beck, Ph.D.
BJS Statistician

Candace Johnson, Ph.D.
Principal Research Scientist, NORC

May 2012, NCJ 237363

Bureau of Justice Statistics
James P. Lynch
Director

BJS Website:
www.bjs.gov

askbjs@usdoj.gov

The Bureau of Justice Statistics is the statistics agency of the U.S. Department of Justice. James P. Lynch is director.

This compendium was written by Allen J. Beck, BJS Statistician, and Candace Johnson, NORC Research Scientist. Jessica Rexroat, BJS intern, verified the report.

BJS statisticians Christopher J. Mumola and Paige M. Harrison, under the supervision of Allen J. Beck, were project managers for the National Former Prisoner Survey. NORC, under a cooperative agreement and in collaboration with BJS staff, developed the survey and collected, processed, and analyzed the data. Candace Johnson with Pam Loose directed the project; Kirk Wolter and Ken Copeland guided sampling, weighting, and other statistical support services; Kris Talley and Patt Maugherman led field operations; Angela Herrmann directed telephone center activities; Mike Cooke managed TACASI development and IT support; Marissa Kiss, Stephanie Poland, Mehera Baugher, and Emily Frizzell assisted throughout the project; and Lynda Okeke and Fang Wang prepared statistical tables.

Vanessa Curto and Jill Thomas edited the report, and Barbara Quinn and Tina Dorsey designed and produced the report, under the supervision of Doris J. James.

May 2012, NCJ 237363

National Former Prisoner Survey, 2008

Sexual Victimization Reported by Former State Prisoners, 2008

Allen J. Beck, Ph.D.
BJS Statistician

Candace Johnson, Ph.D.
Principal Research Scientist, NORC

May 2012, NCJ 237363

Contents

Highlights 5

Incidents of sexual victimization 8

Type of coercion and physical injury 12

Circumstances surrounding victimization 14

Variations by sex of former inmates 15

Variations by other individual-level characteristics 16

Variations by selected facility-level characteristics 20

Prison placements and individual-level risk factors 25

Reporting of sexual victimization 30

Post-release responses to victimization 32

HIV testing and results 33

Methodology 35

Appendix A 40

Appendix B 41

Appendix C 43

Appendix D 44

Appendix E 45

List of tables

Table 1. Former state prisoners reporting sexual victimization during most recent period of incarceration, by type of victimization and facility 8

Table 2. Former state prisoners reporting sexual victimization in a community-based correctional facility 10

Table 3. Criminal history and supervision status of persons under active parole supervision, by sex of former inmate . . .11

Table 4. Type of coercion and physical injury of former state prisoners who reported sexual victimization, by type of incident 12

Table 5. Circumstances surrounding sexual victimization of former state prisoners, by type of incident 14

Table 6. Former state prisoners reporting sexual victimization, by sex of inmate 15

Table 7. Staff sexual misconduct and type of activity, by sex of victim and sex of staff 15

Table 8. Prevalence of sexual victimization, by type of incident and former prisoner demographic characteristics 16

Table 9. Prevalence of sexual victimization, by type of incident and former prisoner criminal justice status and history 17

Table 10. Multivariate logistic regression models of sexual victimization, by type of incident, former prisoner demographic characteristics, and former prisoner criminal justice status and history 19

Table 11. Prison facilities entered and prison placements, by former state prisoners 20

Table 12. Sequence of reported sexual victimization in prison, by sex of victim and type of incident 21

Table 13. Prevalence of sexual victimization during prison placement, by sex of inmate, type of incident, and facility-level characteristics 23

Table 14. Prevalence of sexual victimization during each prison placement, comparing the National Former Prisoner Survey, 2008, and National Inmate Survey, 2008–09 25

Table 15. Prevalence of sexual victimization among male and female placements, by type of incident and former prisoner characteristics 26

Table 16. Final multivariate logistic regression models of sexual victimization among male and female placements, by type of incident and former prisoner and facility characteristics 28

Table 17. Reporting of sexual victimization, by type of incident and persons to whom the incident was reported 30

Table 18. Reasons for not reporting sexual victimization to facility staff, by type of victimization 31

Table 19. Facility responses to the reporting of sexual victimization to staff, by type of incident 31

Table 20. Post-release responses of victims to sexual victimization, by type of incident 32

Table 21. HIV testing and results for former state prisoners, by type of victim 33

Table 22. Current employment, housing, and living arrangements of former inmates under active parole supervision, by victimization status 34

List of appendix tables

Appendix table 1. Standard errors for table 4: Type of coercion and physical injury of former state prisoners who reported sexual victimization, by type of incident 46

Appendix table 2. Standard errors for table 5: Circumstances surrounding sexual victimization of former state prisoners, by type of incident 47

Appendix table 3. Wald-F statistics for former prisoner characteristics in the final multivariate logistic regression models of sexual victimization, by type of incident 48

Appendix table 4. Wald-F statistics for former state prisoner and facility characteristics in the final multivariate logistic regression models of sexual victimization among male and female placements, by type of incident 49

Appendix table 5. Standard errors for table 17: Reporting of sexual victimization, by type of incident and persons to whom the incident was reported 50

Appendix table 6. Standard errors for table 19: Facility responses to the reporting of sexual victimization to staff, by type of incident 50

Appendix table 7. Standard errors for table 20: Post-release responses of victims to sexual victimization, by type of incident 51

Highlights

Prevalence of sexual victimization

- An estimated 9.6% of former state prisoners reported one or more incidents of sexual victimization during the most recent period of incarceration in jail, prison, and post-release community-treatment facility.

- Among all former state prisoners, 1.8% reported experiencing one or more incidents while in a local jail, 7.5% while in a state prison, and 0.1% while in a post-release community-treatment facility.

- About 5.4% of former state prisoners reported an incident that involved another inmate. An estimated 3.7% of former prisoners said they were forced or pressured to have nonconsensual sex with another inmate, including manual stimulation and oral, anal, or vaginal penetration.

- About 5.3% of former state prisoners reported an incident that involved facility staff. An estimated 1.2% of former prisoners reported that they unwillingly had sex or sexual contact with facility staff, and 4.6% reported that they "willingly" had sex or sexual contact with staff.

- Although the rate of sexual victimization in state prison reported by former inmates (7.5%) was higher than the rate reported by inmates in previous BJS surveys (4.8% in 2008-09), the difference may reflect longer exposure periods (39.4 months and 7.9 months, respectively).

Coercion and physical injury

- Among victims of inmate-on-inmate sexual violence, a quarter had been physically held down or restrained, and a quarter had been physically harmed or injured.

- Half of all victims of staff sexual misconduct said they had been offered favors or special privileges; a third said they had been persuaded or talked into it.

- Approximately 16% of victims of unwilling sexual activity with staff, compared to 2% of victims of "willing" sexual activity, reported being physically injured by staff.

Individual risk factors

- The rate of inmate-on-inmate sexual victimization was at least 3 times higher for females (13.7%) than males (4.2%).

- The rate of "willing" sexual activity with staff was higher among males (4.8%) than females (2.6%), and the rate of unwilling sexual activity was higher among females (2.5%) than males (1.1%).

- Among heterosexual males, an estimated 3.5% reported being sexually victimized by another inmate. In comparison, among males who were bisexual, 34% reported being sexually victimized by another inmate. Among males who were homosexual or gay, 39% reported being victimized by another inmate.

- Female heterosexual inmates reported lower rates of inmate-on-inmate victimization (13%) and staff sexual misconduct (4%) than female bisexual inmates (18% and 8%, respectively).

- Among female homosexual or lesbian inmates, the rate of inmate-on-inmate sexual victimization was similar to that for female heterosexual inmates (13%), while the rate of staff sexual victimization was at least double (8%) that for female heterosexual inmates (4%).

- The rate of imate-on-inmate sexual victimization for males was higher among non-Hispanic white inmates (5.9%) and inmates of two or more races (9.5%) than non-Hispanic black inmates (2.9%).

- Among male former state prisoners, the rates of staff sexual misconduct were higher for those of two or more races (11.3%) and black non-Hispanics (6.5%) than for white non-Hispanics (4.5%) and Hispanics (4.0%).

- The rate of staff sexual misconduct was higher for male inmates ages 20 to 24 (7.9%) than for male inmates ages 25 to 34 (5.2%), ages 35 to 44 (3.5%), and age 45 or older (2.0%).

- Among female former state prisoners, rates of staff sexual misconduct were lower for those ages 35 to 44 (3.1%) and age 45 or older (1.6%), compared to those ages 20 to 24 (6.7%).

- Most victims of staff sexual misconduct (87%) reported only perpetrators of the opposite sex.

- Among victims of staff sexual misconduct, 79% were males reporting sexual activity with female staff. An additional 5% were males reporting sexual activity with both female and male staff.

Facility characteristics

- Rates of sexual victimization did not vary among commonly cited characteristics of facilities, including size of facility, facility age, crowding, inmate-to-staff ratios, or gender composition of staff.

- Among male former inmates, inmate-on-inmate and staff-on-inmate victimization rates were higher in facilities under a court order or consent decree, higher in facilities reporting a major disturbance in the 12 months prior to the most recent facility census, higher in facilities with medium or greater security levels, and higher in facilities with a primary function of housing general population than in facilities without these characteristics.

- Among female former inmates, rates of inmate-on-inmate victimization were lower in community corrections centers, in facilities that permitted 50% or more of their inmates to leave unaccompanied during the day, in minimum or low security facilities, and in privately operated facilities than in facilities without these characteristics.

- After controlling for multiple individual-level characteristics—

  ▶ Inmate-on-inmate and staff-on-inmate victimization rates among males were lower in reception and diagnostic centers than in facilities that housed general population, and lower in minimum security facilities than in facilities with higher security levels.

  ▶ Inmate-on-inmate victimization rates among females were lower in facilities that permitted 50% or more of their inmates to leave unaccompanied during the day than in other confinement facilities, lower in medium security facilities than in maximum or high security facilities, and higher in facilities that had a major disturbance in the census year than in facilities that did not.

Sexual victimization and its consequences

- Following their release from prison, 72% of victims of inmate-on-inmate sexual victimization indicated they felt shame or humiliation, and 56% said they felt guilt.

- The majority of victims of staff sexual misconduct involving unwilling activity said they felt shame or humiliation (79%) and guilt (72%) following their release from prison. More than half (54%) reported having difficulty feeling close to friends or family members as a result of the sexual victimization.

- Although the vast majority of victims of staff sexual misconduct (86%) reported at least one incident that they considered "willing," approximately a quarter said they felt guilt (27%) or shame and humiliation (23%) after their release from prison.

- Among former inmates who had been tested for HIV (90%), those who had been sexually victimized by other inmates or by staff had significantly higher percentages for HIV positive (6.5% and 4.6%, respectively) than those who had not been victimized (2.6%).

- Among former inmates under parole supervision, victims and nonvictims did not differ in their current employment (64% employed) or housing arrangements (92% in house, apartment, trailer, or mobile home); however, victims (18%) were somewhat more likely than nonvictims (14%) to be living alone.

Sexual Victimization Reported by Former State Prisoners, 2008

The Bureau of Justice Statistics (BJS) conducted the first-ever National Former Prisoner Survey (NFPS) between January 2008 and October 2008. NORC at the University of Chicago, under a cooperative agreement with BJS, collected the data. A total of 317 parole offices in 40 states were randomly included in the survey sample. A total of 17,738 former state prisoners who were under active supervision (i.e., required to contact a supervisory parole authority regularly in person, by mail, or by telephone) participated in the national survey. Interviews from an additional 788 former prisoners were included from the survey test sites. These former inmates had been randomly selected from 16 offices sampled. Based on 18,526 completed interviews, the survey achieved a 61% response rate. (See *Methodology* for further details.)

The NFPS is part of the National Prison Rape Statistics Program, which collects both administrative records of reported sexual violence and allegations of sexual victimization directly from victims. BJS has collected administrative records annually since 2004. We collected victim reports through surveys of adult inmates in prisons and jails in the National Inmate Survey in 2007 (NIS-1) and in 2008-09 (NIS-2) and through surveys of youth held in juvenile correctional facilities in the National Survey of Youth in Custody in 2008-09 (NSYC-1).

The NFPS collects data on the totality of the prior term of incarceration, including any time in a local jail, state prison, or community correctional facility prior to final discharge. Because the survey is based on a sample of parole offices and not a sample of prisons, the NFPS is not conducive to providing facility estimates or rankings. The NFPS is designed to encourage a fuller reporting of victimization, by surveying only former inmates, who are not subject to the immediate risk of retaliation from perpetrators or a code of silence while in prison. The NFPS may elicit reports of incidents that were unreported in the previous NIS-1 and NIS-2 surveys of prisoners; however, some reports may be untrue. At the same time, some former inmates may remain silent about sexual victimization experienced while incarcerated, despite efforts to assure victims that their responses will be kept confidential.

Other PREA data collections

The Prison Rape Elimination Act of 2003 (PREA; P.L. 108-79) requires the Bureau of Justice Statistics (BJS) to carry out, for each calendar year, a comprehensive statistical review and analysis of the incidence and effects of prison rape. The act further specifies that the review and analysis shall be based on a random sample or other scientifically appropriate sample of not less than 10% of all federal, state, and county prisons and a representative sample of municipal prisons. It requires BJS to use surveys and other statistical studies of current and former inmates. To fully meet these requirements, BJS has developed a multiple measure, multi-mode data collection strategy, in which the NFPS is one component.

National Survey of Youth in Custody (NSYC) provides facility-level estimates of youth reporting sexual victimization in juvenile facilities, as required under PREA. The first NSYC (NSYC-1) was conducted in 2008-09; the second (NSYC-2) is underway and will be completed by September 2012. NSYC-2 will provide estimates for large facilities that house adjudicated youth and for each of the 50 state systems and the District of Columbia.

National Inmate Survey (NIS) gathers data on the incidence of sexual assault in adult prisons and local jail facilities, as reported by inmates. The first NIS (NIS-1) was conducted in 2007, the second (NIS-2) was conducted in 2008-09, and the third (NIS-3) is underway and will be completed by May 2012. Based on inmate allegations, the NIS provides facility-level estimates used to rank facilities as required under PREA.

Survey of Sexual Violence (SSV) collects data annually on the incidence of sexual violence in adult and juvenile correctional facilities. Based on administrative data only, the SSV is limited to incidents reported to correctional officials. Begun in 2004, the SSV provides detailed information on incidents that have been substantiated upon investigation.

Clinical Indicators of Sexual Violence in Custody (CISVC) In 2010–11, in collaboration with the National Institute of Justice (NIJ) and the Centers for Disease Control and Prevention (CDC), BJS conducted a feasibility study using medical indicators and medical surveillance methodologies. As part of routine medical practice, medical staff in 19 prisons and 11 jails completed a surveillance form for adult males who either made an allegation of sexual violence or displayed clinical conditions consistent with sexual victimization. Results of the 12-month pilot study are expected in 2012.

Incidents of sexual victimization

9.6% of former state prisoners reported one or more incidents of sexual victimization during the most recent period of incarceration in jail, prison, or a post-release community-treatment facility

Among the 18,526 former state inmates participating in the NFPS survey, 2,096 reported experiencing one or more incidents of sexual victimization during their most recent period of incarceration, including the combined time in local jails, state prisons, or post-release community-treatment facilities. Because the NFPS is a sample survey, weights were applied to the sampled offices and offenders under their supervision to produce national-level estimates. The estimated number of former state prisoners experiencing sexual victimization totaled 49,000, or 9.6% of all former state prisoners under active supervision at midyear 2008 (table 1).

Among all former state prisoners, 1.8% reported experiencing one or more incidents while in a local jail, 7.5% while in a state prison, and 0.1% while in a post-release community-treatment facility. An estimated 1.4% reported an incident in a facility for which the type could not be determined.

5.4% of former inmates reported an incident with another inmate; 5.3% reported an incident with staff

Among former state prisoners, 5.4% (or an estimated 27,300 prisoners nationwide at midyear 2008) reported an incident that involved another inmate, and 5.3% (27,100) reported an incident that involved facility staff. Some inmates (1.1%) reported sexual victimization by both another inmate and facility staff.

An estimated 3.7% of former prisoners said they had nonconsensual sex with another inmate, including manual stimulation and oral, anal, or vaginal penetration. An additional 1.6% of former prisoners said they had experienced one or more abusive sexual contacts only with another inmate, including unwanted touching of the inmate's buttocks, thigh, penis, breast, or vagina in a sexual way.

An estimated 1.2% of former prisoners reported that they unwillingly had sex or sexual contact with facility staff. An estimated 4.6% said they "willingly" had sex or sexual contact with staff.

TABLE 1
Former state prisoners reporting sexual victimization during most recent period of incarceration, by type of victimization and facility

Type of incident	Estimated number of victims	Percent of former prisoners[a]			Standard errors[b]		
		All[c]	Prison	Jail	All	Prison	Jail
Total	49,000	9.6%	7.5%	1.8%	0.29%	0.26%	0.14%
Inmate-on-inmate	27,300	5.4%	3.7%	1.0%	0.24%	0.19%	0.09%
Nonconsensual sexual acts	18,700	3.7	2.6	0.6	0.17	0.14	0.06
Abusive sexual contacts only	7,900	1.6	0.9	0.2	0.13	0.09	0.04
Staff sexual misconduct	27,100	5.3%	4.7%	1.0%	0.22%	0.22%	0.10%
Unwilling activity	6,300	1.2%	1.0%	0.2%	0.11%	0.11%	0.03%
Excluding touching	5,100	1.0	0.8	0.1	0.10	0.10	0.02
Touching only	1,100	0.2	0.2	0.0	0.05	0.04	0.02
Willing activity	23,300	4.6%	4.0%	0.7%	0.21%	0.21%	0.08%
Excluding touching	22,200	4.3	3.4	0.3	0.21	0.21	0.06
Touching only	1,100	0.2	0.2	0.0	0.04	0.04	0.01

Note: Former prison inmates include only persons who were under active community supervision following a period of incarceration in state prison. See *Methodology* for sample description. Detail may not sum to total because former inmates may have reported more than one type of victimization or victimization in more than one type of facility.

[a]Based on the most recent period of incarceration, which may include time spent in local jail prior to admission to state prison and time spent in a post-release community treatment facility following release from prison.

[b]Standard errors may be used to construct confidence intervals around each estimate. See *Methodology* for calculations.

[c]Includes former inmates victimized in a post-release community-treatment facility (0.1%) and in facilities for which type was not reported (1.4%).

Source: BJS, National Former Prisoner Survey, 2008.

National Former Prisoner Survey Protocol

Active post-custody supervision

Only people who had served time in a state prison, were age 18 or older at the time of the survey, and under active post-release supervision were eligible to be part of the NFPS. The survey includes some people who were under age 18 at the time of their incarceration. These people were sentenced as adults and served time in adult facilities.

In 2008, approximately 85% of all persons under some form of post-custody supervision were considered to be under active supervision. Individuals who were ineligible for the survey included those who had absconded, were re-incarcerated, were in a halfway house or community-based treatment center, had a warrant issued for their arrest, were in violator status, or had been transferred to another parole office. Persons under supervision in small offices (under 40 parolees) in remote areas or in specialty offices (e.g., sex offender supervision or treatment facilities) were also excluded from the survey. Overall, the NFPS is a representative sample of approximately 510,800 former state prisoners under supervision at midyear 2008. (See *Methodology* for sampling information.)

Audio computer-assisted self-interview

The NFPS interviews, which averaged 23 minutes in length, were conducted using computer-assisted personal interviewing (CAPI) and audio computer-assisted self-interviewing (ACASI) data collection methods. Survey interviewers initiated the personal interview using CAPI to obtain demographic and criminal history information. For the remainder of the interview, respondents interacted with a computer-administered questionnaire using a touch-screen and synchronized audio instructions delivered via headphones. Respondents completed the survey in private at the parole office (or satellite office), with the interviewer in the room but unable to see the computer screen. (See *Methodology* for further description of the survey protocol.)

Voluntary participation with incentives

Before the interview, respondents were informed verbally and in writing that participation was voluntary and that all information provided would be held in confidence. They were also informed that if they agreed to participate, they would receive $50 as a token of appreciation for participating in the survey. A second automated consent protocol was administered at the beginning of the ACASI portion of the interview to confirm that the respondent had been properly informed that participating in the survey was voluntary and that they were "ready to continue with the interview."

Measuring sexual victimization

The NFPS first screened for inmate-on-inmate sexual touching "when they didn't want this to happen" and sexual activity "in which they did not want to participate." Respondents were then asked about the specific sexual activity, including oral, anal, or vaginal penetration, and about the specific contact, including touching of buttocks, thighs, breasts, penis, or vagina in an attempt to hurt or arouse the victim or the perpetrator. (See appendix A and B for specific survey questions.) Reports of inmate-on-inmate sexual victimization were classified as either nonconsensual sexual acts or abusive sexual contacts.

The NFPS also asked about staff sexual activity, including staff sexually harrassing the inmate, staring inappropriately at the inmate, and forcing the inmate to undress or brushing private parts when "it was not required by their job." Former inmates were then screened for sexual contact with staff, "whether it was willing or not," or "whether you wanted to have it or not." These contacts may have included oral, anal, or vaginal penetration and other forms of sexual stimulation through rubbing the penis and touching other private parts. (See appendix C and D for specific survey questions.)

Reports of staff sexual misconduct involving physical force, threat of force, fear of bodily injury, and being pressured or made to feel they had no choice were classified as "unwilling." Other reports of staff sexual misconduct in which former inmates reported willingly having sex or sexual contact with staff were classified as "willing" even though any sex or sexual contact between inmates and staff is illegal. (See *Definition of terms* on page 13.)

Former prisoners reported a wide variety of other sexual experiences with staff that were inappropriate:

- An estimated 8.9% reported that staff had hassled or harassed them in a sexual way.
- 27.9% said that staff had stared or watched them at inappropriate times (e.g., while the inmate was dressing or taking a shower).
- 13.5% said that staff had forced them to undress in their presence or had brushed against their private parts when "they did not think it was an accident or it was not required by their job."

Nearly a third (32.4%) of all former inmates reported one or more of these types of experiences. While inappropriate, these lesser forms of staff sexual misconduct were not included in the analysis unless combined with reports of "willingly" or unwillingly having sex or sexual contact with staff. (See appendix D for survey items related to staff-on-inmate sexual victimization.)

Few former inmates reported experiencing sexual victimization while in a community-based correctional facility

Correctional facilities are typically classified as community-based if 50% or more of the residents are regularly permitted to leave unaccompanied by facility staff to work or study in the community. Community-based facilities include entities such as halfway houses, residential treatment centers, restitution centers, and pre-release centers. Although community-based correctional facilities are covered by the Prison Rape Elimination Act (PREA), little data have been available on the rate of sexual victimization in these facilities. Despite the large number of such facilities (529 of the 1,719 state correctional facilities in 2005), they hold few inmates on any single day (54,233 inmates at yearend 2005, or approximately 4% of all state inmates held nationwide) (See *Census of State and Federal Correctional Facilities, 2005*, October 2008, BJS Web, NCJ 222182, appendix tables 2 and 10.) As a result of their small size (an average of 102 inmates per facility) and the relatively short length of stay for most inmates while in community-based facilities, inmates held in these facilities have been excluded from previous PREA-related inmate surveys.

The NFPS provides the first systematic data available on sexual victimization in community-based facilities. An estimated 66,400 former state prisoners (13%) said they had served some time in a community-based treatment facility or halfway house after release from prison. Among those inmates who had served time in such a facility, 0.9% reported experiencing one or more incidents of sexual victimization while in the facility (table 2). Among all former state prisoners, 0.1% said they had been sexually victimized while in a post-release community-treatment facility.

Approximately 65,500 former inmates (13%) reported spending time in a community-based facility before their release from prison. During the time they had been placed in such a facility, 2.0% reported experiencing one or more incidents of sexual victimization: 0.7% reported inmate-on-inmate sexual victimization, while 1.4% reported staff-on-inmate victimization.

Sexual victimization rates differed from those previously reported in the NIS-1 and NIS-2

The rate of sexual victimization reported by former state prisoners (9.6%) was substantially higher than the rates reported in the previous BJS National Inmate Surveys which were based on confined state and federal inmates (e.g., 4.5% in the NIS-1 conducted in 2007 and 4.4% in the NIS-2 conducted in 2008-09). The differences may largely reflect longer average exposure time among former inmates.

Unlike NFPS, the NIS-1 and NIS-2 provide facility-specific estimates of the prevalence of sexual victimization. As required under the PREA of 2003, these surveys are designed to provide a list of prisons and jails ranked by the prevalence of sexual victimization. To eliminate experiences that may have occurred in other facilities or in the distant past and to control for the varying length of stay, the NIS-1 and NIS-2 asked inmates to provide the most recent date of admission to the current facility. To provide comparative rates, if the date of admission was at least 12 months prior to the date of the interview, inmates were asked questions related to their experiences during the past 12 months. If the admission date was less than 12 months prior to the interview, inmates were asked about their experiences since they arrived at the facility.

As a consequence, the average exposure period among state prisoners participating in the NIS-2 was 7.9 months, compared to the average of 39.4 months that the former inmates in the NFPS had served in state prisons prior to their release (excluding time served in a local jail or post-release community-treatment facility). (See *Methodology* for differences in coverage between NFPS and NIS.)

TABLE 2
Former state prisoners reporting sexual victimization in a community-based correctional facility

Type of incident	Percent of former inmates who served time in a community-based facility	
	Before release[a]	After release[b]
Number of former inmates	65,500	66,400
Total	2.0%	0.9%
Inmate-on-inmate	0.7	0.4
Staff sexual misconduct	1.4	0.5

[a]Includes pre-release community-based facilities, such as halfway houses, residential treatment centers, restitution centers, and other pre-release centers.
[b]Includes post-release community-based treatment facilities only.
Source: BJS, National Former Prisoner Survey, 2008.

Criminal history and supervision profile of former inmates

In addition to collecting data on the sexual experiences of former state inmates during their most recent period of confinement, the NFPS gathered information on their criminal histories and their current supervision (table 3). Results from the survey include the following:

- Among former state inmates under active supervision, 47% had been on parole or community supervision for less than 12 months, 24% for 12 to 23 months, 12% for 24 to 35 months, and 17% for 36 months or more.

- About a third of the former inmates under active parole supervision had served time for a violent offense (33%) or a drug offense (30%), a quarter for a property offense (25%), and an eighth for a public-order offense (12%).

- Nearly 21% of the former inmates under active supervision had served time for a probation violation; 21% for a parole violation.

- Nineteen percent of the former state prison inmates had served less than 12 months in prison or jail before their release from prison; 25% had served 12 to 23 months; 16%, 24 to 35 months; 17%, 36 to 59 months; and 23%, 60 months or more.

- More than half of those under supervision (56%) had been released as a result of a parole board decision.

- As a condition of their release, more than 90% of the parolees were required to submit to drug testing; 78% were required to be employed.

- Participation in a treatment or counseling program was also required of 53% of the parolees for drugs; 39% for alcohol; and 26% for issues other than drugs or alcohol.

- Nearly 80% of parolees said they had a face-to-face meeting in the last month with their parole officer in the parole office; 57% said they had a face-to-face meeting outside of the office (at home, at work, or elsewhere); and 48% said they had been contacted by mail, e-mail, or telephone.

TABLE 3
Criminal history and supervision status of persons under active parole supervision, by sex of former inmate

	All[a]	Male	Female
Number under supervison	510,800	449,700	60,700
Time on parole/community supervision			
Less than 12 months	47.2%	47.1%	48.3%
12–23	24.0	23.9	25.1
24–35	11.6	11.7	11.5
36–59	8.2	8.3	7.6
60 months or longer	8.8	9.0	7.5
Most serious offense			
Violent	33.3%	35.0%	20.7%
Property	25.2	23.8	35.2
Drug	29.7	29.0	35.2
Public order	11.5	11.9	8.5
Other	0.3	0.3	0.5
Probation/parole violator			
No	58.8%	59.2%	55.8%
Yes[b]	41.2	40.8	44.2
Probation	20.7	19.7	28.5
Parole	21.0	21.7	16.3
Total time served			
Less than 12 months	19.0%	17.8%	27.6%
12–23	25.3	24.6	30.5
24–35	16.1	16.2	15.7
36–59	16.8	17.1	14.7
60–119	14.6	15.4	8.8
120 months or more	8.2	9.0	2.7
Release type			
Parole board decision	56.0%	56.4%	53.3%
Other release	43.0	42.6	45.4
Don't know[c]	1.0	1.0	1.3
Requirements of supervision			
Be employed	77.5%	78.9%	66.6%
Submit to drug testing	90.9	91.3	88.5
Participate in drug treatment or counseling	53.3	53.2	54.3
Participate in alcohol treatment or counseling	38.6	39.3	32.9
See counselor/therapist for issues other than drugs/alcohol	25.6	25.4	26.7
Contacts with parole officer in last month			
Face-to-face in office			
None	20.6%	19.9%	26.2%
1	50.5	50.4	51.5
2–3	19.9	20.4	16.3
4 or more	8.9	9.3	6.0
Face-to-face outside of office			
None	43.2%	42.4%	49.4%
1	39.5	39.8	37.4
2–3	13.7	14.1	10.4
4 or more	3.6	3.7	2.8
Contact by mail, e-mail, or telephone			
None	51.9%	52.2%	49.4%
1	23.1	23.0	23.9
2–3	17.8	17.8	18.0
4 or more	7.2	7.0	8.7

[a]Includes persons who said they were transgendered.

[b]Detail may not sum to total because some former inmates had violated both probation and parole.

[c]Former inmates said they did not know if they had been released through a parole board decision.

Source: BJS, National Former Prisoner Survey, 2008.

Type of coercion and physical injury

Among victims of inmate-on-inmate sexual violence, a quarter had been physically held down or restrained and a quarter had been physically harmed or injured

Incidents of inmate-on-inmate sexual victimization involved a wide array of acts with differing levels of coercion and force to get the victim to participate. Although many of the victims were not raped, all of the victims had been sexually abused.

Force or threat of force or harm was reported by 59% of victims of inmate-on-inmate sexual victimization—about 3.2% of former state prisoners overall (not shown in table). An estimated 53% said they had been threatened with harm or a weapon; 28% had been physically held down or restrained, and 25% had been physically harmed or injured. (table 4).

The most common form of coercion other than force or threat of force was being "persuaded or being talked into it" (34%) against their will. A quarter of victims (26%) said the inmate perpetrator had given them a bribe or blackmailed them, and a quarter (24%) said they had been offered or given protection from other inmates. In addition, some victims had been given drugs or alcohol to get them drunk or high (9%), and some had sexual contact to pay off or settle a debt that they owed (8%). Overall, 52% of victims reported one or more of these types of coercion.

Among victims of inmate-on-inmate sexual victimization, the most common injuries were anal or vaginal tearing, severe pain or bleeding (12%) and chipped or lost teeth (12%). Although 29% of all victims reported bruises, black eyes, sprains, cuts, scratches, swelling, or welts from one or more incidents involving another inmate, nearly a quarter (23%) also reported more serious injuries.

TABLE 4

Type of coercion and physical injury of former state prisoners who reported sexual victimization, by type of incident

	Inmate-on-inmate		Staff sexual misconduct		
	Total[a]	Nonconsensual sexual acts	Total	Willing activity[b]	Unwilling activity[b]
Number of victims	27,300	18,700	27,100	23,300	6,300
Type of coercion[c]					
Force/threat	58.6%	65.6%	12.3%	5.4%	48.2%
Threatened with harm or a weapon	53.1	59.7	11.0	5.2	43.9
Physically held down or restrained	28.1	34.2	4.9	1.5	19.2
Physically harmed/injured	24.8	30.0	4.1	1.6	15.2
Coercion other than force/threat	51.7%	63.0%	62.4%	61.6%	87.0%
Persuaded/talked into it	34.3	45.4	35.2	33.9	71.9
Offered/given protection from other inmates	24.4	29.4	6.5	5.0	16.5
Given bribe/blackmailed	25.6	31.3	27.2	24.3	60.4
Given drugs/alcohol	9.0	12.0	18.6	19.9	21.0
Pay off debt[d]	8.2	10.8	3.1	2.7	6.5
Offered/given protection from another correctional officer[d]	~	~	13.3	10.3	34.2
Offered favors or special privileges	~	~	49.6	49.1	72.0
Physically injured[c]	29.7%	35.3%	4.1%	2.1%	16.5%
Excluding minor injuries	22.9	28.4	3.2	1.6	13.0
Knife/stab wounds	4.4	5.1	0.6	0.2	2.6
Broken bones	4.3	5.5	0.5	0.5	1.9
Anal/vaginal tearing, severe pain, or bleeding	11.7	17.0	2.1	1.0	8.8
Teeth chipped/knocked out	11.5	13.9	1.6	0.6	6.3
Internal injuries	6.3	7.4	1.2	0.5	4.9
Knocked unconscious	8.4	10.5	0.6	0.4	2.5
Bruises, a black eye, sprains, cuts, scratches, swelling, or welts	28.6	33.8	2.9	1.0	11.8

Note: See appendix table 1 for estimated standard errors.

~Not applicable.

[a]Includes abusive sexual contacts.

[b]Includes touching only.

[c]Detail may not sum to total because multiple responses were allowed for this item.

[d]Not included in the pretest interviews. See *Methodology* for a detailed discussion of the merged pretest and full survey data files.

Source: BJS, National Former Prisoner Survey, 2008.

Half of victims of staff sexual misconduct said they had been offered favors or special privileges; a third had been persuaded or talked into it; a quarter had been bribed or blackmailed

Most victims of staff sexual misconduct said they "willingly" had sex or sexual contact with staff; however, many of these victims also reported sexual contact or activity with staff that involved some form of coercion. Among the estimated 23,300 former prisoners who reported some type of "willing" activity with staff, 11% (2,500) also reported unwilling sexual activity with staff. The most common form of coercion reported by the 23,300 "willing" victims was offers of favors or special privileges by staff (49%), followed by being persuaded or talked into it by staff (34%) and being given a bribe or blackmailed (24%). Overall, 62% of inmates who had engaged in "willing" sex or sexual activity with staff reported some type of coercion or offer of favors, special privileges, or protection by staff.

An estimated 6,300 former state prisoners (1.2%) reported unwilling sexual activity with staff during their most recent period of incarceration. These unwilling victims (48%) were more likely than "willing" victims of staff sexual misconduct (5%) to report having been physically forced or threatened by staff. An estimated 44% of unwilling victims said they had been threatened with harm or a weapon, 19% said they had been physically held down, and 15% said they had been physically harmed or injured.

Nearly 7 of every 8 inmates who reported unwilling sexual activity with staff said that staff had employed other forms of coercion to engage them in sexual activities or have sexual contact. In specific, 72% of the victims were offered favors or special privileges, 72% were persuaded or talked into it, 60% were given bribes or blackmailed, 34% were offered protection from other staff, and 21% were given drugs or alcohol.

These reports suggest that these former inmates experienced a wide array of pressures from staff to have sexual contact against their will. More than 80% of victims who reported force and threat of force also reported one or more of these other forms of coercion (not shown in table).

Four percent of victims of staff sexual misconduct reported that they were physically injured

Approximately 16% of victims of unwilling sexual activity with staff, compared to 2% of victims of "willing" sexual activity, reported being physically injured by staff. Among victims of unwilling activity, the most commonly reported injuries were bruises, black eyes, sprains, cuts, scratches, swelling or welts (11.8%). Most of these victims of unwilling sexual activity also reported more serious injuries, including anal or vaginal tearing (8.8%), loss or chipping of teeth (6.3%), and receiving internal injuries (4.9%). Though few victims of "willing" sexual activity with staff reported being injured, some (1.6%) reported a serious injury.

Definition of terms

Sexual victimization—all types of unwanted sexual activity with other inmates (e.g., oral, anal, or vaginal penetration, hand jobs, or touching of the inmate's buttocks, thighs, penis, breasts, or vagina in a sexual way), abusive sexual contacts with other inmates, and both willing and unwilling sexual activity with staff.

Nonconsensual sexual acts—unwanted contact with another inmate or any contact with staff that involved oral, anal, vaginal penetration, hand jobs, and other sexual acts.

Abusive sexual contacts only—unwanted contact with another inmate or any contact with staff that involved touching of the inmate's buttocks, thighs, penis, breasts, or vagina in a sexual way.

Unwilling activity—incidents of unwanted sexual contact with another inmate or staff.

Willing activity—incidents of willing sexual contacts with staff. These contacts are characterized by the reporting inmates as willing; however, all sexual contacts between inmates and staff are legally nonconsensual.

Staff sexual misconduct—all incidents of willing and unwilling sexual contact with facility staff, and all incidents of sexual activity that involved oral, anal or vaginal penetration, hand jobs, and other sexual acts with facility staff.

Circumstances surrounding victimization

Inmate-on-inmate victimization occurred most often in the victim's cell; staff-on-inmate victimization occurred most often in a closet, office, or other locked room

In the NFPS victims were asked to provide additional information about the circumstances surrounding their victimization, including the number of times it had happened, the number of different perpetrators, when each incident occurred, and where it occurred in each facility.

Data provided by inmates who reported sexual victimization by another inmate revealed that—

- Victimization was more common in the evening (between 6 p.m. and midnight) (52%) than at any other time (table 5).

- Almost two-thirds (62%) of the victims said at least one incident took place in their cell or room, and a quarter said an incident took place in another inmate's cell or room (24%).

- An estimated 46% of inmate-on-inmate victims had been victimized by more than one perpetrator.

- About 42% had been victimized once; 31% had been victimized 3 or more times.

Most victims (86%) of staff sexual misconduct reported more than one incident; 47% reported more than one perpetrator

Data provided by inmates who had been sexually victimized by facility staff also revealed that—

- Reports of staff sexual misconduct were more common between midnight and 6 a.m. (54%) than at any other time.

- More than two-thirds (70%) of the victims said at least one incident had occurred in a closet, office, or other locked room; half (54%) of the victims said an incident had occurred in a work area; and a third (35%) in a shower or bathroom.

- Reports of when and where incidents had occurred were similar among willing and unwilling victims.

TABLE 5
Circumstances surrounding sexual victimization of former state prisoners, by type of incident

Circumstance	Inmate-on-inmate		Staff sexual misconduct		
	Total[a]	Nonconsensual sexual acts	Total	Willing activity[b]	Unwilling activity[b]
Number of victims[c]	27,300	18,700	27,100	23,300	6,300
Time of day[d]					
6 a.m. to noon	30.4%	30.3%	41.7%	41.7%	44.5%
Noon to 6 p.m.	35.5	34.0	37.6	37.7	35.6
6 p.m. to midnight	52.2	56.6	46.4	46.6	50.9
Midnight to 6 a.m.	41.3	52.8	54.5	56.5	51.3
Where occurred[d]					
Victim's cell/room/sleeping area	61.9%	71.3%	42.8%	43.8%	45.9%
Another inmate's cell/room	24.3	31.5	9.0	9.9	8.5
Shower/bathroom	36.7	38.4	35.0	36.5	33.8
Yard/recreation area	21.8	19.2	10.8	10.2	11.8
Workplace	17.9	19.8	54.5	55.8	57.4
Closet, office, or other locked room	13.1	17.2	69.8	71.7	67.0
Classroom/library	9.6	11.3	33.8	34.5	33.6
Elsewhere in facility	11.3	11.6	13.3	13.7	12.1
Off facility grounds[e]	5.4	5.9	9.9	9.9	14.4
Number of perpetrators					
1	53.8%	48.1%	52.8%	52.0%	53.6%
2	25.4	28.0	27.0	27.5	22.0
3 or more	20.8	23.9	20.3	20.5	24.4
Number of times					
1	42.4%	36.4%	14.2%	13.2%	11.0%
2	26.2	26.5	22.3	22.2	19.3
3 or more	31.3	37.1	63.5	64.6	69.7

Note: See appendix table 2 for estimated standard errors.

[a]Includes abusive sexual contacts.

[b]Includes touching only.

[c]Detail may not sum to total because respondents may have reported more than one type of victimization.

[d]Detail may sum to total because multiple responses were allowed for this item.

[e]Includes incidents that occurred in a temporary holding facility, on work release, in a medical facility, in a vehicle, or at a courthouse.

Source: BJS, National Former Prisoner Survey, 2008.

Variations by sex of former inmates

Past BJS surveys of confined prison inmates have consistently found higher rates of inmate-on-inmate victimization among females than males. In the National Inmate Survey, 2008-09, 4.7% of the surveyed female inmates and 1.9% of the male inmates reported being sexually victimized by another inmate. This difference was found to be statistically independent and largely unexplained by covariation with other demographic characteristics (e.g., an inmate's race or Hispanic origin, age, education, marital status, and weight). (See Sexual Victimization in Prisons and Jails Reported by Inmates, 2008-09, tables 6 and 7.) The reports of former prisoners confirm the large and statistically significant difference between male and female rates of inmate-on-inmate sexual victimization (table 6).

The rate of inmate-on-inmate sexual victimization among former state prisoners was 3 times higher among females (13.7%) than males (4.2%)

When the rate of sexual victimization was limited to nonconsensual sexual acts including only incidents of manual stimulation and oral, anal, or vaginal penetration, the difference between females and males was large. An estimated 10.5% of females reported such incidents with other inmates, compared to 2.7% of males.

The rate of "willing" sexual activity with staff was higher among males (4.8%) than females (2.6%), and the rate of unwilling sexual activity was higher among females (2.5%) than males (1.1%)

Most victims of staff sexual misconduct (87%) reported only perpetrators of the opposite sex (table 7). Same-sex victimization was more likely to be reported by victims of unwilling staff sexual misconduct than by victims of "willing." Approximately a quarter of the reports of unwilling sexual activity with staff involved male inmates with male staff only (23%) and female inmates with female staff only (3%).

TABLE 6
Former state prisoners reporting sexual victimization, by sex of inmate

Type of incident	Percent of former prisoners		
	All	Male*	Female
Total[a]	9.6%	8.7%	16.1%**
Inmate-on-inmate	5.4%	4.2%	13.7%**
Nonconsensual sexual acts	3.7	2.7	10.5**
Abusive sexual contacts only	1.6	1.3	3.1**
Staff sexual misconduct	5.3%	5.4%	4.4%
Unwilling activity	1.2%	1.1%	2.5%**
Excluding touching	1.0	0.9	1.7**
Touching only	0.2	0.2	0.7**
Willing activity	4.6%	4.8%	2.6%**
Excluding touching	4.3	4.6	2.2**
Touching only	0.2	0.2	0.4

*Comparison group.

**Difference with comparison group is significant at the 95%-confidence level.

[a]Detail may not sum to total because former inmates may report more than one type of victimization.

Source: BJS, National Former Prisoner Survey, 2008.

TABLE 7
Staff sexual misconduct and type of activity, by sex of victim and sex of staff

	All staff sexual misconduct	Willing activity	Unwilling activity
Total	100%	100%	100%
Male victims			
Female staff only	78.7%	86.0%	42.2%
Male staff only	6.8	4.4	23.1
Both male and female staff	4.6	2.7	10.9
Female victims			
Female staff only	1.3%	1.1%	2.8%
Male staff only	8.1	5.5	19.2
Both male and female staff	0.5	0.3	1.8

Source: BJS, National Former Prisoner Survey, 2008.

Variations by other individual-level characteristics

Large differences in sexual victimization were found among former inmates based on their sexual orientation

An estimated 3.5% of male heterosexual former inmates reported being sexually victimized by another inmate, and 5.2% reported being victimized by staff (table 8). In comparison, 34% of male inmates who were bisexual reported being sexually victimized by another inmate, and 18% reported being sexually victimized by staff. Thirty-nine percent of male inmates who were homosexual or gay indicated they had been victimized by another inmate and 12% by staff.

- Bisexual female former inmates reported a higher rate of inmate-on-inmate victimization (18%) than heterosexual inmates (13%) and lesbian inmates (13%).

- Lesbian inmates and bisexual female former inmates had rates of staff sexual misconduct that were at least double (8%) the rate among heterosexual female former inmates.

TABLE 8
Prevalence of sexual victimization, by type of incident and former prisoner demographic characteristics

Demographic characteristic	Number of male former prisoners	Percent of male former prisoners reporting sexual victimization — Inmate-on-inmate	Percent of male former prisoners reporting sexual victimization — Staff sexual misconduct	Number of female former prisoners	Percent of female former prisoners reporting sexual victimization — Inmate-on-inmate	Percent of female former prisoners reporting sexual victimization — Staff sexual misconduct
Race/Hispanic origin						
White[a]	173,200	5.9%**	4.5%**	29,300	13.2%	4.5%
Black/African American[a]*	171,000	2.9	6.5	17,400	15.2	4.2
Hispanic/Latino	80,500	2.7	4.0**	10,100	12.2	3.8
Other[a,b]	13,500	4.1	6.0	1,800	7.2	2.3
Two or more races[a]	11,100	9.5**	11.3**	1,800	23.9	11.9**
Age at admission						
Under 18	10,200	8.4%	18.6%	800	14.8%	14.9%
18–19	27,000	4.3	9.1	1,700	22.9	10.4
20–24*	91,000	5.3	7.9	8,300	17.1	6.7
25–34	146,600	4.1	5.2**	20,300	14.8	5.1
35–44	107,300	3.7	3.5**	20,100	12.0	3.1**
45 or older	61,500	3.5	2.0**	9,000	10.9	1.6**
Education[c]						
Less than high school[d]*	267,100	4.0%	5.5%	33,200	13.0%	4.5%
High school graduate	89,800	3.2	4.0**	11,300	12.2	2.8
Some college	78,100	5.8	7.0	13,400	16.4	4.8
College degree or more	14,100	5.2	5.2	2,600	15.3	8.1
Marital status[c]						
Married*	90,700	4.8%	6.4%	10,600	12.4%	4.3%
Widowed, divorced, or separated	132,400	4.1	4.5**	25,100	15.4	4.3
Never married	225,500	4.0	5.6	24,900	12.7	4.6
Weight[c,e]						
1st quartile*	121,200	4.9%	4.5%	16,700	14.3%	5.0%
2nd quartile	108,400	4.1	5.3	13,300	12.6	3.5
3rd quartile	118,800	4.0	5.7	15,000	14.1	4.7
4th quartile	101,200	3.8	6.4**	14,900	13.8	4.1
Sexual orientation[c]						
Straight/heterosexual*	435,600	3.5%	5.2%	49,800	13.1%	3.7%
Bisexual	5,500	33.7**	17.5**	7,300	18.1**	7.5**
Lesbian/gay/homosexual	4,200	38.6**	11.8**	3,300	12.8	8.0**

*Comparison group.

**Difference with comparison group is significant at the 95%-confidence level.

[a]Excludes persons of Hispanic or Latino origin.

[b]Includes American Indians, Alaska Natives, Asians, Native Hawaiians, and other Pacific Islanders.

[c]As reported at time of interview.

[d]Includes former prisoners who received a GED while incarcerated.

[e]Weight quartiles are defined by sex: Men—1st quartile (86 to 170 lbs.), 2nd quartile (171 to 190 lbs.), 3rd quartile (191 to 220 lbs.), 4th quartile (more than 220 lbs.). Women—1st quartile (78 to 145 lbs.), 2nd quartile (146 to 169 lbs.), 3rd quartile (170 to 198 lbs.), 4th quartile (more than 198 lbs.).

Source: BJS, National Former Prisoner Survey, 2008.

Rates of inmate-on-inmate sexual victimization among males varied by race and Hispanic origin. Rates of inmate-on-inmate victimization for males were higher among white non-Hispanic inmates (5.9%) and multi-racial inmates (9.5%) than among black non-Hispanic inmates (2.9%). Among females, rates of inmate-on-inmate victimization did not vary significantly across other demographic characteristics.

Patterns of staff sexual misconduct among male former prisoners varied among multiple demographic characteristics. Rates of staff sexual misconduct were higher for those of two or more races (11.3%) and lower for white non-Hispanic inmates (4.5%) and Hispanic inmates (4.0%), when compared to black non-Hispanic inmates (6.5%). Rates of staff sexual misconduct were also higher among younger male inmates (under age 25) than among older male inmates; higher among those with less than a high school education than those who completed high school; and higher for those who were married than those who were widowed, divorced, separated, or never married.

Among female former prisoners, rates of staff sexual misconduct were significantly lower among those ages 35 to 44 (3.1%) and age 45 or older (1.6%), compared to those ages 20 to 24 (6.7%). The only other statistically significant difference among female inmates was that 11.9% of multi-racial inmates reported staff sexual misconduct, which was approximately 2 to 3 times the rate of victimization reported by white non-Hispanic inmates (4.5%), black non-Hispanic inmates (4.2%), and Hispanic inmates (3.8%).

Violent, male sex offenders reported high rates of inmate-on-inmate sexual victimization (13.7%)

Consistent with findings in previous BJS data collections based on inmates held in prisons and local jails, male former state prisoners whose most serious offense was a violent sex offense reported significantly higher rates of inmate-on-inmate sexual victimization than other inmates (table 9). The rate among male sex offenders (13.7%) was more than twice the rate among other violent male offenders (4.9%), 3 times the rate of property offenders (4.4%), 5 times the rate of public-order offenders (2.6%), and 6 times the rate of drug offenders (2.0%). Among female former inmates, no differences were found in rates of inmate-on-inmate sexual victimization by type of offense for which they had been sentenced.

TABLE 9
Prevalence of sexual victimization, by type of incident and former prisoner criminal justice status and history

Criminal justice status and history	Number of male former prisoners	Percent of male former prisoners reporting sexual victimization		Number of female former prisoners	Percent of female former prisoners reporting sexual victimization	
		Inmate-on-inmate	Staff sexual misconduct		Inmate-on-inmate	Staff sexual misconduct
Prior incarcerations						
No prior incarceration*	79,700	6.6%	5.7%	14,200	11.9%	4.4%
1 or more prior incarcerations	370,300	3.7**	5.4	46,500	14.3	4.4
Most serious offense						
Violent sexual offense*	28,500	13.7%	6.5%	500	17.2%	10.4%
Other violent	125,500	4.9**	8.6	11,700	15.5	7.0
Property	104,900	4.4**	5.8	20,900	14.4	4.2
Drug	127,500	2.0**	3.0**	20,900	12.5	3.5
Public order	52,400	2.6**	2.3**	5,100	10.4	2.9
Other	1,500	5.6	7.3	300	8.0	0.0
Total time served[a]						
Less than 12 months*	80,100	1.8%	2.0%	16,800	9.3%	1.3%
12–23	110,500	3.1	3.1	18,500	13.8	3.7**
24–35	72,900	3.6**	3.6**	9,500	13.9	2.2
36–59	76,800	2.8	5.3**	8,900	16.9**	6.2**
60–119	69,000	6.4**	8.3**	5,300	20.9**	11.3**
120 months or longer	40,300	12.3**	17.2**	1,600	16.4	25.4**
Number of facilities[b]						
1*	25,200	2.4%	2.6%	5,100	9.0%	2.2%
2	91,900	3.4	3.9	20,100	13.5	3.6
3	127,000	3.9	4.0	19,800	13.6	3.8
4	92,400	4.3	5.4**	9,800	16.5**	4.4
5	52,400	4.5	6.7**	3,900	14.6	7.7**
6 or more	61,000	6.5**	10.7**	2,000	13.6	17.7**

*Comparison group.

**Difference with comparison group is significant at the 95%-confidence level.

[a]Includes time served in jail, all prison facilities, and post-release community treatment facilities.

[b]Includes all facilities in which the former inmates were held during the most recent period of incarceration.

Source: BJS, National Former Prisoner Survey, 2008.

Rates of sexual victimization increased with the length of time that former inmates had served

Rates of sexual victimization by other inmates and staff increased with the length of time the former inmate had served during the most recent incarceration in jail, prison, or post-release community-treatment facility. Among males, rates for former inmates who had served 5 years or more were at least 3 times higher than for those who had served less than a year. Among males who had served 10 years or longer, 12% reported having been sexually victimized by other inmates and 17% by staff. Among females who had served 5 to 10 years before their release, 21% reported having been sexually victimized by other inmates and 11% by staff. A quarter of the females who had served 10 years or more reported experiencing staff sexual misconduct.

Male inmates with no prior incarceration experience had a higher rate of inmate-on-inmate sexual victimization (6.6%) compared to those with one or more prior incarcerations (3.7%). Rates of staff sexual victimization for males and rates for both inmate and staff sexual victimization for females did not vary by prior incarceration history.

Former state prisoners who had served time in 5 or more facilities during their most recent confinement reported the highest rates of staff sexual misconduct

Staff sexual misconduct rates varied by the number of facilities in which male and female inmates had served time during their most recent period of incarceration. Approximately 25% of the male former state prisoners and 10% of the female state prisoners had served time in five or more facilities before their release. These inmates reported significantly higher rates of staff sexual misconduct (6.7% or more among males and 7.7% or more among females) than those who had served in three or fewer facilities (4.0% or less among males and females).

These differences are consistent with the practice of transferring victims to other facilities in response to substantiated incidents of staff sexual misconduct. In 2006, based on reports by correctional authorities of all substantiated incidents of sexual victimization, nearly a third of the victims of staff sexual misconduct were transferred to another facility—19% of victims in prisons and 48% of victims in jails. (For further details, see *Sexual Violence Reported by Correctional Authorities, 2006*, April 2007, BJS Web, NCJ 218914, table 12.) The increase in sexual victimization rates by number of facilities may also reflect covariation with total time served, with inmates who serve longer sentences being placed in more facilities.

Difference in findings after BJS performed multivariate logistic regressions

Among male former prisoners, after controlling for the effects of other individual-level factors—

- Inmate-on-inmate victimization was higher for white non-Hispanic inmates, persons of two or more races, those age 24 or younger, non-heterosexuals, sex offenders, and those who served 5 years or more than for inmates with other characteristics (table 10).

BJS used multivariate logistic regression models to determine which inmate characteristics were significant predictors of whether the inmate would be sexually victimized in prison

Multivariate logistic regression estimation is a modeling technique used to determine what characteristics are statistically significant for predicting a dichotomous outcome (e.g., an inmate is victimized or not victimized) while controlling for all the other characteristics in the model.

BJS used this technique to determine which inmate characteristics were statistically significant for predicting sexual victimization. Based on four separate models, each representing the type of sexual victimization and sex of the former inmate, the variations in rates of sexual victimization by demographic characteristic, sexual orientation, and criminal justice status were found to be largely statistically independent of one another.

Estimates are displayed in terms of the conditional marginal probabilities, which represent the probability that a former male or female inmate with a particular characteristic has experienced a specific sexual victimization outcome conditional on the former inmate having the mean value for all other predictors in the model. For example, based on models with demographic and criminal justice status characteristics only, a white male former inmate had a 4.0% chance of having been sexually victimized by another inmate, and a female former inmate had a 12.2% chance (conditional on the inmate having the mean value on all of the other characteristics in the model). For characteristics that are categorical, which is the case for every variable in these logistic regression models, the mean value is a weighted value of the joint distribution of all other characteristics in the respective model. (See *Methodology* for a discussion of logistic regression.)

TABLE 10

Multivariate logistic regression models of sexual victimization, by type of incident, former prisoner demographic characteristics, and former prisoner criminal justice status and history

Former prisoner characteristic	Predicted percent of male former prisoners reporting sexual victimization		Predicted percent of female former prisoners reporting sexual victimization	
	Inmate-on-inmate	Staff sexual misconduct	Inmate-on-inmate	Staff sexual misconduct
Race/Hispanic origin				
White[a]	4.0%**	3.4%**	12.2%**	3.2%**
Black/African American[a]*	2.0	4.4	15.0	2.2
Hispanic/Latino	2.1	3.2**	11.6**	2.6
Other[a,b]	3.0	4.9	4.8**	1.7
Two or more races[a]	6.0**	8.3**	24.5**	9.3**
Age at admission				
Under 18	4.9%	11.0%**	14.1%	5.8%
18–19	3.0	6.2	24.4	6.4
20–24*	3.8	6.1	18.6	4.5
25–34	2.6**	4.0**	14.2	3.6
35–44	2.4**	2.9**	10.4**	2.2**
45 or older	2.1**	1.9**	9.3**	1.3**
Education[c]				
Less than high school[d]*	~	~	11.7%	~
High school graduate	~	~	12.1	~
Some college	~	~	15.8**	~
College degree or more	~	~	15.8	~
Marital status[c]				
Married*	~	~	11.8%	~
Widowed, divorced, or separated	~	~	15.8**	~
Never married	~	~	10.6	~
Weight[c,e]				
1st quartile*	~	3.3%	~	~
2nd quartile	~	3.8	~	~
3rd quartile	~	3.9	~	~
4th quartile	~	4.6**	~	~
Sexual orientation[c]				
Straight/heterosexual*	2.6%	3.7%	~	~
Bisexual	28.1**	15.6**	~	~
Lesbian/gay/homosexual	31.8**	10.4**	~	~
Prior incarcerations				
No prior incarceration*	~	2.8%	9.5%	1.9%
1 or more prior incarcerations	~	4.1**	14.0**	3.2**
Most serious offense				
Violent sexual offense*	6.8%	4.0%	~	~
Other violent	2.5**	4.4	~	~
Property	3.2**	5.1	~	~
Drug	2.1**	3.0	~	~
Public order	2.9**	3.0	~	~
Other	4.0	5.3	~	~
Total time served				
Less than 12 months*	1.5%	1.9%	8.9%	1.1%
12–23	2.3	2.8**	13.3**	3.2**
24–35	2.8**	3.3**	13.7**	1.9
36–59	2.0	4.5**	15.8**	5.3**
60–119	4.9**	6.5**	19.2**	10.3**
120 months or longer	9.5**	12.1**	14.4	24.0**

Note: See appendix table 3 for Wald-F statistics for each model.

~Characteristics deleted from model when Wald statistic for each categorical variable was not significant at the 95%-confidence level.

*Comparison group.

**Difference with comparison group is significant at the 95%-confidence level.

[a]Excludes persons of Hispanic or Latino origin.

[b]Includes American Indians, Alaska Natives, Asians, Native Hawaiians, and other Pacific Islanders.

[c]As reported at time of interview.

[d]Includes former prisoners who received a GED while incarcerated.

[e]Weight quartiles are defined by sex: Men—1st quartile (86 to 170 lbs.), 2nd quartile (171 to 190 lbs.), 3rd quartile (191 to 220 lbs.), 4th quartile (more than 220 lbs.). Women—1st quartile (78 to 145 lbs.), 2nd quartile (146 to 169 lbs.), 3rd quartile (170 to 198 lbs.), 4th quartile (more than 198 lbs.).

Source: BJS, National Former Prisoner Survey, 2008.

- Staff sexual misconduct was higher for black non-Hispanic inmates, persons of two or more races, those age 24 or younger, non-heterosexuals, those with one or more prior incarcerations, and those who served 12 months or more than for inmates with other characteristics.

Among female former prisoners, after controlling for the effects of other individual-level factors—

- Inmate-on-inmate victimization was higher for inmates of two or more races, those age 24 or younger, those with some college education, those with one or more prior incarcerations, and those who had served a year or more but less than 10 years than for inmates with other characteristics.

- Staff sexual misconduct was higher for white non-Hispanic inmates, inmates of two or more races, those age 24 or younger, those with one or more prior incarcerations, and those who served 3 years or more than for inmates with other characteristics.

- Sexual victimization either by other inmates or by staff was unrelated to sexual orientation.

For both male and female former prisoners, the number of facilities in which the inmate had served time was no longer related to reports of staff sexual misconduct. For male former inmates, education levels and marital status were no longer correlated with reports of staff sexual victimization.

Variations by selected facility-level characteristics

To understand more fully the correlates of sexual victimization and circumstances surrounding that victimization, BJS included survey questions to identify each of the state facilities in which the inmates had served time during their most recent period of incarceration and asked if the inmates had been sexually victimized (by type of victimization) within each facility. (See appendix E for specific survey questions.) Data collected in prior BJS censuses of state prison facilities (conducted in 1990, 1995, 2000 and 2005) were linked to these reports to determine whether any facility characteristics were associated with variations in rates of sexual victimization. Although data on local jails and post-release community-treatment facilities were also collected, they have been excluded from this analysis. (See *Methodology* for details on linkage of prison census data.)

Three-quarters of former inmates had served time in more than one prison facility; nearly 1 in 8 had served time in 5 or more prison facilities before their release

During their period of incarceration, inmates typically served time in more than one facility. Covering only the last continuous period of incarceration, the 18,526 former prisoners interviewed in NFPS reported 63,813 separate placements. Of these, 16,073 involved jail placements (either prior to prison, as an interim stop or as the only placement for some). In addition, 2,422 placements were to post-release local facilities, and 1,525 were to out-of-state facilities. When weighted by the inverse of the probability of selection, the eligible prison-only placements represented more than 1.3 million separate placements (table 11).

Overall, an estimated 500,400 former prisoners (98%) had served time in a prison facility in the state in which they were currently under parole or post-custody supervision, excluding 10,400 prisoners who had served time only in a local jail. Approximately three-quarters of these inmates had served time in more than one prison facility; nearly an eighth had served time in five or more prison facilities.

TABLE 11
Prison facilities entered and prison placements, by former state prisoners

State prisons entered/ order of placement	Percent of former inmates[a]	Percent of prison placements[b]
Total	100%	100%
1	24.4	37.6
2	32.5	28.5
3	21.4	16.2
4	10.0	8.2
5	5.8	4.4
6 or more	6.0	5.0
Number	500,400	1,329,700

Note: Respondents were asked to identify the names of the facilities in which they had been placed. Among those who entered a prison, the number of prisons ranged from 1 to 15. Facilities were ordered from the first to last by date of entry.

[a]Excludes an estimated 10,400 former prisoners who served time in local jail only.

[b]Based on separate records for each state prison entered during the period of incarceration. Excludes placements in jails and post-release community treatment facilities.

Source: BJS, National Former Prisoner Survey, 2008.

Nearly 44% of male victims and 74% of female victims reported that sexual victimization had occurred in the first prison facility they had entered

Based on the self reports of victims in the NFPS, sexual victimization frequently occurred in the first facility to which the inmates had been admitted. Among victims, nearly half (49%) said they were victimized in the first prison they had entered (table 12). Female victims (74%) were much more likely than male victims (44%) to report having been victimized in the first prison entered. This difference in victimization may be partially explained by differences among males and females in the likelihood of serving time in more than one facility. An estimated 78% of males, compared

to 57% of females, had served time in two or more prison facilities before their release; nearly 25% of males, compared to 7% of females, had served time in four or more prison facilities (not shown in table).

Among victims, sexual victimization by other inmates was more likely than sexual victimization by staff to have occurred in the first facility the inmates had entered. More than half (57%) of the estimated 18,800 prisoners who reported sexual victimization by another inmate indicated that it occurred in the first prison facility they entered. Fewer than half (42%) of the 23,800 victims of staff sexual misconduct indicated it occurred in the first facility.

TABLE 12
Sequence of reported sexual victimization in prison, by sex of victim and type of incident

Sequence	Total	Male*	Female	Inmate-on-inmate*	Staff sexual misconduct
Number victimized in state prison[a]	38,500	31,900	6,600	18,800	23,800
Victimized in first prison entered	49.0%	43.7%	74.5%**	57.1%	41.8%**
Victimized in first prison and subsequent prison(s)	17.0	17.3	16.0	18.8	14.2
Victimized in subsequent prison(s) only	47.6%	52.7%	22.7%**	37.6%	56.3%**
Unable to place victimization	3.4%	3.6%	2.7%	5.3%	1.9%**

Note: Detail may not sum to total because former inmates may report more than one type of victimization.

*Comparison group.

**Difference with comparison group is significant at the 95%-confidence level.

[a]Excludes former state prisoners victimized in local jails only.

Source: BJS, National Former Prisoner Survey, 2008.

Reports of sexual violence did not vary by size of facility, facility age, crowding, inmate-to-staff ratios, or sex composition of staff

Further analysis of prison placements provided a detailed risk profile of facility-level characteristics in conjunction with reported sexual victimization. Overall, few measurable differences at the 95% level of statistical confidence emerged among commonly cited facility risk factors (table 13). Sexual victimization rates (defined by type of victimization and sex of inmate) did not increase with—

- increased size of the facility (based on the average daily population during the 12 months prior to the census closest in time to the inmate's placement)

- increased age of the facility (based on year of original construction)

- facility overcrowding (based on the ratio of the number of inmates the facility actually held to the official rated capacity)

- increased inmate-to-staff ratios in the facility (based on the number of inmates held to the total number of payroll, non-payroll, and contract staff)

- decreased proportion of female to male staff.

Sexual victimization rates varied by type and primary function of the facility and by indicators of facility disorder

Among male former state prisoners, inmate-on-inmate and staff-on-inmate victimization rates were higher in facilities—

- under a court order or consent decree (to limit the number of inmates, to address crowding, or in response to the totality of conditions at the time of the census) than in other facilities

- reporting a major disturbance (involving five or more inmates and which resulted in serious injury or significant property damage) in the 12 months prior to the census than in other facilities

- with medium or greater security levels than in facilities with minimum or low security levels

- with a primary function of housing general population than in facilities with specialized functions (e.g., reception or diagnostic centers, community corrections centers, medical treatment, and alcohol or drug treatment).

Among female former state prisoners, reports of inmate-on-inmate victimization were lower in community corrections centers (1.3%) and facilities that permitted 50% or more of their inmates to leave unaccompanied during the day (1.3%), than in facilities holding general population (5.3%) or in general confinement facilities (5.0%). Inmate-on-inmate sexual victimization rates were also lower in minimum or low security facilities (3.0%) than in medium security facilities (5.6%) and lower in privately operated facilities (2.0%) than in state facilities (5.0%).

Reports of staff sexual misconduct among female former state prisoners did not vary significantly across facility characteristics, except for being lower in minimum or low security facilities (1.0%) than in medium security facilities (3.0%) and higher in facilities under a court order (6.3%) than in other facilities (2.0%).

Whether a facility was publicly operated or privately operated was an inconsistent predictor of victimization. While reports by male former state prisoners of staff sexual misconduct were higher in privately operated facilities (4.6%) than in state facilities (2.5%), reports by female former prisoners did not differ statistically between state and privately operated facilities. Rates of inmate-on-inmate victimization among women, but not among men, were lower in privately operated facilities than in state facilities.

When an inmate had been placed in the facility was a strong predictor of sexual victimization among male former prisoners. As measured by the census year closest to the time of placement, male former state inmates were nearly 4 times more likely to report victimization by another inmate and 3 times more likely to report victimization by staff if they had entered the facility around the 1990 census than if they had entered around the 2005 census. Female inmates who entered the prison facility around 1990 were nearly 8 times more likely to report staff sexual misconduct (12.5%) than if they had entered around 2005 (1.6%). However, rates of inmate-on-inmate sexual victimization among females did not differ by year of placement.

TABLE 13
Prevalence of sexual victimization during prison placement, by sex of inmate, type of incident, and facility-level characteristics

Facility-level characteristic[a]	Number of male placements[b]	Percent of male inmates reporting sexual victimization during placement		Number of female placements[b]	Percent of female inmates reporting sexual victimization during placement	
		Inmate-on-inmate	Staff sexual misconduct		Inmate-on-inmate	Staff sexual misconduct
Average daily population[c]						
860 or less	287,300	1.0%	2.1%	45,100	3.6%	2.1%
861 to 1,350*	287,500	1.5	2.8	22,800	4.9	2.9
1,351 to 2,200	289,000	1.9	2.8	16,700	5.6	2.9
More than 2,200	288,800	1.9	2.5	17,900	6.9	2.2
Type of facility						
General population*	825,500	1.9%	3.1%	89,900	5.3%	2.6%
Reception/diagnostic	162,400	0.9**	1.1**	1,100	4.5	6.0
Community corrections center	66,200	0.6**	1.3**	5,700	1.3**	1.2
Returned to custody[d]	34,700	0.8	1.2**	900	3.1	4.3
Other[e]	52,300	0.9**	1.5**	3,900	0.4**	0.3**
Percent of inmates leaving facility during the day						
Less than 50%*	1,084,800	1.6%	2.6%	96,600	5.0%	2.5%
50% or more	67,700	0.6**	1.2**	5,900	1.3**	1.0
Security level[f]						
Maximum/close/high	394,800	2.1%	3.0%	39,300	5.2%	2.8%
Medium*	488,900	1.6	2.7	38,100	5.6	3.0
Minimum/low	268,800	0.7**	1.7**	25,000	3.0**	1.0**
Who operates facility						
State*	1,087,400	1.6%	2.5%	96,400	5.0%	2.5%
Private	50,800	0.8	4.6**	5,900	2.0**	1.1
Other[g]	14,300	1.4	1.3**	:	:	:
Year built[h]						
Before 1951	277,500	1.8%	2.4%	22,800	4.7%	3.4%
1951–1985*	325,200	1.6	2.7	29,200	3.8	2.7
1986–1990	187,300	1.6	3.0	14,100	5.5	2.4
1991 or after	339,600	1.4	2.4	34,400	5.6	1.6
Facility over capacity[i]						
No*	706,700	1.6%	2.8%	65,100	4.4%	2.4%
Yes	444,200	1.5	2.1	37,400	5.5	2.4
Inmate-to-staff ratio[j]						
Less than 4.0	306,300	1.4%	2.5%	32,000	4.3%	3.3%
4.0–4.9*	200,900	2.0	2.9	19,500	3.9	1.6
5.0–5.9	216,700	1.8	3.3	14,900	5.5	2.3
6.0 or more	279,600	1.6	2.5	18,300	4.2	2.1
Under a court order[k]						
No*	1,001,500	1.4%	2.2%	92,600	4.6%	2.0%
Yes	138,800	3.0**	4.9**	9,800	6.7	6.3**
Major disturbance in census year[l]						
No*	941,800	1.4%	2.4%	90,400	4.5%	2.5%
Yes	171,600	2.4**	3.9**	5,800	8.0	3.2
Percent female staff[m]						
Low	328,000	1.6%	2.1%	18,900	3.8%	3.7%
Medium*	239,800	1.6	2.8	21,900	4.5	1.9
High	261,900	1.7	2.7	20,700	5.1	2.1
Highest	173,800	1.9	4.2	23,300	4.2	2.3
Census year closest to time of placement[n]						
1990	47,600	4.2%**	6.8%**	2,200	4.2%	12.5%**
1995	85,700	2.2**	4.5**	4,700	5.0	6.7**
2000	257,100	2.4**	3.4**	14,600	5.6	4.3**
2005*	762,100	1.0	1.8	80,900	4.6	1.6

Continued on next page

TABLE 13 (continued)
Prevalence of sexual victimization during prison placement, by sex of inmate, type of incident, and facility-level characteristics

Facility-level characteristic[a]	Number of male placements[b]	Percent of male inmates reporting sexual victimization during placement		Number of female placements[b]	Percent of female inmates reporting sexual victimization during placement	
		Inmate-on-inmate	Staff sexual misconduct		Inmate-on-inmate	Staff sexual misconduct
Placement order of facility[o]						
1st*	413,400	1.5%	1.9%	55,200	5.5%	2.6%
2nd	325,700	1.9	2.6**	30,400	4.8	1.9
3rd or higher	413,400	1.4	3.2**	16,900	2.4**	2.8

Note: Based on a separate record for each prison placement for the 18,256 former prison inmates interviewed nationwide. Facility-level data from BJS prison censuses (conducted in 1990, 1995, 2000, and 2005) were merged with each placement record based on the census year closest to the prison placement. After weighting, the number of placements with valid data totaled 1,254,998. (See *Methodology* for further description.)

:Not calculated.

*Comparison group.

**Difference with comparison group is significant at the 95%-confidence level.

[a]Characteristic of the facility is based on the prison census year closest to the time of placement.

[b]Detail may not sum to total because of missing data on facility characteristics in each census year.

[c]Based on the number of inmates for each day during the 12 months prior to the census divided by 365.

[d]Includes facilities whose primary function is to house persons returned to custody (e.g., parole violators).

[e]Includes facilities whose primary function is boot camp, medical treatment/hospitalization confinement, mental health/psychiatric confinement, alcohol/drug treatment confinement, housing youthful offenders, and geriatric care.

[f]The physical security level that best describes the facility.

[g]Includes facilities under joint state and local authority.

[h]Based on year of original construction. If more than one building, based on the oldest building used to house inmates.

[i]Based on the ratio of the number of inmates housed on the day of census to the rated capacity.

[j]Based on the ratio of the inmate population on the day of census divided by the number of payroll and non-payroll, full-time, part-time, and contract staff, excluding volunteers.

[k]Includes state or federal court order or consent decree to limit the number of inmates, crowding, and totality of conditions at time of the census.

[l]Represents facilities that reported one or more major disturbances in the 12 months prior to the census. Major disturbances are incidents involving five or more inmates which result in serious injury or significant property damage.

[m]Categories are specific to sex: For males, low is less than 15%, medium is 15% to 21%, high is 22% to 34%, and highest is 35% or more. For females, low is less than 35%, medium is 35% to 49%, high is 50% to 69%, and highest is 70% or more.

[n]Prison census year closest to the time of placement.

[o]Placement order of the facility during the period of incarceration: 1st placement, 2nd placement, and 3rd placement or higher.

Source: BJS, National Former Prisoner Survey, 2008.

Prison placements and individual-level risk factors

While individual-level factors related to sexual victimization have been examined by type of victimization and sex of inmate for the entire period of incarceration, they may also be examined for each prison placement. Such a placement-based examination takes into account the risk of victimization related to individual-level factors, regardless of the duration of time served during a specific prison placement, and permits analysis of the independent contribution of individual-level and facility-level factors. Unlike the earlier analysis based on individuals (510,800 former inmates nationwide), the placement analysis is based on prison placements (more than 1.25 million prison placements). Individuals are represented multiple times, based on their number of separate prison placements (up to a maximum of 15 times per inmate).

An incident of sexual victimization was reported in 4.0% of prison placements

Among the estimated 1.15 million placements of male inmates, 1.6% involved inmate-on-inmate sexual victimization and 2.6% involved staff-on-inmate victimization (table 14). Among the estimated 102,500 placements of female inmates, 4.8% involved sexual victimization by another inmate and 2.4% involved sexual victimization by staff. Overall, in 4.0% of the more than 1.25 million prison placements, former prisoners reported at least one experience of sexual victimization by another inmate or facility staff.

TABLE 14
Prevalence of sexual victimization, comparing results from the National Former Prisoner Survey, 2008, and National Inmate Survey, 2008–09

Sex of inmate and type of incident	Percent of inmates reporting sexual victimization	
	Among all prison placements[a]	Among all inmates at time of survey[b]
Total	4.0%	4.8%
Male inmates		
Inmate-on-inmate	1.6	2.0
Staff sexual misconduct	2.6	3.2
Female inmates		
Inmate-on-inmate	4.8	5.1
Staff sexual misconduct	2.4	2.3

[a]Based on the experience reported by former state prisoners during each prison placement while incarcerated in NFPS.

[b]Based on the experience reported by state prisoners in the last 12 months, or since admission to the facility, if shorter in NIS-2.

Source: BJS, National Former Prisoner Survey, 2008, and National Inmate Survey, 2008–09.

These rates of victimization among all prison placements are similar to those reported by inmates in NIS-2 based on the current facility (during the last 12 months or since admission, if shorter). Based on the NIS-2, 2.0% of currently confined male inmates reported sexual victimization by another inmate and 3.2% by staff; 5.1% of currently confined female inmates reported sexual victimization by another inmate and 2.3% by staff.

Patterns of sexual victimization based on prison placements also resembled those observed for individuals based on their entire period of incarceration in NFPS, except that the rates were somewhat lower across categories defined by demographic and criminal justice characteristics:

- Large differences in sexual victimization during prison placement were found among inmates based on their sexual orientation (table 15).

- Among male former inmates, reports of inmate-on-inmate sexual victimization during prison placement varied by race and Hispanic origin. Reports were higher among white non-Hispanic inmates (2.4%) and multi-racial inmates (4.0%) than among black non-Hispanic inmates (0.9%).

- Among male inmates, violent sex offenders reported higher rates of inmate-on-inmate sexual victimization (5.9%) than other violent offenders (1.4%), property offenders (1.7%), public-order offenders (1.0%), and drug offenders (0.8%).

- Among male former inmates, those with a prior incarceration (1.4%) were less likely to be victims of other inmates than those with no prior incarceration (2.5%).

- Among female former inmates, rates of inmate-on-inmate victimization during prison placement did not significantly vary across demographic characteristics, except among inmates of two or more races.

- Among placements of male former prisoners, reports of staff sexual misconduct were higher among black non-Hispanic inmates (3.3%) than among white non-Hispanic inmates (2.0%) and Hispanic inmates (1.7%). The rates were also higher among younger male inmates (under age 25) than among older male inmates (age 35 or older).

- Among placements of female former prisoners, rates of staff sexual misconduct were significantly lower among those ages 35 to 44 (1.5%) and age 45 or older (1.1%), compared to those ages 20 to 24 (4.0%).

- The only other statistically significant difference among placements of female former inmates was that 8.1% of multi-racial inmates reported staff sexual misconduct, compared to 2.4% or lower among inmates who were white, black, or Hispanic.

TABLE 15
Prevalence of sexual victimization among male and female placements, by type of incident and former prisoner characteristics

Former prisoner characteristic	Number of male placements	Percent of male inmates reporting sexual victimization during placement		Number of female placements	Percent of female inmates reporting sexual victimization during placement	
		Inmate-on-inmate	Staff sexual misconduct		Inmate-on-inmate	Staff sexual misconduct
Race/Hispanic origin						
White[a]	433,700	2.4%**	2.0%**	48,700	4.9%	2.4%
Black/African American[a]*	449,900	0.9	3.3	30,400	3.5	2.3
Hispanic/Latino	203,200	0.8	1.7**	17,400	5.9	2.1
Other[a,b]	31,900	1.2	2.3	2,900	2.1	1.1
Two or more races[a]	31,300	4.0**	5.1	2,800	12.0**	8.1**
Age at admission						
Under 18	39,900	2.0%	5.7%	1,700	5.9%	4.1%
18–19	84,200	1.4	3.5	2,700	6.8	6.5
20–24*	253,600	1.8	3.6	14,300	6.0	4.0
25–34	374,300	1.6	2.6	34,900	4.9	2.8
35–44	258,600	1.3	1.7**	34,000	4.5	1.5**
45 or older	128,900	1.4	0.8**	14,300	3.8	1.1**
Education[c]						
Less than high school[d]*	693,300	1.5%	2.4%	55,200	4.7%	2.3%
High school graduate	210,500	1.3	1.8	18,200	4.1	1.3
Some college	209,000	2.1	3.8**	23,800	5.3	2.9
College degree or more	37,600	1.9	2.1	5,100	6.2	5.7
Marital status[c]						
Married*	237,900	2.0%	3.1%	18,400	4.4%	2.1%
Widowed, divorced, or separated	325,600	1.4	2.2	41,100	5.9	2.4
Never married	584,900	1.5	2.5	43,000	3.9	2.6
Weight[c,e]						
1st quartile*	303,300	1.7%	2.2%	28,000	5.8%	3.1%
2nd quartile	279,100	1.7	2.4	22,300	3.6	1.9
3rd quartile	309,800	1.4	2.6	26,100	5.1	2.8
4th quartile	259,100	1.4	3.0	24,600	4.4	1.6
Sexual orientation[c]						
Straight/heterosexual*	1,118,200	1.2%	2.5%	84,200	4.3%	2.0%
Bisexual	13,100	18.1**	9.2**	11,900	7.8	4.2**
Lesbian/gay/homosexual	9,600	19.3**	5.6**	5,700	5.4	5.5**
Prior incarcerations						
No prior incarceration*	211,400	2.5%	2.5%	25,200	3.3%	2.4%
1 or more prior incarcerations	941,100	1.4**	2.6	77,300	5.3	2.4
Most serious offense						
Violent sexual offense*	78,300	5.9%	2.9%	900	6.2%	5.3%
Violent	385,200	1.4**	3.8	22,300	3.7	3.7
Property	259,600	1.7**	2.5	34,300	6.0	2.3
Drug	297,300	0.8**	1.5	35,000	4.4	2.0
Public order	112,500	1.0**	0.9**	8,000	4.0	1.6
Other	3,200	1.7	3.3	300	2.0	0.0
Total time served						
Less than 12 months*	129,000	0.9%	1.2%	22,200	3.6%	0.8%
12–23	233,700	0.9	1.1	30,000	4.6	1.6
24–35	177,100	1.4	1.8	16,900	4.5	1.2
36–59	215,000	0.8	2.0	17,500	6.0	2.9**
60–119	226,800	1.9**	2.9**	11,700	6.2	5.4**
120 months or longer	170,500	3.5**	6.6**	4,200	5.6	11.8**

*Comparison group.

**Difference with comparison group is significant at the 95%-confidence level.

[a]Excludes persons of Hispanic or Latino origin.

[b]Includes American Indians, Alaska Natives, Asians, Native Hawaiians, and other Pacific Islanders.

[c]As reported at time of interview.

[d]Includes former prisoners who received a GED while incarcerated.

[e]Weight quartiles are defined by sex: Men—1st quartile (86 to 170 lbs.), 2nd quartile (171 to 190 lbs.), 3rd quartile (191 to 220 lbs.), 4th quartile (more than 220 lbs.). Women—1st quartile (78 to 145 lbs.), 2nd quartile (146 to 169 lbs.), 3rd quartile (170 to 198 lbs.), 4th quartile (more than 198 lbs.).

Source: BJS, National Former Prisoner Survey, 2008.

Independent contributions of individual-level and facility-level factors to victimization

Variations in rates of sexual victimization among groups of inmates based on the characteristics of facilities in which they were placed overlap somewhat with variations based on individual risk factors. Multivariate regression models were developed to incorporate selected individual-level and facility-level factors. Models for each type of sexual victimization were developed separately for male and female former prisoners based on prison placements (table 16).

In each of the logistic regression models, the conditional probabilities represent the probability that a former inmate during a prison placement with a particular individual or facility characteristic experienced sexual victimization, conditional on the inmate having the mean value for all other predictors in the model. For example, based on the final multivariate model, a male former state prisoner who served time for a violent sex offense had a 2.2% chance of having been sexually victimized by another inmate during a prison placement, given that he was at the mean of the joint distribution of other individual characteristics (i.e., race or Hispanic origin, marital status, sexual orientation, and time served) and facility characteristics (i.e., type, security level, census year closest to placement, and placement order).

Variations in sexual victimization rates were strongly related to sexual orientation after controlling for other factors

An inmate's sexual orientation remained an important correlate of victimization, except for staff sexual misconduct reported by females. Male inmates who identified themselves as bisexual were at least 13 times more likely to report being sexually victimized by another inmate and 4 times more likely to report being sexually victimized by staff than male inmates who identified themselves as straight or heterosexual.

After controlling for other factors, an inmate's race or Hispanic origin remained an important predicator of sexual victimization. Based on the multivariate placement models for male former inmates—

- White non-Hispanic inmates (1.4%) and inmates of two or more races (2.0%) had higher rates of inmate-on-inmate victimization than black non-Hispanic and Hispanic inmates (each 0.6%).

- Black non-Hispanic inmates (2.0%) had higher rates of staff-on-inmate victimization than white non-Hispanic (1.4%) and Hispanic inmates (1.2%).

Based on the multivariate placement models for female former inmates—

- Inmate-on-inmate victimization rates were lower for black non-Hispanic inmates (2.8%) than for white non-Hispanic inmates (3.9%), Hispanic inmates (4.6%) and inmates of two or more races (8.7%)

- Staff-on-inmate victimization rates were higher for inmates of two or more races (6.1%) than for white non-Hispanic (1.7%), black non-Hispanic (1.1%) and Hispanic inmates (1.1%).

Facitily-level factors remained significant after controlling for inmate characteristics

- Among male former inmates, inmate-on-inmate and staff-on-inmate victimization rates were lower in reception or diagnostic centers than in facilities that housed general population. For inmate-on-inmate victimizations, rates were lower in minimum security facilities than in facilities with higher security levels.

- Among female former inmates, the inmate-on-inmate victimization rate was lower in facilities that permitted 50% or more of their inmates to leave unaccompanied during the day (than in other confinement facilities), lower in medium security facilities (than in facilities with maximum, close, or high security levels), higher in facilities that had been built before 1951 or after 1985 (than in facilities built between 1951 and 1985), and higher in facilities that had a major disturbance in the census year (than in those that did not).

- Among female former inmates, few facility-level factors were linked to staff sexual misconduct. Rates were lower in minimum or low security facilities than in medium security facilities, and lower in facilities built between 1951 and 1985 than in facilities built before 1951.

The final regression models confirm that the best predictor of staff sexual misconduct among female former inmates was length of time served, with the rate of staff sexual misconduct during prison placements generally increasing with total time served.

TABLE 16

Final multivariate logistic regression models of sexual victimization among male and female placements, by type of incident and former prisoner and facility characteristics

Former prisoner/facility characteristic	Predicted percent of male placements in which sexual victimization was reported		Predicted percent of female placements in which sexual victimization was reported	
	Inmate-on-inmate	Staff sexual misconduct	Inmate-on-inmate	Staff sexual misconduct
Race/Hispanic origin				
White[a]	1.4%**	1.4%**	3.9%**	1.7%
Black/African American[a]*	0.6	2.0	2.8	1.1
Hispanic	0.6	1.2**	4.6**	1.1
Other[a,b]	0.6	1.6	1.8	0.8
Two or more races[a]	2.0**	3.3	8.7**	6.1**
Age at admission				
Under 18	~	3.1%	~	1.4%
18–19	~	2.3	~	3.4
20–24*	~	2.5	~	2.2
25–34	~	1.7**	~	1.8
35–44	~	1.3**	~	1.0
45 or older	~	0.6**	~	0.8
Education[c]				
Less than high school[d]*	~	1.5%	~	~
High school graduate	~	1.4	~	~
Some college	~	2.6**	~	~
College degree or more	~	1.4	~	~
Marital status[c]				
Married*	1.1%	~	3.5%	~
Widowed, divorced, or separated	0.6**	~	4.4	~
Never married	0.9	~	3.0	~
Sexual orientation[c]				
Straight/heterosexual*	0.8%	1.6%	3.4%	~
Bisexual	10.6**	7.2**	5.6**	~
Gay/homosexual	9.6**	3.8	4.0	~
Prior incarcerations				
No prior incarceration*	~	1.2%	2.5%	~
1 or more prior incarcerations	~	1.7**	4.1**	~
Most serious offense				
Violent sexual offense*	2.2%	1.7%	~	~
Other violent	0.7**	1.8	~	~
Property	1.1**	1.9	~	~
Drug	0.8**	1.3	~	~
Public order	0.8**	1.2	~	~
Other	0.9	2.6	~	~
Total time served				
Less than 12 months*	0.7%	1.1%	2.1%	0.6%
12–23	0.7	1.0	3.3	1.4**
24–35	0.9	1.6	3.5	1.0
36–59	0.5	1.6	5.2**	2.2**
60–119	1.0	2.0**	6.1**	3.4**
120 months or longer	1.9**	3.6**	7.1	6.1**
Type of facility				
General population*	1.0%	2.0%	4.0%	~
Reception/diagnostic	0.4**	0.8**	2.7	~
Community corrections center	0.6	0.8**	3.9	~
Returned to custody[e]	0.8	1.6	2.0	~
Other[f]	0.7	1.2	0.4**	~

Continued on next page

TABLE 16 (continued)
Final multivariate logistic regression models of sexual victimization among male and female placements, by type of incident and former prisoner and facility characteristics

Former prisoner/facility characteristic	Predicted percent of male placements in which sexual victimization was reported		Predicted percent of female placements in which sexual victimization was reported	
	Inmate-on-inmate	Staff sexual misconduct	Inmate-on-inmate	Staff sexual misconduct
Percent of inmates leaving the facility during the day[g]				
Less than 50%*	~	~	3.8%	~
50% or more	~	~	1.7**	~
Security level[h]				
Maximum/close/high	1.1%	~	4.6%**	1.6
Medium*	0.9	~	3.1	2.0
Minimum	0.5**	~	3.2	0.6**
Who operates facility				
State*	~	1.6%	~	~
Private	~	3.2**	~	~
Other	~	1.4	~	~
Year built[i]				
Before 1951	~	1.5%**	4.4%**	2.2%**
1951–1985*	~	1.8	2.6	1.1
1986–1990	~	2.0	3.4**	1.6
1991 or after	~	1.5**	4.4**	1.1
Inmate-to-staff ratio[j]				
Less than 4.0	~	~	3.1%	~
4.0–4.9*	~	~	2.7	~
5.0–5.9	~	~	3.7	~
6.0 or more	~	~	3.4	~
Under court order[k]				
No*	~	1.6%	~	~
Yes	~	1.9	~	~
Major disturbance in census year[l]				
No*	~	~	3.4%	~
Yes	~	~	7.6**	~
Percent female staff[m]				
0% to less than 15%	~	1.2%**	~	~
15% to less than 22%*	~	1.6	~	~
22% to less than 35%	~	1.7	~	~
35% or more	~	3.1**	~	~
Census year closest to time of placement[n]				
1990	1.3%	~	~	~
1995	0.8	~	~	~
2000	1.2**	~	~	~
2005*	0.7	~	~	~
Placement order of facility[o]				
1st*	0.8%	~	3.9%	~
2nd	1.1**	~	4.2	~
3rd or higher	0.7	~	2.1**	~

Note: See appendix table 4 for Wald-F statistics for each model. See table 15 for footnotes a–d. For the remaining footnotes describing facility characteristics, see table 13.

~Characteristics deleted from model when Wald statistic was not significant at the 95%-confidence level.

*Comparison group.

** Difference with comparison group is significant at the 95%-confidence level.

Source: BJS, National Former Prisoner Survey, 2008.

Reporting of sexual victimization

In addition to identifying key individual-level and facility-level risk factors associated with variations in sexual victimization rates, the former inmate survey provided data on the responses of victims and the impact on victims while they were still in prison and after their release from prison. The survey included questions about reporting victimization to facility staff and persons other than facility staff, reasons for not reporting and what happened if they did report to facility staff, and the continued impact on the victims following their release from prison.

Two-thirds of victims of inmate-on-inmate sexual victimization said they reported at least one incident to facility staff or someone else

Detailed data suggest that victims of inmate-on-inmate victimization were most likely to have reported at least one incident to another inmate (49%), followed by having reported to a family member or friend outside the facility (28%) and to correctional officers (24%). Few victims (1.4%) had reported their experience on a telephone hotline (table 17).

An estimated 37% of victims of inmate-on-inmate sexual victimization reported at least one incident to facility staff—58% of those injured, compared to 29% of those not injured (not shown in table). Reporting to medical and healthcare staff was even less common (14% of the victims said they reported an incident to medical personnel). Among those physically injured by another inmate, a third (33%) said they reported to medical staff (not shown in table).

22% of unwilling victims of sexual activity with staff, compared to 3% of "willing" victims, said they had reported an incident to facility staff or someone else

"Willing" sexual activity with staff was rarely reported to any facility staff (2%) or to other persons (2%). When sexual activity with staff was reported, it was typically unwilling and divided nearly equally between reporting to staff (21%) and someone other than staff (20%).

TABLE 17
Reporting of sexual victimization, by type of incident and persons to whom the incident was reported

| | Inmate-on-inmate | | Staff sexual misconduct | | |
	Total[a]	Nonconsensual sexual acts	Total	Willing activity[b]	Unwilling activity[b]
Number of victims	27,300	18,700	27,100	23,300	6,300
Percent of victims reporting at least one incident of sexual victimization	65.9%	66.6%	6.8%	3.3%	22.1%
Percent reporting to any facility staff[c]	37.4%	38.2%	5.8%	2.5%	20.7%
Correctional officer	24.0	24.2	2.7	0.9	10.1
Administrative staff	16.5	16.2	4.8	1.8	18.0
Medical/healthcare staff	13.5	15.1	2.1	0.9	7.5
Instructor/teacher	4.3	5.3	1.4	0.6	5.1
Counselor/case manager	12.1	12.8	2.9	1.2	10.4
Chaplain/other religious leader	8.0	9.4	1.4	0.6	5.1
Volunteer	4.0	3.3	1.3	0.3	4.7
Someone else at the facility[d]	13.5	13.7	3.1	1.2	11.3
Percent reporting to someone other than facility staff[c]	60.0%	60.6%	5.2%	2.1%	19.7%
Telephone hotline	1.4	1.6	0.5	0.2	2.3
Another inmate	49.0	48.2	3.6	1.3	14.6
Family/friend outside the facility	28.1	28.8	4.5	1.4	17.3
Someone else outside the facility	14.6	17.3	~	~	~

Note: See appendix table 5 for estimated standard errors.
~Category not included in the survey.
[a]Includes abusive sexual contacts.
[b]Includes touching only.
[c]Detail may not sum to total because victim may have reported to more than one person inside or outside the facility.
[d]Category not included in the pretest interviews. See *Methodology* for a detailed discussion of merged data files.
Source: BJS, National Former Prisoner Survey, 2008.

Most common reasons for not reporting sexual victimization by other inmates linked to embarrassment, shame, and not wanting others to know

Victims who never reported their experience of sexual victimization to anyone at the facility were asked their reasons for not reporting. The most common reason for victims not reporting sexual victimization by another inmate was that they "didn't want anyone else to know about it" (70%), followed by feeling "embarrassed or ashamed that it happened" (68%) (table 18). The most common reasons for not reporting staff sexual misconduct were that they "had the sex or sexual contact willingly" (80%) and they "didn't want the staff person to get in trouble" (71%). Almost 40% of victims of inmate-on-inmate sexual victimization and staff sexual misconduct said they were afraid of being punished by staff. Nearly a quarter of inmates victimized by another inmate or by staff said they were afraid of being charged with making a false report.

37% of victims who reported being victimized by other inmates said facility staff did not respond

Among victims who reported inmate-on-inmate sexual victimization to authorities—

- 34% were moved to administrative segregation or protective housing, 24% were confined to their cell, 14% were assigned a higher level of custody, and 11% were placed in a medical unit or hospital.
- 18% were offered a transfer to another facility.
- More than a quarter (29%) said they were written up; and 28% said they spoke to an investigator (table 19).

Though few in number, 86% of the victims who reported staff sexual misconduct to authorities said the facility responded: more than half (54%) of the victims spoke to an investigator, and nearly half (46%) said that they were "written up" for the incident. More than 40% said they were moved to administrative segregation or protective housing.

TABLE 18
Reasons for not reporting sexual victimization to facility staff, by type of victimization

Reason for not reporting	Inmate-on-inmate	Staff sexual misconduct
Number of victims not reporting victimization to staff*	16,870	25,200
Afraid/scared of perpetrator	51.6%	~%
Afraid of being punished by staff	40.7	38.3
Afraid of being charged with making a false report	24.9	25.4
Didn't want anyone to know	70.1	~
Embarrassed/ashamed	68.5	14.6
Thought staff would not investigate	43.3	21.9
Thought perpetrator would not be punished	40.6	~
Didn't want staff to get in trouble	~	70.5
Had sex or sexual contact willingly	~	79.8

~Not asked of victims.

*Represents the item with largest number of valid responses.

Source: BJS, National Former Prisoner Survey, 2008.

TABLE 19
Facility responses to the reporting of sexual victimization to staff, by type of incident

	Inmate-on-inmate	Staff sexual misconduct
Number of victims reporting to facility staff	10,200	1,600
Facility response to reported sexual victimization[a]	63.0%	85.5%
Moved victim to administrative segregation/protective housing	34.3	41.2
Placed victim in medical unit/ward/hospital	10.9	12.2
Confined victim to cell	24.3	35.2
Assigned victim to higher level of custody to victim	14.3	26.6
Offered victim a transfer	17.6	39.1
Victim written up	28.5	46.3
Victim spoke to investigator[b]	28.3	53.9
Perpetrator punished/segregated	28.6	~
No facility response reported by victim	37.0%	14.5%

Note: An additional 200 victims of inmate-on-inmate victimization reported that someone else reported his/her victimization to staff. See appendix table 6 for estimated standard errors.

~Not asked of victims of staff sexual misconduct.

[a]Detail may not sum to total because multiple responses were allowed for this item.

[b]Category not included in the pretest interviews. See *Methodology* for a detailed discussion of merged data files.

Source: BJS, National Former Prisoner Survey, 2008.

Post-release responses to victimization

Following their release from prison, victims of inmate-on-inmate sexual victimization—

- had feelings of shame or humiliation (72%) and guilt (56%) (table 20)

- discussed their victimization with intimate partners (27%) or friends (26%)

- saw a therapist or counselor (15%), participated in a self-help group for emotional or mental health problems (14%), or enrolled in a treatment program other than counseling (8%).

Victims of staff sexual misconduct that involved unwilling activity reported many similar feelings or thoughts about their victimization following their release from prison:

- 79% said they felt shame or humiliation.

- 72% said they felt guilt.

- 54% reported having difficulty feeling close to friends or family members.

Although the vast majority of victims (86%) of staff sexual misconduct said they had at least one incident that they considered "willing," more than a quarter (27%) said they felt guilt and 23% said they felt shame or humiliation after their release from prison.

TABLE 20
Post-release responses of victims to sexual victimization, by type of incident

| | All victims | Inmate-on-inmate | | Staff sexual misconduct | | |
		Total[a]	Nonconsensual sexual acts	Total	Willing activity[b]	Unwilling activity[b]
Number of victims[c,d]	47,000	26,200	18,000	26,100	22,500	5,900
Discussed victimization with at least one individual[d]	51.4%	43.7%	44.6%	56.8%	60.1%	35.9%
Husband/wife, boyfriend/girlfriend, or other partner	30.9	26.9	27.0	33.7	35.0	25.8
Children	2.7	2.9	2.5	2.4	2.4	3.5
Parents	14.7	13.0	10.7	15.6	15.5	12.9
Other family member	26.3	15.5	14.8	34.9	38.2	16.1
Friends	38.4	26.0	26.7	47.8	52.4	20.2
Minister or other religious leader	5.6	7.7	7.7	3.4	2.7	9.4
Therapist or treatment professional	11.7	16.1	17.3	7.1	6.6	12.9
Parole officer	3.5	4.9	5.9	2.0	1.4	4.1
Another inmate	29.6	22.7	22.4	34.5	37.0	17.0
Had feelings or thoughts about victimization[d]						
Guilt	40.5%	55.7%	67.2%	31.3%	26.9%	72.2%
Shame or humiliation	47.9	71.9	79.8	29.6	22.6	79.1
Revenge against someone victim was angry with	15.3	23.2	24.9	9.5	6.8	27.6
Difficulty feeling close to friends/family members	24.9	37.0	44.7	17.9	13.1	54.1
Participated in treatment to deal with victimization[d]	13.3%	20.5%	23.5%	7.8%	6.6%	16.6%
Saw therapist or counselor	9.7	15.4	17.3	5.8	5.1	12.1
Participated in self-help group for emotional/mental health problems	9.6	14.5	16.2	6.1	4.9	14.2
Enrolled in treatment program (other than counseling) for emotional/mental health problems	5.4	8.5	10.5	3.4	2.7	7.4
Took medication to treat emotional/mental health problems	6.9	10.5	12.2	4.1	2.7	12.3
Hospitalized for emotional/mental health problems	2.7	4.1	4.9	1.4	1.2	3.0

Note: See appendix table 7 for estimated standard errors.

[a]Includes abusive sexual contacts.

[b]Includes touching only.

[c]Detail may not sum to total because respondents may report more than one type of victimization.

[d]Interviews conducted in the pretest were excluded due to changes in the questionnaire design. See *Methodology* for a detailed discussion of merged data files.

Source: BJS, National Former Prisoner Survey, 2008.

HIV testing and results

The former inmate survey also provided self-report data on HIV testing and outcomes for victims of inmate-on-inmate and staff-on-inmate sexual victimization.

- Among former inmates tested for HIV, a significantly higher percentage of those who had been sexually victimized by other inmates (6.5%) or by staff (4.6%) were HIV-positive, compared to those who had not been victimized (2.6%) (table 21).

- Among all victims tested for HIV, 5.1% of males and 3.9% of females were HIV-positive (not shown in table).

- Among all victims tested for HIV, 15.5% of non-heterosexual inmates were HIV-positive, compared to 3.8% of heterosexual victims (not shown in table).

Although the rates of HIV infection are high among former prisoners, when these inmates contracted HIV is unknown. Inmates were not asked if they became HIV-positive while incarcerated.

Through the National Prisoner Statistics program, BJS has collected data on the number of inmates HIV-positive and the number with confirmed acquired immune deficiency syndrome (AIDS) since 1991. At yearend 2008, 20,499 inmates in state prisons (or 1.6% of all inmates in custody) were known to be HIV-positive or had confirmed AIDS. (See *HIV in Prisons, 2007-08*, NCJ 228307, BJS Web, December 2009.) Data are not available on the percentage of inmates who were HIV-positive when they were admitted to prison.

TABLE 21
HIV testing and results for former state prisoners, by type of victim

	All former state prisoners	Nonvictims	Inmate-on-inmate victims	Staff-on-inmate victims
Number	510,800	461,800	27,300	27,100
Tested for HIV				
Percent	89.9%	89.5%	93.0%	95.0%
Standard error	0.39%	0.43%	0.92%	0.89%
Tested positive for HIV				
Percent	2.8%	2.6%	6.5%	4.6%
Standard error	0.16%	0.16%	0.93%	0.88%

Source: BJS, National Former Prisoner Survey, 2008.

Current employment, housing, and living arrangements of former inmates

Following their release from prison, victims and nonvictims did not differ in their employment and housing arrangements, but victims were more likely than nonvictims to be living alone

The NFPS asked former prisoners about their current employment status, housing, and living arrangements while on post-release supervision. Except for a slightly higher percent of victims living alone (18%) than nonvictims (14%), few differences were reported in their current employment status or housing arrangements:

- Two-thirds of both victims and nonvictims were employed; at least half of each group were employed full-time.

- A quarter of victims and nonvictims were looking for work.

- More than 90% of victims and nonvictims were currently living in a house, apartment, trailer or mobile home.

- An estimated 2% of victims and nonvictims said they were in a shelter, homeless, or on the street (table 22).

TABLE 22
Current employment, housing, and living arrangements of former inmates under active parole supervision, by victimization status

	All	Victims	Nonvictims*
Number under supervison[a]	510,800	49,000	461,800
Current employment status			
Employed[b]	64.4%	63.6%	64.5%
Full-time	52.1	52.9	52.0
Part-time	8.8	7.2	8.9
Occasional	3.5	3.4	3.5
Not employed[b]	35.6%	36.4%	35.5%
Looking for work	24.5	22.9	24.7
Not looking	11.0	13.2	10.7
Current housing			
In house, apartment, trailer, or mobile home	92.1%	92.1%	92.1%
In rooming house, hotel, or motel	3.6	3.4	3.7
In hospital/treatment center	0.9	0.6	0.9
In a shelter/homeless	2.0	2.0	2.0
Other	1.4	1.9	1.4
Current living arrangements			
Alone	14.9%	18.0%**	14.5%
With others[c]	85.1%	82.0%**	85.5%
Spouse/girlfriend/boyfriend	41.7	45.0**	41.3
Children	27.6	25.8	27.8
Parents	25.2	20.3**	25.7
Other family members	22.5	16.8**	23.1
Friends	11.3	10.5	11.4

*Comparison group.

**Difference with comparison group is significant the 95%-confidence level.

[a]Number of victims and nonvictims were rounded to the nearest 100.

[b]Detail may not sum to total because of missing data.

[c]Detail sums to more than total because the former inmates may be living with more than one person.

Source: BJS, National Former Prisoner Survey, 2008.

The National Former Prisoner Survey (NFPS) was conducted between January 2008 and October 2008. The data were collected by the NORC at the University of Chicago under a cooperative agreement with the Bureau of Justice Statistics. A total of 317 total parole offices in 40 states were included in the survey sample. Within each of the sampled offices, respondents were selected at random from rosters of eligible former prisoners. A total of 17,738 former state prisoners under active supervision participated in the survey. An additional 788 former prisoners were included from survey test offices. These former inmates had been randomly selected from 16 sampled offices. Based on 18,526 completed interviews, the survey achieved a 61% response rate.

The interviews, which averaged 23 minutes in length, were conducted using computer-assisted personal interviewing (CAPI) and audio computer-assisted self-interviewing (ACASI) data collection methods. Survey interviewers initiated the personal interview using CAPI to obtain demographic and criminal history information. For the remainder of the interview, respondents interacted with a computer-administered questionnaire using a touch-screen and synchronized audio instructions delivered via headphones. Respondents completed the survey in private at the parole office (or satellite office), with the interviewer in the room but unable to see the computer screen.

The interviews were completed in 13 rounds of data collection. The survey was typically scheduled for 2 weeks at each parole office. Approximately 2 to 3 weeks before each round of interviews, sampled respondents were contacted by mail. The respondents were introduced to the survey, provided an approximate data collection date, informed of the nature of the survey, and given a toll-free number to set up an appointment. Two weeks prior to the interview period, NORC appointment setters called respondents to set up interview appointments with those respondents who had not used the toll-free number.

Before the interview, respondents were informed verbally and in writing that participation was voluntary and that all information provided would be held in confidence. They were also informed that if they agreed to participate, they would receive $50 as a token of appreciation for participation in the survey. A second automated consent protocol was administered at the beginning of the ACASI portion of the interview to confirm that the respondent had been properly informed that participation in the survey was voluntary and that they were "ready to continue with the interview."

Interviews were conducted in either English (99.4%) or Spanish (0.6%). Twenty interviews (0.1%) were lost because the sample parolee could not speak English or Spanish.

Sample design

The NFPS used a multistage stratified sample design with probabilities of selection proportionate-to-size (PPS). The sampling frame was developed based on the 2006 Census of State Parole Supervising Agencies, conducted by the U.S. Census Bureau on behalf of BJS. The original sampling frame consisted of two subframes: a field office group (FOG) level frame of 800 field office groups and a district level frame of 101 districts. Each of these subframes was sampled separately to produce the sampled offices. A two-stage stratified sample design was used for selection from the office subframe, while a three-stage design was used for the district subframe.

Sampling from the field office subframe

Prior to selection of offices, the field office sampling frame was modified:

- 40 offices were considered ineligible and deleted, including administrative offices not actively supervising parolees; specialty offices, such as those supervising sex offenders only; and offices supervising only individuals committed to treatment or other confinement facilities.

- 8 offices in the District of Columbia were deleted, as most parolees had served time in federal facilities; 10 offices in Alaska and 4 offices in Hawaii, except for the largest in each state, were deleted.

- 34 offices, with a parolee population under 40 and that had no other in-state office within 75 miles, were deleted.

- 27 offices included in the sample frame for the NFPS pretest were excluded. (See page 36 for details on the inclusion of pretest sample data in the final survey.)

- Offices with a parolee population under 40 were combined with another office within 75 miles for sampling purposes to form FOGs.

Field offices and FOGs were selected from the remaining frame of 800 offices using a PPS sampling procedure:

- 34 FOGs were selected with certainty, due to their large size, and allocated a sample size of 260 parolees.

- 117 FOGs were selected with non-certainty and allocated a sample size of 130 for offices with populations of 130 or greater, or the actual population sizes for offices with populations of less than 130.

- 37 additional FOGs were selected as reserve offices and activated in order of selection as needed to offset office refusals and potential ineligible offices on the frame.

A total of 151 FOGs (including 7 involving combined offices) were selected. Data collection was completed in 157 FOGs (after exclusion of 4 ineligible administrative offices and inclusion of 10 reserve sample offices.) All eligible sampled offices agreed to participate.

Sampling from the district office sub-frame

The 2006 census provided data only at the district or regional office in 19 states. A total of 50 districts were selected from the list of 101 offices using PPS sampling procedures (including 35 certainty and 15 non-certainty districts). An additional 20 reserve districts were selected to offset potential refusals and ineligible listings. Eleven of the districts on the reserve list were activated. All sampled state offices granted approval to participate in the survey; however, one sampled district was excluded due to lateness of the request.

Following selection of district offices, field offices and population sizes within each selected district were enumerated. The same grouping and elimination criteria as listed above for parole offices were used for FOGs within each district, except that the distance cutoff was increased to 120 miles. Offices with fewer than 40 parolees were only eliminated if there was no other office with 120 miles for grouping. Three offices were deleted due to the distance and size criteria. Access to one office was denied by the district and was replaced by another randomly selected office within that district.

The remaining eligible FOGs within each sampled district were selected using PPS sampling procedures. A total of 81 FOGs were selected (including 21 with combined field offices).

Parolee selection

After approvals from states and offices were received, a roster was requested of eligible former prisoners under active supervision by the parole office. Only persons who had served time in a state prison and were age 18 or older were eligible. Individuals who had absconded, were reincarcerated or committed, were in a halfway house or community treatment center, had a warrant issued for their arrest, were in violator status, or had been transferred to another parole office were ineligible.

Prior to sample selection, each roster was sorted by sex. Males and females were then randomly selected for inclusion in the survey. The target sample size was 260 (196 males and 64 females) in large field offices and 130 (98 males and 32 females) in smaller offices. Female former prisoners were sampled at a higher rate than males to ensure that sufficient numbers were included to provide reliable national estimates. For offices with 130 or fewer eligible parolees, all former prisoners were selected. In total, 34,782 former prisoners were selected.

Response rates

Of the total number of former prisoners selected for the national survey, 17,738 eligible and available respondents completed the CAPI and ACASI portions of the interview:

- 4,318 (12.4%) refused to participate in the survey for reasons such as work, no transportation to the office, unwillingness to discuss prison experiences, wanting to avoid the parole office, dissatisfaction with the system, in trouble, health issues, and other unknown reasons.

- 5,664 (16.3%) could not be reached due to absence of working phone numbers, wrong phone numbers, failure to return phone messages, or lack of interest communicated by the parole officer or another person.

- 3,338 (9.6%) were found to be ineligible for reasons such as death; deportation; under age 18; not on parole; under warrant or absconder status; transferred to another office; incarcerated at time of sample selection; or under warrant, violator or absconder status after sample selection.

- 2,151 (6.2%) were unavailable due to change in status after sample selection, primarily due to incarceration, transfer, or completion of parole supervision.

- 1,571 (4.5%) did not participate for other reasons, primarily due to missing scheduled appointments.

Overall, 60.6% of eligible and available sampled former prisoners participated in the survey.

Inclusion of pretest sample sites and respondents

Due to the extensive and burdensome nature of the pretest, and the similarities in the pretest and national survey design and content, data from the pretest were included in the final survey results. PPS sampling methods were employed:

- 16 offices from a list of 29 offices responsible for supervision of post-release offenders were selected using PPS sampling methods.

- The initial protocol called for randomly sampling 75 cases from each office, with a goal of obtaining 50 completed interviews per office.

- A reserve sample of 50 former prisoners per office was drawn for activation in case of high numbers of ineligible cases and non-response.

- After interviewing in 8 offices, the initial sample sizes were increased to 100 to address the large numbers of ineligible cases on the office rosters.

- Sample sizes varied from 100 to 135 across 15 of the sampled offices. One office, with a population of 67, had a sample size equal to its population.

In total, 1,745 former prisoners were selected in the pretest. Interviews were completed by 788 parolees (representing 64.5% of the 1,222 eligible sampled cases).

Weighting and non-response adjustments

Responses from interviewed former prisoners were weighted to provide national-level estimates. The construction of parolee base weights took into account the probability of selection at each stage, reflecting two stages in the field office subframe and three stages in the district subframe:

- Within the district sample, selection probabilities were adjusted at the district and office levels for non-response.

- Within the field office sample, all selected FOGs participated.

- Probabilities of selection from each subframe took into account the impact of certainty and non-certainty districts and offices.

- Within selected FOGs in both subframes, males and females were selected at different rates; consequently, the probabilities of selection were computed separately.

- The final parolee base weights in the district sample represent the inverse of the product of the non-response adjusted probabilities from the district and FOG stages times the probability of selection of male and female parolees within field offices. The base weights in the field office subframe represent the inverse of the product of the probability of selection at the FOG and parolee stages.

A series of adjustments were applied to the initial base weights to compensate for non-response among sampled parolees. To produce final weights, the initial weights given to sampled parolees who did not respond to the survey were distributed to responding cases. A response propensity model was constructed and used to form adjustment cells within which these weights were reallocated:

- Variables used in the non-response adjustments were race, age, years in prison, years since release, and required number of office visits per month.

- Predicted probabilities obtained from the model were used to construct five non-response groupings, based on the quintiles of the probability distribution.

- Subsequent weight adjustment was done within each group, so that the weights of nonresponding individuals within a range of propensities were allocated to like individuals.

Following procedures to address undesirably large weights, final post-stratification was introduced to adjust the weights to known control totals. All states in the sample frame were divided into seven strata, and control totals for each stratum were produced based on the midyear 2008 parolee counts.

The final weights in the national survey (including pretest offices) averaged 27.57, resulting in a national estimate of approximately 510,800.

Standard errors and confidence intervals

As with any survey estimates, the NFPS estimates are subject to error arising from the fact that they are based on a sample rather than a complete enumeration. A common way to express this sampling error is to construct a 95%-confidence interval around each survey estimate. Typically, multiplying the standard error by 1.96 and then adding or subtracting the result from the estimate produces the confidence interval. This interval expresses the range of values that could result among 95% of the different samples that could be drawn.

To facilitate the analysis, rather than provide the detailed estimates for every standard error, differences in the estimates of sexual victimization for subgroups in these tables have been tested and notated for significance at the 95%-level confidence. For example, the difference in the rate of inmate-on-inmate sexual victimization among female prisoners (13.7%), compared to male prisoners (4.2%), is statistically significant at the 95% level of confidence. (See table 6 on page 15.) In all tables providing detailed comparisons, statistically significant differences at the 95% level of confidence or greater have been designated with two asterisks (**).

Measurement of sexual victimization

The survey of sexual victimization relied on former inmates reporting their direct experience, rather than reporting on the experience of other inmates. Questions related to inmate-on-inmate sexual activity were asked separately from questions related to staff sexual misconduct.

The ACASI survey began with a series of questions that screened for general unwanted sexual activities with other inmates. To fully measure all sexual activities, a question related to touching of specific body parts in a sexual way was followed by a general question regarding any sexual activity with another inmate in which the respondent did not want to participate. (For specific screening questions, see appendix A.)

Respondents who answered "yes" to either of the sex-specific screener questions were then asked questions related to the touching of body parts in a sexual way and questions related to acts of oral, anal, and vaginal sex. (For survey items related to specific inmate-on-inmate victimization categories, see appendix B.) The nature of coercion (including physical force, pressure, and other forms of coercion) was measured for each type of reported sexual activity.

ACASI survey items related to staff sexual misconduct were asked somewhat differently. Respondents were first asked if during their confinement staff had sexually harassed them, watched them at an inappropriate time while dressing or taking a shower, or forced them to undress or touched their private parts in an inappropriate way. (See survey items in appendix C.)

Regardless of the responses to the initial questions, all respondents were then asked two screener questions to determine if they ever "willingly" or unwillingly had sex or sexual contact with any facility staff. Respondents who answered "yes" to either of the screener questions were then asked questions related to "willing" and unwilling sex or sexual contacts, the nature of coercion, and the specific types of sexual contacts including oral, anal, and vaginal sex. (For survey items related to specific staff-on-inmate victimization categories, see appendix D.)

Based on their responses to the survey items, victims were classified in each of four general variables: (1) inmate-on-inmate nonconsensual acts, (2) inmate-on-inmate abusive sexual contacts only, (3) staff sexual misconduct—unwilling; and (4) staff sexual misconduct—willing.

The entire ACASI questionnaire (listed as the National Former Prisoner Survey) is available on the BJS website at http://www.bjs.gov.

Prison placements

In order to assess the impact of facility factors on the likelihood of a former prisoner reporting inmate-on-inmate sexual victimization and staff sexual misconduct, a separate record for each prison placement was constructed. Overall, the 18,526 former prisoners in the survey reported entering separate prison facilities 45,318 times during the period of incarceration prior to their release from custody. Depending on the number of state prisons entered, each respondent is represented between 0 and 15 times. Facility-level data from BJS prison censuses conducted in 1990, 1995, 2000, and 2005 were merged to each placement record, based on the census closest to the period of incarceration.

Individual-level victimization variables and other individual-level characteristics reported in the survey were included with each placement. Of all 45,318 prison placements, 96% were matched to an appropriate census data file. When weighted to reflect initial probabilities of selection and non-response adjustments, data were available for 1,254,998 of the prison placements (approximately 94% of all placements). Local jail placements (prior to prison, as an interim stop, or as the only placement) were excluded. Placements in hospitals and out-of-state facilities were also excluded.

Linkage of placements to prison census data

Prison facilities were identified from an initial list provided by the 2000 Census of State and Federal Correctional Facilities. Information on these facilities was enhanced by the 1990 and 1995 censuses and contacts in departments of correction in each state. The final list was programmed to appear in the CAPI portion of the survey prior to the start of ACASI. If the respondent provided a facility name that could not be identified on the list after attempts to locate the facility by name of city, the interviewer added the facility to the list.

Initial rules were used to define the most appropriate census file for linking the facility information. Each inmate provided admission and release dates for the most recent period of incarceration, not for individual facilities. The following rules were applied to determine the reference year for linkage, either the year of admission or the average year (i.e., the midpoint between the admission and release date):

- If the victim was placed in only one facility, the average year was used.
- If the victim was in multiple facilities, the admission year was used for the first facility placement and the average year for all other placements.

If the reference year was—

- 1992 or earlier, facility characteristics were drawn from the 1990 census
- 1993-1997, facility characteristics were drawn from the 1995 census
- 1998-2002, facility characteristics were drawn from the 2000 census
- 2003 or later, facility characteristics were drawn from the 2005 census.

All unmatched facilities from the interviewer entry list were identified and linked to an appropriate census file.

Logistic regression models

Multivariate logistic regression estimation is a modeling technique used to determine what characteristics are statistically significant for predicting a dichotomous outcome (e.g., victimized or not victimized) while controlling for all the other characteristics in the model.

NFPS used this technique to determine what inmate-level characteristics were significant predictors of inmate-on-inmate sexual victimization and staff sexual misconduct over the entire period of confinement. For each type of victimization, and for males and females separately, selected parolee characteristics were examined, including demographic characteristics, sexual orientation and history, and criminal justice status and history. For each type of victimization, a logistic model was iteratively run under a backwards selection technique until only predictors that were significant at the 95% level of confidence remained. (See table 10 on page 19.)

NFPS also used this technique to determine what facility-level and inmate-level characteristics were significant predictors of inmate-on-inmate sexual victimization and staff sexual misconduct in each of the state prisons where the former inmates had served time. Based on a separate record for each prison placement for the 18,526 former prison inmates interviewed, logistic regression models were developed to model the effects of individual and prison-level characteristics. For each type of victimization, a logistic model was developed to isolate specific individual and facility factors that remain significant at the 95% level of confidence. (See table 16 on page 28.)

Conditional marginal probabilities

In each of the logistic regression models, the conditional marginal probability represents the probability that an inmate with a particular characteristic has experienced sexual victimization (by type) conditional on the inmate having the mean value for all other predictors in the model. For example, based on a combination of individual characteristics only, a white male former prisoner had a 4.0% chance of being victimized by another inmate given that he was at the mean of the joint distribution of age, sexual orientation, offense, and total time served.

For purposes of estimating the conditional marginal probabilities, the overall log odds of incurring the event for a given level of race/Hispanic origin was calculated from the estimated linear model by specifying the value of the race/Hispanic origin variable as the level of interest and then specifying all other variables in the model to be the weighted mean in the population. For example, the simple logistic model for the binary variable Y (experienced sexual victimization or not) is

$$\log\left(\frac{P(Y_i=1)}{1-P(Y_i=1)}\right) = \alpha_i + x'_{ij}\beta$$

where, α_i is the parameter of the race/Hispanic origin category for the individual i ($i=1 \dots n$, n is the total number of respondents).

To calculate the log odds for a specific race/Hispanic origin = r; use fixed α_r and $\bar{x}$,

$$\log\left(\frac{M_r}{1-M_r}\right) = \alpha_r + \bar{x}'\beta$$

where, $\bar{x} = \sum_{i=1}^{n} \frac{w_i x_i}{\sum_i w_i}$.

For other categorical covariates x except race/Hispanic origin, the mean value for each dummy variable is the weighted percentage of the corresponding level.

Based on the obtained log odds, the conditional marginal probability was then calculated for the specific level of the race/Hispanic = r as

$$M_r = \frac{e^{\alpha_r + \bar{x}'\beta}}{1 + e^{\alpha_r + \bar{x}'\beta}}$$

These estimates (M_r) represent the expected risk of victimization for a former inmate, conditional on the inmate belonging to a particular group (defined by each characteristic in the model) and having the mean value on all of the other characteristics in the model. The conditional marginal assumes that $\bar{x}$ is constant, and the variance is due to the variances of β.

Significance tests

For each of the regression models, variances for the estimates took into account the NFPS sample design. These variances were computed with weighted data in SUDAAN using the Taylor Linearization method. Wald F-statistics were calculated to test for statistical significance of the effects of each individual-level and facility-level characteristic (appendix tables 3 and 4). The Wald F-statistics were used to test the null hypothesis that all regression coefficients are equal to zero for each characteristic (i.e., the probability of experiencing victimization is the same across all categories of the selected characteristic), conditional on all other inmate or facility-level characteristics being included in the model.

NFPS and NIS sample differences

Findings in the NFPS are limited to persons released from state prison to a period of post-custody supervision (including parole, probation following incarceration, community supervised release, or other form of supervision). Approximately 24% of all sentenced state prisoners released in 2008 were released unconditionally. These former inmates, some of whom may have experienced sexual victimization while in prison, were not surveyed. Because these former inmates were not subject to post-custody supervision, and correctional authorities lacked their current addresses or phone numbers, they could not be easily contacted and interviewed after their release from prison.

The NFPS findings should not be generalized to all former prisoners. Based on selected demographic characteristics reported in BJS's National Corrections Reporting Program in 2008, inmates released conditionally were similar to those released unconditionally. Nearly the same percentage were male (89.2% compared to 89.4%), under age 30 (34.9% compared to 35.2%), age 50 or older (10.1% compared to 10.2%), and sentenced for a violent offense

(25.4% compared to 26.6%). However, inmates released unconditionally had served significantly longer in prison than those released conditionally. An estimated 23.2% of inmates released unconditionally had served more than 3 years, compared to 15.9% of inmates released conditionally. In addition, 12.5% of unconditional releases had served fewer than 6 months, compared to 32.5% of conditional releases.

Caution is also recommended when comparing NFPS findings with NIS-1 and NIS-2 findings, due to differences in coverage and differences in composition among former and current inmates. In contrast with the NIS sample, the NFPS sample does not include inmates who may never be released. (Based on data from the 1997 Survey of Inmates in State Prison, approximately 5% of all inmates in state prison were not expected to ever be released.) In addition, the cross-section of former inmates is comprised of less serious offenders with shorter maximum sentences than the cross-section of inmates in the NIS sample. For example, 33% of former inmates in NFPS had served time for a violent offense, compared to 56% of state inmates in NIS-2 who were serving time for a violent offense.

Appendix A

Survey items that screen for inmate-on-inmate sexual victimization, National Former Prisoner Survey, 2008

C11. [MALES] During your confinement, did another inmate touch your butt, thighs, penis, or other private parts in a sexual way or did you touch theirs, when you did not want this to happen?

C11a. [FEMALES] During your confinement, did another inmate touch your butt, thighs, breasts, vagina, or other private parts in a sexual way or did you touch theirs, when you did not want this to happen?

[IF C11 NE Yes or C11a NE YES] We recognize that you may find questions regarding sexual activity sensitive. However, no one will know how you answered these questions. Please remember that your responses are confidential.

C11b. During your confinement, were you involved in any sexual activity with another inmate in which you did not want to participate?

Survey items related to inmate-on-inmate sexual victimization categories, National Former Prisoner Survey, 2008

Males	Females
Nonconsensual sexual activity—oral sex	
C12. Did the sexual activity ever involve oral sex or a blow job in which your mouth was on another inmate's penis or other private parts?	C12d. Did the sexual activity ever involve oral sex in which your mouth was on another inmate's vagina or other private parts?
You indicated that you were involved in unwanted sexual incidents, but that oral and anal sex did not occur. During the unwanted sexual incident or incidents, which of the following things happened? Please indicate all that happened.	You indicated that you were involved in unwanted sexual incidents but [if applicable] oral, [if applicable] vaginal, or [if applicable] anal sex did not occur. During the unwanted sexual incident or incidents, which of the following happened? Please indicate all that happened.
C15f. Another inmate put their mouth on your penis or other private parts.	C16g. Another inmate put their mouth on your vagina or other private parts.
C15g. You put your mouth on another inmate's butt or thighs.	C16h. You put your mouth on another inmate's butt or thighs.
Nonconsensual sexual activity—anal sex	
C14. Did the sexual activity ever involve anal sex in which another inmate inserted their finger, penis, or an object into your butt?	C14a. Did the sexual activity involve anal sex in which another inmate inserted their finger or an object into your butt?
You indicated that you were involved in unwanted sexual incidents, but that oral and anal sex did not occur. During the unwanted sexual incident or incidents, which of the following things happened? Please indicate all that happened.	You indicated that you were involved in unwanted sexual incidents but [if applicable] oral, [if applicable] vaginal, or [if applicable] anal sex did not occur. During the unwanted sexual incident or incidents, which of the following happened? Please indicate all that happened.
C15h. You inserted your finger, penis, or an object into another inmate's butt.	C16j. You inserted your finger or an object into another inmate's butt.
Nonconsensual sexual activity—vaginal sex	
	C13. Did the sexual activity ever involve vaginal sex in which another inmate inserted their finger or an object into your vagina?
	You indicated that you were involved in unwanted sexual incidents but [if applicable] oral, [if applicable] vaginal, or [if applicable] anal sex did not occur. During the unwanted sexual incident or incidents, which of the following happened? Please indicate all that happened.
	C16i. You inserted your finger or an object into another inmate's vagina.

Survey items related to inmate-on-inmate sexual victimization categories, National Former Prisoner Survey, 2008

Males	Females
Nonconsensual sexual activity—manual/hand job	

You indicated that you were involved in unwanted sexual incidents, but that oral and anal sex did not occur. During the unwanted sexual incident or incidents, which of the following things happened? Please indicate all that happened.

You indicated that you were involved in unwanted sexual incidents but [if applicable] oral, [if applicable] vaginal, or [if applicable] anal sex did not occur. During the unwanted sexual incident or incidents, which of the following happened? Please indicate all that happened.

C15d. Another inmate rubbed your penis in an attempt to arouse you.

C16e. Another inmate rubbed your breasts, butt, or vagina in an attempt to arouse you.

C15e. You rubbed another inmate's penis with your hand.

C16f. You rubbed another inmate's breasts or vagina with your hand.

C15i. You were forced to masturbate while someone watched.

Abusive sexual contact only

You indicated that you were involved in unwanted sexual incidents, but that oral and anal sex did not occur. During the unwanted sexual incident or incidents, which of the following things happened? Please indicate all that happened.

You indicated that you were involved in unwanted sexual incidents but [if applicable] oral, [if applicable] vaginal, or [if applicable] anal sex did not occur. During the unwanted sexual incident or incidents, which of the following happened? Please indicate all that happened.

C15a. Another inmate touched your butt or thighs.

C16a. Another inmate touched your butt or thighs.

C15b. Another inmate touched your penis or scrotum.

C16b. Another inmate touched your breasts.

C15c. Another inmate violently grabbed or touched your penis or scrotum in an attempt to hurt you.

C16c. Another inmate touched your vagina.

C16d. Another inmate violently grabbed or touched your breasts or vagina in an attempt to hurt you.

Survey items related to staff sexual misconduct, National Former Prisoner Survey, 2008

E1. During your confinement, did staff hassle or harass you in a sexual way?

E2. Did staff ever stare at you or watch you at inappropriate times (for example, while you were dressing or taking a shower)?

E3. [FEMALES] Did a staff member ever force you to undress in their presence or hit or brush against your breast or other private parts when you did not think it was an accident or it was not required by their job?

E3b. [MALES] Did a staff member ever force you to undress in their presence or hit or brush against your private parts when you did not think it was an accident or it was not required by their job?

E4. Did you ever willingly or unwillingly have sex or sexual contact with any facility staff person?

[IF E4 NE Yes] Please remember that your responses are confidential. Neither you nor the staff person involved will be identified through this survey. No one will know you answered these questions.

E4a. During your confinement did you have sex or any sexual contact with a staff person, whether it was willing or not?

Survey items related to staff-on-inmate sexual victimization categories, National Former Prisoner Survey, 2008

Males	Females
Nonconsensual sexual activity—oral sex	
E15. Did the sexual contact involve oral sex or a blow job in which your mouth was on the male staff person's penis or other private parts or his mouth was on your private parts?	E15b. Did the sexual contact involve oral sex in which your mouth was on the male staff person's penis or other private parts or his mouth was on your private parts?
E15a. Did the sexual contact involve oral sex or a blow job in which the female staff person's mouth was on your penis or other private parts or in which your mouth was on her private parts?	E15c. Did the sexual contact involve oral sex in which your mouth was on the female staff person's breasts, vagina, or other private parts or her mouth was on your private parts?
Nonconsensual sexual activity—anal sex	
E16. Did it involve anal sex in which the male staff person inserted his finger, penis, or an object into your butt or you inserted your finger, penis, or object into his?	E16b. Did it involve anal sex in which the male staff person inserted his finger, penis, or an object into your butt or you inserted your finger or an object into his?
E16a. Did it involve anal sex in which the female staff person inserted her finger or an object into your butt or you inserted your finger, penis, or an object into hers?	E16c. Did it involve anal sex in which the female staff person inserted her finger or an object into your butt or you inserted your finger or an object into hers?
Nonconsensual sexual activity—vaginal sex	
	E13. Did you have vaginal sex with a female staff person in which your penis, finger, or an object was inserted into her vagina?
	E13a. Were you involved in vaginal sex in which a male staff person inserted his penis, finger, or an object into your vagina?
	E13b. Were you involved in vaginal sex with a female staff person in which she inserted her finger or an object into your vagina or you inserted your finger or an object into hers?
Nonconsensual sexual activity—manual/hand job	
E14. Did you give or receive a hand job in which a male staff person rubbed your penis with his hand or you rubbed his?	E14b. Did you give the male staff person a hand job in which you rubbed his penis with your hand?
E14a. Did you receive a hand job in which a female staff person rubbed your penis with her hand?	
Abusive sexual contact only	
E12. Did a male staff person touch your penis or other private parts in a sexual way or did you touch his?	E12b. Did a male staff person touch your breasts, vagina, or other private parts in a sexual way or did you touch his private parts?
E12a. Did a female staff person touch your penis or other private parts in a sexual way or did you touch her private parts?	E12c. Did a female staff person touch your breasts, vagina, or other private parts or did you touch hers?

Survey items that identify prison placements and measure sexual victimization in each facility, National Former Prisoner Survey, 2008

B5. What was the name of the facility in which you were placed in [Month/Year]?

B6. Were you placed in any other facilities between [date of admission] and your release in [Month/Year]?

B5. [REPEAT, up to 25 times] What was the name of another facility in which you were placed?

For each type of inmate-on-inmate sexual victimization

FBM12a. [MALES] You indicated you had unwanted [oral sex or gave a blow job because you were physically forced, afraid, or someone threatened to hurt you physically]. Where did this unwanted [oral sex or blow job occur]? [READ LIST OF FACILITIES]

FBM12b. [FEMALES] You indicated you had unwanted [oral sex because you were physically forced, afraid, or someone threatened to hurt you physically]. Where did this unwanted [oral sex] occur? [READ LIST OF FACILITIES]

For all forms of staff-on-inmate sexual victimization

E6. At which facility or facilities did you have sexual contact with staff? [READ LIST OF FACILITIES]

APPENDIX TABLE 1

Standard errors for table 4: Type of coercion and physical injury of former state prisoners who reported sexual victimization, by type of incident

	Inmate-on-inmate		Staff sexual misconduct		
	Total[a]	Nonconsensual sexual acts	Total	Willing activity[b]	Unwilling activity[b]
Type of coercion					
Force/threat	1.73%	1.92%	1.49%	0.99%	4.28%
Threatened with harm or a weapon	1.76	1.86	1.43	1.00	4.84
Persuaded/talked into it	1.73	2.26	1.82	1.93	3.73
Physically held down or restrained	1.84	2.51	0.96	0.57	3.65
Physically harmed/injured	1.39	1.76	1.02	0.58	3.84
Coercion other than force/threat	1.57%	1.91%	1.78%	1.90%	2.69%
Offered/given protection from other inmates	1.67	2.07	1.13	0.95	2.84
Given bribe/blackmailed	1.74	2.30	1.68	1.75	3.51
Given drugs/alcohol	1.05	1.35	1.31	1.37	3.53
Pay off debt[c]	0.98	1.28	0.71	0.78	2.08
Offered/given protection from another correctional officer[c]	~	~	2.12	1.74	5.97
Offered favors or special privileges	~	~	1.83	1.83	4.04
Physically injured	1.62%	2.03%	0.79%	0.68%	3.00%
Excluding minor injuries	1.36	1.81	0.74	0.64	2.84
Knife/stab wounds	0.77	1.05	0.30	0.21	1.28
Broken bones	0.83	1.13	0.26	0.29	1.05
Anal/vaginal tearing, severe pain, or bleeding	1.25	1.91	0.65	0.55	2.60
Teeth chipped/knocked out	1.19	1.68	0.53	0.31	2.16
Internal injuries	0.95	1.31	0.37	0.29	1.50
Knocked unconscious	1.11	1.53	0.25	0.20	1.08
Bruises, a black eye, sprains, cuts, scratches, swelling, or welts	1.60	2.04	0.62	0.39	2.48

~Not applicable.

[a]Includes abusive sexual contacts.

[b]Includes touching only.

[c]Not included in the pretest interviews. See *Methodology* for a detailed discussion of the merged data files.

Source: BJS, National Former Prisoner Survey, 2008.

Standard errors for table 5: Circumstances surrounding sexual victimization of former state prisoners, by type of incident

Circumstance	Inmate-on-inmate		Staff sexual misconduct		
	Total[a]	Nonconsensual sexual acts	Total	Willing activity[b]	Unwilling activity[b]
Time of day					
6 a.m. to noon	2.01%	2.55%	2.00%	2.18%	4.25%
Noon to 6 p.m.	1.72	1.93	2.08	2.20	4.60
6 p.m. to midnight	1.90	2.18	2.02	2.28	4.86
Midnight to 6 a.m.	1.90	2.16	2.04	2.38	3.05
Where occurred					
Victim's cell/room/sleeping area	1.81%	2.03%	1.92%	2.24%	3.61%
Another inmate's cell/room	1.83	2.64	1.07	1.22	2.29
Shower/bathroom	1.72	2.17	1.93	2.07	4.20
Yard/recreation area	1.50	1.65	1.12	1.20	2.55
Workplace	1.37	1.74	2.19	2.43	4.46
Closet, office, or other locked room	1.35	1.96	1.71	1.70	4.19
Classroom/library	1.17	1.49	1.89	1.97	4.35
Elsewhere in facility	1.15	1.41	1.37	1.53	2.42
Off facility grounds[c]	1.06	1.20	1.37	1.44	3.34
Number of perpetrators					
1	2.02%	2.55%	1.62%	1.83%	3.10%
2	1.81	2.41	1.84	1.92	3.52
3 or more	1.51	1.87	1.72	1.98	3.30
Number of times					
1	2.28%	2.48%	1.31%	1.32%	2.31%
2	1.59	1.99	1.75	1.83	3.62
3 or more	1.89	2.14	2.01	2.05	4.29

[a]Includes abusive sexual contacts.

[b]Includes touching only.

[c]Includes incidents that occurred in a temporary holding facility, on work release, in a medical facility, in a vehicle, or at a courthouse.

Source: BJS, National Former Prisoner Survey, 2008.

Wald-F statistics for former prisoner characteristics in the final multivariate logistic regression models of sexual victimization, by type of incident

Former prisoner characteristic	Degrees of freedom All models*	Wald-F statistics for male sexual victimization in prison		Wald-F statistics for female sexual victimization in prison	
		Inmate-on-inmate	Staff sexual misconduct	Inmate-on-inmate	Staff sexual misconduct
Race/Hispanic origin	4	8.80	4.05	6.31	4.80
Age at admission	5	3.22	13.94	5.43	4.69
Education	3	~	~	2.68	~
Marital status	2	~	~	6.63	~
Weight	3	~	2.61	~	~
Sexual orientation	2	105.48	17.58	~	~
Prior incarcerations	1	~	14.02	10.22	7.02
Most serious offense	5	9.06	4.13	~	~
Total time served	5	20.30	26.68	4.16	21.28

Note: Wald-F tests were conducted to test for the statistical significance of each former state prisoner characteristic in the final models presented in table 10. For each characteristic, the Wald-F tests the null hypothesis that all regression coefficients are equal to zero (i.e., the probability of experiencing a victimization is the same across all categories of the selected characteristic), conditional on all other former state prisoner characteristics being included in the model. The Wald-F statistic is calculated by comparing the maximum likelihood estimate for the characteristic to an estimate of its standard error. Though varying by the number of degrees of freedom, statistics greater than 2.0 (for 1 degree of freedom) are statistically significant at the 95%-confidence level.

~Characteristics deleted from model when Wald statistic was not significant at the 95%-confidence level.

*For each former prisoner characteristic, the degrees of freedom represent the number of categories minus 1.

Source: BJS, National Former Prisoner Survey, 2008.

Wald-F statistics for former state prisoner and facility characteristics in the final multivariate logistic regression models of sexual victimization among male and female placements, by type of incident

Characteristic	Degrees of freedom All models*	Wald-F statistics for sexual victimization among male placements in prison		Wald-F statistics for sexual victimization among female placements in prison	
		Inmate-on-inmate	Staff sexual misconduct	Inmate-on-inmate	Staff sexual misconduct
Former prisoner characteristic					
Race/Hispanic origin	4	9.11	4.48	4.75	6.82
Age at admission	5	~	8.98	~	3.24
Education	3	~	6.03	~	~
Marital status	2	3.91	~	3.19	~
Weight	3	~	~	~	~
Sexual orientation	2	73.46	15.23	3.72	~
Prior incarcerations	1	~	5.53	8.73	~
Most serious offense	6	4.49	2.55	~	~
Total time served	5	4.94	8.75	3.75	7.54
Facility characteristic[c]					
Type of facility	4	3.85	11.5	2.61	~
Percent of inmates leaving facility during the day	1	~	~	6.37	~
Security level	2	7.06	~	3.74	12.03
Who operates facility	2	~	9.04	~	~
Year built	4	~	2.96	2.94	2.90
Inmate-to-staff ratio	4	~	~	3.14	~
Under court order	2	~	3.89	~	~
Major disturbance in census year	2	~	~	4.06	~
Percent of female staff	4	~	11.28	~	~
Census year closest to time of placement	3	3.73	~	~	3.83
Placement order of facility	2	7.77	~	4.40	~

Note: Wald-F tests were conducted to test for the statistical significance of each former state prisoner characteristic in the final models presented in table 16. For each characteristic, the Wald-F tests the null hypothesis that all regression coefficients are equal to zero (i.e., the probability of experiencing a victimization is the same across all categories of the selected characteristic), conditional on all other former state prisoner characteristics being included in the model. The Wald-F statistic is calculated by comparing the maximum likelihood estimate for the characteristic to an estimate of its standard error. Though varying by the number of degrees of freedom, statistics greater than 2.0 (for 1 degree of freedom) are statistically significant at the 95%-confidence level.

~Characteristic deleted from the model when Wald statistic was not significant at the 95%-confidence level.

*For each former state prisoner characteristic, the degrees of freedom represent the number of categories minus 1.

Source: BJS, National Former Prisoner Survey, 2008.

APPENDIX TABLE 5
Standard errors for table 17: Reporting of sexual victimization, by type of incident and persons to whom the incident was reported

	Inmate-on-inmate		Staff sexual misconduct		
	Total	Nonconsensual sexual acts	Total	Willing activity	Unwilling activity
Percent of victims reporting at least one incident of sexual victimization	1.77%	2.11%	0.97%	0.80%	3.66%
Percent reporting to any facility staff	2.02%	2.20%	0.88%	0.61%	3.54%
Correctional officer	1.71	1.83	0.71	0.31	2.87
Administrative staff	1.41	1.65	0.84	0.52	3.42
Medical/healthcare staff	1.31	1.71	0.60	0.33	2.35
Instructor/teacher	0.74	0.99	0.54	0.26	2.15
Counselor/case manager	1.29	1.63	0.66	0.35	2.56
Chaplain/other religious leader	0.88	1.19	0.38	0.27	1.49
Volunteer	0.72	0.71	0.55	0.20	2.19
Someone else at the facility[a]	1.46	1.68	0.67	0.35	2.48
Percent reporting to someone other than facility staff	1.99%	2.30%	0.97%	0.62%	3.77%
Telephone hotline	0.38	0.48	0.26	0.19	1.16
Another inmate	1.65	2.15	0.82	0.52	3.38
Family/friend outside the facility	1.94	2.10	0.88	0.45	3.45
Someone else outside the facility	1.31	2.00	~	~	~

~Category not included in the survey.

[a]Category not included in the pretest interviews.

Source: BJS, National Former Prisoner Survey, 2008.

APPENDIX TABLE 6
Standard errors for table 19: Facility responses to the reporting of sexual victimization to staff, by type of incident

	Inmate-on-inmate	Staff sexual misconduct
Facility response to reported sexual victimization	2.95%	4.92%
Moved Victim to administrative segregation/protective housing	2.67	8.27
Placed victim in medical unit/ward/hospital	1.88	4.09
Confined victim to cell	2.57	7.85
Assigned vicctim to a higher level of custody	2.02	6.56
Offered victim a transfe	2.21	7.88
Victim written up	2.62	8.27
Victim spoke to investigator[a]	2.95	8.61
Perpetrator punished/segregated	2.74	~
No facility response reported by victim	2.95%	4.92%

~Not asked of victims of staff sexual misconduct.

[a]Category not included in the pretest interviews.

Source: BJS, National Former Prisoner Survey, 2008.

Standard errors for table 20: Post-release responses of victims to sexual victimization, by type of incident

		Inmate-on-inmate		Staff sexual misconduct		
	All victims	Total	Nonconsensual sexual acts	Total	Willing activity	Unwilling activity
Discussed victimization with at least one individual[a]	1.61%	2.27%	2.27%	2.07%	2.28%	4.53%
Husband/wife, boyfriend/girlfriend, or other partner	1.51	2.16	2.27	1.92	2.09	4.46
Children	0.42	0.63	0.50	0.49	0.53	1.27
Parents	1.09	1.32	1.43	1.50	1.57	3.01
Other family member	1.22	1.36	1.60	1.92	2.32	2.77
Friend(s)	1.47	1.61	1.74	1.98	2.10	3.35
Minister or other religious leader	0.67	1.02	1.12	0.64	0.63	2.14
Therapist or treatment professional	0.86	1.34	1.67	0.98	1.06	2.62
Parole officer	0.56	0.91	1.16	0.57	0.42	2.05
Another inmate	1.28	1.52	1.82	1.84	2.13	2.67
Had feelings or thoughts about victimization[a]						
Guilt	1.30%	1.86%	2.12%	1.84%	1.74%	4.39%
Shame or humiliation	1.44	1.67	1.87	1.74	1.63	3.76
Revenge against someone victim was angry with	1.01	1.52	2.07	1.22	1.15	4.06
Difficulty feeling close to friends/family members	1.22	1.89	2.00	1.60	1.41	4.63
Participated in treatment to deal with victimization[a]	0.98%	1.57%	2.33%	1.06%	1.11%	3.07%
Saw therapist or counselor	0.86	1.44	2.12	1.00	1.07	2.54
Participated in self-help group for emotional/mental health problems	0.82	1.20	1.65	1.00	1.00	2.96
Enrolled in treatment program (other than counseling) for emotional/mental health problems	0.64	1.09	1.45	0.79	0.72	2.36
Took medication to treat emotional/mental health problems	0.68	1.11	1.60	0.78	0.60	2.95
Hospitalized for emotional/mental health problems	0.42	0.70	0.90	0.37	0.38	1.06

[a]Interviews conducted in the pretest were excluded due to changes in the questionnaire design.

Source: BJS, National Former Prisoner Survey, 2008.

NCJ 237363

Office of Justice Programs
Innovation • Partnerships • Safer Neighborhoods
www.ojp.usdoj.gov

The Eight ReEntry Partnership Initiatives:
Plans, Early Results, & Conceptual Framework

National Institute of Justice
Data Resources Program Workshop
Prisoner Reentry and Community Justice

June 18-22, 2001

Faye S. Taxman, Ph.D.
Douglas Young, M.A.
James M. Byrne, Ph.D.
Alex Hoslinger, Ph.D.
Donald Anspach, Ph.D.
Meridith Thanner, M.A.
Rebecca Silverman, M.A.

Bureau of Governmental Research
University of Maryland, College Park

This project is sponsored by the National Institute of Justice under grant 2000IJCX0045. All opinions are those of the authors and do not reflect the opinion of the sponsoring agency. All questions should be directed to Dr. Taxman or Mr. Young at bgr@bgr.umd.edu or 301 403 4403.

1

What is Reentry?

- Transitional Services/Discharge Planning

- "Program" (structured services)

- System Reform

- Offender Processing

What is the Goal(s) of Reentry?

- Prison Safety/Correctional Management

- *Public* Safety

- Quality of Life Improvements

Research Findings on Effective Interventions

- Begin process in prison, emphasize internal motivation and lifestyle changes

- Accountability (external controls) is strengthened when coupled with interventions

- Utilize needs/risk assessment to determine types of services; target high risk offenders

- Duration (and dosage and intensity) are critical—12-24 months of structured processes, if appropriate

- Emphasize prison, structured reentry (transition), reintegration; continuity of care

- Develop support mechanisms (informal social controls)

- Communication of offender responsibility and expectations

- Quality of services is critical (e.g. staff, program design, partnerships, etc.)

ReEntry Partnership Initiatives

- 8 Sites: Baltimore, Burlington, Columbia, Kansas City, Lake City (FLA), Las Vegas, Lowell, Spokane

- Process Evaluation/Action Research

- OJP Technical Assistance for 2 Years

BGR's Recidivism Reduction Laboratory: Model to Improve Outcome

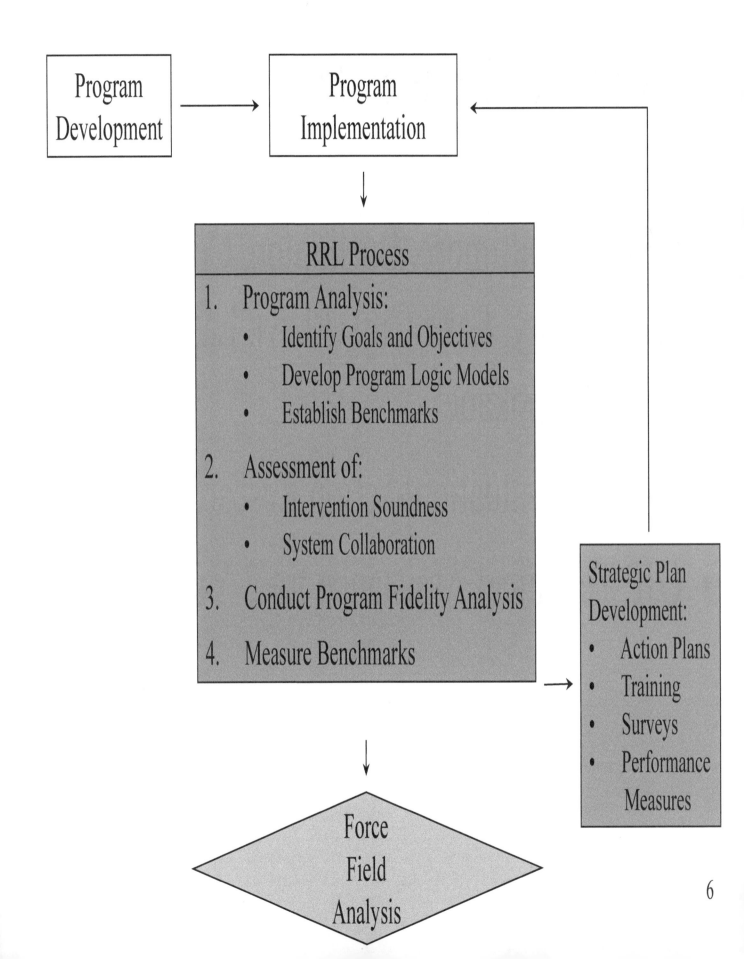

Reentry Partnership Continuum

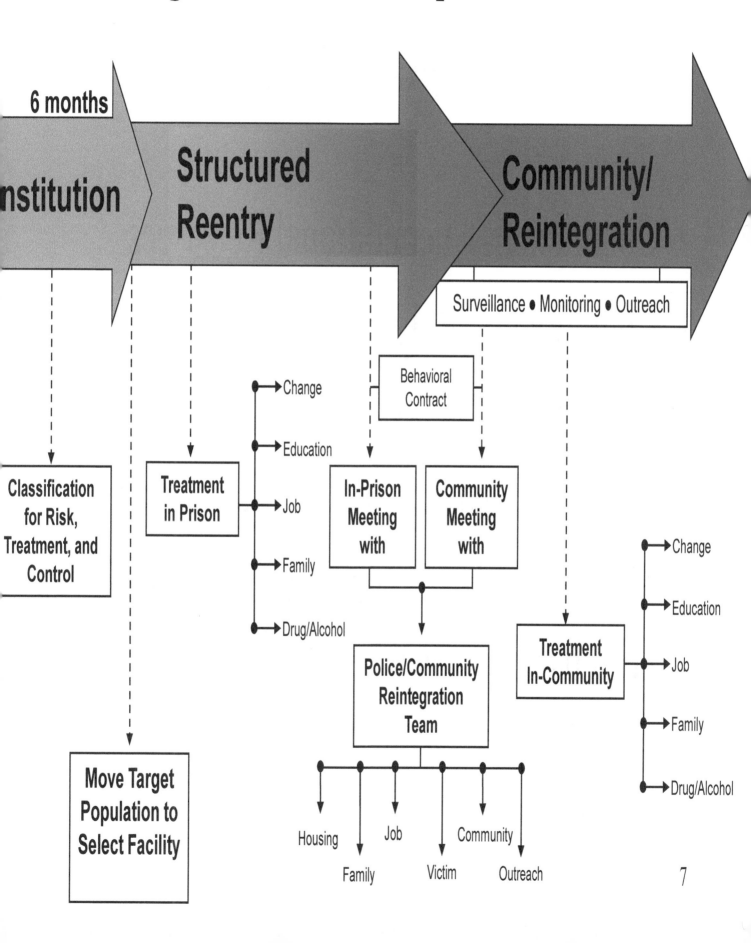

7

Targeting Issues

- Conditional, Unconditional Releasees

- Conditional—Rely on Formal/Informal Social Control Agencies

- Unconditional—Informal Social Control

- Many offenders do not need the services but need basic survival

Fidelity Measures: Building Infrastructure

- Measures degree to which partnerships focused on building infrastructure in each domain

- Uses evidence-based principles (e.g. criminal justice, intervention, and behavior management literature)

- Scale scores: 0—not in plan, 1—in plan, 2—in plan with research-based foundation, 3—in plan & begun implementation

- Reflects weighted average on key domains across the eight partnership sites

Implementation Plan for Institutional Phase:
Target Offenders Returning to Select Communities

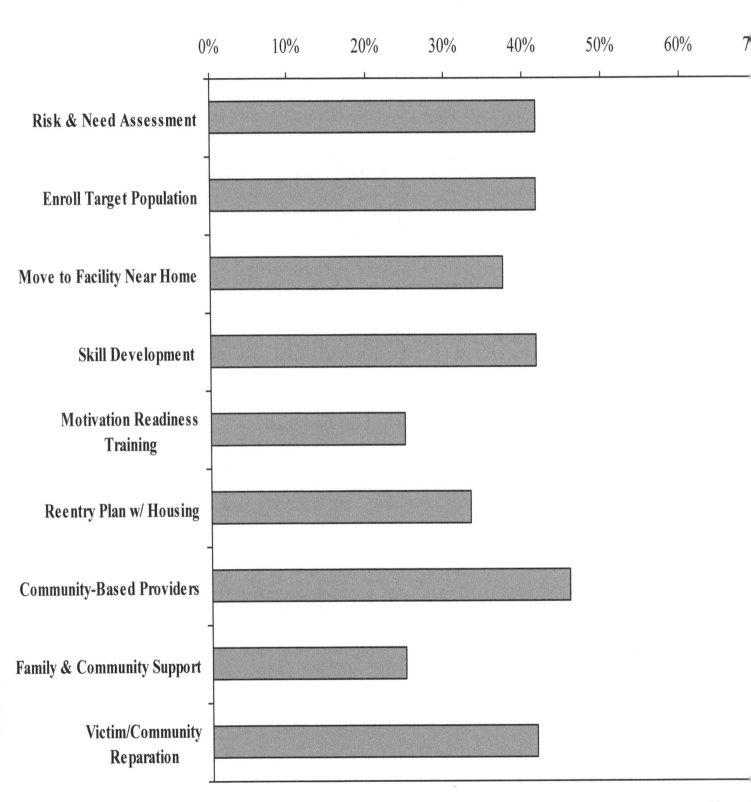

% Focused on Building Infrastructure

10

Implementation of Structured Reentry (Pre-Release)

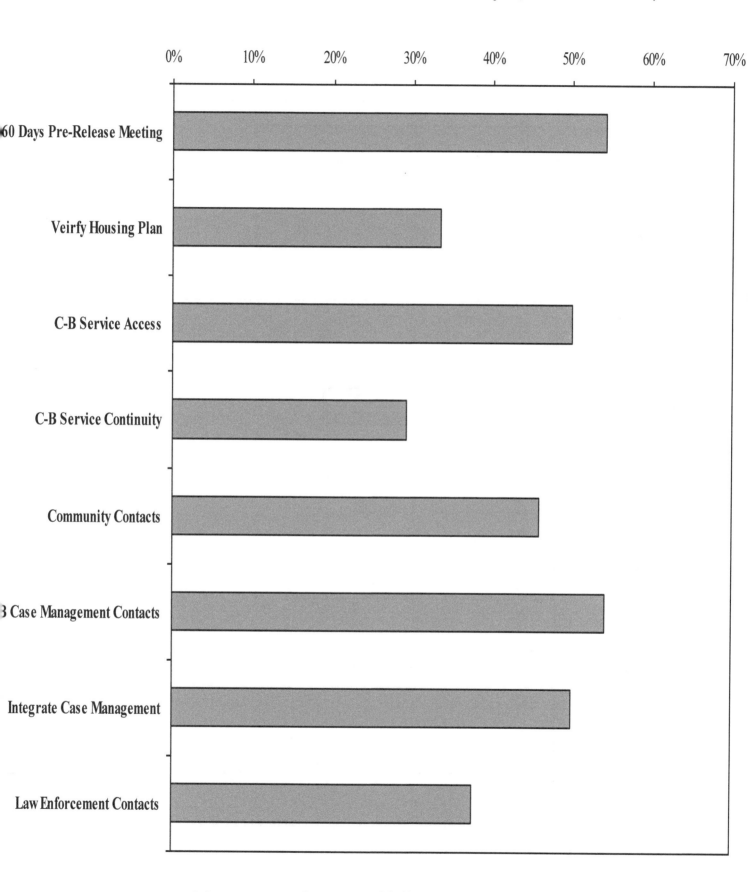

% Focused on Building Infrastructure   11

Implementation of Structured Reentry (Post-Release)

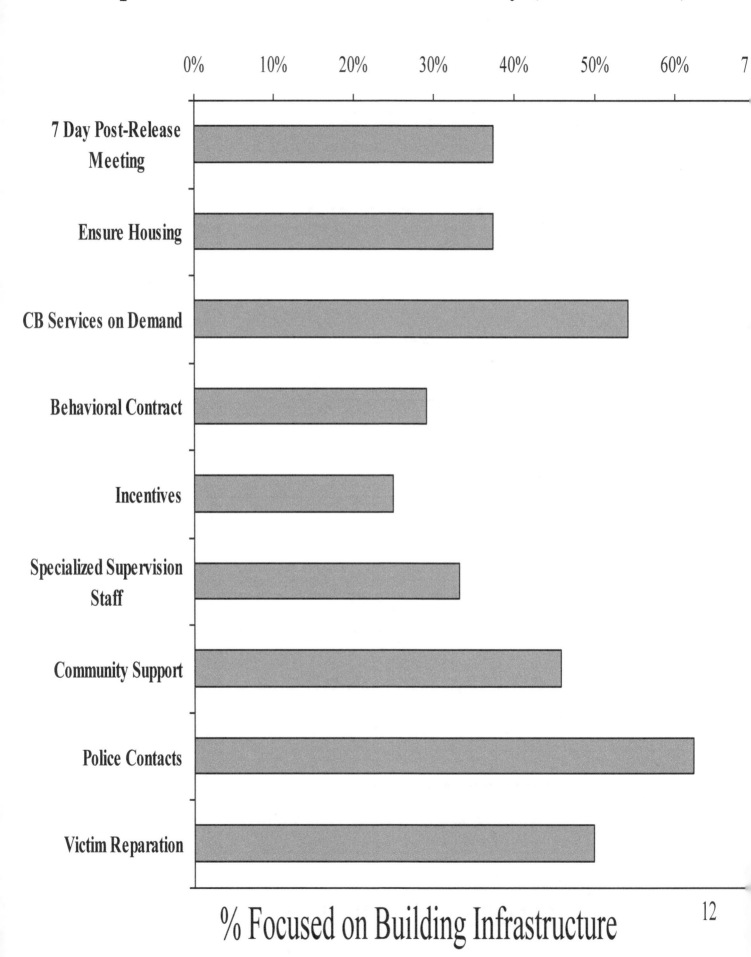

% Focused on Building Infrastructure

12

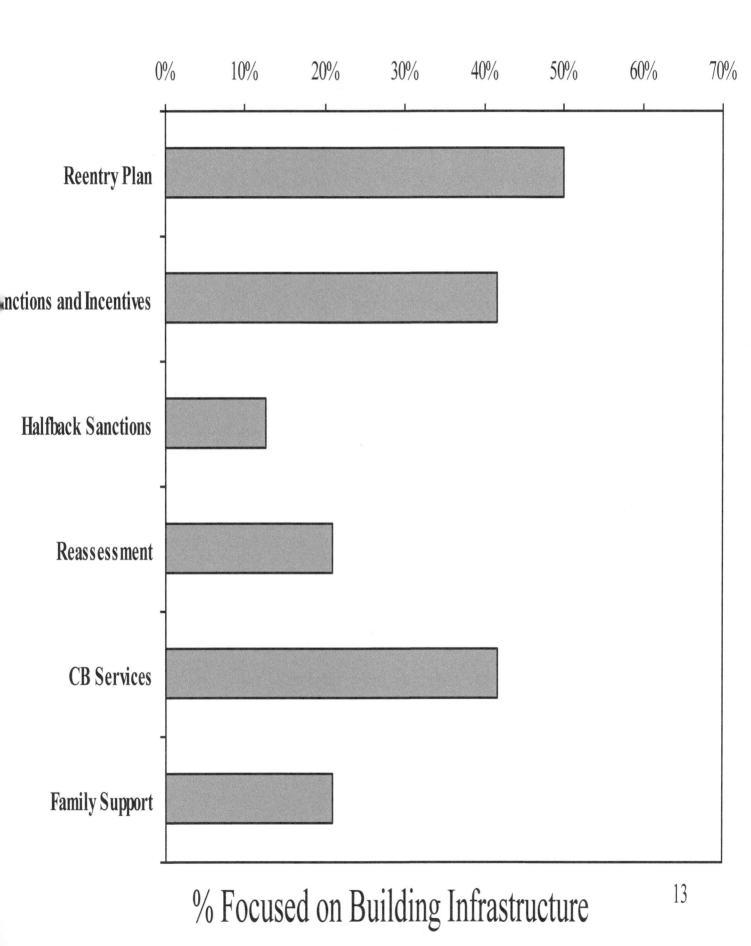

Implementation of Reintegration (Community)

% Focused on Building Infrastructure

13

Implementation Plan for System Collaboration

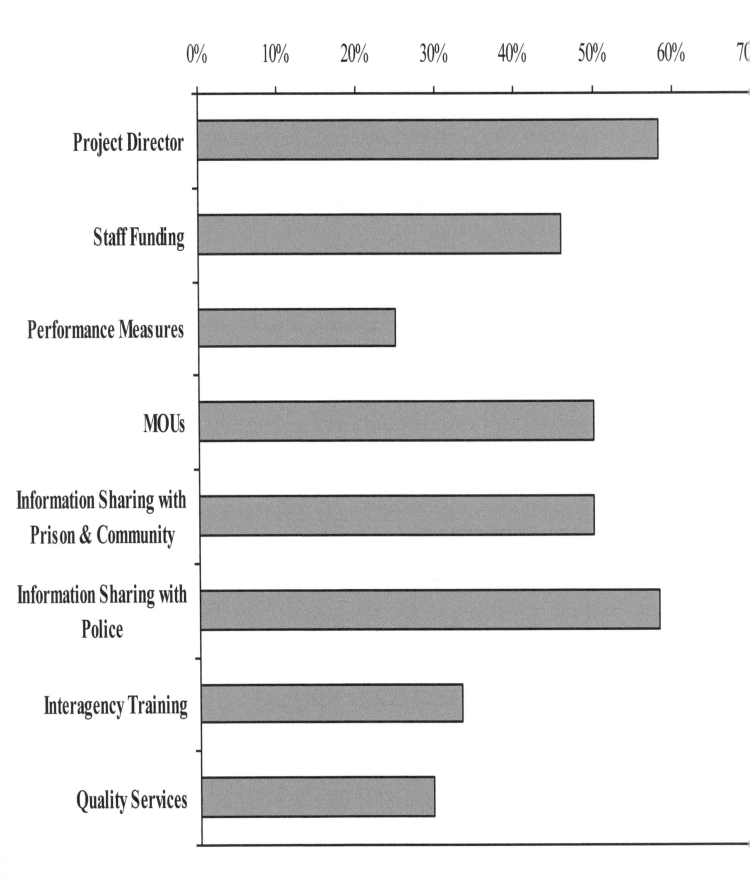

% Focused on Building Infrastructure

14

Overall Emphasis of the Partnership Sites

- Reflects areas in which the site has devoted efforts to build infrastructure

- Sites tend to build on strengths

- Sites built informal social controls such as community advocates, guardians, and others to supplement community attachments

Plans for Building the Reentry Infrastructure

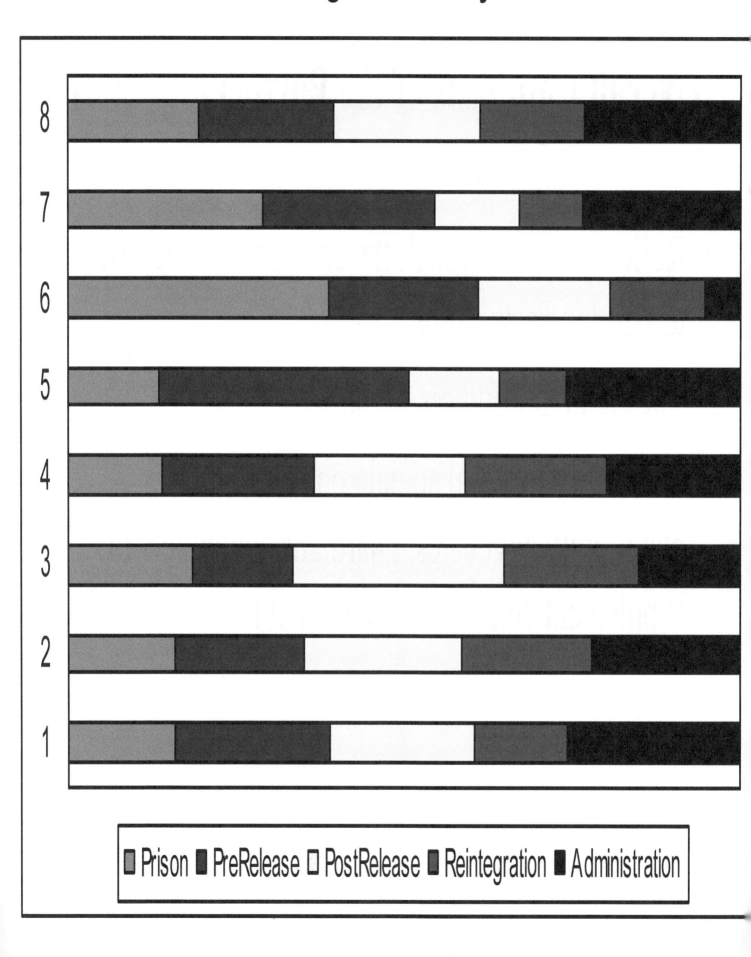

Prison ■ PreRelease □ PostRelease ■ Reintegration ■ Administration

Components of Collaboration

• Leadership

•Authority

•Ownership

•Resources

•Interagency Involvement

•Interagency Support

•Collaborative Problem Solving

•Anticipating and Identifying Implementation Issues

•Willingness to Make Changes

17

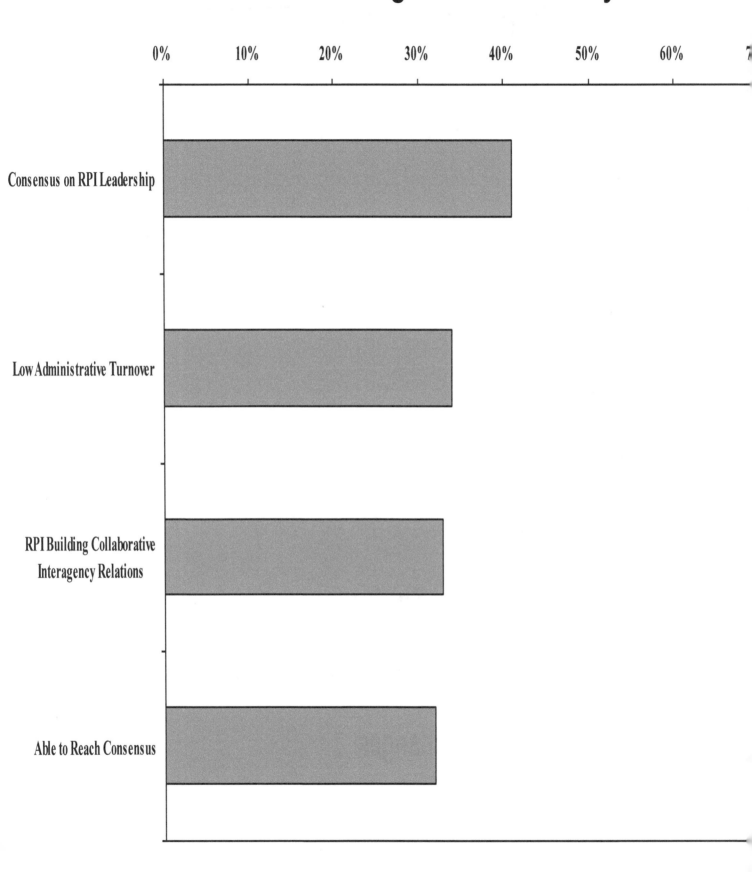

Collaboration Strengths—Site Surveys

% of Very Positive Responses

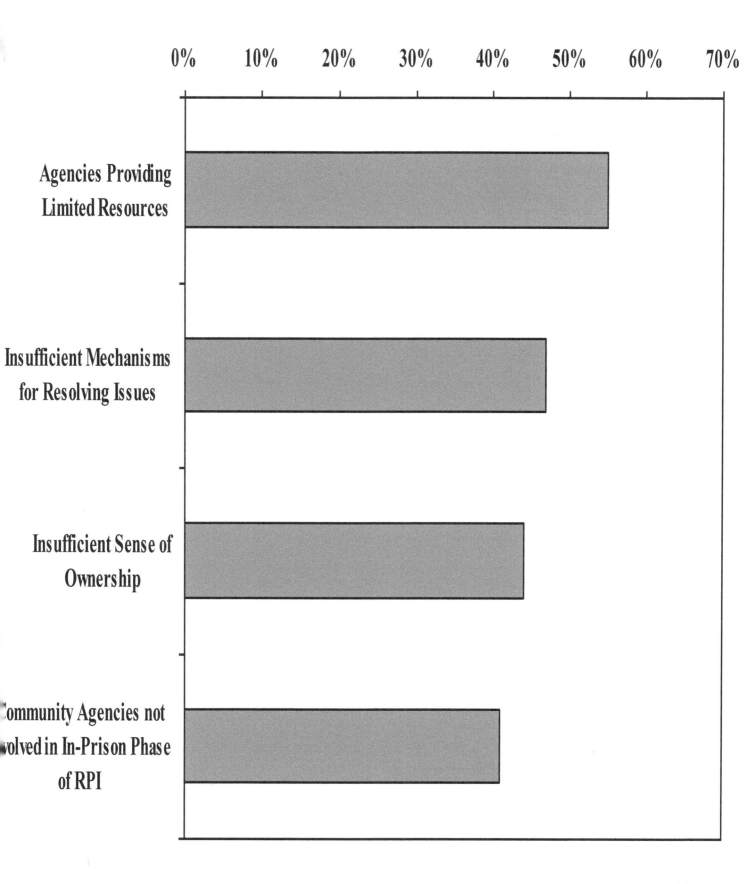

Collaboration Weaknesses—Site Surveys

% of Negative Responses

19

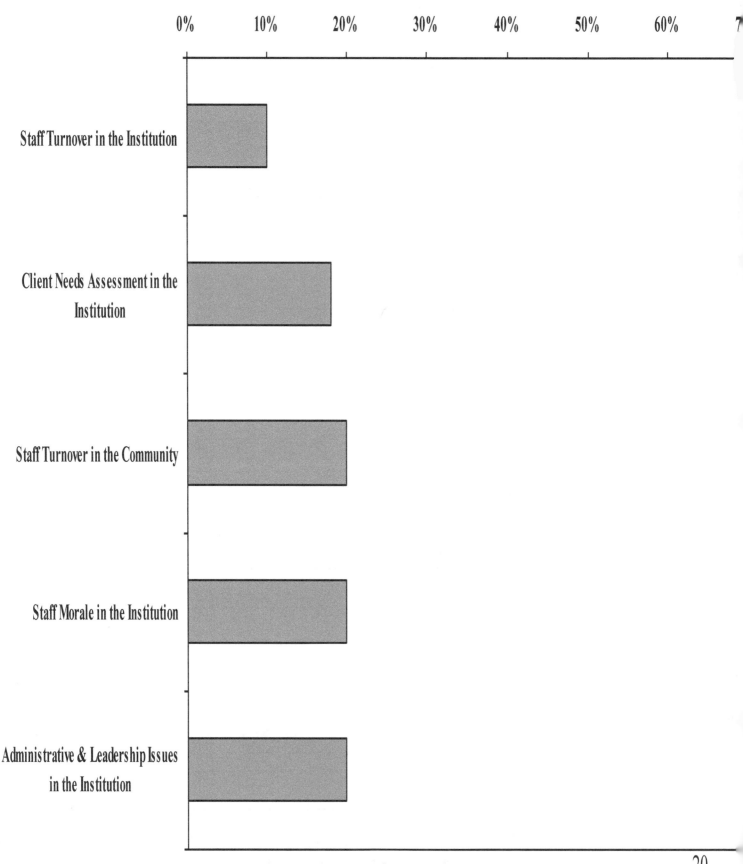

Implementation Areas of Least Concern to RPI Sites

% of Responses

20

Implementation Areas of Greatest Concern to RPI Sites

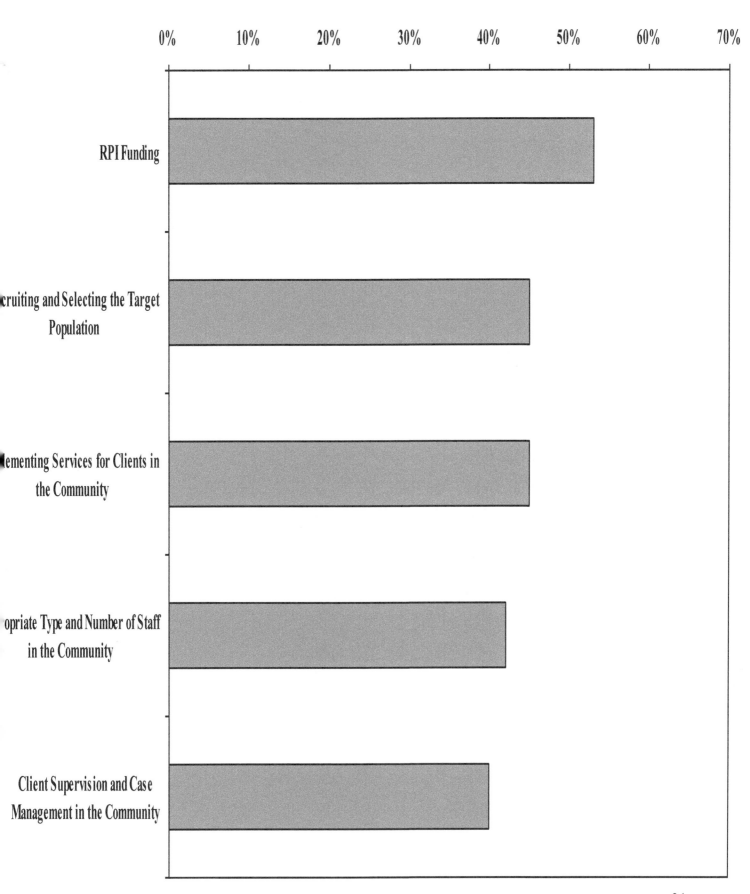

21

Building Reentry Infrastructures

Prison

Reassign to Facility Close to Home (work release/prerelease/transition)

Provide Motivation Readiness Training

Strengthen Transition Plan to be *Community Supervision* Oriented

Structured Reentry

Verify Transition Plan & Work with Offender on Housing and Employment

Identify Community Services & Begin Linkages

Strengthen Family/Support System Affiliations

View Reentry as a Support Team, Not Simply Supervision & Surveillance Agencies

Community/Reintegration

Address Housing Issues

Establish Outreach Efforts

Address "Reintegration Anxiety"

Provide Treatment & Employment Assistance at "No Cost" to Offenders

Provide Linkage to Family, Informal Community Supports

Provide Guardian, Community Advocates, Support Agencies

Provide Incentives to Compliance

Address Victim, Community Reparation

Partner with Law Enforcement to Strengthen "Monitoring"

Community Normalization

Encourage, Support Self-Sustenance

Strengthen Community Support

Strengthen Role as Parent/Partner

Sustain Services as Needed

Offender Focus Groups

- Offender's role in society (e.g. stigma)

- Offender's acknowledgement of harm to family and community

- Offender's doubts about being self-sufficient, self-supporting, contributor

- Offender's willingness to ask for help

Sensitive Issues in the Reentry Process

Socio-Psychological state of the offender
- Shaming
- Adaptation to the community
- Distrust of social control agencies

Community Reentry Problems
- Acceptance of the ex-offender
- "Best fit"
- Mentoring/socialization

Law enforcement/Probation (Supervision)
- Role
- Past History
- New Futures

Private/Non-Profits
- Ex-Offender As a Target Population
- Priorities

Critical Junctures in Reentry Processes

...cture	Goals	Activities	Partnership Agencies
...onths ...to ...se ...son— ...try)	• Motivate offender for crime free lifestyle • Identify risks and needs • Identify and build key community supports (protective factors) • Develop reentry plans • Address responsibility for harms to community	• Move offender to correctional facility close to reentry community • Provide motivation readiness interventions • Conduct/update comprehensive risk and needs assessments • Identify appropriate treatment/service providers in community • Identify resources to address housing, vocational needs • Facilitate family contacts, visits; identify parental role if appropriate • Identify community supports (formal and informal) • Address "shame" of being an ex-offender • Provide victim impact/awareness groups	Corrections Community Supervision Community Treatment Housing Agencies Vocational Agencies Families Community Supports Victim Representatives
...0 days ...to ...se ...on— ...ctured ...ry)	• Verify and confirm reentry plans • Integrate supervision and service roles, responsibilities • Ensure continuity of pre- and post-release services • Strengthen formal and informal social controls	• Share information; confirm consensus on reentry plan and priorities: prison → community supervision → supports → treatment → enforcement · Confirm access to specified community services/treatment · Verify housing plans; ensure stable housing · Identify employment options · Facilitate family/community support visits; specify community supports (guardians, sponsors) · Address community responsibility issues · Facilitate communication with formal supervision agencies including local law enforcement	Corrections Community Supervision Community Treatment Housing Agencies Vocational Agencies Families Community Supports Victim Representatives Law Enforcement

25

Unanswered Questions?

- Can the values, attitudes, beliefs of cj actors change?

- Will offenders participate?

- Will the community stay involved (with minimal money)? Address hard times?

- Can basic survival services obviate the need for further services?

- Will offenders assume roles as member of the community?

- Can offenders change?

Critical Junctures in Reentry Processes

ncture	Goals	Activities	Partnership Agencies
ys After ase ctured ntry)	· Verify housing/living arrangements · Identify risk/protective factors · Link with community network · Emphasize role in the community	· Coordinate case management · Provide housing services · Make employment connections · Verify supervision plan/informal network plans · Meet with community agencies (networks) · Outreach to "wrap-up"/EOS offenders (mandatory releasees) · Provide incentives to engage in community treatment services	Community Supervision Community Treatment Housing Agencies Vocational Agencies Families Community Supports Victim Representatives Law Enforcement
ays After ase ctured ntry)	· Identify risk & protective factors · Link with community network · Readjust plan of supervision · Outreach to releasees	· Reaffirm housing/employment/services connections · Modify supervision plan · Utilize incentives and rewards for participation in support services · Strengthen family/community issues · Address non-compliant issues that present risk factors · Provide outreach to offenders in "crisis" · Provide routine drug testing and, if needed, treatment services	Community Supervision Community Treatment Housing Agencies Vocational Agencies Families Community Supports Victim Representatives Law Enforcement
30 days Release ctured ntry)	· Identify risk & protective factors · Link with network in community · Readjust supervision plan · Outreach to releasees	· Reaffirm housing/employment · Modify supervision plan · Utilize incentives and rewards · Strengthen family/community issues · Address non-compliant issues that present risk factors · Provide routine drug testing and, if needed, treatment services	Community Supervision Community Treatment Housing Agencies Vocational Agencies Families Community Supports Victim Representatives Law Enforcement
720 days ervision)	· Readjust supervision · Outreach to releasees · Enhance quality of life	· Strengthen informal social controls · Strengthen prosocial activities · Provide halfback processes	Community Supervision Community Treatment Families Housing Agencies 27 Law Enforcement